Commercial Law

6th edition

Sir Gordon Borrie, QC, LLM,

Master of the Bench of the Middle Temple
Director General of Fair Trading

Butterworths
London
1988

United Kingdom	Butterworth & Co (Publishers) Ltd, 88 Kingsway, LONDON WC2B 6AB and 61A North Castle Street, EDINBURGH EH2 3LJ
Australia	Butterworths Pty Ltd, SYDNEY, MELBOURNE, BRISBANE, ADELAIDE, PERTH, CANBERRA and HOBART
Canada	Butterworths. A division of Reed Inc., TORONTO and VANCOUVER
New Zealand	Butterworths of New Zealand Ltd, WELLINGTON and AUCKLAND
Singapore	Butterworth & Co (Asia) Pte Ltd, SINGAPORE
USA	Butterworths Legal Publishers, ST PAUL, Minnesota, SEATTLE, Washington, BOSTON, Massachusetts, AUSTIN, Texas and D & S Publishers, CLEARWATER, Florida

© Butterworth & Co (Publishers) Ltd 1988

British Library Cataloguing in Publication Data

Borrie, *Sir* Gordon
  Commercial law.—6th ed.
  1. Commercial law—England
  I. Title
  344.206'7   KD1629

ISBN Hardcover 0 406 55845 0
ISBN Softcover 0 406 55846 9

Phototypeset by Cotswold Typesetting Ltd, Gloucester
Printed in Great Britain by Mackays of Chatham Ltd

LAW

Preface to the sixth edition

The first edition of this book (published in 1962) was written primarily to meet the needs of students preparing for the Commercial Law paper in Part II of the Law Society's Qualifying Examination. The extended treatment given to many matters in subsequent editions was intended to make it useful as a basic textbook for the many advanced courses in universities, polytechnics and elsewhere which include Commercial Law (or parts of it such as Sale of Goods or Insurance) in their syllabus.

Commercial Law does, of course, range over a wide variety of topics but the five selected here are among the most important. The attempt has been made to consider all the key problems they give rise to, though it would be impossible to provide an exhaustive treatment in a book of this size. Indeed, it is probable that each of the present chapters would have to be expanded to the length of a whole book before it could be regarded as a comprehensive exposition of the law. If this were done, such a *magnum opus* would be so daunting even to the most diligent student that its purpose as a basic textbook would be defeated. I have endeavoured, however, by means of footnotes, to refer the reader to the various detailed works on particular aspects of Commercial Law, so that having grasped the essentials he or she may proceed to as intensive a study of any branch of the subject as he or she may wish.

Some emphasis is placed throughout the text on the facts of decided cases. They are fascinating material and it is thought that their study helps to illuminate the legal principles involved much better than if the legal principles are merely stated in the text and, for the facts, the reader has to follow up a bleak footnote reference. The facts of cases are the very stuff of the law and, wherever possible, use is made of them.

Since the last edition there have been many developments in both case law and statute law. Further changes have been made in the modern growth of consumer protection legislation such as the Supply of Goods and Services Act 1982 and the Consumer Protection Act 1987. The Consumer Credit Act 1974 finally came into full operation in 1985 after 11 years of draft regulations, an extensive consultation process and final regulations. The Act applies to many different types of consumer credit agreement but I have adopted a method of exposition which deals first with Hire Purchase—both common law and statutory rules—and then turns to the other principal kinds of consumer credit agreement. It is hoped that this will assist in explaining the complexities of the current law.

The law is given as it stood on 1 December 1987 but any reader wishing to keep absolutely up to date must keep his or her eye open for new cases and new statutes.

I am indebted to the publishers for their invaluable help.

Abbots Morton   G.B.
Worcestershire
December 1987

Contents

Table of statutes

References in this Table to *Statutes* are to Halsbury's Statutes of England (Fourth Edition) showing the volume and page at which the annotated text of the Act may be found.

List of cases

PAGE

Somes v British Empire Shipping
Co (1860) 143
Sorrell v Finch (1976) . . 31, 32
Sparenborg v Edinburgh Life
Assurance Co (1912) . . . 308
Spector v Ageda (1973) . . . 13
Spellman v Spellman (1961) . . 165
Spiro v Lintern (1973) . . 34
Springer v Great Western Rly
Co (1921) 38
Stadium Finance Ltd v Robbins
(or Robins) (1962) 85
Staffs Motor Guarantee Ltd v
British Wagon Co Ltd (1934) . 87
Sterns Ltd v Vickers Ltd (1923) . 70
Stevenson v Beverley Bentinck
Ltd (1976) 94
Stewart v Reavell's Garage
(1952) 54
Stone v Reliance Mutual
Insurance Society Ltd (1972) . 311
Stoneham v Ocean Railway and
General Accident Insurance Co
(1887) 310
Stoneleigh Finance Ltd v Phillips
(1965) 79, 159
Stuart v Freeman (1903) . . . 296
Suisse Atlantique Société
d'Armement Maritime SA v
Rotterdamsche Kolen Centrale
NV (1967) 116
Sumner, Permain & Co v Webb
& Co (1922) 105
Swinfen v Lord Chelmsford
(1860) 32

T

Tai Hing Cotton Mill Ltd v
Kamsing Knitting Factory
(1979) 138
Tai Hing Cotton Mill Ltd v Liu
Chong Hing Bank Ltd (1986) . 271
Tailby v Official Receiver
(1888) 58
Tappenden v Artus (1964) . . 162
Tarling v Baxter (1827) . . . 61
Tattersall v Drysdale (1935) . . 342
Taxation Comrs v English,
Scottish and Australian Bank
(1920) 280
Taylor v Allon (1966) . . 296, 332

PAGE

Taylor v Brewer (1813) . . . 23
Teheran-Europe Co Ltd v S T
Belton (Tractors) Ltd (1968) . 39
Thackwell v Barclays Bank plc
(1986) 284
Thames and Mersey Marine
Insurance Co v Gunford Ship
Co (1911) 324
Theobald v Railway Passengers
Assurance Co (1854) . . . 294
Thompson (W L) Ltd v
Robinson (Gunmakers) Ltd
(1955) 133, 134
Thornett and Fehr v Beers &
Son (1919) 107
Tiedemann and Ledermann
Frères, Re (1899) 35
Tournier v National Provincial
and Union Bank of England
(1924) 274
Travers (Joseph) & Sons Ltd v
Cooper (1915) 177, 205
Tredegar Iron and Coal Co Ltd
v Hawthorn Bros & Co
(1902) 135
Tsakiroglou & Co Ltd v Noblee
Thorl GmbH (1962) . . . 75
Tucker v Farm and General
Investment Trust Ltd (1966) . 152
Turley v Bates (1863) . . . 63
Turnbull v Garden (1869) . . 15
Turner v Goldsmith (1891) . . 45
Turpin v Bilton (1843) 6

U

UCB Leasing Ltd v Holtom
(1987) 171, 172
UGS Finance Ltd v National
Mortgage Bank of Greece and
National Bank of Greece SA
(1964) 117
Underwood (A L) Ltd v Bank of
Liverpool and Martins
(1924) 282, 285
Underwood Ltd v Burgh Castle
Brick and Cement Syndicate
(1922) 62
Union Transport Finance Ltd v
British Car Auctions Ltd
(1978) 161

Chapter 1

Agency

CREATION OF THE CONTRACT OF AGENCY

Purpose of agency

Countless commercial transactions in the modern world are carried out through intermediaries or agents. A sale of goods by exporters in this country may be brought about through the services of an overseas agent who has found the purchaser; a newspaper may obtain orders for advertisements through the work of a representative whose task it is to seek out such orders. These are but two examples of the many contracts that are brought about through the intervention of an agent. The agent may be called by any one of a number of different names—a representative, a broker, a factor—but whatever name he is in practice given, he is in law an agent if he is employed to effect the legal relations of his principal, usually by bringing about a contract between his principal and a third party. The use of an agent in order to effect a contract is common not only in commerce but also in more private transactions. A man may arrange a holiday tour through a travel agency and this will mean that the agency, on his behalf, will make such contracts as he wishes to enter into with hotels, airlines or shipping companies. If he wishes to sell his house, the contract of sale may be effected through the intervention of an estate agent whom he asks to find a purchaser. It may be that both parties to a contract employ agents to bring it about, as where the seller of shares employs a broker to arrange the sale and the buyer of the shares instructs another broker to effect the purchase.

In all these examples, the function of the agent is to act on behalf of his principal in bringing about a contract between his principal and a third party. The word 'agent' does have other wider meanings in common usage. For example, sometimes a car dealer is referred to as an agent or distributor of a certain make of car. Indeed, he may be described as the manufacturer's sole agent in a given area. That, however, does not necessarily mean that when the dealer sells a car to a customer he is acting in law as 'agent' for the manufacturer, bringing about contractual relations between the manufacturer and the customer. In practice, such a car dealer buys the cars from the manufacturer and sells on his own account to purchasers, so that he is selling not as an agent at all but as his own principal and no privity of contract exists between the manufacturer and the ultimate purchaser. Similarly, it seems established as a matter of trade custom that an advertising agency is a principal in its relations with advertisers and publishers and there is no privity of contract brought about between publisher and the advertiser when the latter engages the services of an advertising agency. Only the agency is liable to the publisher and the agency must pay the publisher whether or not it has itself been paid by the advertiser.[1] Keeping, therefore, to the narrower usage in law, the term 'agent' normally means someone whose purpose is to establish contractual relations between his principal and a third party.

An agent may be a servant of his principal or an independent contractor. Examples of agents who are under contracts of service with their principals are sales representatives, canvassers, and commercial travellers, if they are under the control of their principals as to how they do their work. On the other hand, many agents are their own masters, independent contractors, a familiar example being estate agents. The distinction between a servant and an independent contractor, important if the possibility of vicarious liability for an agent's tort is being considered, is not relevant to this chapter. Suffice to say that an agent may be either the one or the other.

Once the contractual relationship between the principal and the third party has been established by the agent A, A generally drops out of the picture—his task, that of bringing P (his principal) and T (the third party) together has been fulfilled—and the rights and obligations contained in the contract created between P and T belong solely to P and T. A has generally no rights or liabilities under that contract.

Whereas, however, that is the general rule, it is subject to exceptions. For example, if when acting on behalf of P and with P's authority, A makes a contract to buy goods from T, and does not disclose he is acting for another person, T has a right to claim the

---

1 *Press and General Publicity Services v Percy Bilton*; Judge Ruttle [1979] *CLY* 26.

price of the goods from either A or P. Problems may arise in such a case over the limits of T's rights against P and P's rights against T. Further, when a contract has been effected by A between his principal P and T, problems may arise as to whether A had authority (express or implied) to make such contract, and if not, whether P has ratified A's actions, or whether P is estopped from denying A's authority. All these problems concern the effect of any agency relationship that may exist between P and A on the contract made by A with T. The law relating to these matters will be examined later, but first we are concerned with the obligations between P and A themselves.

Capacity

It is not necessary for someone to have full contractual capacity in order to be the agent of another person; a minor (someone under 18), therefore, can effectively bring about contractual relations between his principal and a third party. However, a minor can only appoint an agent to make a contract on his behalf if the contract is one which he could validly make himself, for example, a contract to purchase necessaries.[2] If a minor does appoint an agent, eg, to purchase necessaries, what of the principal–agent relationship? One leading work favours the view that such relationship can constitute a valid contract analogous to a contract of service.[3]

Where, in order to be enforceable, a contract has to be evidenced by a note or memorandum in writing, signed by the party to be charged or his agent, such as a contract for the sale of land or a contract of guarantee, it is not possible for one party to act as agent of the other. However, one person, for example an auctioneer or solicitor, may act as agent for both parties for this purpose.[4]

Consensual relationship

The relationship between a principal and his agent is normally a consensual one so that no one can claim to be P's agent unless P

2 *G (A) v G (T)* [1970] 2 QB 643, 652, [1970] 3 All ER 546, 549; per Lord Denning, MR. But Lord Denning said that a minor cannot appoint an agent to dispose of property so as to bind him irrevocably: a disposition by an agent for a minor is voidable so long as it is avoided within a reasonable time after attaining full age.
3 *Bowstead on Agency* (15th edn, 1985), p 31.
4 *Bird v Boulter* (1833) 4 B & Ad 443 and *Gavaghan v Edwards* [1961] 2 QB 220, [1961] 2 All ER 477.

consents to the agency. In *White v Lucas*[5] a firm of estate agents were anxious to act on behalf of the owner of certain property whom they knew was wanting to sell. The owner told the estate agents in clear terms not to put the property on their books. The property was sold to someone introduced by these estate agents. The court held that the estate agents had no right to claim any remuneration since the property owner had never agreed to their acting on his behalf. Exceptionally, however, an agent's authority to bind a principal can arise by virtue of the doctrine of estoppel, ie a person may so act as to be precluded from denying that he has given authority to another to act on his behalf, and in certain cases an agent's authority can arise because of 'necessity'. Both of these possibilities are discussed below.[6]

Returning to the normal position, namely, that the principal-agent relationship is consensual, the relationship can arise in the following ways:

(i) By *contract* under seal;
(ii) By *contract* in writing or verbal;
(iii) By *contract* implied from the conduct or situation of the parties;
(iv) By *consent* express or implied where there is no contract as the agent is acting gratuitously;
(v) By *ratification*—this is where A has no authority but purports eg to make a contract with T on P's behalf and P later ratifies expressly or impliedly what A has done.

Although all these methods of establishing a principal-agent relationship depend on the consent of the principal and the agent, it is clear from (iii), (iv) and (v) above that such consent may be implied. Lord Pearson in *Garnac Grain Co Inc v H M Faure and Fairclough and Bunge Corpn*[7] said:

'The relationship of principal and agent can only be established by the consent of the principal and the agent. They will be held to have consented if they have agreed to what amounts in law to such a relationship, even if they do not recognize it themselves and even if they have professed to disclaim it . . . Primarily one looks to what they said and did at the time of the alleged creation of the agency. Earlier words and conduct may afford evidence of a course of dealing in existence at that time and may be taken into account more generally as historical background.'

5 (1887) 3 TLR 516.
6 See post, p 32 and p 37.
7 [1968] AC 1130n, 1137, [1967] 2 All ER 353, 358.

Although the relationship of principal and agent is normally based on mutual consent, the agreement does not have to be in any particular form. For example, A does not have to be appointed in writing merely because his task is to bring about a contract with T which itself has to be evidenced in writing. In *Heard v Pilley*,[8] an agent was orally appointed to obtain the lease of a house, remuneration to be a share of the profit expected to be made on a resale. The agent entered into a written agreement for the lease in his own name and then refused to give his principal the benefit of the lease. The court held that the agreement for the lease vested the equitable estate in the principal and he was entitled to a decree of specific performance against the vendor.[9]

However, if an agent is required to execute a deed such as a conveyance or a lease of land for a period over three years, he must himself be appointed by deed, called a power of attorney, unless he executes the deed in the presence of his principal and with his authority.

Normally, it will be expressly agreed or impliedly understood that the principal will pay the agent for his services but, as has been noted, a principal-agent relationship also exists where A agrees without any consideration to effect a contract on P's behalf. If A has agreed to act gratuitously he is not liable for non-feasance, that is for not doing what he promised to do, assuming his promise is not embodied in a deed. However, if he does in fact proceed to effect a contract on P's behalf, A is under the same duty to exercise care and skill in carrying out P's instructions, to account to him, and not to make any secret profit as if he were receiving a commission or some other consideration for doing the work. Possibly, if an agent undertakes gratuitously to make, say, a contract of insurance on his principal's behalf, and he does not in fact make the contract, he is under a duty to inform the principal so that the latter can take steps to effect the insurance by other means.[10]

OBLIGATIONS OF THE AGENT TO HIS PRINCIPAL

An agency agreement may contain terms setting forth the express obligations of an agent to his principal. Subject to such express

8 (1869) 4 Ch App 548.
9 If the vendor had already conveyed the legal estate to the agent, the agent would hold it on an implied trust for the principal: *Rochefoucauld v Boustead* [1897] 1 Ch 196. By s 53(1) of the Law of Property Act 1925, an agent can only create or dispose of an interest in land if he has been lawfully authorised in writing.
10 Stoljar *The Law of Agency* (1961) pp 271–273.

terms, the agent owes a number of implied duties or obligations to his principal. It is the agency relationship as such that gives rise to these obligations so that, subject to certain qualifications that will be referred to, they fall as much on the gratuitous agent as on the paid agent. A draft EEC directive on the Law relating to Commercial Agents was strongly criticised by the Law Commission in a Report published in 1977.[11] The Law Commission considered that there was no case for special rules applicable only to 'commercial agents' and that the proposed mandatory rules to protect such agents were one-sided and cumbersome. Instead of clarifying the law, the Law Commission felt the rules contained in the EEC draft directive were full of uncertainties and inconsistent and would distort the common law of agency.

1. To obey the lawful instructions of his principal

If an agent (not being a gratuitous agent) has agreed to effect a certain contract on behalf of his principal and he fails to do so, there is a breach of contract. The agent is liable in damages and has no claim to any agreed remuneration. In *Turpin v Bilton*,[12] for example, an insurance broker agreed for consideration to cause an insurance to be made on the plaintiff's ship, but he failed to do so and the ship was lost. The broker was held liable to the plaintiff. Similarly, in *Fraser v B N Furman (Productions) Ltd*,[13] insurance brokers agreed for consideration to effect an employer's liability policy and failed to do so. The employer was held liable for £3,000 damages in an action brought against him by an employee for breach of the Factories Act and the Court of Appeal held that the brokers must indemnify the employer in that sum for breach of contract. However, an agent is not liable if he agrees to effect an illegal contract and fails to do so. In *Cohen v Kittell*,[14] the defendant undertook to place bets on certain horses on the plaintiff's behalf. The defendant in fact failed to place these bets and the plaintiff sued him, claiming as damages the money he would have obtained if the bets had been placed. The court held that since, by virtue of the Gaming Act 1845, the bets would not have been recoverable at law, the claim must fail.

Whether an agent is acting gratuitously or not, if he proceeds to carry out the agency he must do so as agreed and comply with his

11 Cmnd 6948; Law Com No 84.
12 (1843) 5 Man & G 455.
13 [1967] 3 All ER 57, [1967] 1 WLR 898.
14 (1889) 22 QBD 680.

principal's lawful instructions and is liable in damages to his principal if he does not. An agent does not commit any breach of duty if P gives an order to A in such uncertain terms as to be susceptible of two different meanings and A bona fide accepts one of them and acts upon it.[15]

2. To exercise due care and skill

It has alrady been noted that even a gratuitous agent must, if he chooses to act on behalf of his principal, exercise due care and skill. There is some doubt whether an agent for reward owes a higher duty of care than a gratuitous agent. Professor Powell thought that any distinction is 'unsound in principle' since only slight consideration suffices to make a relationship contractual.[16] Professor Fridman, on the other hand, in his work on the law of agency, says that the cases do show a distinction and that while an agent for reward by implication holds himself out to be as skilful and as careful as people in his trade or profession normally are, a gratuitous agent does not imply that he is any more skilful or careful than he actually is. Only an agent for reward undertakes to possess a certain skill, measured objectively in terms of what is to be expected from agents in his position.[17] However, this distinction may now be subject to the House of Lords decision in *Hedley Byrne & Co Ltd v Heller and Partners Ltd*.[18] It may now be the position, that if a gratuitous agent expressly or by implication asserts that he has a certain skill and this statement is reasonably relied on by his principal, the agent is liable for any loss which may arise from his failure to exercise such skill. But the same decision shows that a gratuitous agent can unilaterally disclaim any obligation to take care.

A simple example of an agent's duty to exercise due care and skill is his duty, if he is an agent to sell property, to obtain the best price that is reasonably obtainable. In *Keppel v Wheeler*[19] agents were employed to sell a block of flats and received an offer from X which the owners accepted 'subject to contract'. Subsequently, the agents received a higher offer from Y, but instead of transmitting this to the owners, arranged a resale from X to Y after the original sale to X was effected. The Court of Appeal held that the agents owed the

15 *Ireland v Livingston* (1872) LR 5 HL 395.
16 Powell *The Law of Agency* (2nd edn, 1961) p 304.
17 Fridman *The Law of Agency* (5th edn, 1983) p 143.
18 [1964] AC 465, [1963] 2 All ER 575. See also *Mutual Life and Citizens' Assurance Co Ltd v Evatt* [1971] AC 793, [1971] 1 All ER 150, PC.
19 [1927] 1 KB 577.

owners a duty to obtain the best price reasonably obtainable, which included a duty to communicate any better offers than the one received from X, and that that duty continued until a binding contract of sale was effected. The agents were made liable in damages for breach of their implied duty, damages being the difference between X's offer and Y's offer. The agents were, however, successful in their counterclaim for commission agreed since the court held that they had bona fide believed that their duties as agents ceased when the owners accepted X's offer 'subject to contract'. Likewise, an independent insurance intermediary must exercise skill, care and diligence to produce the deal which is to his client's best advantage. This is known as the 'best execution' principle.

There was a similar breach of the duty to exercise due care and skill in *Heath v Parkinson*.[20] An estate agent was instructed by the defendant to find a purchaser for the lease of the defendant's business premises which were held under a covenant against carrying on any business other than music selling. The agent received an assurance from the landlords that, despite the covenant, they would consent to a tailoring business but failed to disclose that assurance to the defendant and the lease was sold for a lower price than could have been obtained. The court held that the agent was in breach of his duty of care and was not entitled to any commission on the sale as he had deliberately taken advantage of the defendant's ignorance about the landlords' willingness to relax the covenant, in order to persuade the defendant to take a lower price than he could have obtained elsewhere.

A charge of negligence on the part of estate agents in valuing property was clearly made out in *Baxter v Gapp & Co Ltd*.[1] The agents made an excessive valuation of freehold property which was relied on by the plaintiff when advancing money on a mortgage to the owner of the property. The Court of Appeal was satisfied that the agents were in breach of their duty of care and skill and allowed the plaintiff to recover as damages the actual loss suffered as a result of lending the money. Damages awarded included the difference between the sum advanced by the plaintiff and that received by him when he sold it after entering into possession of the property, the amount of interest the mortgagor had failed to pay, and the expenses both of maintaining the property while in the plaintiff's possession and of selling it.

---

20 (1926) 42 TLR 693.
1 [1939] 2 KB 271, [1939] 2 All ER 752.

No action will lie against the agent in respect of his failure to exercise reasonable care in relation to his principal's affairs unless that carelessness is the effective cause of loss suffered by the principal.[2]

It is possible that this duty of an agent to exercise due care and skill can come into conflict with his duty to obey his principal's lawful instructions. Normally, if an agent obeys his principal's lawful instructions, he will not be liable even though following those instructions is against the principal's best interests. Presumably however, if an agent is, say, a solicitor or other person who is in the position of a professional adviser, such agent would, under his duty to exercise care and skill, owe a duty to warn his principal that the instructions are unwise or might cause the principal loss.

3. To act personally

Unless an agent has been expressly or impliedly authorised to delegate the work to another person, he owes a duty to his principal to act personally: *'delegatus non potest delegare'*. If the agent contravenes this duty, the principal is not bound by any contract effected on his behalf by the sub-agent, and the agent is liable for breach of duty. In *John McCann & Co v Pow*[3] the Court of Appeal held that an estate agent had no implied authority to appoint a sub-agent because the agent's functions required skill and competence to perform.

Where a principal expressly gives authority to his agent to delegate, delegation is, of course, permissible. In *De Bussche v Alt*[4] for example, A was appointed by P to sell a ship in China at an agreed price. A was unable to effect such a sale and obtained P's permission for the appointment by A of a sub-agent to sell the ship in Japan. The court held there was no breach of duty by A in appointing a sub-agent as delegation was expressly agreed. Similarly, delegation may be impliedly authorised by trade usage, by having been authorised in similar dealings between the parties in the past, or in an emergency such as the agent's illness. If a client instructs a country solicitor, that country solicitor is impliedly authorised by his client to delegate work, such as work concerning litigation in London, to 'London agents'. An agent may also delegate a purely ministerial duty such as a duty to sign letters. In *Allam & Co Ltd v*

2 See *O'Connor v B D B Kirby & Co* [1972] 1 QB 90, [1971] 2 All ER 1415, CA. See post, p 312.
3 [1975] 1 All ER 129, [1974] 1 WLR 1643, CA.
4 (1878) 8 Ch D 286.

Europa Postal Services Ltd,[5] site owners authorised the defendant company who were outdoor advertising contractors to serve notice on the plaintiff company (also outdoor advertising contractors) terminating their licences from the site owner to use sites for advertising purposes. The defendant company instructed a firm of solicitors to serve formal notice on the plaintiffs. Buckley J held that the defendant company, like any incorporated company, must act through agents and could validly give notice of termination by way of a notice signed by its solicitors as distinct from one of its directors, as this was a purely ministerial act. The solicitors were 'no more than an amanuensis in transmitting the notice . . .', said Buckley J.[6]

When delegation by the agent A has been expressly or impliedly authorised by P then, as a general rule, the sub-agent is A's agent and no privity of contract is created between P and the sub-agent. In consequence, the sub-agent cannot normally claim remuneration or an indemnity from P, and P cannot normally claim directly against the sub-agent if the latter has displayed a lack of due care. It was held by Wright J in *Calico Printers' Association Ltd v Barclays Bank Ltd*[7] that if the sub-agent has been negligent, P's remedy is against A not against the sub-agent.[8] Of course, this decision predates the House of Lords decision in *Hedley Byrne & Co Ltd v Heller & Partners Ltd*[9] and it may be now that the absence of a contract between P and the sub-agent would not prevent P suing the sub-agent direct, eg in respect of a negligent statement relied on by P. It is clear that the absence of contract between a bailor and sub-bailee does not prevent the bailor suing the sub-bailee direct for negligence and by analogy P may now sue a sub-agent direct.[10] Certainly it seems that if a sub-agent is aware he is being employed by A on behalf of P, he stands in a fiduciary relationship with P and will be accountable to P for any secret profit he may make even though there is no privity of contract between him and P.[11]

---

5   [1968] 1 All ER 826, [1968] 1 WLR 638.

6   [1968] 1 All ER 826, 832.

7   (1931) 145 LT 51.

8   However, Atkin LJ said obiter in one case that A may not be responsible for the sub-agent's negligence if A used reasonable care in the selection of the sub-agent:— *Cheshire & Co v Vaughan Bros & Co* [1920] 3 KB 240, 259.

9   [1964] AC 465, [1963] 2 All ER 575.

10   *Morris v C W Martin & Sons Ltd* [1966] 1 QB 716, [1965] 2 All ER 725, and *Gilchrist Watt and Sanderson Pty Ltd v York Products Pty Ltd* [1970] 3 All ER 825, [1970] 1 WLR 1262. Contra, *Balsamo v Medici* [1984] 2 All ER 304, [1984] 1 WLR 951. See *Bowstead on Agency*, p 134.

11   *Powell and Thomas v Evan Jones & Co* [1905] 1 KB 11. For a discussion of secret profits, see post, p 14.

Although generally, any sub-agent appointed by A is not in contractual relationship with P, it may be that A is clearly authorised not only to appoint a sub-agent but also to bring about a contract of agency between P and the sub-agent.[12] There would then be a novation, ie, the contract of agency between P and A would be replaced by one between P and the sub-agent. A's agency is really confined here to selecting a sub-agent and bringing him into privity of contract with P, and A's only liability to P is the obligation to take due care in the selection of the sub-agent. When that is done, the sub-agent (and not A) is directly liable to P for any breach of his duties of exercising care and skill and of good faith, and he has a direct claim against P for an indemnity and any remuneration agreed.

4. To act in good faith

Under this head we will examine a number of duties that arise from the fiduciary nature of the principal-agent relationship.

(a) *Not to permit a conflict of interest and the duty of disclosure*—An agent must keep before him, all the time he is engaged on his principal's business, the rule that he should at no time allow his own personal interests to come into conflict with the interests of his principal. If the agent has any personal interest that might conflict with his principal's interest, he must disclose it and the principal must consent to the agent continuing to act for him. If the agent breaks this duty, his principal may set aside any transaction effected by the agent and claim any profit made by the agent. It follows, therefore, that if an agent is required to sell his principal's property he must not himself buy it (without full disclosure) because if he did so he would be allowing his personal interest (to pay a low price for the property) to come into conflict with the duty to his principal to obtain the best price reasonably obtainable. In *McPherson v Watt*,[13] a solicitor acted as the agent for two ladies who wished to sell certain houses. The solicitor himself purchased the property though nominally the property was bought in the name of his brother. The

12 As is the case in *De Bussche v Alt* (1878) 8 ChD 286. Wright J in *Calico Printers' Association v Barclays Bank Ltd* (1931) 145 LT 51, 55, said: 'To create privity it must be established not only that the principal contemplated that a sub-agent would perform part of the contract, but also that the principal authorised the agent to create privity of contract between the principal and the sub-agent, which is a very different matter requiring precise proof.'
13 (1877) 3 App Cas 254.

House of Lords refused to grant the solicitor specific performance of the contract of sale. Such a breach of duty would, however, be waived if the agent makes a full disclosure of his interest to the principal and the latter is still willing to proceed with the transaction.

If an agent is employed to buy property for his principal, he must not sell his own property to his principal unless he discloses this fact. In *Lucifero v Castel*,[14] an agent was asked to purchase a yacht for his principal. The agent bought a yacht for himself and then resold it to his principal at a profit. The principal was unaware that he was buying the agent's own property. The court held that the agent must give up the profit he had made and that he be allowed to retain only the price he had paid for the yacht and his commission. *Kimber v Barber*[15] is a similar case. Here, A became aware that B wanted to obtain shares in a certain company and told B that he, A, could procure a certain number of these shares at £3 a share. B agreed to purchase through A at that price and the shares were then transferred, B paying A £3 a share. Later B learned that A was in fact the owner of the shares at the time of the transfer, having just bought them himself at £2 a share. The court held that A must pay B the difference of £1 on each share bought.

It makes no difference that the contract effected by the agent on his principal's behalf is made without intent to defraud and is a fair one as, for example, where an agent to buy sells his own property to his principal at the ordinary market price—such a contract could still be set aside by the principal.[16] The point is, as Romilly MR put it in *Bentley v Craven*,[17] that the law will not allow an agent to place himself in a situation which, under ordinary circumstances, would tempt a man to do that which is not the best for his principal. Nor does it make any difference that the contract has been executed, for example, by the formal transfer of shares,[18] or that a long time has passed before the principal discovers that there has been a breach of duty, unless he ought to have discovered it earlier.[19] In each of these cases the transactions can be set aside by the principal if the agent has permitted the possibility of a conflict of interest.

An independent insurance intermediary must avoid putting himself in a position where his duties to his client conflict with his

---

14 (1887) 3 TLR 371.
15 (1872) 8 Ch App 56.
16 *Armstrong v Jackson* [1917] 2 KB 822.
17 (1853) 18 Beav 75, 76–77.
18 *Armstrong v Jackson* [1917] 2 KB 822, [1916–17] All ER Rep 1117.
19 *Oelkers v Ellis* [1914] 2 KB 139.

own interests unless the circumstances have been explained to and accepted by the client. This is known as the 'subordination of interest' requirement. The client's interests are paramount.

For the same reason, it is a breach of duty for an agent to act for both sides in any particular transaction unless there is full disclosure to both parties and their informed consent obtained. In *Fullwood v Hurley*,[20] a hotel broker A was instructed by the owner of a hotel, P, to sell his hotel for him. A arranged to sell the hotel to T on the terms of a letter which concluded: 'if business is done, we shall act for you at the usual brokerage'. The sale having been made, P paid A a commission and, in this action, A claimed a second commission from T. The Court of Appeal rejected the claim on the ground that the terms of the letter were not sufficient to establish a contract by T to pay A a double commission and that, in any case, since A was acting as agent for the vendor he was not entitled to enter into such a contract with T without full disclosure to both parties. Scrutton LJ said: 'No agent who has accepted an employment from one principal can in law accept an engagement inconsistent with his duty to his first principal, unless he makes the fullest disclosure to each principal of his interest, and obtains the consent of each principal to the double employment'. This case may be contrasted with *Harrods Ltd v Lemon*,[1] where the plaintiffs were acting as estate agents for the vendor of property through one of their departments and as surveyors for the purchaser through another department. When the position was discovered by the plaintiffs, they made full disclosure to the vendor and suggested she engage an independent surveyor but she allowed them to continue acting for her. This was held to be a waiver by the vendor of Harrods' breach of duty in acting also for the other side, and Harrods were entitled to claim their commission from the vendor. By the Estate Agents Act 1979 s 21, an estate agent who has a personal interest in land shall not enter into negotiations with any person with respect to the acquisition or disposal by that person of any interest unless he has disclosed the nature and extent of his personal interest. Failure to comply with s 21 will not constitute a ground for any civil claim but

20 [1928] 1 KB 498, [1927] All ER Rep 610; followed by Megaw J in *Anglo-African Merchants Ltd v Bayley* [1970] 1 QB 311, [1969] 2 All ER 421, and by Donaldson J in *North and South Trust Co v Berkeley* [1971] 1 All ER 980, [1971] 1 WLR 470. Both of these cases concerned the practice of Lloyd's insurance brokers, agents of the insured, acting also for the underwriters. See also *Spector v Ageda* [1973] Ch 30, [1971] 3 All ER 417, (solicitor acting for a client in a transaction to which the solicitor was also a party).
1 [1931] 2 KB 157, [1931] All ER Rep 285.

may be taken into account by the Director General of Fair Trading in considering whether to exercise his powers under s 3 of the Act to make an order prohibiting anyone from doing estate agency work.

The agent's obligation not to allow his personal interest to conflict with the interests of his principal may continue after the relationship of agency has terminated if the agent is making use of knowledge acquired while acting as agent. In *Carter v Palmer*,[2] A had been a confidential legal adviser to a property owner, P, and after the principal-agent relationship between them had come to an end, A purchased some of P's property and made a profit on the resale. The House of Lords held that A had to give up to P the profit he had made, since he had used for his own private gain knowledge he had acquired while acting as a confidential agent for P. A contrasting case is *Nordisk Insulinlaboratorium v C L Bencard (1934) Ltd*.[3] Here, the defendants had been selling agents for the plaintiffs before the 1939 war. In 1940 the plaintiffs' assets, including stocks of insulin, vested in the Custodian of Enemy Property. The defendants bought the insulin from the Custodian and sold it at a profit. The Court of Appeal held that the defendants did not have to hand over that profit to the plaintiffs. They were no longer the plaintiffs' agents and had not acquired any special knowledge of the plaintiffs' business while acting as agents for them. One may add that the defendants had never been in any close confidential relationship with the plaintiffs.

(b) *Not to make any secret profit or take a bribe*—Any agent who uses his position as agent to acquire a benefit for himself is in breach of his duty of good faith. In *Boardman v Phipps*[4] a trust held 8,000 shares in a private company, and X, the solicitor to the trustees (together with one of the beneficiaries, Y) attended the annual general meeting of the company on behalf of the trustees and negotiated with directors of the company to improve the value of the trust holding. Using information they had received while so acting for the trustees which satisfied them that a purchase of shares in the company would be a good investment, and having the opportunity to acquire them which they obtained as representatives of the trustees, X and Y acquired some 21,000 shares for themselves personally and made a substantial profit. The House of Lords held that by attending the company's AGM and conducting negotiations with the company's directors, X and Y were put in a fiduciary

2 (1841) 8 Cl & Fin 657.
3 [1953] Ch 430, [1953] 1 All ER 986.
4 [1967] 2 AC 46, [1966] 3 All ER 721. See also *Bowstead on Agency* pp 179–185.

position. They had made a profit by using such fiduciary position and must account for it to the trust.[5]

Any gain made by an agent in the course of carrying out his principal's work, which is kept secret from his principal, is a secret profit and recoverable by the principal. *Lucifero v Castel*,[6] already referred to, where an agent, instructed to buy a yacht, bought one for himself and then resold it to his principal, is a simple example of a case where a principal recovered his agent's secret profit. It makes no difference that A agreed to act for P without remuneration.[7] A bribe is one particular kind of secret profit—it is a payment to A by a third party who knows A is acting as an agent, the payment being kept secret from his principal. The purpose of such a payment to A by a third party will, no doubt, be an inducement to A to act in the third party's favour in the making of some contract between the third party and P, but proof of corrupt motive is unnecessary. In *Industries and General Mortgage Co v Lewis*,[8] the defendant wanted to arrange a loan and employed an agent to obtain it for him. The plaintiffs, who agreed to provide the loan, made a promise to the defendant's agent that he would receive one-half of the commission that they would charge the defendant. In an action for interest due on the loan, the defendant counterclaimed for the amount of the bribe as damages. Slade J assumed that the defendant had suffered damage because, probably, the interest the defendant was obliged to pay was higher than it would have been so as to cover the plaintiffs' payment of a bribe to the defendant's agent, and the defendant's counterclaim was upheld. The learned judge found that the plaintiffs had no dishonest intention to cause the agent to persuade his principal (the defendant) to accept the rate of commission demanded or to urge the principal to act disadvantageously to his interest. Nevertheless, he held that once a bribe is established there is an irrebuttable presumption that it was given

5 Professor Fridman has argued that there was no justification for treating the facts in terms of agency because (i) X and Y were never instructed to enter into legal relations with anyone on behalf of the trustees but merely to *represent* the trustees at the A.G.M. and in negotiations, and (ii) there was no evidence of any valid creation of agency by the trustees. Fridman suggested it was better to treat the case as one of constructive trusteeship: 'Establishing Agency' (1968) 84 LQR 224, 237. Slade J in *English v Dedham Vale Properties Ltd* [1978] 1 All ER 382, [1978] 1 WLR 93, referred with approval to the Court of Appeal's decision in *Boardman v Phipps* (upheld on different grounds by the House of Lords) where X and Y were considered to be *self-appointed* agents and liable as such to be under a fiduciary duty to account.
6 (1887) 3 TLR 371.
7 *Turnbull v Garden* (1869) 38 LJ Ch 331.
8 [1949] 2 All ER 573.

with an intention to induce the agent to act favourably to the payer and, therefore, unfavourably to the principal. Support for the decision is found in the following words of Romer LJ in an earlier case:—[9]

> 'If a gift be made to a confidential agent with the view of inducing the agent to act in favour of the donor in relation to transactions between the donor and the agent's principal and that gift is secret as between the donor and the agent—that is to say, without the knowledge and consent of the principal—then the gift is a bribe in the eyes of the law. If a bribe be once established to the court's satisfaction . . . the court will not inquire into the donor's motive in giving the bribe, nor allow evidence to be gone into as to motive.'

A payment made by T to A is still a bribe although in fact it does not induce A to show any preference towards T. Thus, if P has entrusted A with the task of placing a certain contract and T makes some gift or payment to A, knowing A is P's agent, and the payment is made without P's knowledge, the payment is a bribe irrespective of whether A does place the contract with T or with someone else.

The principal has a number of civil remedies when he discovers that his agent has received a secret profit or taken a bribe.[10] Certainly, he may dismiss A summarily.[11] P may also recover the secret profit or bribe from A or T in an action for money had and received. In *Andrews v Ramsay & Co*,[12] an owner of certain property instructed estate agents to find a purchaser for the property at £2,500 and agreed that if the agents sold it at that price he would pay them £50 as commission. The agents managed to arrange a sale of the property at £2,100 and, when the purchaser paid the agents £100 as a deposit, the owner agreed that the agents could retain £50 out of that sum as commission due. Later the owner discovered that the purchaser had made a secret payment of £20 to the agents. When the owner brought an action against the agents, the agents paid the £20 into court but the court held that the owner was entitled in addition to the £50 which the agents had retained as commission.[13] The same kind of action lies where A is not strictly an

---

9 *Hovenden & Sons v Millhoff* (1900) 83 LT 41, 43.

10 There is also the possibility of a criminal prosecution under the Prevention of Corruption Acts 1906 and 1916 against the agent or the third party, or both, where a bribe has been paid, but the prosecution must prove that the payment was made or received corruptly. See *R v Barrett* [1976] 3 All ER 895, [1976] 1 WLR 946, CA.

11 *Boston Deep Sea Fishing and Ice Co v Ansell* (1888) 39 ChD 339.

12 [1903] 2 KB 635.

13 The agents were not entitled to their commission because they were not in a position to say to their principal: 'I have been acting as your agent and I have done my duty by you'.

agent, but is in a similar fiduciary relationship to P, as in *Reading v A-G.* [14] In that case Sergeant Reading, wearing his uniform, drove a civilian lorry in Cairo laden with brandy and whisky. He received £20,000 for this work, and what was left of this money was seized by the military authorities, on behalf of the Crown, when Reading was court-martialled. After the war, Reading claimed the return of the money, but the House of Lords held that Reading had been in a fiduciary relationship with the Crown and that he had received the money solely because of his service uniform. The Crown had lost nothing by Reading's activities, but since Reading had made a secret profit from his Army service, the Crown, like any other principal, could claim or retain the secret profit so made.

Where A has acted bona fide, although he will have to give up to his principal any secret profit, he may be permitted to retain his remuneration. In *Hippisley v Knee Bros,* [15] the plaintiff employed the defendants who were auctioneers to sell some pictures for him by auction, on the terms that they were to be paid a lump sum as commission and 'all out of pocket expenses' including the expenses of printing and advertising. In due course the defendants sold the plaintiff's pictures. When rendering their account of expenses, the defendants debited the plaintiff with the gross amount of the printers' bill and the cost of newspaper advertising although they had received discounts from both the printers and the newspaper proprietors. The plaintiff had no knowledge of these discounts. The court held the amounts of these discounts to be a secret profit made by the defendants and, therefore, recoverable by the plaintiff. However, the court also held, expressly distinguishing *Andrews v Ramsay & Co,* [16] that the defendants should be permitted to retain their commission as they had acted without fraud and their neglect to account was purely incidental to the contract they were employed to make.

Where A has taken a bribe from T, P, as an alternative to his remedy of obtaining the amount from A or T in an action for money had and received, may bring an action against A and T (they are jointly and severally liable) for deceit or conspiracy to defraud. In *Salford Corpn v Lever,* [17] the Corporation invited tenders for the supply of coal, and the defendant agreed to pay the Corporation's agent 1*s* a ton if the defendant's tender was accepted. The defendant

14 [1951] AC 507, [1951] 1 All ER 617.
15 [1905] 1 KB 1.
16 [1903] 2 KB 635.
17 [1891] 1 QB 168.

intended to suffer no loss from these payments since he increased his price by 1*s* a ton. His tender was accepted. When the bribe was discovered, the Corporation's agent entered into an agreement with the Corporation to assist it in bringing an action against the defendant and deposited certain securities in a bank on the Corporation's behalf. The defendant was held liable to pay the amount of the bribe as damages for deceit, it being assumed by the Court of Appeal that since the price had been raised by 1*s* a ton, this was the extent of the Corporation's loss. The Court of Appeal ruled that P has two distinct and cumulative remedies: he may recover from A the amount of the bribe A has received and he may also recover from A and T, jointly and severally, damages for loss without allowing any deduction in respect of what he has recovered from A under the former head. As Professor Powell said, the odd result of that ruling was that 'the principal may recover more loss than he has suffered', and added, 'if the result of this is to reduce the amount of bribery, so much the better'.[18] In fact, there does not seem to have been any actual double recovery in any of the cases— in *Lever* the agent put up certain securities but was to be released progressively by the amounts recovered by P by way of damages from T. In *Mahesan v Malaysia Government Officers' Co-operative Housing Society Ltd*,[19] the Judicial Committee reviewed the authorities and disapproved of dicta in *Lever* to the effect that double recovery was possible. In the Judicial Committee's view, P has, against both A and T, the alternative remedies of claiming the amount of the bribe as money had and received *or* claiming damages for fraud in the amount of the actual loss sustained as a consequence of entering into the transaction in respect of which the bribe had been given.

A further remedy for a principal who learns that his agent has been bribed is to rescind the contract made with the third party who has paid the bribe. In *Shipway v Broadwood*,[20] the defendant agreed to buy a pair of horses from the plaintiff, provided the defendant's agent, a veterinary surgeon, passed them as sound. The agent did certify the horses as sound and the defendant sent the plaintiff a cheque for the price. After the horses were delivered to the defendant they were found to be unsound, whereupon the

18 *Powell* p 318.
19 [1979] AC 374, [1978] 2 All ER 405, PC. For an article arguing that the decision is 'misconceived', see Tettenborn *Bribery, Corruption and Restitution—the Strange Case of Mr. Mahesan* (1979) 95 LQR 68.
20 [1899] 1 QB 369.

defendant returned them and stopped payment of the cheque. At the trial, it was learned that the plaintiff had bribed the defendant's agent. The Court of Appeal held that the defendant was not bound by the contract of sale and that it was immaterial whether his agent had been influenced in his judgment of the horses by the bribe. Of course, if despite a bribe having been paid to his agent, a principal prefers to go on with the contract made with the third party who has paid the bribe, he will affirm the contract and pursue his other remedies. In any case, the principal would not be entitled to rescind if more than a reasonable time had elapsed since the contract was made.

(c) *Not to misuse confidential information*—It is a breach of an agent's general duty of good faith if he uses information, acquired while acting as an agent, for his own personal advantage or for the benefit of a third party. This applies even after the agency ceases. Thus, in *Robb v Green*,[1] an injunction was obtained against a former manager of a business to prevent him using for his own purposes a list of customers of the business which he had copied out while he was the manager. The Court of Appeal in the recent case of *Faccenda Chicken Ltd v Fowler*[2] said that the duty of good faith is broken if an employee makes or copies a list of his employer's customers for use after his employment ends or deliberately memorises such a list even though, except in special circumstances, there is no general restriction on an ex-employee canvassing or doing business with customers of his former employer. Employers do frequently, of course, protect their trade secrets and trade connection by an express clause in their contracts of employment, which clause will be upheld provided it is no more than reasonable to protect the employers' interests.[3]

5. To account

There is a duty on the agent to keep proper accounts of all transactions he enters into on his principal's behalf, and to keep

---

1 [1895] 2 QB 315, [1895–9] All ER Rep 1053; see also *Lamb v Evans* [1893] 1 Ch 218 and *Measures Bros v Measures* [1910] 1 Ch 336.
2 [1986] 1 All ER 617, 625, [1986] 3 WLR 288.
3 See Cheshire and Fifoot *Law of Contract* (11th edn, 1986) pp 380–409. If there is no express restriction and the agent does not take a list of customers away with him, he is legally entitled, when the agency is terminated, to canvass the customers of his former principal on his own behalf: *Roberts v Elwells Engineering Ltd* [1972] 2 QB 586, [1972] 2 All ER 890, CA, post, p 28.

'agency money' apart from his own. As Roskill LJ said in *Aluminium Industrie Vaassen BV v Romalpa Aluminium*:—[4]

> 'If an agent lawfully sells his principal's goods, he stands in a fiduciary relationship to his principal and remains accountable to his principal for those goods and their proceeds.'

Should he not keep money belonging to his principal separate from his own, there is a presumption that the whole amount belongs to the principal.[5] Where A holds money belonging to P, then unless A has been specifically permitted to keep the interest, any interest earned belongs to P.[6] But, except as provided by the Solicitors' Accounts (Deposit Interest) Rules 1975, a solicitor is not liable to account to a client for any interest received on money deposited at a bank being money received or held on account of his clients generally.[7] Further, it has been held that if an estate agent, engaged by the owners of property to find a purchaser, receives a deposit from a prospective purchaser as a stakeholder, while being bound should negotiations break down to return the deposit, he is under no obligation to account for any interest obtained on the deposit.[8] The Estate Agents Act 1979 s 13, declares that any money received in the course of estate agency work is held on trust irrespective of whether the money is held as agent or stakeholder or in any other capacity. The money must be paid into a client account and, subject to Accounts Regulations, the estate agent must account for interest earned but need not generally do so in respect of interest received on money held on account of clients generally.[9] The Regulations do not require payment of interest on money received as a stakeholder.

The agent is bound to account to his principal for money received on behalf of his principal, even if there is an adverse claim to it by someone else and even though it is received under an illegal or void contract. Thus, in *De Mattos v Benjamin*[10] it was held that if an agent

4   [1976] 2 All ER 552, 563, [1976] 1 WLR 676.

5   *Gray v Haig* (1854) 20 Beav 219.

6   *Brown v IR Comrs* [1965] AC 244, [1964] 3 All ER 119.

7   Solicitors Act 1974 s 33 (3). The 1975 Rules provide in brief that interest ought to be paid to a client when the amount received by the solicitor exceeds £500 and is unlikely to be disbursed within a period of two months of receipt.

8   *Potters v Loppert* [1973] Ch 399, [1973] 1 All ER 658. Professor Goode explains this on the basis that there is an implied term established by usage that the estate agent can retain the interest as a reward for his duties as a stakeholder: *Rights to trace in commercial transactions* (1976) 92 LQR 360, 371.

9   Estate Agents Act 1979 ss 14 and 15; Estate Agents (Accounts) Regulations 1981, SI 1981/1520.

10   (1894) 63 LJQB 248.

makes bets on behalf of his principal and the agent receives the resulting winnings, he is bound to hand over the winnings to his principal, and an action for money had and received lies against him if he does not. However, if the relation between P and A is itself illegal, no action could be maintained by P against A requiring A to account for money received on P's behalf. That was the position in the case of *Harry Parker Ltd v Mason*,[11] where P conspired with A, turf commission agents, to make sham bets on the course and bets with street bookmakers contrary to the existing law. A had failed to apply, as agreed, the money that P handed to him and the Court of Appeal held that P could not recover it from A on the general principle that money paid under an illegal contract is irrecoverable.

As a general rule, an agent has no right to deny his principal's title. In *Blaustein v Maltz, Mitchell & Co*,[12] the plaintiff received a cheque from his prospective father-in-law for the deposit on a house, the amount of the cheque being a gift conditional upon the marriage taking place. The plaintiff paid the cheque into his bank account and drew a cheque for the same amount in favour of the defendant solicitors who were engaged to effect the house purchase. The marriage did not take place and the plaintiff sought to recover the money from the defendants. The Court of Appeal held that the defendants had no right to refuse to return the money although the father-in-law directed the defendants to account to him. The agents were estopped from denying their principal's title to *money* held by them on account of their principal. Until the law was altered by statute, an agent who was a bailee of *goods* had no right to deny the bailor's title (ie his principal's title) to the goods unless he could show he was defending the action on behalf of a third party.[13] Now, however, by s 8(1) of the Torts (Interference with Goods) Act 1977, such agent or bailee is entitled to show that a third party has a better right or title than the principal or bailor and 'any rule of law (sometimes called *jus tertii*) to the contrary is abolished'. If the agent or bailee is sued by the principal, he should apply to the court for joinder of the third party.

RIGHTS OF THE AGENT

1. Indemnity

Subject to any express terms in the agency agreement, an agent has a right to claim from his principal an indemnity against all expenses

11 [1940] 2 KB 590, [1940] 4 All ER 199.
12 [1937] 2 KB 142, [1937] 1 All ER 497.
13 *Rogers, Sons & Co v Lambert & Co* [1891] 1 QB 318.

or loss incurred in acting on the principal's behalf. In *Hichens, Harrison, Woolston & Co v Jackson & Sons*,[14] the defendant solicitors instructed the plaintiff stockbrokers to sell certain shares. The stockbrokers did make a contract to sell the shares, but incurred liability to the intended purchaser because the solicitors' client declined to execute a transfer of the shares. The House of Lords held the stockbrokers entitled to claim an indemnity from the solicitors, the amount of the indemnity being the cost of obtaining substituted stock for the intended purchaser. This right to an indemnity exists whether the agent is acting for remuneration or is acting gratuitously, but if someone purports to act as P's agent without P's consent he has, as we have seen, no claim for an indemnity against P since an agency relationship cannot normally arise except on a consensual basis.[15]

An agent has no right to claim an indemnity in respect of unauthorised actions unless they are subsequently ratified, nor has the agent any right to an indemnity for loss caused by the agent's own default or negligence. In *Duncan v Hill*,[16] brokers bought shares for P on a running account. The brokers became defaulters, their transactions were closed in accordance with the rules of the Stock Exchange, and the shares were sold at a loss. It was held that such loss could not be recovered from P as it was caused by the agents' own default in becoming insolvent.

There is a right to an indemnity if the agent incurs a loss in acting on his principal's behalf even where the agent's action has been unlawful, provided the agent was unaware of the illegality. In *Adamson v Jarvis*[17] an auctioneer sold goods for P, unaware that P had no right to dispose of them. The auctioneer was made liable in damages in conversion to the true owner, but it was held that the auctioneer had a right to an indemnity for such damages from his principal. Further, an agent may claim an indemnity for a payment made on his principal's behalf, though neither he nor his principal was legally liable to make the payment, if non-payment might have subjected the agent to some personal difficulties. In *Rhodes v Fielder, Jones and Harrison*,[18] a London solicitor, acting as agent for a country solicitor, paid counsel his fees. Neither solicitor could, of course, have been sued for such fees. Nevertheless, the court held the

---

14   [1943] AC 266, [1943] 1 All ER 128.
15   See p 4, ante.
16   (1873) LR 8 Exch 242.
17   (1827) 4 Bing 66.
18   (1919) 89 LJKB 15.

London solicitor entitled to claim the payments as an indemnity from the country solicitor. If the London solicitor had not paid the fees after undertaking to do so, he would have been guilty of professional misconduct. Since the Gaming Act 1892, an agent cannot recover his commission or any indemnity for gaming or wagering losses incurred as a result of carrying out a principal's instructions.

2. Remuneration

An agent has no right to claim any remuneration from his principal unless such right has been expressly or impliedly agreed. We have noted that the agency relationship can exist although the agent's services are given gratuitously. An agent's agreement to take 'such remuneration as may be deemed right' has been held to entitle him to no remuneration.[19]

An agreement to pay some remuneration, however, may be readily implied from the nature of an agent's services, especially if a professional agent is employed. Then, if no amount is specified, a quantum meruit can be claimed for work done and this is also the case where no final concluded contract has been reached but work is done under the intended contract.[20] A quantum meruit cannot, however, be claimed if that would be inconsistent with the express terms of an existing contract. In *John Meacock & Co v Abrahams*,[1] P, as mortgagee of certain houses, gave notice to exercise his power of sale and instructed A, a firm of auctioneers, to sell by auction. It was agreed between P and A that if a sale of the property, whether arranged by the auctioneer or not, were effected before the date of the auction, commission was payable to the auctioneer on the same scale as for a sale by auction. The day before the date of the auction, the mortgagor, having entered into contracts of sale to sitting tenants of the houses, redeemed the mortgage so that the sale envisaged by the mortgagee was not effected. The Court of Appeal held that, on the terms of the agreement, no scale fee was payable on a sale made not by P or an agent of his, but by a third party over whom P had no control (the mortgagor), and a claim for a quantum meruit could not be entertained as the terms of remuneration were covered by express words.

If a principal has agreed to pay his agent remuneration on the

19 *Taylor v Brewer* (1813) 1 M & S 290.
20 *British Bank for Foreign Trade Ltd v Novinex Ltd* [1949] 1 KB 623, [1949] 1 All ER 155.
1 [1956] 3 All ER 660, [1956] 1 WLR 1463.

happening of a certain event, eg, a sale of the principal's property, then the agent is entitled to remuneration only if he has been the effective cause of the event upon which remuneration becomes payable. In *Burchell v Gowrie and Blockhouse Collieries Ltd*,[2] the appellant agent introduced the ultimate purchasers of his principals' property, though the principals sold the property behind his back on terms he advised them not to accept. The Judicial Committee held that the agent was entitled to claim the commission; he had directly brought about the sale. On the other hand, in *Nightingale v Parsons*[3] the plaintiff was employed as an agent to find a tenant for a house owned by the defendant. He did find a tenant and was paid commission for doing so. Three years later the tenant's wife bought the house from the defendant. The plaintiff had nothing to do with the negotiations leading to the sale, and the Court of Appeal held that since the plaintiff's original introduction of the tenant was not the effective cause of the subsequent sale, the plaintiff had no right to a commission on the sale.

If an agent effects a contract on his principal's behalf that is not precisely the contract he was required to make, the question arises whether he may nevertheless be entitled to the agreed commission. He will be so entitled if it can reasonably be said that he has substantially done what he undertook to do. In *Rimmer v Knowles*,[4] for example, the owner of an estate agreed to pay A £50 if he obtained a purchaser for the estate. A found someone who agreed to take a lease of the estate for 999 years with an option to complete within 20 years, and the court held that A was entitled to the agreed remuneration of £50.

Commission payable by vendor of property, eg estate agents' commission—
If an intending vendor of property puts his property on the books of an estate agent and agrees with the estate agent to pay him commission on the sale of the property, the general rule is that no commission is payable till the sale is completed through the agent, and if the vendor himself or another agent negotiates the sale, or no sale is completed at all, the agent is not entitled to any commission.[5] As Lawton LJ put it in *Alpha Trading Ltd v Dunshaw-Patten Ltd*[6]

2 [1910] AC 614.
3 [1914] 2 KB 621, [1914–15] All ER Rep 551.
4 (1874) 30 LT 496.
5 *Luxor (Eastbourne) Ltd v Cooper* [1941] AC 108, [1941] 1 All ER 33. For a very useful summary of the law relating to estate agents' commission, see the Appendix to Fridman, pp 369–378.
6 [1981] QB 290, [1981] 1 All ER 482, 493.

'The life of an agent in commerce is a precarious one. He is like the groom who takes a horse to the water-trough. He may get his principal to the negotiating table but when he gets there there is nothing he can do to make the principal sign, any more than the groom can make the horse drink.'

Lord Denning has said that it is the 'common understanding of men' that the agents' commission is payable out of the purchase price,[7] so that clear and unequivocal language is needed for the estate agent to be able to claim commission at some earlier stage than a completed sale. More recently, Cairns and James LJJ have preferred to say that when commission is payable depends on the terms of the contract and on the ordinary rules of construction.[8] The estate agent impliedly waives any right to an indemnity for expenses incurred, in return for substantial remuneration if the sale is completed. At the same time, the agent is under no obligation to use any effort to effect a sale.

Generally, if the commision is payable 'on introducing a person ready, able and willing to purchase', commission will be payable only if the person introduced shows his willingness and ability to buy (not necessarily by a binding contract) and remains so willing and able up to the time of completion. If the purchaser does not complete, no commission is payable even if the purchaser's deposit is forfeited by the vendor. Nor is the vendor bound to claim specific performance of any binding contract.[9]

Once there is a binding contract of sale, however, the vendor cannot withdraw from it except at the risk of having to pay his agent commission, because it is his own fault that the sale has not been completed. In order to give business efficacy to an agency contract under which commission is payable on the agent introducing a buyer, there is an implied term that once a sale contract is concluded with a buyer introduced by the agent, the principal (vendor) will not commit a breach of contract with the buyer which would deprive the agent of his commission.[10] Moreover, if a person who is able to purchase is introduced and expresses readiness and

7 *McCullum v Hicks* [1950] 2 KB 271, 274, [1950] 1 All ER 864, 865.
8 *Christie Owen and Davies Ltd v Rapacioli* [1974] QB 781, [1974] 2 All ER 311, CA.
9 *Boots v E Christopher & Co* [1952] 1 KB 89, [1951] 2 All ER 1045.
10 Per Templeman LJ in *Alpha Trading Ltd v Dunshaw-Patten Ltd* [1981] 1 All ER 482, 491, who added that it was necessary to imply such a term to prevent a vendor from 'playing a dirty trick on the agent with impunity after making use of the services provided by that agent'. He saw no sensible distinction between an agency contract relating to the sale of real property and other agency contracts in this context.

willingness by an unqualified offer to purchase, though such offer has not been accepted by the vendor and could be withdrawn, and the vendor withdraws, commission is payable.[11] If it is not the vendor but the purchaser who withdraws, the case is entirely different and no commission is payable.[12] Where commission was payable on introducing someone 'willing and able to purchase' leasehold property, and after contract the landlord refused consent to the assignment, the Court of Appeal held that the agent was not entitled to commission because, although the person introduced was able financially to effect the purchase, he was not suitable and acceptable on other grounds and therefore not 'able' to purchase.[13]

In *Midgley Estates Ltd v Hand*[14] commission was payable to the agents as soon a someone introduced by them 'shall have signed a legally binding contract effected within a period of three months from this date'. The person introduced signed a legally binding contract within that period but was unable to raise the money to complete the purchase. The Court of Appeal ruled that, on the terms of the agents' contract, they had earned their commission; the terms were clear and unambiguous. In *Peter Long & Partners v Burns*,[15] however, where commission was payable on similar terms, since the person introduced had a right to rescind the contract of purchase on the ground of misrepresentation, the contract was not 'legally binding', so the agent was held not entitled to claim commission. In *Wilkinson Ltd v Brown*[16] the Court of Appeal held that payment of commission on the introduction of someone 'prepared to enter into a contract' means payment when someone is introduced who is 'ready, willing and able' to enter into such a contract. The court had already held in *Ackroyd & Sons v Hasan*[17] that this form of wording implies that commission is payable if such a person is introduced even if no binding contract is actually entered into.

Where the estate agent is to be paid commission 'on securing an offer to purchase', normally at not less than a specified price,

11 *Christie Owen and Davies Ltd v Rapacioli* [1974] QB 781, [1974] 2 All ER 311, CA.
12 *Dennis Reed Ltd v Goody* [1950] 2 KB 277, [1950] 1 All ER 919.
13 *Dellafiorá v Lester* [1962] 3 All ER 393, [1962] 1 WLR 1208.
14 [1952] 2 QB 432, [1952] 1 All ER 1394.
15 [1956] 3 All ER 207, [1956] 1 WLR 1083. Cf *Sheggia v Gradwell* [1963] 3 All ER 114, [1963] 1 WLR 1049 where A was entitled to commission on bringing about a legally binding contract. A did find T who signed such a contract but later T wrongly repudiated the contract—A was held entitled to commission.
16 [1966] 1 All ER 509, [1966] 1 WLR 194.
17 [1960] 2 QB 144, [1960] 2 All ER 254.

commission is payable as soon as such an offer is made. So too, where the estate agent is to be paid commission when a 'prospective purchaser' signs a 'purchaser's agreement', commission is payable as soon as someone who has the question of buying in bona fide prospect is prepared to sign such 'purchaser's agreement', though he may not be in a position to complete the purchase: *Drewery v Ware-Lane*.[18]

Sometimes an agent may be appointed a 'sole agent'. A sole agent is under a duty to use his best endeavours to effect a sale[19] and commission is payable even if the ultimate purchaser is introduced by another agent (to whom a commission may also be payable) but not if the vendor himself sells.[20] If the agent is given the 'sole right to sell' or the 'sole and exclusive right to sell' it would seem that the agent may claim commission even if the owner himself sells.

The point has already been made that since the general rule is that commission is payable on a completed sale, only clear language in the terms of contract between the intending vendor and the estate agent will entitle the agent to commission at an earlier point of time. It follows that if the clause covering remuneration is uncertain in its meaning it will be unenforceable.[1]

The Estate Agents Act 1979 s 18, requires an estate agent to give to his client particulars of the circumstances in which the client will become liable to pay remuneration to the agent and particulars of the amount or of the manner in which the remuneration will be calculated. Failure to comply with this obligation means that the contract is not enforceable except pursuant to an order of the court.

3. Lien

An agent who is entitled to claim an indemnity and remuneration, or both, from his principal may exercise a lien on any goods belonging to the principal which are in his lawful possession as an agent until his claims are met. Liens are either general or particular;

---

18 [1960] 3 All ER 529, [1960] 1 WLR 1204.

19 *E Christopher & Co v Essig* [1948] WN 461; *Mendoza & Co v Bell* (1952) 159 Estates' Gazette 372. But it has been pointed out that neither of these cases is the subject of a full report and doubt is cast upon the underlying reason. See Murdoch *The Nature of Estate Agency* (1975] 91 LQR 357, 365. Mr Murdoch considers that whether or not a sole agent is legally obliged to take positive action on behalf of his client cannot be regarded as settled.

20 *Bentall, Horsley and Baldry v Vicary* [1931] 1 KB 253. See also *John McCann & Co v Pow* [1975] 1 All ER 129; [1974] 1 WLR 1643, CA.

1 *Jaques v Lloyd D George & Partners* [1968] 2 All ER 187, [1968] 1 WLR 265, CA.

a particular lien is a right to retain possession of goods only in respect of any debts due in connection with those goods. A general lien is a right to retain possession of goods in respect of any debts owed by the owner whether in connection with those goods or not. General liens arise by express agreement or by trade usage, as in the case of factors, bankers and solicitors. Subject to such express agreement or usage, the agent's lien is a particular one. For example, if A is instructed to purchase goods for P, A has a particular lien over goods purchased by him for P till his expenses and agreed remuneration are paid. Since the right of lien is based on possession, it is lost if the agent gives up possession.

By the Estate Agents Act 1979 s 13 (5), it is stated that nothing in s 13 declaring that clients' money is held by an estate agent on trust prevents a lien being given effect.

Continuing commission

As a general rule, when a contract of agency is terminated, no further commission or other remuneration is payable to the agent even though the principal obtains the benefit of making contracts with persons introduced by the agent before such termination.[2] However, it is a matter of construction of the contract. In *Wilson v Harper, Son & Co*[3] an agreement was made by the defendants to pay an agent 5 per cent commission on all business done with persons introduced by the agent 'as long as we do business'. Neville J granted a declaration that commission on accounts introduced by the agent continued to be payable to his executors after his death so long as the defendants continued to do business with the persons introduced by him. In *Roberts v Elwells Engineers, Ltd*,[4] however, the Court of Appeal ruled that normally damages were a more appropriate remedy than a declaration or an account. An agreement had been made by the defendants to pay an agent $2\frac{1}{2}$ per cent commission on all orders received by the defendants from customers introduced by the plaintiff. After the agency was terminated, the plaintiff contended he was entitled to an account for commission due on all orders received from customers introduced by him for all time—to the 'crack of doom'. This was held to be an inappropriate remedy because the plaintiff was no longer obliged to visit customers but might do so for his own benefit

---

2 *Naylor v Yearsley* (1860) 2 F & F 41.
3 [1908] 2 Ch 370.
4 [1972] 2 QB 586, [1972] 2 All ER 890, CA.

and the defendants would be obliged to engage another representative to do the visiting on their behalf. Instead, compensation should be assessed on the basis that the plaintiff was entitled to go on receiving commission on repeat orders but that allowance should be made, inter alia, for the fact that the plaintiff no longer had the expenses of visiting customers and that the defendants would have to engage another representative.

A rather more complicated case is *Sellers v London Counties Newspapers Ltd.*[5] The plaintiff was employed by the defendants as an advertising representative at a salary of £3 a week, and on the terms that on all advertisements that he obtained he was to be paid a commission when the advertisements appeared in one of their newspapers. Sometimes, orders for advertisement space obtained by the plaintiff were orders for a series of advertisements continuing for a definite period or, alternatively, until cancelled. The plaintiff was dismissed from his employment and he claimed to be entitled to commission on advertisements he had obtained before his dismissal but published by the defendants subsequently. The Court of Appeal held that the plaintiff earned his commission when he obtained an order for an advertisement which the defendants later published, and the defendants could not, by terminating his employment, deprive him of the commission he had thus earned. In consequence, in respect of orders obtained by the plaintiff for advertisements to continue for a definite period or until cancelled, he was entitled to his commission whenever the advertisements were published.

THE AGENT'S AUTHORITY

As was mentioned earlier, once the agent A has performed his task of bringing about a contract between his principal P and the third party T, A generally drops out of the picture, and the rights and obligations in the contract created between P and T belong solely to P and T—A has no rights or liabilities under that contract.

The assumption behind this is that A did have *authority* from P to effect the contract with T and was therefore capable of binding P to it. It is the purpose of this part of the chapter to discuss the various ways in which P is bound by a contract effected by A.

The distinction is drawn between *actual authority*,, ie the authority that is *expressly* given by P to A or which is *implied* from the conduct of the parties and the circumstances of the case, and *apparent*

5 [1951] 1 KB 784, [1951] 1 All ER 544.

authority, ie the authority which A appears to others to have as a result of some representation or conduct by P intended to be acted upon by T.[6]

1. Express authority

If A is given by P express authority to make a certain contract or type of contract with T and, acting in accordance with that express authority A does make such a contract with T, P is bound by it. It has already been said that A does not have to be given his authority in any particular form. He does not have to be appointed in writing merely because his task is to bring about a contract with T which itself has to be evidenced in writing.[7] However, if an agent is required to execute a deed such as a conveyance or a lease of land for a period over three years he must himself be appointed by deed, called a power of attorney, unless he executes the deed in the presence of his principal and with his authority.

2. Implied and usual authority

P is also bound by any act done or contract made by A if it is necessary for or reasonably incidental to carrying out the authority expressly given to A or is of a type that someone in A's trade or profession usually does have authority to do or make. This may be so even if P has expressly informed A that he has no such authority *unless* T knew of that exclusion. In *Watteau v Fenwick*,[8] P, the owner of the business of a beerhouse appointed A as manager of the business and by agreement with him forbad him from purchasing certain articles for the business, including cigars. In contravention

6 Per Diplock LJ in *Freeman and Lockyer v Buckhurst Park Properties (Magnal) Ltd* [1964] 2 QB 480, 502, [1964] 1 All ER 630, 644.
7 *Heard v Pilley* (1869) 4 Ch App 548. See ante, p 5.
8 [1893] 1 QB 346. It is not surprising that the case has been much criticised by writers on partnership law because Wills J was incorrect when he said that no secret limitation of authority as between a dormant partner and an active partner will prevent the dormant partner being bound by contracts made within the ordinary authority of the active partner. By s 5 of the Partnership Act 1890, such limitation of authority *will* prevent the dormant partner being bound if the third party does not know or believe the active partner is a partner. If the decision in *Watteau v Fenwick* is correct that P was bound although T did not know or believe A to be an agent, the liability of an ordinary undisclosed principal differs from the liability of a dormant partner: See *Powell* pp 73–74. *Bowstead* p 97, describes the decision in *Watteau v Fenwick* as 'dubious'.

of his instructions, the manager in his own name did buy such articles for use in the business from T. When T learned who the real owners of the business were, he sued P for the price of the articles and the Divisional Court held that P was liable—A's purchase was considered to be an act within the authority usually conferred upon an agent of his particular character, and T did not know of the agreement between P and A expressly excluding such authority.

An estate agent normally has no authority to effect a contract of sale on behalf of his principal (the vendor) nor to receive a pre-contract deposit as agent for the vendor. In *Hill v Harris*[9] Diplock LJ pointed out that an estate agent may well have implied authority to make representations about the state of the vendor's premises but not as to permitted user.

Where A is engaged to act for P in a particular market, he is impliedly authorised to act according to the custom of that market, unless the custom is inconsistent with the instructions given by P to A.

Until the House of Lords ruled to the contrary in 1976 there was authority for saying that it was within the usual practice of an estate agent to receive a deposit from a potential purchaser as agent for the vendor.[10] In *Sorrell v Finch*;[11] P arranged to sell his house through A. Nothing was said about the taking of deposits from prospective purchasers prior to contract. T was interested in buying the house and paid a deposit to A of 10 per cent of the purchase price. A gave T a receipt signed by himself on his firm's writing paper. No indication was given as to whether A received the deposit as agent for P or as stakeholder. Subsequently A disappeared and T sued P for the return of the deposit contending that it had been received by A as agent for P. The House of Lords held that when a prospective vendor engages an estate agent this does not confer on the estate agent any implied authority to receive as agent for the vendor a pre-contract deposit from a would-be purchaser. When a deposit was paid to A in such circumstances, A holds it as a stakeholder, the purchaser was at all times until contract the only person with any claim or right to the deposit moneys and his was a right on demand; the vendor had no such claim or right and no control over the deposit moneys. It followed that as P had not expressly authorised A

9 [1965] 2 QB 601, [1965] 2 All ER 358, CA. Also Lord Russell of Killowen in *Sorrell v Finch* [1976] 2 All ER 371, 383. The Misrepresentation Act 1967 s 3, (p 95, post) does not prevent P making known to T that A has no such authority: *Overbrooke Estates Ltd v Glencombe Properties Ltd* [1974] 3 All ER 511, [1974] 1 WLR 1335.

10 *Burt v Claude Cousins & Co Ltd* [1971] 2 QB, 426, [1971] 2 All ER 611, CA.

11 [1977] AC 728, [1976] 2 All ER 371, HL.

to receive the deposit on his behalf, he was not under any liability to T to repay it following A's default. Lord Russell of Killowen referred[12] to the argument that 'in justice' the one of two innocent people to suffer should be the vendor who chose the estate agent. He pointed out that a would-be purchaser is not obliged to pay a pre-contract deposit and can in any event require that it be paid into joint names. Lord Russell of Killowen added that his own opinion was not intended to cast doubt on the liability of a vendor for the default of a stakeholder auctioneer—in such cases the deposit is paid on contract and the purchaser is required by the vendor to make the payment, he has no option.

Under the Estate Agents Act 1979, no estate agent may seek a pre-contract deposit in excess of a prescribed amount. Failure to comply with this provision may be taken into account by the Director General of Fair Trading in considering whether to exercise his powers under s 3 of the Act to make an order prohibiting anyone from doing estate agency work.

In litigation, it is well established that the solicitor or counsel retained in the action has implied authority to compromise the suit without reference to the client provided that the compromise does not involve matter 'collateral to the action'.[13]

3. Agency by estoppel and apparent or ostensible authority

If someone (P) has so acted as from his words or conduct to lead another to believe that he has appointed A to act as his agent or that A has authority from P, and A purports to act as P's agent, P will generally be estopped from denying A's authority though in fact no agency really existed.[14] A is said to have apparent or ostensible authority. Thus, where P appoints A as his agent to purchase goods and A does purchase goods from T, if subsequently P dismisses A, P will still be liable on later contracts made by A with T where A purports to act on P's behalf (even though A is acting fraudulently for his own benefit) unless T has knowledge that A no longer has authority. Similarly, all members of a partnershp are agents of the partnership for the purpose of the business of the partnership. If one partner retires, he is bound by any contract made by the remaining

---

12 [1976] 2 All ER 371, 384.

13 *Swinfen v Lord Chelmsford* (1860) 5 H & N 890, 157 ER 1436; *Prestwich v Poley* (1865) 18 CBNS 809, 144 ER 662; *Waugh v H B Clifford & Sons Ltd* [1982] Ch 374, [1982] 1 All ER 1095, CA.

14 See Lord Cranworth in *Pole v Leask* (1863) 33 LJ Ch 155, 161–162.

partners with anyone who had previously dealt with the partnership unless that person knew of the retirement.[15]

It is well established that the solicitor or counsel retained in litigation has not only implied authority to compromise suit without reference to the client but also ostensible authority to do this, provided in each case that the compromise does not involve matter 'collateral to the action'. Counsel or solicitor are often said to be 'clothed' by the client with the apparent authority to do everything he thinks best for the interests of his client in the conduct of the case. In *Waugh v H B Clifford and Sons*,[16] Brightman LJ emphasised that the ostensible authority of counsel or solicitor may be wider than his implied authority. He suggested that in a defamation suit the defendant's solicitor, for example, may offer to settle for £100,000 and the plaintiff may desire to accept that offer. That offer would bind the defendant on the basis of his solicitor's ostensible authority despite the large sum involved. However, it would not follow that the solicitor would have implied authority to agree damages on that scale without the defendant's agreement—in the light of the solicitor's knowledge of the defendant's cash position, it might be unreasonable to commit the defendant to such a burden without enquiring if it were acceptable. Thus, a solicitor may have ostensible authority where he has no implied authority.

It is important to appreciate that T may not claim that A has apparent authority from P simply on the basis of a representation by A. Diplock LJ said in *Freeman & lockyer v Buckhurst Park Properties*:—[17]

'... where the agent on whose "apparent" authority the contractor relies has no actual authority from the corporation to enter into a particular kind of contract with the contractor on behalf of the corporation, the contractor cannot rely on the agent's own representation as to his actual authority. He can rely only on a representation by a person or persons who have actual authority to manage or conduct that part of the business of the corporation to which the contract relates'.

The House of Lords followed that proposition in the recent case of *Armagas Ltd v Mundogas SA*[18] and ruled that where A is known to have no general authority to enter into transactions of a certain type but A falsely represented to T that he had obtained from P specific

---

15 A notice in the *London Gazette* will suffice as regards persons who have had no dealings with the firm before the retirement: Partnership Act 1890 s 36 (1), (2).
16 [1982] 1 All ER 1095, 1105, [1982] Ch 374, CA.
17 [1964] 1 All ER 630, 645, [1964] 2 QB 480, 505.
18 [1986] 2 All ER 385.

authority to enter into a one-off transaction of that type, A could not, in the absence of any representation by P concerning A's authority, reasonably be believed to have authority to enter into that transaction and P was not bound by A's actions.

In *Spiro v Lintern*[19] the owner of a house asked his wife to put it into the hands of estate agents with a view to sale. She had no authority to instruct the estate agents to enter into a binding contract of sale but a contract was made, signed by the plaintiff as purchaser and by the estate agents 'as agents for the vendor'. Subsequently, the owner treated the plaintiff as the purchaser, allowing him to engage a builder to carry out repairs on the house, but the owner refused to complete. The Court of Appeal held that when the owner learned that the plaintiff believed the owner was under a binding obligation to him, the owner was under a duty to disclose the non-existence of that obligation—failure to disclose that his wife had acted without authority amounted to a representation by conduct that she had that authority and the owner was estopped from asserting that the contract had been entered into without authority. The plaintiff was entitled to specific performance of the contract.

4. Ratification

Where A has no authority but purports to contract with T on P's behalf, P may later ratify the contract and the ratification then relates back to the making of the contract by A. Ratification is the express adoption by P of the contract, or conduct showing unequivocally that he adopts A's acts.

Suppose that on Day 1, T makes an offer to sell goods which A at once unconditionally accepts on behalf of P (but without any authority from P to do so), on Day 2, T purports to revoke his offer and on Day 3, P ratifies A's acceptance of the offer. Since ratification relates back to the making of the contract by A, the contract is considered to have been complete on Day 1, and therefore, T's purported revocation is of no effect—the contract is binding on T and P.[20] However, if A's acceptance on Day 1 had

19 [1973] 3 All ER 319, [1973] 1 WLR 1002, CA.

20 *Bolton & Partners Ltd v Lambert* (1889) 41 ChD 295, CA. In the result T seems to be treated rather unfairly by the law because from the moment A accepts his offer unconditionally, T is bound if P chooses to ratify A's acceptance but P is not bound to ratify. However, if P does not ratify, T 'could sue A for breach of warranty of authority. It was held in *Kidderminister Corpn v Hardwicke* (1873) LR 9 Exch 13, that P has no right of action against T in respect of any breach committed before ratification but this case was prior to *Bolton & Partners v Lambert* and difficult to reconcile with it.

been expressly or impliedly *conditional* on P ratifying it, there would have been no completed contract on that date and any revocation by T and P ratified would have been effective.[1]

For ratification to be effective, certain conditions must be satisfied:—

(i) *Contract made expressly on behalf of P.*—There is no question of P ratifying a contract made by A without P's authority unless, when making the contract, A purported to contract as an agent and named or clearly identified P as the person for whom he was acting. In *Keighley, Maxsted & Co v Durant*[2] P authorised A to buy wheat on a joint account for A and P at a certain price. A was unable to buy at the authorised price and, without authority, bought wheat from T at a higher price. A bought in his own name though intending it to be on a joint account for P and himself. The following day P agreed with A to take this wheat on a joint account with A, but both P and A refused to take delivery of the wheat. The House of Lords held P could not be made liable for breach of contract as A had not, when acting without authority, professed to be acting for a principal and P's purported ratification was ineffective.[3]

If, however, A does make the contract in the name of P (without authority) but with the intention of fraudulently taking the benefit of the contract for himself, P may ratify and enforce the contract.[4]

(ii) *P in existence and with capacity at date of contract.*—P may only ratify a contract made on his behalf by A without authority if, at the time A made the contract P was in existence and had capacity to enter into the contract. If P was an enemy alien at the time, clearly he cannot ratify.[5] In *Kelner v Baxter*,[6] the promoters of a company that was to be formed in order to run a hotel agreed on behalf of the proposed company to purchase some wine from the plaintiff, and when the company was formed, the company purported to ratify

1 *Watson v Davies* [1931] 1 Ch 455; *Warehousing and Forwarding Co of East Africa Ltd v Jafferali & Sons Ltd* [1964] AC 1, [1963] 3 All ER 571.

2 [1901] AC 240, [1900–3] All ER Rep 40.

3 The price at which A bought was so slightly above the authorised price that one may wonder why A was not treated as having a general authority to go slightly beyond the original figure. *Stoljar* p 200.

4 *Re Tiedemann and Ledermann Freres* [1899] 2 QB 66.

5 *Boston Deep Sea Fishing & Ice Co Ltd v Farnham* [1957] 3 All ER 204; [1957] 1 WLR 1051.

6 (1866) LR 2 CP 174.

that agreement. It was held that the promoters of the company were personally liable on the contract—the company itself could not be made liable as its purported ratification was ineffective, but the promoters were made liable so as to give some real effect to the contract. Now, as an incidental result of Britain joining the EEC, this is the general rule. By s 9 (2) of the European Communities Act 1972 (now s 36 (4) of the Companies Act 1985):

> 'Where a contract purports to be made by a company, or by a person as agent for a company, at a time when the company has not been formed, then subject to any agreement to the contrary the contract has effect as one entered into by the person purporting to act for the company or as agent for it, and he is personally liable on the contract accordingly.'

The Court of Appeal held in *Phonogram Ltd v Lane*[7] that a contract was 'purported' to be made on behalf of an unformed company, even though both parties knew that the company had not then been formed and accordingly, there did not have to be a representation that the company was already in existence.

(iii) *Ratification within proper time.*—Ratification must be within any period of time fixed for ratification and in the absence of any such fixed period of time, within a reasonable period. Ratification after the contract is intended to commence is ineffective because a reasonable time cannot extend beyond the date when the contract is to commence. This was said by Fry LJ in *Metropolitan Asylums Board Managers v Kingham & Son*,[8] where there was an acceptance by A on P's behalf (without authority) of an offer by T to sell eggs, supplies to be made as from 30 September. P purported to ratify A's acceptance on 6 October but it was held to be too late and, therefore, P was unable to claim damages for non-delivery. Certainly, ratification must be at a time when it is would be lawful for P to make the contract himself. In *Grover and Grover Ltd v Mathews*[9] a contract of fire insurance had been taken out by A on P's behalf (without authority) and P purported to ratify this contract *after* a fire had taken place. The purported ratification was held to be ineffective.

---

7 [1982] QB 938, [1981] 3 All ER 182.

8 (1890) 6 TLR 217, 218. However, Parker J said more recently that no authority was cited by Fry LJ for his statement and 'I know of no principle to sustain it': *Bedford Insurance Co Ltd v Instituto de Resseguros de Brasil* [1985] QB 966, [1984] 3 All ER 766, 776.

9 [1910] 2 KB 401. Cf the rule in marine insurance: Marine Insurance Act 1906 s 86.

(iv) *Void contracts not ratifiable.*—Void contracts cannot be ratified. If directors of a company purport to make a contract which is ultra vires the company, it cannot be ratified by the shareholders of the company even after altering the memorandum of association to increase its powers, because the principle of ratification rests on the assumption that at the time of the agent's unauthorised action, authority could have been given but was not.[10]

It is believed that a forged signature cannot be ratified because a forger does not purport to act as an agent.[11]

(v) *P aware of facts.*—Finally, P can only ratify if he is aware of all the material facts, or can be shown to have adopted A's acts, whatever they were.[12] Clearly, if without P's authority A agrees to sell P's goods for £100 but informs P that he has sold them for £200, any 'ratification' by P of A's action will be ineffective if made without knowledge of the true facts.

5. Agency of necessity

In certain limited circumstances a person may be bound by a contract made on his behalf without authority and which he declines to ratify. Thus the master of a ship, in times of emergency, may contract for provisions and urgent repairs and bind the owner of the ship to such a contract. If the master signs an agreement for salvage services on behalf of the cargo owner, assuming such salvage services are necessary for the preservation of the cargo, the relationship between the master and the owner of the cargo may be an agency of necessity.[13] In *Great Northern Rail Co v Swaffield*[14] the railway company had carried a horse to its destination and there being no one to receive it and no appropriate accommodation for it on the company's premises, the horse was placed with a stable keeper and the company paid the stable keeper's charges. It was held that although the company had no express or implied

---

10 *Ashbury Railway Carriage and Iron Co v Riche* (1875) LR 7 HL 653. But an issue of shares intra vires the company, though voidable because made by the directors for improper motives is ratifiable by the company: *Bamford v Bamford* [1970] Ch 212, [1969] 1 All ER 969, CA. By the Companies Act 1985 s 35, in favour of a person dealing with a company in good faith, any transaction decided on by the directors shall be deemed to be one which it is within the capacity of the company to enter into.

11 *Brook v Hook* (1871) LR 6 Exch 89.

12 *Marsh v Joseph* [1897] 1 Ch 213, [1895–9] All ER Rep 977.

13 *China Pacific SA v Food Corpn of India, The Winston* [1982] AC 939, [1981] 3 All ER 688, HL.

14 (1874) LR 9 Exch 132.

authority to incur such charges, it had acted in an emergency as an agent of necessity and was therefore entitled to claim an indemnity from the owner of the horse.

It is not possible to claim to be an agent of necessity unless it is impossible or impracticable to communicate with the alleged principal in time. With modern means of communication, this must limit considerably the occasions when anyone can successfully claim to be an agent of necessity. In *Springer v Great Western Rly Co*[15] a consignment of tomatoes had arrived at Weymouth from Jersey after some delay due to storm at sea, and there was a railway strike which would cause further delay in their delivery to the consignees. The railway company decided to sell the tomatoes locally and were sued in damages by the consignees. The company had no express or implied authority to sell and the Court of Appeal held that they could not claim to have sold as agents of necessity because they could have communicated with the consignees to obtain instructions.

In any case, any action taken or contract made must have been reasonably necessary in the circumstances[16] and taken in good faith in the interest of the principal.[17]

The former law, that a deserted wife was an agent of necessity with authority to pledge her husband's credit, was abrogated by the Matrimonial Proceedings and Property Act 1970 s 41. The repeal of this section by the Matrimonial Causes Act 1973 s 54 (1) (b) and Sch 3, has not revived the old common law rule.

WHO CAN SUE AND BE SUED?

1. Where A has authority to bind P and P's existence is disclosed to T

Provided that A has express, implied or usual authority to bind P, if P's existence is disclosed to T, the general rule is that P and T, and only P and T, have rights and liabilities under the contract effected by A. Exceptionally, A may expressly or by implication from the contract (or by reference to trade usage) be a party to the contract either in addition to[18] or in place of P.[19] There is also a technical rule

15 [1921] 1 KB 257, [1920] All ER Rep 361, CA.

16 *Prager v Blatspiel, Stamp and Heacock Ltd* [1924] 1 KB 566, [1924] All ER Rep 524.

17 *Sachs v Miklos* [1948] 2 KB 23, [1948] 1 All ER 67; *China Pacific SA v Food Corpn of India, The Winston* [1982] AC 939, [1981] 3 All ER 688, HL.

18 *Rusholme and Bolton and Roberts Hadfield Ltd v S G Read & Co* [1955] 1 All ER 180, [1955] 1 WLR 146.

19 *Paterson v Gandasequi* (1812) 2 Smith LC (13th edn) 322.

that if A executes a deed, P can neither sue nor be sued upon it—
only A can sue and be sued even when A is described as acting for
someone else, *unless* P is described in the deed as a party to it and the
deed is executed in the name of P, or it can be established that A
contracted as trustee for P. There is too, a statutory provision to the
effect that if A is appointed by a *power of attorney*, any deed executed
by A is effectual in law as if it had been executed by A in the name
and with the signature and seal of P.[20]

It is thought that an intention that the agent shall be a
contracting party is more readily inferred if the name of the
principal has not been given. It is still, however, a matter of
construction and if the signature of A is accompanied by such words
as 'agent', clearly this negatives any personal liability on the part of
A.[1] At one time it was understood that if A contracted for a foreign
principal there was a presumption that A alone could sue and be
sued. The continued existence of such a presumption was doubted
by Bray J in 1917[2] and the Court of Appeal in 1968 held that the
usage alleged to the effect that only the agent for a foreign principal
could sue and be sued was no longer law. The Court of Appeal in
Teheran-Europe Ltd v S T Belton Ltd,[3] ruled that P's nationality was
merely one factor in determining the intention of the parties as to
whether P was a party to the contract with T and, if so, whether A
was also a party. As regards the creation of privity between P and T
the weight of this factor may be minimal, particularly where no
credit is extended by T—it may have considerably more weight in
determining whether A should be personally liable to be sued as
well as P, particularly if credit has been extended by T.

2. Where A has authority to bind P but P's existence is not disclosed to T

Suppose that P gives A authority to sell P's furniture and A does
effect a contract to sell the furniture to T without disclosing the
existence of P, ie, by purporting to sell on his own behalf, then
provided A *intended* to contract on P's behalf, (i) A can enforce the
contract against T, (ii) P can enforce the contract against T, and
(iii) T generally has a right to elect to sue either A or P.

Point (ii), the right of P to enforce the contract against T must be

20 Powers of Attorney Act 1971 s 7.
1 *Universal Steam Navigation Co Ltd v James McKelvie & Co* [1923] AC 492.
2 *Miller Gibb & Co v Smith and Tyrer Ltd* [1917] 2 KB 141.
3 [1968] 2 QB 545, [1968] 2 All ER 886.

examined further. It is a rule of business convenience that the 'undisclosed' principal should be permitted to sue and the so-called 'doctrine' of the undisclosed principal is a unique feature of the common law systems.[4] For example, on the facts given above, if A were to become bankrupt, permitting P to sue T direct ensures that P does not merely have a right to a dividend in A's bankruptcy.[5]

P may not sue T if the terms of the contract made by A with T are inconsistent with the existence of an agency. Thus, if P gave A authority to engage a maidservant and A, without disclosing that he was contracting merely as an agent, agreed to engage T, P could not enforce such contract against T because it is a personal contract. A company is entitled to consider the personality of an applicant for shares before deciding whether or not to allot shares to him, so if a broker applies for shares without disclosing he is acting for another person, the undisclosed principal would not have rights under any contract of allotment made by the company with the broker and could not, therefore, seek rescission of the contract for misrepresentation.[6] In *Humble v Hunter*,[7] P authorised A to make a contract of charter in relation to a ship owned by P. A did make such a contract with T, without disclosing that he was acting for a principal and describing himself in the charterparty as 'owner' of the 'Good Ship Ann'. It was held that P could not enforce the contract. To allow evidence that P was really the owner would be to contradict the terms of the contract and A had impliedly contracted that he was the only P.[8] But where P authorised A to obtain a charter of a ship owned by T and A made such a contract without disclosing he was acting for a principal and simply signing himself as 'charterer', the House of Lords held that P was entitled to enforce the charterparty.[9] Viscount Haldane said the term 'charterer' is

4 *Bowstead* p 3.

5 Diplock LJ said the rule can be rationalised as avoiding circuity of action for P could in equity compel A to lend his name in an action to enforce the contract against T, and would at common law be liable to indemnify A in respect of the performance of the obligations assumed by A under the contract; *Freeman and Lockyer v Buckhurst Park Properties (Magnae) Ltd* [1964] 2 QB 480, 502, [1964] 1 All ER 630, 644.

6 *Collins v Associated Greyhound Racecourses* [1930] 1 Ch 1.

7 (1848) 12 QB 310. If A misrepresents the identity of P or falsely says there is no principal, P cannot sue T, but mere non-disclosure of the existence of P is no defence to T unless the facts show that T would never have made the contract had he known of P's identity *and* the contract is a personal one: *Said v Butt* [1920] 3 KB 497, [1920] All ER Rep 232.

8 See *Powell* p 155.

9 *Fred Drughorn Ltd v Rederiakt Transatlantic* [1919] AC 203, [1918–19] All ER-Rep 1122.

very different from the term 'owner', that the term 'charterer' merely indicates someone who is entering into a contract and that to allow evidence to show that the 'charterer' merely contracted as an agent is not to contradict the terms of the contract.

On point (iii), the right of T to elect to sue either A or P, there are exceptions to his right to sue P. He cannot sue P if the terms of the contract are inconsistent with A having contracted as an agent. Nor can T sue P if T has obtained a judgment against A, whether or not he had previously discovered P's existence.[10] However, should the judgment be unsatisfied, T may seek to have the judgment set aside and then be free to sue P. Furthermore, wherever T having discovered P's existence does any unequivocal act which shows an intention to hold A liable, T has exercised his right of election and may not then sue P. Similarly, if T shows clearly that he is holding P liable on the contract, he cannot thereafter sue A. In *Clarkson Booker Ltd v Andjel*,[11] T sold goods to A who did not disclose he was purchasing them on behalf of P but T later discovered this. Letters were written by T's solicitors to both P and A threatening proceedings in respect of the price of the goods and a writ was then issued against P. When P went into liquidation, a writ was issued against A and judgment obtained against him. The Court of Appeal upheld the judgment. The court pointed out that the institution of proceedings against either A or P did not amount as a matter of law to a binding election so as to bar proceedings against the other. The institution of proceedings was normally strong evidence of such election but as T had never withdrawn the threat to sue A, T had not by suing P unequivocally elected to hold P alone liable for the price.

3. Where A has no authority to act for anyone but purports to act for a principal

A may, when contracting for himself purport to be acting for another, perhaps in order to obtain brokerage fees or for some other reason. Clearly T is entitled in these circumstances to hold A liable on the contract.

---

10 *Kendall v Hamilton* (1879) 4 App Cas 504. In so far as the rule is based on the view that P and A are joint debtors, the rule would seem to be reversed by the Civil Liability (Contribution) Act 1978 s 3. However, the rule also arises from the view that P's liability is in a sense a windfall and T cannot complain if the windfall turns out to be of limited value. It seems that the rule can only be changed by the House of Lords (*Bowstead* pp 346–347).

11 [1964] 2 QB 775, [1964] 3 All ER 260.

Moreover, A may sue T provided that A did not name a principal, or if he did, the name was fictitious or immaterial to T. In *Schmaltz v Avery*[12] T, the owner of a ship chartered it to A who was described in the charterparty as acting as agent for unnamed freighters. A was in fact acting for himself and was permitted to enforce the contract against T.

SETTLEMENT WITH THE AGENT

1. Payment to A by P

The general rule is that if P owes T money under a contract made by A on P's behalf, eg, a contract to purchase goods from 'l', should P pay A and A defaults, P is still liable to T. Of course, if T has directed P to pay by settling with A, or T has led P to believe that he (T) is looking to A alone for payment or that he has already been paid by A, P's settlement with A discharges P from any further liability. Thus, if T gives A a receipt for the price of the goods and P, on seeing this, naturally believes that T has been paid and settles with A, P is discharged.[13] In *Irvine & Co v Watson & Sons*,[14] P engaged A to buy oil for him and A made a contract to buy oil from T informing T that he was acting for a principal but without naming his principal. The terms of the sale were 'cash on delivery', but T delivered the oil without insisting on prepayment. P, believing that A had paid T for the oil, paid A. A defaulted and T sued P. The Court of Appeal held that the mere omission on the part of T to insist on prepayment was not, in the absence of an invariable custom to that effect, such conduct that could reasonably induce in P a belief that T had been paid by A. P was therefore liable to T.

The cases are conflicting as to whether the rule is any different where the existence of P is not disclosed. In *Armstrong v Stokes*[15] P engaged A & Co commission merchants, to buy goods on P's behalf. A & Co sometimes acted for themselves and sometimes as agents. A & Co bought the goods from T who had dealt with A & Co in the past and A & Co gave no indication that, on this occasion, they were acting as agents. P paid A & Co the price of the goods but A & Co did not pay T and T now sued P for the price, but it was held that P was not liable on the ground that P's payment to A & Co was

12 (1851) 16 QB 655.
13 *Wyatt v Marquis of Hertford* (1802) 3 East 147.
14 (1879) 4 QBD 102; affd (1880) 5 QBD 414.
15 (1872) LR 7 QB 598.

made at a time when T looked to A & Co alone for payment, and when T did not know of P's existence. The authority of the case is, however, doubted because it conflicts with the earlier case of *Heald v Kenworthy*[16] and was criticised by the Court of Appeal in *Irvine & Co v Watson & Sons*.[17]

2. Payment to A by T

(*a*) *T knows A to be an agent.*—Suppose that P engages A to sell goods to T and T, knowing A to be an agent, pays A the price of the goods, and A fails to account to P. Is T discharged or may P sue him for the price? The answer is that T is liable to P unless A was authorised to receive payment of the price and as a general rule, an agent to sell goods does not have authority to receive payment[18] T will only avoid having to pay twice in these circumstances if he can show that A had express, implied or apparent authority to receive payment. A factor has implied authority and so has an auctioneer when selling goods. If A is authorised, he may only be authorised to take cash.[19]

(*b*) *T does not know A to be an agent.*—It would seem to be grossly unfair to T in this case if, having paid A before he discovers P's existence, he could be made to pay over again to P unless T is aware A might be an agent. He may, however, have to pay over again if P had not authorised A to act in his own name or to receive payment of the price.[20]

3. Set-off

Where P authorises A to sell goods and A sells them to T and A owes a personal debt to T, can T set-off this private debt against the price of the goods? The answer is clearly no if T knows A to be an agent. Nor does T have a right of set-off if he knows A sometimes acts as agent and sometimes on his own account but does not enquire as to whether or not it is acting as an agent on this occasion.[1] If, however,

16 (1855) 10 Exch 739.
17 (1880) 5 QBD 414, 421.
18 *Butwick v Grant* [1924] 2 KB 483, [1924] All ER Rep 274.
19 *Williams v Evans* (1866) LR 1 QB 352. *s.q.* now cheques are common—see *Stoljar* p 81.
20 *Drakeford v Piercy* (1866) 7 B & S 515.
1 *Cooke & Sons v Eshelby* (1887) 12 App Cas 271.

T believes he is dealing with A alone and there is nothing to make him enquire as to whether A may be acting as agent, T can claim a right of set-off.[2]

BREACH OF WARRANTY OF AUTHORITY

Where A purports to have authority to act for P but does not in fact have such authority, A can be sued in the tort of deceit by anyone who relies on his representation and suffers loss if A had no honest belief in its truth.

But even where deceit cannot be proved A can be sued in damages for breach of warranty of authority. In *Collen v Wright*[3] A, believing wrongly that he had the authority of the owner of a farm to lease it, agreed to lease it to T. A was held liable in damages to T for breach of warranty of authority.[4]

A WIFE AS AGENT

By virtue of cohabitation, a man's wife (or mistress) is presumed to have authority to pledge the man's credit for necessaries. In determining whether goods supplied are necessaries, regard is had to the man's style of living rather than to his actual means.[5]

However, a man is not liable on contracts made by his wife for necessaries if:

(a) the trader has been warned expressly not to supply goods to the wife on credit;
(b) the wife has been forbidden to pledge her husband's credit;
(c) the wife was supplied with sufficient means to purchase necessaries without pledging her husband's credit;
(d) the trader gave credit exclusively to the wife; or
(e) the household already had a sufficient supply of the goods bought.

However, where a man has in the past held out his wife to a trader as having his authority to pledge his credit (for necessaries or otherwise), for example, by regularly paying his wife's debts to that trader, the husband will be liable on any later contract made by his

2 *Rabone v Williams* (1785) 7 Term Rep 360. Quaere the position where P has not authorised A to act in his own name. *Baring v Corrie* (1818) 2 B & Ald 137.
3 (1857) 8 E & B 647.
4 See also *Yonge v Toynbee* [1910] 1 KB 215, [1908–10] All ER Rep 204, p 47, post.
5 *Phillipson v Hayter* (1870) LR 6 CP 38.

wife unless the trader has knowledge that the authority has been withdrawn.[6]

A deserted wife can no longer be an agent of necessity.[7]

TERMINATION OF THE CONTRACT

By act of parties

The parties to an agency contract may at any time mutually agree to bring it to an end. Further, there is normally a right in both the principal and the agent unilaterally to revoke the agency contract at any time before the agency has been completely performed by giving notice. Thus, irrespective of any express words in the contract, the principal can revoke A's authority so that any further acts by A, purporting to be on P's behalf, will render A liable to third parties for pretending to have an authority that has been withdrawn from him—ie, for breach of warranty of authority, and of course, A cannot claim an indemnity or any remuneration for acts done after the termination of his authority. Revocation of A's authority requires no formality so that even a deed containing a power of attorney can be revoked orally. However, such unilateral withdrawal or revocation of A's authority may well be a breach of the agency contract and P can be made liable in damages to A for such breach. Damages may include loss of prospective earnings, but since an agency contract is one of personal service a court will not make an order of specific performance. In *Turner v Goldsmith*[8] a shirt manufacturer G expressly agreed to engage A as a traveller for five years certain on a commission basis. A was required to do his utmost to sell any shirts or other goods manufactured or sold by G. After two years the manufacturer's factory was burned down and he did not resume business. It was held that A was entitled to damages for breach of the express term that he was engaged for five years and the measure of damages represented what A would probably have earned by way of commission in the remainder of the five-year period. There was no evidence that G was unable to carry on his business altogether.

6 This is merely another example of agency by estoppel examined earlier ante, p 32.

7 Matrimonial Proceedings and Property Act 1970 s 41. The repeal of this section by the Matrimonial Causes Act 1973 s 54 (1) (b) and Sch 3, has not revived the old common law rule.

8 [1891] 1 QB 544. Contra, *Rhodes v Forwood* (1876) 1 App Cas 256, where there was no express agreement to employ the agent for any particular period.

It all depends on the terms of the agency contract whether a revocation by either the principal or his agent gives rise to liability for breach of contract. It should be appreciated that even though a principal has revoked an agent's authority, the principal may still be liable on a later contract made by the agent on his behalf with a third party who relies on the agent's previous authority and has not been informed that the authority has been terminated.[9]

If the agency contract is also a contract of service and no fixed term is provided for, the need for reasonable notice is implied and failure to give it will be a breach of contract.[10] Moreover, if the agency contract is analogous to a service contract, again reasonable notice will be required to terminate the contract. Thus in *Martin-Baker Aircraft Co Ltd v Murison*[11] P & Co, appointed A their sole selling agent in North America, A was required to devote considerable time and money in his duties and A was not permitted to become interested in the sale of competitive products. No time limit was provided for in their contract. McNair J held that a term would be implied that either side must give 12 months' notice to terminate the contract.

By operation of law

Subject to exceptions depending upon the special terms of the appointment and the types of irrevocable agency referred to below, an agency is normally terminated automatically in the following circumstances—

1. *End of fixed period or execution of authority.*—If the agency is expressed (or can be implied by trade usage) to be for a fixed period, the contract of agency terminates at the end of that period. Where no time has been laid down, the contract ends when the agent has completed all he has been authorised to do. Having discharged his duty, the agent is said to be 'functus officio'.[12]

2. *Death, mental incapacity, or bankruptcy of either party.*—Since the agency relationship is a personal one, the death, mental incapacity, or bankruptcy of either the principal or the agent (assuming the

9 See ante, pp 32–34.
10 *Bauman v Hulton Press* [1952] 2 All ER 1121.
11 [1955] 2 QB 556, [1955] 2 All ER 722.
12 It is not always easy to say when an agent has become functus officio. See *Keppel v Wheeler* [1927] 1 KB 577, p 7, ante.

agent is unfit to continue his duties) brings the contract to an end and notice of such event to the other party is immaterial. In *Yonge v Toynbee*[13] a solicitor started legal proceedings on behalf of a client. The client was later certified insane and without knowledge of this, the solicitor continued to act for him and took certain steps in the litigation. The solicitor-agent was liable to the third party for breach or warranty of authority—ie, purporting to have an authority which he no longer had by reason of his principal having become insane.[14] However, by s 45 of the Bankruptcy Act 1914, where a principal becomes bankrupt, the agent is not liable for breach of warranty of authority in respect of a contract made by him before the date of the receiving order, without notice of any act of bankruptcy. If the principal is a company, a winding-up order will terminate the authority of its agents.

3. *Supervening illegality or frustration.*—Like any other contract, an agency contract may be discharged by frustration. The general law of contract applies so that, for example, if a principal is conscripted for military service,[15] or if an estate agent is instructed to sell a house and the house is burned down before the sale is effected, the contract of agency is discharged by frustration.

Irrevocable authority

Common law. It has long been a rule that where an agent has been given authority to act for his principal as a security for some debt or obligation by the principal to the agent, the authority is irrevocable without the agent's agreement. It was expressed in *Smart v Sandars*[16] to be 'an authority coupled with an interest'. Thus, if P owes A £100 and then, as security for that liability, P appoints A his agent to sell goods on P's behalf, allowing A to retain £100 out of the proceeds, such authority is irrevocable without A's consent.

In *Smart v Sandars* itself, however, it was held that where P appointed A his agent to sell goods on his behalf, handing over possession of the goods to A, and subsequently A made advances to

13 [1910] 1 KB 215, [1908–10] All ER Rep 204.
14 The principal may be liable by reason of estoppel if the third party has no knowledge of the insanity: *Drew v Nunn* (1879) 4 QBD 661. Possibly a principal's personal representatives are *not* liable by reason of estoppel if the principal dies and subsequently the agent enters into a contract with a third party who is unaware of the death: *Blades v Free* (1829) 9 B & C 167.
15 *Morgan v Manser* [1948] 1 KB 184, [1947] 2 All ER 666.
16 (1848) 5 CB 895.

P, A's authority was revocable. After P withdrew A's authority, therefore, A had no right to sell the goods in order to recoup himself out of the proceeds for the advances he had made to P. The ratio of the decision was that at the time A was given authority to sell he did not then have an interest.

It should be added that an authority coupled with an interest is irrevocable by the death, insanity or bankruptcy of the principal, which events do normally terminate an agency by operation of law, as has been seen above.

Statute. By virtue of s 5 of the Powers of Attorney Act 1971, the donee of a power of attorney who acts in pursuance of the power at a time when it has been revoked shall not, by reason of the revocation, incur any liability (either to the donor or to any other person) if at the time he did not know that the power had been revoked. Where a power of attorney has been revoked and a person without knowledge of the revocation deals with the donee of the power, the transaction between them shall, in favour of that person, be as valid as if the power had been in existence.

By virtue of the Enduring Powers of Attorney Act 1985,[17] a person may appoint an attorney whose authority is *not* terminated by that person's subsequent mental incapacity. The Act requires certain formalities to be followed in the creation of an enduring power of attorney, ie the instrument creating the power must be in the prescribed form, it must be executed in the prescribed manner by both P and A and it must incorporate at the time of execution by P the prescribed explanatory information (s 2). By s 4, if A, having an 'enduring power', has reason to believe that P is or is becoming mentally incapable, he must as soon as practicable make an application to the Court of Protection to register the instrument creating the power, first giving notice of his intention to do so to certain relatives of P and to P himself. While P remains mentally capable, the 'enduring power' operates as an ordinary power of attorney except that A may not disclaim otherwise than by written notice given to P. In the event of P's incapacity, A's power is suspended until he has applied to the Court of Protection to register the instrument creating the power, on which event A has limited authority to maintain P and prevent loss to P's estate. Section 5 of the Powers of Attorney Act 1971 applies to protect P and third parties. Then, if no successful objection is made by specified

17 See Practice Direction [1986] 2 All ER 41, [1986] 1 WLR 419.

relatives, the Court registers the instrument and A once more has full authority under the instrument. While the instrument remains registered, P may not (even if mentally capable) revoke the power without the Court's confirmation and A may disclaim only by notice to the Court (s 7).

Chapter 2

Sale of goods

A CONTRACT OF SALE OF GOODS

Codification and consolidation of the law

One of the most important types of contract at the present day is a contract for the sale of goods. The purpose of such a contract is readily understood—it is to transfer the ownership of goods from one person, the seller, to another, the buyer. To a large extent, the law relating to contracts of sale of goods was codified by the Sale of Goods Act 1893,[1] but this Act was amended, particularly by the Supply of Goods (Implied Terms) Act 1973 and the law has now been consolidated in the Sale of Goods Act 1979 which came into force on 1 January 1980. For those accustomed to the section numbers of the 1893 Act it is convenient that *most* of the section numbers of the 1979 Act are the same. Unless otherwise stated, references in this chapter to sections are to sections of the Sale of Goods Act 1979. The Act applies to contracts made on or after 1 January 1894 but in relation to contracts made on certain dates the Act applies subject to the modification of certain of its sections as mentioned in Sch 1. Any such modification is indicated in the section concerned by a reference to Sch 1.

The general principles of law that are applicable to all contracts still apply to contracts of sale of goods, unless those principles are inconsistent with the express provisions of the Act. Section 62 (2) of

---

1 In interpreting a codifying Act, Lord Herschell in *Bank of England v Vagliano Bros* [1891] AC 107, 144, said that 'the proper course is in the first instance to examine the language of the statute and to ask what is its natural meaning, uninfluenced by any consideration derived from the previous state of the law. . . .' Cases on sale of goods decided prior to 1893 may be referred to, however, in order to resolve any ambiguity in the Sale of Goods Act or to illustrate a technical meaning.

the Sale of Goods Act shows how a contract of sale of goods fits into the general framework of contract law:—

> 'The rules of the common law, including the law merchant, except in so far as they are inconsistent with the provisions of this Act, and in particular the rules relating to the law of principal and agent and the effect of fraud, misrepresentation, duress or coercion, mistake, or other invalidating cause, apply to contracts for the sale of goods.'

Many of the non-statutory rules governing, eg misrepresentation and mistake, are rules not of the *common law* but of *equity*. It seems certain that the rules of equity as well as those of the common law apply to contracts of sale of goods unless they are inconsistent with the Act.

By virtue of certain provisions in the Act, a number of terms and conditions are implied in contracts of sale of goods. Inter alia there is an implied term that if the purpose for which goods are required is made known expressly or impliedly to the seller, the goods supplied will be reasonably fit for that purpose (s 14). Similarly, there are provisions in s 29 which determine the duties of the seller with regard to the delivery of goods sold. Until the Act was amended by the Supply of Goods (Implied Terms) Act 1973 (followed by the Unfair Contract Terms Act 1977), it was clear that the various rights and duties implied by the provisions of the Act could always be excluded or modified. But s 55 (1) now reads as follows—with the key qualification in brackets:—

> 'Where a right, duty or liability would arise under a contract of sale of goods by implication of law it may (subject to the Unfair Contract Terms Act 1977) be negatived or varied by express agreement, or by the course of dealing between the parties, or by such usage as binds both parties to the contract.'

The phrase 'course of dealing' means that past business between the parties may raise 'an implication as to the terms to be implied in a fresh contract where no express provision is made on the point at issue'.[2] Thus, if in the past the parties have contracted on the basis that the seller would deliver the goods at the buyer's place of business, a court may imply that the parties intended to contract on the same basis in the present transaction. The 'course of dealing' between the parties would prevail over the general rule set out in s 29 (2) that the place of delivery is the seller's place of business. Similarly, if it is shown that the parties intended to contract according to the usage of a particular trade, that usage prevails over

---

2 Per McCardie J in *Pocahontas Fuel Co v Ambatielos* (1922) 27 Com Cas 148, 152.

terms implied by the Act. In *Cointat v Myham*,[3] for example, a butcher bought the carcase of a pig from a salesman in Smithfield Market. The meat was subsequently condemned as unfit for food. Evidence was admitted to show that, by the usage of the market, no term as to fitness for food was implied, and that usage was held by the court to govern the transaction rather than s 14 of the Act.

Later in this chapter, under the head 'Terms of the Contract', we shall examine the implied obligations of the seller and note how contracting out of these obligations is now considerably restricted, especially if it is a consumer sale, by the Unfair Contract Terms Act 1977.

FORMATION OF THE CONTRACT

Definition

Section 2 (1) of the Sale of Goods Act defines a contract of sale of goods as follows:—

> 'A contract of sale of goods is a contract by which the seller transfers or agrees to transfer the property in goods to the buyer for a money consideration, called the price.'

There may be a contract of sale between one part owner and another and the contract may be absolute or conditional.

Where the transfer of property takes place at once, the contract is called a sale, and where the transfer of property is to take place at a future time or subject to some condition that has to be fulfilled, such as payment of the price, the contract is an agreement to sell. An agreement to sell becomes a sale when the time elapses or the conditions are fulfilled subject to which the property in the goods is to be transferred (s 2 (6)).

The Act does not apply to a mortgage transaction even though it may, on the face of it, appear to be an ordinary sale of goods.[4]

'Goods' are defined in s 61 as including:—

> 'all personal chattels other than things in action and money and . . . includes emblements, industrial growing crops, and things attached to or forming part of the land which are agreed to be severed before sale or under the contract of sale'.

3 (1914) 110 LT 749, 30 TLR 282.
4 Section 62 (4). See *Polsky v S and A Services* [1951] 1 All ER 185, affd, [1951] 1 All ER 1062n.

It follows from the definition that sales of ships[5] or animals are included but sales of real property or chattels real (leaseholds) are not sales of goods; nor is a sale of minerals unless they are already detached from the land. It was held in *Morgan v Russell & Sons*[6] that the sale of cinders and slag, which were not in definite or detached heaps resting on the ground, was not a sale of goods but a sale of an interest in land itself. 'Things in action' like shares and negotiable instruments are not goods, but money would be goods if dealt with as a curio, like an 1897 Jubilee £5 gold piece.[7] 'Emblements' and 'industrial growing crops' (*fructus industriales*) are crops like potatoes or wheat that are not naturally growing but are grown by the industry of man.[8] Even common law regarded these crops as goods and not as interests in land so that a contract to sell wheat, entered into even before it is harvested, has always been a contract for the sale of goods. 'Things attached to or forming part of the land' include things that are growing naturally on the land (*fructus naturales*) such as timber or grass, as well as fixtures. Common law treated a sale of *fructus naturales* as a sale of goods only if the subject-matter was to be severed before or very soon after the contract was made. Now, by the Sale of Goods Act, so long as, say, timber is to be severed before sale or 'under the contract of sale', it is a contract of sale of goods and it is thought that it does not matter how long a delay there is before severance is effected.[9]

Contracts for work and supply of materials. It used to be a matter of some considerable importance to distinguish between a contract of sale of goods and a contract for work or skill, because until the Law Reform (Enforcement of Contracts) Act 1954, contracts for the sale

5 *Behnke v Bede Shipping Co* [1927] 1 KB 649, 659, [1927] All ER Rep 689, per Wright J.
6 [1909] 1 KB 357.
7 *Moss v Hancock* [1899] 2 QB 111.
8 'Industrial growing crops' has a wider meaning than 'emblements' because it includes a crop not maturing within 12 months, eg, clover.
9 This view may, however, be doubted. Suppose, for example, A is given by contract a right for 10 years to take the annual crop of B's field. Could not that be interpreted as a contract to take a 'right, privilege or benefit in, or over, or derived from land', which things are comprised in the definition of 'Land' in s 205 (1) (ix) of the Law of Property Act 1925, a later Act of Parliament than the Sale of Goods Act? The point may be important because by s 40 of the Law of Property Act, a sale of an interest in land is unenforceable unless there is a note or memorandum in writing of the contract, signed by the party to be charged. Perhaps the correct view is that such a contract is both a sale of goods and a sale of an interest in land (Atiyah *Sale of Goods* (7th edn, 1985) p 42).

of goods of the value of £10 and upwards were unenforceable unless, for example, evidenced in writing. The Court of Appeal in *Robinson v Graves*[10] held that a contract to paint a portrait was a contract for skill and not a contract for the sale of goods. The reasoning of the court was that the 'substance of the contract' was the skill and experience of the artist in producing the picture, and it was only ancillary that there would pass to the customer some materials, namely the paint and canvas, in addition to the skill involved in the production of the portrait. The distinction still exists because, in contracts of sale of goods, there are certain conditions implied by the Sale of Goods Act, such as under s 14 that goods sold are reasonably fit for the purpose for which the buyer requires them if he has made known such purpose expressly or impliedly to the seller. In a contract for the repair of a car, where the substance of the contract is skill and labour and it is only ancillary that materials or new parts are supplied, s 14 of the Sale of Goods Act cannot be invoked if these materials supplied are not fit for the purpose, as it is not a contract for the sale of goods. However, case law and (in 1982) statute intervened to introduce similar implied terms. In the 1960s it was held by the House of Lords that in a contract for work and the supply of materials, terms are implied that the materials supplied be of reasonable fitness for their purpose and of reasonable quality. In *Young and Marten Ltd v McManus Childs Ltd*,[11] building contractors subcontracted some roofing work to the appellants and specified they should use 'Somerset 13' tiles. These tiles were made by only one manufacturer and the appellants used these tiles in the roofing

---

10 [1935] 1 KB 579, [1935] All ER Rep 935. In earlier cases, like *Lee v Griffin* (1861) 1 B & S 272, it was held that if a contract resulted in the transfer of goods from one person to another, it must be a contract of sale.

11 [1969] 1 AC 454,[1968] 2 All ER 1169. See also *Gloucestershire County Council v Richardson* [1969] 1 AC 480, [1968] 2 All ER 1181, HL. In *Stewart v Reavell's Garage* [1952] 2 QB 545, [1952] 1 All ER 1191, the plaintiff took his car to a firm of motor repairers to have the braking system repaired and agreed, on the recommendation of the repairers, that certain parts of the brakes should be sent to a particular specialist for relining. The car was later damaged in an accident owing to unsuitable brake linings and faulty work carried out by the specialist. The court held the repairers liable for the damage on the ground that there can be implied in a contract for work done and materials supplied in repairing a motor car an absolute warranty of fitness for the intended purpose of the work, if the circumstances show, as they did here, that the work was of the type which the repairers held themselves out to perform (either by themselves or by sub-contractors) and the purpose was made known to the repairers. See also *Ingham v Emes* [1955] 2 QB 366, [1955] 2 All ER 740, where the defendant hairdresser was held not liable to a customer who, knowing she was allergic to a certain dye, failed to disclose this fact to the defendant before he used the dye on her.

work—after exposure to weather, defects in the tiles became apparent and the building contractors sued the appellants for damages. The House of Lords held that on the facts the appellants were liable in damages because the materials supplied were not of good quality.

By the Supply of Goods and Services Act 1982, in a contract for the transfer of property in goods that is analogous to a sale of goods contract, such as a contract for work and the supply of materials, terms are implied as to title, description, fitness for purpose and quality. The detailed provisions of Pt I of the Act which deal with these matters are modelled on ss 12–15 of the Sale of Goods Act, discussed below. Contractual terms which seek to exclude or restrict liability for breach of obligations arising under the 1982 Act are subject to the provisions of the Unfair Contract Terms Act 1977.[12]

Capacity

Capacity to buy and sell is regulated by the general law concerning capacity to contract and to transfer and acquire property (s 3).

A minor's liability to pay a reasonable price for 'necessaries' sold and delivered to him (as also that of a person who by reason of mental incapacity or drunkenness is incompetent to contract) is put into statutory form by s 3, which also defines 'necessaries' as 'goods suitable to the condition in life of the minor or other person concerned and to his actual requirements at the time of the sale and delivery.' It is for the seller to prove that the goods are necessaries. Probably, a minor is not liable on an executory contract of sale and, in consequence, if a minor orders a suit of clothes to be made for him, it seems that there is no liability on him if he cancels the order at any time before delivery is made of the suit. By the Family Law Reform Act 1969, the age of majority was reduced from 21 to 18 as from 1 January 1970.

Price

From the definition of a contract for the sale of goods, it is apparent that the consideration must be money and a barter transaction is not within the Act. However, if part of the consideration is in the form of money, the contract seems to be one of sale of goods. In *Aldridge v Johnson*,[13] a contract for the exchange of 52 bullocks with

12 See pp 118–119, post.
13 (1857) 7 E & B 885.

100 quarters of barley, the difference in value to be made up in cash, was accepted as being a contract of sale. So too, if a man when buying a new car from a dealer hands over his old one in 'part exchange', making up the balance in the form of money, the sale of the new car is a sale of goods. It has been suggested that the transaction relating to the old car is also a sale though no money passes if, as is usual, the parties fix a notional price which is set off against the price of the new car.[14]

By s 8 (1), the price in a contract of sale of goods may be fixed by the contract, or left to be fixed in an agreed manner, for example, by a third party valuer, or determined by the course of dealing between the parties. Thus, if although the parties have not agreed expressly on the price nor agreed that it be settled by a valuer or by arbitration, a court may be able to imply the price the parties intended should be paid by reference to the price paid in earlier similar transactions between the same parties. The price is determined by the 'course of dealing' between the parties. Section 8 (2) adds that where the price is not determined in accordance with the provisions of s 8 (1), the buyer must pay a reasonable price; what is a reasonable price is a question of fact dependant on the circumstances of each particular case.

Section 8 presupposes that a contract of sale has been finally concluded. In *May and Butcher Ltd v R*,[15] an agreement for the sale of tentage at a price to be fixed by the parties at a later date was held by the House of Lords not to be a concluded contract at all. The *only* provision in the agreement for determining the price required further discussion between the parties so that the parties were really still in the process of negotiation. On the other hand, if nothing had been said as to price in the agreement, there would have been a concluded contract and by s 8 (2) a 'reasonable price' would have been payable.

Where parties do agree that the price is to be fixed by the

14 *Atiyah* p 7. The Law Commission, in its *Report on Implied Terms in Contracts for the Supply of Goods* (Law Com No 95, 1979), after saying that barter is sometimes used in substantial commercial transactions and that retail sales promotion by way of coupons, vouchers, etc brings about transactions on the borderline of sale and barter, recommended that the supplier by barter should be under the same implied obligations as to title, quality, etc as a seller of goods. The recommendation was implemented by the Supply of Goods and Services Act 1982.

15 [1934] 2 KB 17n. The case can be contrasted with *Foley v Classique Coaches Ltd* [1934] 2 KB 1, [1934] All ER Rep 8, where there was an agreement to buy petrol at a price to be agreed by the parties in writing from time to time and a provision for the submission of any dispute to arbitration. The Court of Appeal held that there was a concluded contract because the price could be determined otherwise than by the parties themselves, ie, by arbitration.

valuation of a third party and such third party cannot or does not make the valuation, the agreement is avoided, provided that if the goods or any part of them have been delivered to and appropriated by the buyer he must pay a reasonable price for them (s 9 (1)). Where the third party is prevented from making the valuation by the fault of the seller or buyer, the party not in fault may maintain an action in damages against the party in fault (s 9 (2)). That would be the position where the seller refuses to allow the valuer to examine the goods so that the latter cannot make the valuation.

Form of contract

There is now no general rule requiring any contract of sale of goods of any value to be in any particular form (s 4). Exceptional cases are contracts for the sale of a British ship or a share therein, within s 24 of the Merchant Shipping Act 1894, and certain contracts of conditional sale or credit sale, which are examined later.[16] By the Bills of Sale Act 1878, if a sale is effected in writing and the seller retains possession, the sale is ineffective against the seller's trustee in bankruptcy and persons seizing goods in execution, unless the sale has been registered as a bill of sale.

TRANSFER OF PROPERTY TO THE BUYER

Sections 16 to 20 of the Sale of Goods Act are preceded by the heading: 'Transfer of property as between seller and buyer'. The object of any contract of sale of goods is to transfer the ownership of goods from the seller to the buyer and the word 'property' in this heading, as indeed in the actual provisions of the Act, is used synonymously with 'ownership'. Sections 16 to 19 contain rules for determining *when* the property or ownership in goods is transferred to the buyer. One of the reasons why it may be important to know at what particular moment of time ownership is transferred is because at that moment, by virtue of s 20, the risk of any loss or damage to the goods generally passes to the buyer. So long as the ownership rests with the seller the goods are still at his risk. This principle and the exceptions to it are examined below in the section on 'Risk of Loss'. Further, it is only when ownership has passed to the buyer that the seller is generally entitled to sue him for the price.

It should be emphasised that if the ownership or property in

16 See pp 201–203, post.

goods has passed to the buyer, that does not necessarily mean that he is entitled to delivery of the goods. Unless the seller has agreed to give the buyer credit, s 28 makes it clear that the buyer is entitled to delivery only if he has tendered the price for the goods.[17] The reverse side of the same principle is that just because the seller has not yet delivered the goods to the buyer, that does not necessarily mean that the ownership and risk of loss remain with the seller.

Classification of goods

The rules, now to be considered, as to when the property in goods passes to a buyer depend on whether the goods are specific goods, or are unascertained or future goods. 'Specific goods' are defined in s 61 as goods identified and agreed on at the time a contract of sale is made. 'Unascertained goods' are not defined in the Act. An example of a sale of unascertained goods would be a sale by a dealer of a new Ford Sierra 1987 model; until one particular car of the model specified is appropriated or earmarked to the contract, the goods are unascertained goods. It is a sale of goods of a kind—a sale of 'generic' goods. Also, a sale of part only of a quantity of timber in the seller's yard, or a sale of a given proportion of spirit contained in a storage tank is a sale of unascertained goods. In *Re Wait*,[18] a sale of 500 tons of wheat out of a quantity of 1,000 tons of wheat on board a ship was held to be a sale of unascertained goods. The buyers paid in advance of delivery of the goods and the seller went bankrupt. Since, as we shall now see, the property in unascertained goods cannot pass until the goods are ascertained, the buyers had no right to claim the goods and could only prove as unsecured creditors in the seller's bankruptcy. Prior to the Sale of Goods Act there had been a rule of equity[19] that goods were ascertained if they were capable of being identified as the thing sold but it seems clear since *Re Wait* that this no longer exists. Atkin LJ in that case said that the rules in the Sale of Goods Act for the transfer of property appeared to be complete and exclusive statements of the legal relations between the seller and the buyer.[20]

'Future goods' are defined in s 5 (1) as goods 'to be manufactured or acquired' by the seller after the making of the contract of sale. Generally, future goods will also be unascertained goods; in the

17 See p 123, post.
18 [1927] 1 Ch 606, [1926] All ER Rep 433.
19 *Tailby v Official Receiver* (1888) 13 App Cas 523, 533, per Lord Watson.
20 [1927] 1 Ch 606, 635–636.

example just given of a sale by a dealer of a new Ford Sierra 1987 model, that will be a sale of future goods, assuming the seller has not yet acquired the actual car that will in due course be earmarked to the contract; it is also a sale of unascertained goods. An agreement for the sale of goods not yet acquired by the seller could, however, be an agreement for the sale of specific goods already identified by the seller with the buyer's implied agreement: the 'future goods' here would be specific not unascertained goods. Thus, suppose B wants to purchase from S, an antique dealer, a table of a particular type. S does not have one in stock but knows that T, another dealer, does have just one. S makes an agreement with B to sell him that particular table. It is a sale of 'future goods' because S has not himself yet acquired ownership and it is also a sale of specific goods because the subject-matter of the sale has already been identified by S with B's implied agreement. If S were uncertain as to whether T would be willing to sell the table, then the agreement between S and B may have expressly been made contingent on T selling the table to S. Such a contract between S and B is still a contract of sale of goods. Section 5 (2) provides:—

> 'There may be a contract for the sale of goods the acquisition of which by the seller depends on a contingency which may or may not happen.'

The non-happening of the contingency brings the contract to an end. By s 5 (3):—

> 'Where by a contract of sale the seller purports to effect a present sale of future goods, the contract operates as an agreement to sell the goods.'

This means that if, say, S agrees to build a ship for B, the property in the ship will, as a general rule, only pass to B when the ship's construction is complete and the ship is appropriated to B. However, S and B might agree that B should pay the price by instalments and that on payment of the first instalment, the vessel and all materials purchased for its construction should become B's absolute property.[1]

The basic rules

By s 16, where there is a contract for the sale of unascertained goods, no property in the goods is transferred to the buyer unless and until the goods are ascertained, ie, identified after the contract as being in

---

1 *Re Blyth Shipbuilding and Dry Docks Co* [1926] Ch 494, [1926] All ER Rep 373, CA.

accordance with the agreement. In *Healy v Howlett & Sons*,[2] the plaintiff, a fish exporter carrying on business in Ireland, agreed to sell to the defendants 20 boxes of mackerel. The plaintiff despatched 190 boxes of mackerel by rail, instructing the railway officials to deliver 20 of the boxes to the defendants. The fish deteriorated before those instructions were carried out, that is, before any of the 190 boxes were earmarked for the defendants. It was held that the property in all the boxes remained in the plaintiff. The boxes were, therefore, still at his risk, and the defendants were not liable for the price. Contrast *Wardar's (Import and Export) Co Ltd v W Norwood & Sons Ltd*[3] where S who had 1,500 cartons of kidneys in a cold store in London sold 600 of these cartons to B. S gave B's carrier a delivery note authorising him to collect 600 cartons and, when the carrier arrived at S's cold store, 600 cartons had already been placed on the pavement. B's carrier having produced his delivery note, these cartons were loaded in to the carrier's lorry and when they arrived at B's premises in Glasgow the kidneys were found to be unfit for human consumption. There was no evidence that the kidneys had deteriorated before the carrier loaded them. The Court of Appeal held that the goods were ascertained from the time the carrier loaded the goods, the property passed to B at that time and the goods were no longer at S's risk. Hence B was obliged to pay for them. Mustill J held in *Karlshamns Oljefabriker v Eastport Navigation*[4] that the issue of 'ascertainment' under s 16 must be interpreted broadly and where there were parallel contracts between the parties encompassing the whole of a consignment of unascertained goods passing from a seller to a buyer or from different sellers to the buyer, the goods are 'ascertained' when the whole of the consignment covered by all the contracts was ascertained in bulk, without any necessity for the goods to be physically allocated between the separate contracts or for the buyer to nominate which particular goods come from which particular source.

The other basic rule is that, where there is a contract for the sale of specific or ascertained goods, the property in them is transferred to the buyer at such time as the parties to the contract intend it to be transferred. For the purpose of ascertaining the intention of the parties, regard is had to the terms of the contract, the conduct of the parties, and the circumstances of the case (s 17). Diplock LJ, said in *R V Ward Ltd v Bignall*:[5] 'in modern times very little is needed to give

2 [1917] 1 KB 337.
3 [1968] 2 QB 663, [1968] 2 All ER 602, CA.
4 [1982] 1 All ER 208.
5 [1967] 1 QB 534, [1967] 2 All ER 449, 453, CA.

rise to the inference that the property in specific goods is to pass only on delivery or payment'. Clearly, the parties to a contract for the sale of specific goods can expressly agree on the exact time at which the property in them is to pass. It is not, however, normal to do so and s 18 provides that, unless a different intention appears, 'the following are rules for ascertaining the intention of the parties as to the time at which the property in the goods is to pass to the buyer'. There then follow the five rules in s 18.

The Rules in section 18

Rule 1.—'Where there is an unconditional contract for the sale of specific goods in a deliverable state the property in the goods passes to the buyer when the contract is made, and it is immaterial whether the time of payment or the time of delivery, or both, be postponed.'

In *Tarling v Baxter*,[6] there was a sale of a haystack. Before the buyer took it away, it was burned down. It was held that the loss fell on the buyer and he still had to pay the price because the property had passed to him at the time of the contract, and the fact that the buyer had not yet taken delivery was immaterial.

If, *after* a contract has been made for the sale of goods, the parties agree that the property is not to pass until a certain time, such agreement will have no effect if the property has already passed by reason of the operation of this rule. In *Dennant v Skinner and Collom*[7] a car was knocked down at an auction to a crook named King, who had given a false name and address, and he asked to take away the car in return for a cheque. King was only allowed to do this after signing a document in which it was agreed that the title to the vehicle should not pass until the cheque had been met. King resold the car to the defendant. It was held that, since there was no agreement to the contrary at the time of the sale, which was effected when the auctioneer knocked down the car to King, the property in the car passed to King there and then under rule 1 of s 18, and the subsequently signed document had no effect. The defendant therefore had acquired a good title to the car by buying from the owner of it.[8]

Goods are in a 'deliverable state' by s 61 (5) when they are in such a state that the buyer would under the contract be bound to

---

6 (1827) 6 B & C 360.
7 [1948] 2 KB 164, [1948] 2 All ER 29.
8 Presumably, in any case, the defendant could have relied on what is now s 25 (1); see p 88, post.

take delivery of them. In *Underwood Ltd v Burgh Castle Brick and Cement Syndicate*[9] a condensing engine, weighing 30 tons and embedded in a flooring of concrete, was sold to the defendants. It had to be detached from its base and dismantled by the plaintiffs before it was in such state that the buyer would be bound to take delivery. The property did not pass under rule 1 as the goods were not at the time of the contract in a deliverable state. There has been some suggestion that an 'unconditional contract' in the words of the rule mean a contract not containing any important terms, but the better view seems to be that it means that the contract is not subject to any condition precedent (or subsequent) in contrast to the type of contract covered by rules 2, 3 and 4.[10]

Rule 2.—'Where there is a contract for the sale of specific goods and the seller is bound to do something to the goods, for the purpose of putting them into a deliverable state, the property does not pass until such thing is done and the buyer has notice that it has been done.'

In the *Underwood* case just referred to, the engine was broken while being loaded on to a railway track. The Court of Appeal held that it was not in a 'deliverable state', ie, the buyer was not bound to take delivery of it, until it was completely and without mishap put on the truck, and the plaintiffs had no right to claim the price of the engine as the risk of loss was still on them—the property had not passed under rule 2. In any contract of sale where the seller agrees to repair or alter goods for the buyer, they will not be in a 'deliverable state' until the repairs or alterations are done. The property in the goods will only pass when such repairs or alterations have been done and the buyer has notice of that fact. The Act does not specify that the seller must *give* notice and therefore the knowledge of the buyer may be enough.

Rule 3.—'Where there is a contract for the sale of specific goods in a deliverable state but the seller is bound to weigh, measure, test, or do some other act or thing with reference to the goods for the purpose of ascertaining the price, the property does not pass until such act or thing is done and the buyer has notice that it has been done.'

If, for example, there is a sale of a sack of coffee at so much per

9 [1922] 1 KB 343, [1921] All ER Rep 515.

10 See *Atiyah* pp 224–225. It has also been suggested that goods are not in a deliverable state if, eg they are unmerchantable: Fridman *The Sale of Goods* (1966) p 71. Sed queare *Atiyah* p 226.

pound, and it is agreed that the seller weigh the coffee to ascertain the total price payable, the property in the sack does not pass until that is done and the buyer has notice.[11] If, however, it were agreed that the buyer do the weighing or measuring, the property would pass at the time of the contract under rule 1.[12]

Rule 4.—'When goods are delivered to the buyer on approval or on sale or return or other similar terms the property in the goods passes to the buyer:—

   (a) when he signifies his approval or acceptance to the seller or does any other act adopting the transaction;

   (b) if he does not signify his approval or acceptance to the seller but retains the goods without giving notice of rejection, then, if a time has been fixed for the return of the goods, on the expiration of that time, and, if no time has been fixed, on the expiration of a reasonable time.'

Considering first part (a) of this rule, obviously as soon as the person taking goods on 'approval or on sale or return' informs the seller that he wants to buy them, the property passes. Further, it has been held that if the person taking the goods does any act in relation to the goods consistent only with his having become the purchaser, such as selling or pledging them, then that is an 'act adopting the transaction' and the property in the goods passes to him. In *Kirkham v Attenborough*[13] the plaintiff let X have jewellery on sale or return and X pawned the jewellery with the defendants. The plaintiff's action for the recovery of the jewellery failed as X's act in pawning the jewellery was held to be an 'act adopting the transaction', the property in the goods thereby passed to X, and X, therefore, was able to give rights under a pledge to the defendants. As a reminder that all these rules in s 18 are only applicable if there is no contrary

11 If there is a sale of all the seller's stock of a certain article and it is agreed that the seller count the stock to ascertain the price payable, it is uncertain whether the property cannot pass until the seller completes the counting and informs the buyer of the result. In a case decided before the Sale of Goods Act, the property was held not to pass in such circumstances until the counting was completed: *Zagury v Furnell* (1809) 2 Camp 240. Contra, Lord Alverstone CJ, obiter in *R v Tideswell* [1905] 2 KB 273, 277.

12 *Turley v Bates* (1863) 2 H & C 200.

13 [1897] 1 QB 201. Other examples are *Genn v Winkel* (1912) 28 TLR 483, and *London Jewellers Ltd v Attenborough* [1934] 2 KB 206, [1934] All ER Rep 270. Fridman shows the difference of approach of the courts in these two cases: in the former, stress was laid on keeping the goods more than a reasonable time; in the latter, stress was laid on behaving or acting as a buyer: *Fridman* pp 80–81.

intention in the contract, we may mention the case of *Weiner v Gill*.[14] Here again, jewellery was delivered to X on sale or return, but on the terms of a document which stated that the goods remained the plaintiff's property until the goods were paid for. X pledged the jewellery with the defendant, but never paid for the jewellery. An action for recovery of the jewellery succeeded, because, on the express terms of the sale or return agreement, the property in the jewellery had not passed to X.

Part (b) of rule 4 embodies the effect of *Elphick v Barnes*,[15] where a horse was handed over on approval for eight days and died on the third day. The property was held not to have passed because the eight-day period had not expired and the risk, therefore, remained in the seller. In *Re Ferrier, ex p Trustee v Donald*[16] furniture was delivered to Mrs F on sale or return within a week, and after two days the furniture was seized in an execution by the sheriff. The sheriff retained the goods for a month. It was held that the property had not passed to Mrs F under rule 4 (b) because it was not Mrs F who had retained the goods beyond the one-week period. In *Poole v Smith's Car Sales (Balham) Ltd*,[17] the plaintiff arranged in August, 1960 to leave a second-hand car with the defendant dealers and gave them authority to sell it for not less than £325, the defendants being entitled to retain any excess. On November 7, the plaintiff demanded the return of the car within three days or the payment of £325. The car was only returned at the end of November and in a badly damaged condition having been involved in an accident whilst being used by the defendants' employees without authority. The plaintiff refused to accept it. The Court of Appeal found that the parties had regarded the transaction as one of sale or return and the court accepted that it was a sale or return contract, pointing out that a contract could be a sale or return contract whether or not the recipient of the goods intended to buy them himself or to sell them to third parties. Applying s 18, rule 4 (b), and bearing in mind the rapid deterioration of second-hand car values in the autumn, the court held that more than a reasonable time had elapsed, the property in the car had therefore passed to the defendants, and the defendants were liable for the price, £325.

14 [1906] 2 KB 574, [1904–7] All ER Rep 773. If, however, X had been a retailer, given possession as an agent with a view to finding a buyer for the owner (and not as a *buyer* himself) and X had sold or pledged the goods to the defendant, the defendant may have obtained a good title to the goods under s 2 of the Factors Act 1889: *Weiner v Harris* [1910] 1 KB 285, [1908–10] All ER Rep 405. See p 78.

15 (1880) 5 CPD 321.

16 [1944] Ch 295.

17 [1962] 2 All ER 482, [1962] 1 WLR 744.

Rule 5.—'(1) Where there is a contract for the sale of unascertained or future goods by description, and goods of that description and in a deliverable state are unconditionally appropriated to the contract, either by the seller with the assent of the buyer or by the buyer with the assent of the seller, the property in the goods then passes to the buyer and the assent may be express or implied, and may be given either before or after the appropriation is made.

(2) Where, in pursuance of the contract, the seller delivers the goods to the buyer or to a carrier or other bailee or custodier (whether named by the buyer or not) for the purpose of transmission to the buyer, and does not reserve the right of disposal, he is deemed to have unconditionally appropriated the goods to the contract.'

The basic rule in s 16, already referred to, is that in a contract for the sale of unascertained goods, no property in the goods is transferred to the buyer unless and until the goods are ascertained. Rule 5 shows that, generally, the goods are 'ascertained' when goods of the description agreed and in a deliverable state are unconditionally appropriated to the contract. We have said, as an example, that a sale of a new Ford Sierra 1987 is a sale of unascertained goods; no property will pass until one car of the description given and in a deliverable state is, in some way, irrevocably set aside or earmarked for this particular contract; the car is then said to be 'appropriated' to the contract. It will be appropriation by the seller with the buyer's assent. Similarly, if B orders goods of a certain description from S by post, the despatch by S of goods corresponding with that description, amounts to appropriation by S with B's consent.[18] In a sale of a given proportion of spirit contained in a storage tank, there is no appropriation until the proportion sold is separated from the bulk. It is difficult to be precise as to the meaning of 'appropriation' and in every case, the court must consider all the facts and circumstances. Pearson J pointed out in *Carlos Federspiel & Co S A v Charles Twigg & Co Ltd*,[19] that

> 'the setting apart or selection by the seller of the goods which he *expects* to use in performance of the contract is not enough. If that is all, he can change his mind and use those goods in performance of some other contract and use some other goods in performance of this contract' (our italics).

Nevertheless, if the 'setting apart' by the seller of certain goods is an

18 *Badische Anilin und Soda Fabrik v Basle Chemical Works Bindschedler* [1898] AC 200.
19 [1957] 1 Lloyd's Rep 240, 255–256.

unambiguous and irrevocable act, that will amount to appropriation although delivery of the goods to the buyer only takes place later.[20] In *Edwards v Ddin*,[1] the Divisional Court held that, when a garage attendant fills someone's car tank with petrol and the petrol is therefore mixed with petrol already in the tank, the petrol is unconditionally appropriated to the contract with the assent of both parties. (Should the car owner drive off without paying he cannot be convicted of theft because the property is his and the garage could not be said to have reserved the right of disposal. But the Theft Act 1978 s 3, creates a new offence of making off without payment, commonly known as 'bilking'.)

If there is an agreement for the sale of specific future goods, that is, goods not yet acquired by the seller but already identified by him with the buyer's implied agreement, as in the example of the antique table referred to above,[2] rule 5 applies. This means that the property will pass to the buyer as soon as he, the seller, acquires the ownership—that will, in effect, be an appropriation of the goods by the seller with the buyer's implied assent.

Rule 5 (2) is a particular example of the application of rule 5 (1). If a seller, having agreed to sell unascertained goods, say 500 tons of wheat out of his larger stock of wheat, delivers 500 tons of wheat as ordered to a carrier for transmission to the buyer, that is an unconditional appropriation of the goods to the contract and the ownership in the 500 tons passes at once to the buyer.[3] If, however, the appropriation of the 500 tons to the contract was subject to a condition, for example as to payment, the property will not pass to the buyer until he has fulfilled the condition. This is the effect of s 19, which section also covers sales of specific goods in a deliverable state where rule 1 has no application because the sale is not unconditional. Rule 5 is of course subject to the parties indicating a contrary intention and it was held in *Karlshamns Oljefabriker v Eastport Navigation Corpn, The Elafi*[4] that goods were ascertained by a process of exhaustion after prior deliveries to other buyers at intermediate ports and before arrival at the final port where the buyers were entitled to take delivery of all remaining goods on

20 *Furby v Hoey* [1947] 1 All ER 236.

1 [1976] 3 All ER 705, [1976] 1 WLR 942, DC.

2 See ante, p 59. Although the goods are specific goods, the property could not pass under rule 1 at the time of the contract, because the seller is not them himself the owner.

3 Presumably this is not so if the carrier is an agent or servant of the seller. See also s 32 (1), post, p 128.

4 [1982] 1 All ER 208.

board. Property passed before the goods were appropriated to particular contracts of sale with the residuary buyers.

Reservation of Right of Disposal.—Section 19 (1) enacts:—

'Where there is a contract for the sale of specific goods or where goods are subsequently appropriated to the contract, the seller may, by the terms of the contract or appropriation, reserve the right of disposal of the goods until certain conditions are fulfilled; and in such case, notwithstanding the delivery of the goods to the buyer, or to a carrier or other bailee or custodier for the purpose of transmission to the buyer, the property in the goods does not pass until the conditions imposed by the seller are fulfilled.'

In consequence, if a seller of specific goods 'reserves the right of disposal' of the goods (i.e. reserves the property in the goods to himself) until some condition is satisfied, for example, that the purchase price be paid, the property in the goods cannot pass until that condition is fulfilled. So too, if a seller imposes a similar condition when he is appropriating goods to a contract for the sale of unascertained goods. Section 19 (2) is a particular application of this principle:—

'Where goods are shipped, and by the bill of lading the goods are deliverable to the order of the seller or his agent, the seller is prima facie to be taken to reserve the right of disposal'.[5]

A bill of lading is the document signed by the master of a ship on which goods are being carried and it acknowledges receipt of the goods on board. By virtue of s 19 (2), if a bill of lading is made out to the order of the seller or his agent instead of to the order of the buyer, the property in the goods shipped remains with the seller until he indorses the bill of lading to the buyer and the price is paid or tendered.

As will be seen, the reservation of a right of disposal does not usually protect the seller against the buyer being able (if he acquires possession) to confer a good title on a sub-buyer who is in good faith.[6] However, the important Court of Appeal decision in *Aluminium Industrie Vaasen BV v Romalpa Aluminium Ltd*[7] to the effect that the seller can ensure himself prior rights in the event of the buyer's insolvency has given rise to the emergence of many

---

5 Section 19 (3) is considered p 90, post, together with the important case of *Cahn v Pockett's Bristol Channel Steam Packet Co Ltd* [1899] 1 QB 643.
6 See p 88, post.
7 [1976] 2 All ER 552, [1976] 1 WLR 676, CA.

'Romalpa clauses' in sale contracts. In the *Romalpa* case, the plaintiff Dutch manufacturers sold aluminium foil to the defendant English buyers and a key term of the contract specified that ownership of material delivered would be transferred only on full payment. The defendants got into financial difficulties and the receiver who was appointed by debenture holders certified that he held £35,000 as proceeds of sale of foil supplied by the plaintiffs and sold by the defendants to third parties. The Court of Appeal construed the term referred to as meaning that the defendants sold as agents for the plaintiffs and, by virtue of their fiduciary relationship, they remained fully accountable for the proceeds of sale. The plaintiffs were entitled to trace the proceeds and to recover them in priority to secured and unsecured creditors.[8]

So-called Romalpa clauses have come before the courts on several occasions but they differ materially and to some extent each of the decisions turns upon its own facts. In *Borden (UK) Ltd v Scottish Timber Products Ltd*,[9] the property sold by the sellers (resin for use in making chipboard) was agreed to pass only on payment in full for all resin supplied. The Court of Appeal held that, once the resin was used in manufacture, it ceased to be a separable constituent of the chipboard and the sellers could not claim any property in the chipboard or in the proceeds of sale of the chipboard. In *Re Peachdart Ltd*,[10] the retention of title clause sought to retain for the sellers the property not only in the raw material supplied (leather) but in the goods manufactured by the buyer with that raw material (handbags) and the proceeds of sale of the handbags. Vinelott J held, however, that once the buyer appropriated a piece of leather and began to turn it into a handbag, it ceased to be the property of the seller but instead the seller had a charge on the handbags and on any proceeds of sale. As the charge had not been registered under the Companies Act, the seller was merely an unregistered creditor on the appointment of a receiver of the buyer.

In *Clough Mills Ltd v Martin*,[11] sellers of yarn stipulated that

---

8 See also *Re Bond Worth* [1980] Ch 228, [1979] 3 All ER 919; where Slade J came to the contrary conclusion in relation to a condition of sale where only 'equitable and beneficial' ownership was retained by the seller until full payment and the condition had not been registered as a charge under s 95 of the Companies Act 1948, now Companies Act 1985 ss 395–398.

9 [1981] Ch 25, [1979] 3 All ER 961.

10 [1984] Ch 131, [1983] 3 All ER 204.

11 [1984] 3 All ER 982, [1985] 1 WLR 111. See also *Hendy Lennox (Industrial Engines) Ltd v Grahame Puttick Ltd* [1984] 2 All ER 152 and *Airborne Accessories Ltd v Goodman* [1984] 3 All ER 407.

ownership was to remain in the sellers until full payment was received or until the buyers sold the yarn to customers and that, if the yarn was incorporated into other goods before payment, the property in the whole of such goods remained in the sellers until such payment was made or the other goods sold and the sellers' rights extended to those other goods. The buyers became insolvent before they paid for or used all the yarn. The Court of Appeal held that the sellers had retained title in yarn after delivery to the buyers (as sellers are entitled to do under s 19 (1) of the Sale of Goods Act) until they were paid for it or the buyers resold the material. The sellers were, therefore, entitled on the buyers' insolvency to assert their legal title to yarn that was identifiable, unused and unpaid for. As the buyers never acquired any title to the yarn they were never in a position to confer a charge over the yarn in favour of the sellers so the question of whether such a charge was void for non-registration under the Companies Act did not arise.

RISK OF LOSS

General Rule

When someone is an owner of goods, the goods are said to be 'at his risk'.If they are, say, destroyed by fire or any other accidental destruction, since he is the owner he must himself bear the loss (unless he has insured them against such loss) and cannot, of course, recover the price of the goods from the person from whom he bought them even if the sale was only a short time before. Further, if in such case, the owner of the goods has not yet paid the full price for them, he is still obliged to do so.

By s 20 'Unless otherwise agreed, the goods remain at the seller's risk until the property in them is transferred to the buyer, but when the property in them is transferred to the buyer the goods are at the buyer's risk whether delivery has been made or not'. In other words, unless otherwise agreed, the risk passes with the ownership of the goods, since the word 'property' is used here, as we have seen, synonymously with 'ownership'.

Exceptions

In cif contracts, where the price agreed covers the cost of the goods, insurance and freight charges, the property in the goods does not generally pass until the shipping documents relating to the goods (the bill of lading, insurance documents and invoice) are handed over to the buyer,[12] but the risk passes as soon as the goods cross the ship's rail at the port of shipment. In consequence, when the shipping documents are tendered to the buyer, he is bound to pay for the goods even though they have already been lost at sea. They are at the buyer's risk from the moment they are put on board.[13]

Another exceptional instance where the risk may pass before the ownership of the goods is exemplified by the case of *Sterns Ltd v Vickers Ltd*.[14] The defendants sold to the plaintiffs 120,000 gallons of spirit, being part of a larger quantity of spirit contained in a storage tank belonging to a third party. The defendants obtained a delivery warrant from the third party whereby the spirit sold was made deliverable to the plaintiffs' order and handed it to the plaintiffs. The plaintiffs, however, left the spirit in the tank for the time being, and before they took delivery the quality of the spirit in the tank deteriorated. The ownership of the spirit bought had not passed to the plaintiffs because it had not been separated from the larger quantity in the tank and appropriated to the contract. Nevertheless, the Court of Appeal held that the risk had passed to the plaintiffs from the moment that the third party acknowledged the plaintiffs' rights to 120,000 gallons of the spirit by signing a delivery warrant in their favour, and the plaintiffs must therefore, bear the loss. Where goods are sent to someone on approval on the express terms that the goods are at the risk of the person who ordered them while in his hands, again the risk passes before the property in the goods passes.[15]

In contrast, the property in goods may pass before the risk. By s 33, where the seller of goods agrees to deliver them at his own risk at a place other than that where they are when sold, the buyer must nevertheless (unless otherwise agreed) take any risk of deterioration in the goods necessarily incident to the course of transit. For deterioration not caused by the transit, the seller may be liable for breach of the implied condition of merchantable quality; to that extent, the goods are still at the seller's risk till delivery is completed

12 Even then it is only a *conditional* property that passes—it is conditional on the buyer having the right to examine the goods on arrival and being entitled to reject them if they do not conform to the contract: per Devlin J in *Kwei Tek Chao v British Traders and Shippers Ltd* [1954] 2 QB 459, [1954] 1 All ER 779. See also post, p 131.

13 *C Groom Ltd v Barber* [1915] 1 KB 316, [1914–15] All ER Rep 194.

14 [1923] 1 KB 78, [1922] All ER Rep 126.

15 A usage to this effect in the fur trade was recognised in *Bevington and Morris v Dale & Co Ltd* (1902) 7 Com Cas 112.

although the ownership may have passed earlier. For example, suppose a seller of rabbits agrees to deliver them at his own risk in Brighton and, although they are fit for consumption when they leave London, they are putrid and valueless when they are delivered in Brighton. If the deterioration has not arisen because of anything incident to the transit such as a train crash, then the seller will be held liable for the deterioration even though the ownership in the rabbits may have passed to the buyer either before or at the commencement of the transit.[16]

There are also two qualifications to the general rule that risk passes with ownership in s 20 itself. By s 20 (2), where delivery has been delayed through the fault of either buyer or seller, the goods are at the risk of the party in fault as regards any loss which might not have occurred but for such fault. In *Demby Hamilton Co v Barden Ltd*,[17] a manufacturer contracted to supply to a wine merchant 30 tons of apple juice in accordance with a sample, the juice to be delivered in weekly truckloads. The seller crushed the apples, put the juice in casks, and kept it pending delivery. The court found as a fact that it would have been difficult to supply apple juice complying with the sample unless all the apples had been crushed at one time and that the juice was rightly kept for the fulfilment of the contract, but that the property in the juice had not passed to the buyer. After 20½ tons had been delivered, notwithstanding requests by the seller for delivery instructions for the remainder, no further deliveries were accepted. In due course the undelivered juice went putrid and had to be thrown away. The court held that delivery had been delayed through the fault of the buyer and the loss might not have occurred but for such fault. Applying s 20 (2) (or rather what was under the 1893 Act a proviso to s 20), the court held the buyer liable in damages for the loss.

Section 20 (3) provides that nothing in the section is to affect the duties or liabilities of either seller or buyer as a bailee of the goods of the other party. For example, if after the property in goods has passed to the buyer the seller remains in possession as the buyer's bailee, agreeing perhaps to provide safe custody for the goods for a certain period, and the goods are lost or damaged during the time of the bailment, the seller is liable unless he can disprove negligence on his part. That is the ordinary common law liability of anyone who is a bailee of goods.

---

16 *Beer v Walker* (1877) 46 LJQB 677. See also *Mash and Murrell Ltd v Joseph I Emanuel Ltd* [1961] 1 All ER 485, [1961] 1 WLR 862, discussed pp 105–106, post.
17 [1949] 1 All ER 435.

MISTAKE AND FRUSTRATION OF CONTRACT

Specific goods

Section 62 (2) expressly provides that the rules of common law, save in so far as they are inconsistent with the Act, shall continue to apply to contracts of sale of goods, and it refers, inter alia, to the common law on the effect of mistake on contracts. The Act itself puts into statutory form only part of the common law rule on the effect of common mistake on contracts for the sale of specific goods. By s 6, where there is a contract for the sale of specific goods, and the goods without the knowledge of the seller have perished at the time when the contract is made, the contract is void. If it is alleged that a contract for the sale of specific goods is void for some other kind of mistake, eg, mistaken identity, then the ordinary common law rules apply. It would seem that s 6 cannot apply where the goods have never existed at any time—they will not have 'perished', but at common law, the contract would prima facie be void.

The 'perishing' of goods means their complete physical destruction or theft, or their not being merchantable according to the contract description. In *Asfar & Co Ltd v Blundell*[18] there was a sale of dates and, unknown to the seller, the dates were at the time of the contract of sale a mass of pulpy matter impregnated with sewage and in a state of fermentation through having been under water for two days. The contract was held to be void. It is a matter of degree whether the state of the goods at the time of the contract is such that they may be considered as having perished and slight deterioration would not be enough.[19]

In *Barrow, Lane and Ballard Ltd v Phillip Phillips & Co Ltd*[20] there was a sale of 700 bags of nuts thought to be lying in certain warehouses. Actually, 109 of the bags had already disappeared, presumably because of theft. As the court considered the contract was for an indivisible parcel of goods, it held the contract void under s 6 although only part of the goods sold had ben stolen.

It is thought that s 6 has no application to a contract of sale of goods where the seller expressly or by implication promises that the

18 [1896] 1 QB 123.
19 In *Horn v Minister of Food* [1948] 2 All ER 1036, Morris J said that potatoes that had rotted had not 'perished' within the meaning of s 7, but this view was stated obiter and seems doubtful.
20 [1929] 1 KB 574, [1928] All ER Rep 74.

subject-matter of the contract is, in fact, in existence. If it is later discovered that the subject matter of the contract was not in existence when the contract was made and had never been in existence the seller will be liable in damages for breach of contract.[1] The same result seems to follow if the goods did once exist but have perished by the time the contract is made.[2]

By s 7, where there is an agreement to sell specific goods, and subsequently the goods, without any fault on the part of the seller or buyer, perish before the risk passes to the buyer, the agreement is avoided. The word 'perish' has the same meaning as for s 6 and s 7 puts into statutory effect the common law relating to frustration of a contract for sale of specific goods where the goods are destroyed after the contract has been made but before the property and the risk pass to the buyer. Section 7 cannot apply if the property in the goods passes to the buyer at the time of the contract, for example, where rule 1 of s 18 applies. Section 7 will be applicable, however, where the property passes according to rule 2 or rule 3 of s 18. The effect of such frustration of contract is not governed by the Law Reform (Frustrated Contracts) Act 1943, which expressly excludes 'any contract to which s 7 of the Sale of Goods Act . . . applies'.[3] Instead, the common law rules on the effect of frustration, as established in the *Fibrosa* case[4] apply—any money paid by the buyer, before frustration of the contract occurs, is recoverable if there has been a total failure of consideration, and there is no set off for any expenses the seller may have incurred under the contract before frustration. As an example, suppose S agrees to sell B a table and undertakes to have it repaired and repainted. At the time of the contract B makes a part payment towards the purchase price. The table will not be in a 'deliverable state', ie, B will not be bound to take delivery till the repairing and repainting have been done, and by virtue of rule 2 of s 18 the property and the risk in the table will not pass to B until the work is completed and he is given notice. Before the work is

1 *McRae v Commonwealth Disposals Commission* (1951) 84 CLR 377, is a decision of the High Court of Australia to this effect, but it has not been universally approved; see, eg Cheshire and Fifoot *The Law of Contract* (11th edn, 1986) pp 222–223.
2 See *Atiyah* pp 64–65.
3 Section 2 (5) (c) of the 1943 Act also excludes from the Act's operation any contract for the sale of specific goods where the contract is frustrated by reason of the fact that the goods have perished. It is difficult to see how this phrase adds to the words quoted in the text.
4 *Fibrosa Spolka Akcyjna v Fairbairn Lawson Combe Barbour Ltd* [1943] AC 32, [1942] 2 All ER 122.

done the table is destroyed accidentally by fire. The contract is avoided by s 7 and B is entitled to recover the part of the purchase price he has paid because there has been a total failure of consideration. S has no right of set-off for any expenses he may have already incurred in carrying out work on the table.

If, after a contract of sale of specific goods has been made, but before the risk in the goods passes to the buyer, some event occurs other than the destruction or theft of the goods, for example, outbreak of war making further performance of the contract illegal, or the requisitioning of goods, or the closing of the usual transit route, then whether the contract is frustrated depends on ordinary common law principles and s 7 has no application. The effect of any such frustration will be governed by the terms of the Law Reform (Frustrated Contracts) Act 1943.[5]

Unascertained goods

Sections 6 and 7 have no application to sales of unascertained goods. If the sale is of a dozen bottles of champagne and the seller's whole stock of champagne from which he intended to meet the order is, unknown to him, destroyed at the time of the sale, the contract is not void for mistake at common law and the seller will be liable for breach of contract on failure to deliver. However, if the sale is of a dozen bottles of champagne out of the two dozen bottles in a particular cellar and the whole cellar and its contents is, unknown to the seller, destroyed at the time of the sale, the contract would seem to be void at common law.

A contract for the sale of unascertained goods may be frustrated by destruction of goods after the contract has been made and before the risk passes, if they are goods to be manufactured or grown by the

---

5 The principal provision is contained in s 1 (2) of this Act:

'All sums paid or payable to any party in pursuance of the contract before the time when the parties were so discharged (in this Act referred to as "the time of discharge") shall, in the case of sums so paid, be recoverable from him as money received by him for the use of the party by whom the sums were paid, and, in the case of sums so payable, cease to be so payable.'

There then follows a proviso:

'Provided that, if the party to whom the sums were so paid or so payable incurred expenses before the time of discharge in or for the purpose of the performance of the contract, the court may, if it considers it just to do so having regard to all the circumstances of the case, allow him to retain or, as the case may be, to recover the whole or any part of the sums so paid or payable, not being an amount in excess of the expenses so incurred.'

seller[6] or a sale of part of a given quantity of goods, but not if it is a sale of generic goods, ie, a sale of goods of a kind. The distinction is important. Suppose S agrees to make a bookcase for B and sell it to him. Should the bookcase be accidentally destroyed before it is completed, the contract of sale will be frustrated. This was the position in *Appleby v Myers*[7] where a contract to make machinery was frustrated when the machinery was destroyed before the date of its completion. On the other hand, if S agrees to sell B a car of a certain make (generic goods), intending to obtain a car of that make from a particular source, he cannot claim the contract is frustrated just because he cannot in fact obtain a car of the make required in the place he expected because that source of supply has been destroyed since the agreement was made. He will be liable in damages for non-delivery.

Any contract for the sale of unascertained goods may be frustrated by other events than the perishing of goods, for example, by the outbreak of war, but that depends on ordinary common law principles.[8] Whatever the reason for the frustration of a contract for the sale of *unascertained* goods, the Law Reform (Frustrated Contracts) Act 1943 will govern the effect.

6 *Howell v Coupland* (1876) 1 QBD 258. A contract for the sale of a crop of potatoes to be grown on a particular piece of land was held to be discharged by frustration when the crop failed. The court said the contract was for the sale of specific goods but that would not now accord with the definition of specific goods in the Sale of Goods Act. Nevertheless the decision can be considered to represent a common law rule retained by s 62 (2) of the Sale of Goods Act and, as Atkin LJ, pointed out in *Re Wait* [1927] 1 Ch 606, 631, [1926] All ER Rep 433, the case is also covered now by s 5 (2) of the Sale of Goods Act. See ante, p 58. It was held in *H R and S Sainsbury Ltd v Street* [1972] 3 All ER 1127, [1972] 1 WLR 834, where part of the crop failed, that a term could be implied that the buyer had the option of accepting part delivery. Failure to deliver the crop actually harvested when the buyer was willing to accept it rendered the seller liable in damages. However, the seller would not be liable for failure to deliver the remainder.

7 (1867) LR 2 CP 651.

8 In *Re Badische Co Ltd* [1921] 2 Ch 331, a contract for the sale of unascertained goods, namely dyestuffs which could only be obtained from Germany was held frustrated by the outbreak of the 1914–1918 war. On the other hand, in the case of *Tsakiroglou & Co Ltd v Noblee Thorl GmbH* [1962] AC 93, [1961] 2 All ER 179, the House of Lords held that a contract of the sale of unascertained goods, namely groundnuts, from the Sudan to Europe, was not frustrated by the closing of the Suez Canal for some six months although it meant that the seller would, under the terms of the contract, incur additional expense by having to despatch the goods via the Cape of Good Hope. The House of Lords took the view that though the route via the Cape involved a change in the method of performance of the contract, it was not such a fundamental change from that undertaken under the contract as to entitle the seller to say the contract was frustrated.

TRANSFER OF TITLE

Basic rule

Nemo dat quod non habet.—As a general rule, if a buyer buys goods from someone other than the owner of the goods, he will not obtain a good title to them, and it makes no difference that he was in good faith and without knowledge of the lack of title in the seller. In other words, no one can obtain a good title to goods if he buys from a thief because only the owner of goods can pass a good title to them. The owner with an immediate right to possession is entitled to sue a buyer who has not acquired a good title to them in conversion. The court may award damages or, in its discretion, order specific restitution of the goods. In the latter case, the court may order the owner to compensate the defendant for any improvement effected by the defendant to the goods while they were in his possession.[9]

There are, however, a number of exceptions to this basic rule because, whereas the basic rule upholds the principle that ownership should be protected, it is in conflict with another principle, namely, that the buyer of goods who is in good faith should be protected. Lord Denning has explained the conflict in these terms:[10]

'In the development of our law, two principles have striven for mastery. The first is the protection of property. No one can give a better title than he himself possesses. The second is the protection of commercial transactions. The person who takes in good faith and for value without notice should get a good title. The first principle has held sway for a long time, but it has been modified by common law itself and by statute so as to meet the needs of our times.'

The basic rule is embodied in s 21 (1):—

'Subject to this Act, where goods are sold by a person who is not their owner, and who does not sell them under the authority or with the consent of the owner, the buyer acquires no better title to the goods than the seller had, unless the owner of the goods is by his conduct precluded from denying the seller's authority to sell.'

General exceptions

1. *Agency.*—If the seller of goods sells them under the authority of or with the consent of the owner, the buyer obtains a good title.

9 *Greenwood v Bennett* [1973] QB 195, [1972] 3 All ER 586, CA.
10 In *Bishopsgate Motor Finance Corpn v Transport Brakes Ltd* [1949] 1 KB 322, 336–337, [1949] 1 All ER 37, 46.

Moreover, a buyer obtains a good title if the owner of goods is precluded by his conduct from denying the seller's authority to sell (s 21 (1)). In *Henderson & Co v Williams*,[11] the owner of goods lying at a warehouse was induced by the fraud of S to instruct the warehouseman to transfer the goods to the order of S, and the goods were accordingly placed at S's disposal. S then sold the goods to an innocent purchaser who obtained a statement from the warehouseman that he held the goods at the purchaser's order. When S's fraud was discovered, the warehouseman refused to deliver the goods to the purchaser. In an action by the purchaser against the warehouseman, the Court of Appeal held that as the warehouseman had attorned to the purchaser, ie, acknowledged his rights, he was estopped from denying the purchaser's title to the goods and the refusal to deliver amounted to conversion. Lord Halsbury asserted further, that the owner of goods was estopped from denying S's authority to sell as he had allowed S to hold himself out as the owner of the goods, with the result that the bona fide purchaser for value obtained a good title that prevailed against anybody.

However, merely permitting another person to have possession of goods does not estop the owner from denying his authority to sell. For example, when the owner of goods allows someone to take possession of them under a hire purchase agreement, that does not prevent the owner denying the debtor's authority to sell, and as a general rule, no one buying the goods from the debtor can claim to have a good title. Another example is the case of *Central Newbury Car Auctions Ltd v Unity Finance Ltd*.[12] A personable stranger S approached the plaintiffs with a view to taking a car owned by them on hire purchase. It was arranged that the plaintiffs would sell the car to a finance company who would let it out on hire purchase to S. The plaintiffs allowed S to take away the car, together with its registration book, before the hire purchase forms were submitted to the finance company. S sold the car to T who in turn sold it to the defendants. In a claim in damages for conversion the defendants pleaded that the plaintiffs were estopped from denying S's authority to sell the car as they had permitted him to take away possession of the car and the registration book without making sufficient enquiries. The Court of Appeal held by a majority that the plaintiffs were not estopped from denying S's authority to sell the car. 'If the owner of a car gives mere possession of it to another,'

---

11 [1895] 1 QB 521. Cf *Farquharson Bros & Co v King & Co* [1902] AC 325, [1900–3] All ER Rep 120.
12 [1957] 1 QB 371, [1956] 3 All ER 905.

said Morris LJ, 'he does not hold out or represent that other person as being entitled to sell.' It had been argued that handing over the registration book made a difference, but a car registration book contains a clear warning that the person in whose name a car is registered may not be the legal owner. In a recent case, the Court of Appeal has made it clear that the proviso to s 21 (1) can only apply if S actually sells the goods.[13] It does not apply where S merely agrees to sell the goods.

A difficult case is *Mercantile Credit Co Ltd v Hamblin*[14] where the defendant owner of a Jaguar car wished to make arrangements through a car dealer for the loan of £1,000 on the security of the car. The dealer said he would contact various finance companies and gave the defendant a blank cheque which she could fill in for the amount of the loan when it was finally approved, and at the dealer's suggestion, she signed certain documents, including one of the plaintiff finance company's hire purchase proposal forms. The dealer filled in the blanks in these documents so that it appeared that the defendant was offering to take the Jaguar on hire purchase, and he also certified that he, the dealer, had an absolute title to the Jaguar which he purported to sell to the company. The company accepted the defendant's purported offer contained in the proposal form and paid the dealer £800 for the car. The defendant refused to pay the instalments due under the agreement. The Court of Appeal held that the company could only succeed in its claim in detinue and conversion if it could establish that it had a good title to the Jaguar and that this involved showing that the defendant was precluded by her conduct from denying the dealer's authority to sell within the meaning of s 21 (1). As Pearson LJ put it,[15] to establish such an estoppel, the company had to show '(i) that the defendant owed to them a duty to be careful, (ii) that in breach of that duty she was negligent, (iii) that her negligence was the proximate or real cause of the plaintiffs being induced to part with £800 to the dealer.' On the facts, the court felt that the defendant did owe a duty of care in respect of the documents submitted to the company by the dealer. 'She must have contemplated someone to whom the documents would ultimately go'.[16] However, she was not in breach of that duty because she was acquainted with the dealer, who was an apparently respectable and prosperous dealer, and his blank

13 *Shaw v Natalegawa* [1987] 3 All ER 405, CA.
14 [1965] 2 QB 242, [1964] 3 All ER 592.
15 [1964] 3 All ER 592, 602.
16 Per Sellers LJ at p 606.

cheque must have led her to believe that she could rely on his due performance of the arrangement he had made.

The great majority of finance houses are members of Hire Purchase Information Ltd (HPI) and it is their practice to inform HPI of any hire-purchase agreement they enter into in relation to a car. About 98 per cent of all hire-purchase agreements relating to cars are registered with HPI and car dealers, when offered a car for sale, normally contact HPI to see if it is the subject of a hire-purchase agreement. In *Moorgate Mercantile Co Ltd v Twitchings*,[17] the plaintiff finance company let a car on hire-purchase to S and by reason of some unidentified mistake or oversight in the company's office HPI were not informed of the agreement between the plaintiffs and S. S offered the car for sale to the defendant dealer. The defendant contacted HPI who informed him that, according to their records, the car was not registered with them and the defendant bought the car from S. The House of Lords, by a majority, upheld a county court judgment in conversion against the defendant, holding that when HPI replied to the defendant's enquiry, HPI was not making a positive representation that no hire-purchase agreement existed in relation to the car and in any case was not acting as the plaintiffs' agent. Further, as the plaintiffs were under no legal duty to the defendant to register or take care in registering the agreement with HPI, the plaintiffs were not estopped from pursuing their claim against the defendant.

One may contrast the earlier case of *Eastern Distributors Ltd v Goldring*[18] where the owner of a van, A, signed hire purchase documents and expressly agreed that S, a dealer, should pretend to be the owner, with the intention that the documents should be shown to a finance company. The documents *were* presented to a finance company who bought the van from S. The Court of Appeal held that A was precluded from denying S's authority to sell and the finance company, therefore, acquired a good title to the van that prevailed against any other claimant.

2. *Sale under any special common law or statutory power of sale or under the order of a court of competent jurisdiction.*—By s 21 (2) (a), nothing in

17 [1977] AC 890, [1976] 2 All ER 641, HL. Since this decision, HPI's rules have been altered so that members are now obliged to register agreements with it. It follows that a member company suffering loss through an unregistered agreement should be able to claim title by estoppel: *Atiyah* p 305.

18 [1957] 2 QB 600, [1957] 2 All ER 525, followed in *Lloyds and Scottish Finance Ltd v Williamson* [1965] 1 All ER 641 [1965] 1 WLR 404, CA. See also *Stoneleigh Finance Ltd v Phillips* [1965] 2 QB 537, [1965] 1 All ER 513, CA.

the Act is to affect 'any enactment enabling the apparent owner of goods to dispose of them as if he were their true owner'.[19]

By s 21 (2) (b), nothing in the Act is to affect 'the validity of any contract of sale under any special common law or statutory power of sale or under the order of a court of competent jurisdiction.' As a result, the sale by a pledgee of an unredeemed pledge at common law and the sale of a guest's goods by an innkeeper under the provisions of the Innkeepers Act 1878 give the purchaser a good title *as against* the pledgor or guest respectively. This does not mean necessarily, a good title against the whole world because the sale does not cure any inherent defects of title in the goods that may exist. Thus, in *Burrows v Barnes*[20] it was held that where O had hired out a bicycle to H and H pledged the bicycle with X, the sale by X of the bicycle as an unredeemed pledge did not give the purchaser a good title as against O.

On the other hand, a sale by a sheriff of goods seized by way of execution under the Bankruptcy and Deeds of Arrangement Act 1913 s 15, is effective to pass a good title to a bona fide purchaser and this title is valid against the whole world, provided that no claim was made by the original owner before the sale.[1] A court has wide powers under the Rules of the Supreme Court to order the sale of goods, eg, goods which are of a perishable nature or likely to injure from keeping, and presumably the sale cures any inherent defects of title.[2]

Special exceptions

1. *Market overt.*—Market overt is every 'open public and legally constituted market'.[3] By s 22, where goods are sold in market overt, according to the usage of the market,[4] the buyer acquires a good

19 This seems to be a reference to the reputed ownership clause of the Bankruptcy Act 1914: *Atiyah* p 279. However, the definition of a bankrupt's estate in s 130 of the Insolvency Act 1985 no longer includes goods in the bankrupt's reputed ownership. See now s 283 of the Insolvency Act 1986.

20 (1900) 82 LT 721. Similarly, a sale by a bailee, who has properly given notice of intention to sell goods in his possession under s 12 of the Torts (Interference with Goods) Act 1977, does not cure an inherent defect of title. The same is true of a sale authorised by the court under s 13 of that Act.

1 *Curtis v Maloney* [1951] 1 KB 736, [1950] 2 All ER 982. The proviso to s 15 enables the original owner to claim the proceeds of sale from the execution creditor.

2 RSC Ord 29 r 14.

3 *Lee v Bayes* (1856) 18 CB 599, 601, per Jervis CJ.

4 The sale must take place between sunrise and sunset: *Reid v Metropolitan Police Comr* [1973] QB 551, [1973] 2 All ER 97.

title to the goods, provided he buys them in good faith and without notice of any defect or want of title on the part of the seller. Every shop in the city of London is market overt and a sale in such a shop is a sale in market overt, provided it is a sale *by* the shopkeeper in the public part of the premises during ordinary business hours on a business day, and provided it is a sale of goods of the kind normally sold by the shop. The whole transaction must be in market overt, so that it is not enough for a sample alone to be exposed for sale.[5] An illustration of a sale in market overt outside the city of London is the case of *Bishopsgate Motor Finance Corpn v Transport Brakes Ltd.*[6] There, B had a car on hire purchase from the plaintiffs and took it to Maidstone market where he handed it to auctioneers for sale. As it failed to obtain the reserve price specified by B, B sold it in the area of the market by private treaty to C who was in good faith and had no knowledge of the hire purchase agreement affecting the car. C sold it to the defendants. The Court of Appeal held that the sale by private treaty was according to the usage of the market and the market itself was constituted by a Royal Charter. In consequence, the defendants obtained a good title to the car under s 22. Horses were excluded by a provision in the Sale of Goods Act 1893 but this was repeated by the Criminal Justice Act 1967.

Until the Theft Act 1968, it was the rule that if goods were stolen and the offender prosecuted to conviction, the title in the goods so stolen revested in the original owner, notwithstanding any intermediate dealing with them, whether by sale in market overt or otherwise.[7] Now, conviction cannot affect the title to goods—that is a matter for the civil law. However, by s 28 of the Theft Act 1968, as amended by the Criminal Justice Act 1972 s 6, where goods have been stolen and a person is convicted of any offence with reference to the theft (or such offence is taken into consideration in determining sentence) a court does have power

(a) to order anyone having possession of the goods to restore them to the owner; *or*

(b) on the application of the owner to order the convicted person to transfer to the owner any other goods directly or indirectly representing the goods stolen, being the proceeds of any disposal of the goods stolen; *or*

(c) to order that a sum not exceeding the value of the goods shall be paid out of any money of the person convicted which was

5 *Crane v London Dock Co* (1864) 5 B & S 313.
6 [1949] 1 KB 322, [1949] 1 All ER 37.
7 Sale of Goods Act 1893 s 24; repealed by the Theft Act 1968 ss 33 (3) and Sch 3.

taken out of his possession on his apprehension to any person who, if those goods were in the possession of the person convicted, would be entitled to recover them from him.

By s 28 (3) if an innocent purchaser of the goods (who does not obtain title under the civil law) is ordered to restore the goods to the true owner, the court may order that there shall be paid to such innocent purchaser, out of any money of the person convicted which was taken out of his possession on apprehension, a sum not exceeding the amount paid for the purchase.

A court will not in practice exercise its powers under s 28 unless there is no real dispute as to the ownership of the goods.

2. *Sale under a voidable title.*—'When the seller of goods has a voidable title to them, but his title has not been avoided at the time of the sale, the buyer acquires a good title to the goods, provided he buys them in good faith and without notice of the seller's defect of title' (s 23). The onus of proof lies on the original owner to prove want of good faith on the part of the purchaser.[8]

If B buys goods from A by a misrepresentation, B's title is *voidable*, but if before B's title has been avoided he sells the goods to C who buys them in good faith and without notice of B's defect of title, C will obtain a good title. On the other hand, if B had no title at all because the contract of sale between A and B is *void* for say, mistaken identity, and B resells to C, C cannot claim a good title under s 23.[9]

An example of a case where s 23 was unsuccessfully pleaded is *Car and Universal Finance Co Ltd v Caldwell.*[10] The defendant owner of a car sold it to N in return for a cheque which was dishonoured on presentation. Immediately, the defendant informed the police and the Automobile Association of the fraudulent transaction. N purported to sell the car to a firm of motor dealers who had notice that N had acquired it fraudulently and, after two further transactions it was bought by the plaintiffs in good faith and without notice of any defect in title. The Court of Appeal held that the defendant, in informing the police and the AA of the fraud had clearly evinced an intention to avoid the contract of sale. Upjohn LJ said that,

'if one party, by absconding, deliberately puts it out of the power of the other to communicate his intention to rescind . . . he can no longer insist on his right to be made aware of the election to determine the contract

8 *Whitehorn Bros v Davison* [1911] 1 KB 463, [1908–10] All ER Rep 885.
9 *Cundy v Lindsay* (1878) 3 App Cas 459, *Ingram v Little* [1961] 1 QB 31, [1960] 3 All ER 332, CA; cf *Lewis v Averay* [1972] 1 QB 198, [1971] 3 All ER 907, CA.
10 [1965] 1 QB 525, [1964] 1 All ER 290, CA.

... The law must allow the innocent party to exercise his right of rescission otherwise than by communication or repossession'.[11]

In the circumstances the property in the car revested in the defendant when he went to the police and the plaintiffs could not claim a good title under s. 23.[12]

3. *Sale by a mercantile agent.*—A mercantile agent is defined in the Factors Act 1889, as—

'a mercantile agent having in the customary course of his business as such agent authority either to sell goods, or to consign goods for the purpose of sale, or to buy goods, or to raise money on the security of goods.'

Under the Factors Act, where a mercantile agent is, with the consent of the owner, in possession of goods or of the documents of title to goods, any sale, pledge, or other disposition of the goods, made by him when acting in the ordinary course of business of a mercantile agent shall be as valid as if he were expressly authorised by the owner of the goods to make the same, provided that the person taking under the disposition acts in good faith and has not at the time of the disposition notice that the person making the disposition has not authority to make the same, and provided he has given consideration (ss 2 and 5). It seems that the burden of proof is on the purchaser to show his good faith etc.[13]

If A entrusts an antique to a dealer B for display with a view to sale, and B is instructed not to effect a sale without reference back to A, a sale by B contrary to these instructions to C who is in good faith and gives value will confer on C a good title to the antique, provided B acts in the ordinary course of business. These provisions would not operate to give C a good title if B was in possession of the antique simply as a bailee, for example, for the purpose of safe custody or repair, but only if B is in possession for some purpose connected with a possible sale, ie, for some purpose in his capacity as a mercantile agent or factor.[14] As Willes J said in *Hayman v Flewker*,[15] the term

11 [1964] 1 All ER 290, 296.

12 N was a buyer of goods in possession 'with the consent of' the defendant but N's sale to the motor dealers did not pass a good title under the Factors Act s 9, because the dealers were not in good faith: cf *Newtons of Wembley Ltd v Williams* [1965] 1 QB 560, [1964] 3 All ER 532, post, p 91.

13 *Heap v Motorists Advisory Agency Ltd* [1923] 1 KB 577. Contrast the position under the previous head of Sale under a voidable title.

14 *Pearson v Rose and Young Ltd* [1951] 1 KB 275, 288, [1950] 2 All ER 1027, 1032, per Denning LJ, followed by Chapman J in *Astley Industrial Trust Ltd v Miller* [1968] 2 All ER 36, and by Donaldson J in *Belvoir Finance Co Ltd v Harold G Cole & Co Ltd* [1969] 2 All ER 904, [1969] 1 WLR 1877.

15 (1863) 13 CB NS 519.

'mercantile agent' does not include 'a mere servant or caretaker, or one who has possession of goods for carriage, safe custody, or otherwise as an independent contracting party'. Winn LJ in *Rolls Razor Ltd v Cox*[16] said it would be surprising if travelling salesmen in possession of goods belonging to the company that engaged them as independent contractors were factors. Similarly, these provisions have no application if B, while casually in possession of A's goods because B has told A that he (B) thinks that a friend of his might be interested in buying the goods, sells them to an innocent purchaser.[17]

However, as Wright J pointed out in *Lowther v Harris*[18] a man may be a mercantile agent though he does not have a general occupation as an agent but acts for one principal only in one transaction. He must, however, to be a mercantile agent, act as a business proposition and not merely as a personal friend.[19] In *Lowther v Harris*, an art dealer given possession of certain furniture and tapestry, in order to sell it on a commission basis, was held to be a mercantile agent.

The provisions only apply if B is, or was originally, in possession of the goods or documents of title with the consent of the owner A, but later withdrawal of A's consent will not affect a purchaser who had no notice of the withdrawal (s 2 (2)). However, 'consent of the owner shall be presumed in the absence of evidence to the contrary' and it has been held that the provisions apply although consent has been obtained by fraud[20] or as a result of larceny by a trick, offences which by s 15 of the Theft Act 1968 are now called obtaining property by deception. In *Pearson v Rose and Young Ltd*,[1] the owner of a car left it with a dealer B to see what offers would be made for it. The dealer intended to sell the car as soon as possible and misappropriate the proceeds. The owner produced the car's registration book and while B was looking at it, he induced the owner to leave on a bogus errand so that the owner forgot that he had left the custody of the registration book in B's hands. On the

---

16 [1967] 1 QB 552, [1967] 1 All ER 397, 409.

17 *Heap v Motorists' Advisory Agency Ltd* [1923] 1 KB 577, [1922] All ER Rep 251. It made no difference that *after* A gave possession of his car to B, B became a car salesman for a firm of motor engineers. See also *Jerome v Bentley & Co* [1952] 2 All ER 114.

18 [1927] 1 KB 393, [1926] All ER Rep 352.

19 In *Budberg v Jerwood and Ward* (1934) 51 TLR 99, the owner of a necklace entrusted it with a view to sale, to a lawyer simply as a friend.

20 *Folkes v King*, [1923] 1 KB 282.

1 [1951] 1 KB 275, [1950] 2 All ER 1027.

same day B sold the car to C, who bought it in good faith and was given possession of both the car and the registration book. The Court of Appeal took the view that although B obtained possession of the car by means of larceny by a trick he was nevertheless in possession of it 'with the consent of the owner'. However, the owner had never consented to B being in possession of the registration book. Since B did not have possession of *both* the car and its registration book with the owner's consent and a sale without the registration book would not be a sale in the ordinary course of business, C did not obtain a good title to the car when he bought from B. It follows from this decision that if the owner of a car hands over possession of it to a dealer with a view to its being displayed for sale, but retains possession of the car's registration book, no buyer of the car from the dealer could claim to have a good title to it under the Factors Act. This decision was followed by the Court of Appeal in *Stadium Finance Ltd v Robbins*,[2] where a car dealer was given possession of a car for display in the dealer's showrooms with a view to finding a purchaser and the dealer obtained possession of the registration book by breaking open the glove compartment in the car which the owner had locked. A purchaser from the dealer was held not to have obtained a good title under the Factors Act.

By s 4 of the Factors Act, where a mercantile agent *pledges* goods as security for a debt or liability due from him to the pledgee, the pledgee acquires no further right to the goods than could have been enforced by the mercantile agent at the time of the pledge. It follows that in such a case, the pledgee has no rights against the owner unless, say, the mercantile agent had a lien on the goods at the time of the pledge because the owner owed him money in which event the pledgee would have the same right of lien against the owner.

'Documents of title' are defined by s 1 (4) of the Factors Act as:

'any bill of lading, dock warrant, warehousekeeper's certificate, and warrant or order for the delivery of goods, and any other document used in the ordinary course of business as proof of the possession or control of

---

2 [1962] 2 QB 664, [1962] 2 All ER 633, Professor J A Hornby has made the sound criticism of these cases that whether a mercantile agent has obtained possession of a car with the owner's consent has obviously to be decided in the light of the circumstances at the time that the goods are obtained, but whether a subsequent disposition by him is in the ordinary course of business of a mercantile agent should depend on the circumstances surrounding the disposition, and for this purpose it is irrelevant whether the car or its registration book had been obtained by unlawful means. In neither the *Pearson* case nor the *Robbins* case was the car deficient with regard to the registration book at the time of the dealer's disposition of the car (1962) 25 MLR 722. See also dicta of Chapman J in *Astley Industrial Trust Ltd v Miller* [1968] 2 All ER 36, 42–43.

goods, or authorising or purporting to authorise, either by endorsement or by delivery, the possessor of the documents to transfer or receive the goods thereby represented.'

One type of document referred to in the definition, a bill of lading, is the receipt by the master of a ship for goods taken on board and, in effect, it represents the goods. A mercantile agent in possession of a document of title, like a bill of lading, with the consent of the owner of the goods it represents, can pass a good title to the goods to anyone taking the document in good faith and for value, who is unaware of any lack of authority on the part of the agent.

By s 2 (3) of the Factors Act, if a mercantile agent is in possession of any documents of title by reason of being or having been, with the owner's consent, in possession of the goods represented thereby or any other documents of title to the goods, his possession of the first-mentioned documents are deemed to be with the consent of the owner. Thus, suppose owners of a cargo of tobacco indorse the bill of lading relating to the cargo to a mercantile agent and the agent is thereby able to have a dock warrant made out in his name. If the agent then pledges the goods to X by handing the warrant to him and X honestly believes the agent is the owner of the cargo, the pledge will be valid because, by s 2 (3), the agent is deemed to have been in possession of the dock warrant with the owner's consent.[3]

4. *Second sale by seller left in possesion.*—Section 8 of the Factors Act and what is now s 24 of the Sale of Goods Act 1979 (formerly s 25 (1) of the 1893 Act) are identical subject to the omission of a few words in s 24. By s 8 of the Factors Act,

'Where a person, having sold goods continues or is in possession of the goods or of the documents of title to the goods, the delivery or transfer by that person, or by a mercantile agent acting for him, of the goods or documents of title under any sale, pledge, or other disposition thereof (or under any agreement for sale, pledge, or other disposition thereof), to any person receiving the same in good faith and without notice of the previous sale, shall have the same effect as if the person making the delivery or transfer were expressly authorised by the owner of the goods to make the same.'

The bracketed words are inexplicably omitted in s 24 of the 1979 Act and s 24 has slightly altered the wording of s 25 (1) of the 1893 Act by substituting 'has' for 'shall have' in the final phrase. If S sells

3 The facts given in the example are based on those in *Phillips v Huth* (1840) 6 M & W 572, where the decision of the court was different from what it would now be since the law was changed in the Factors Act 1842, re-enacted by s 2 (3) of the 1889 Act.

goods to B and B leaves them in S's possession, and then S resells *and* delivers them to X who takes them in good faith and without notice of the first sale to B (for example, the goods are not marked 'Sold') X obtains a good title. It does not matter if S is in possession with B's consent or not. S would not obtain a good title if he had not taken delivery of the goods (or the transfer of any documents of title relating to them). In *Nicholson v Harper*[4] a merchant sold a certain quantity of wine (specific goods) which was stored in a warehouse, and later the merchant purported to pledge the wine to the warehouseman who made certain advances to the merchant in good faith and without notice of the sale. It was held that, there having been no delivery of the wine to the warehouseman or transfer to him of any document of title relating to the wine, he could claim no rights over the wine by virtue of this provision.

In *Staffs Motor Guarantee Ltd v British Wagon Co Ltd*,[5] S sold a lorry to B and B agreed to hire it out to S on hire purchase; the lorry had never actually left S's possession. S then resold the lorry to X and delivered it to X. When S fell into arrears with his hire-purchase instalments to B, B retook possession of the lorry. X claimed to have a good title to it under s 8 of the Factors Act, but Mackinnon J found against him, as S was not in possession of the lorry as a seller when he resold it to X but as a hirer under a hire-purchase agreement. The effect of his decision is that s 8 only applies if, after sale, the seller remains in possession *as* a seller and not in some other capacity such as that of a bailee. The Court of Appeal in *Eastern Distributors Ltd v Goldring*[6] on one point in a complicated case, accepted and followed this decision without discussion but the Judicial Committee in the later case of *Pacific Motor Auctions Property Ltd v Motor Credits (Hire Finance) Ltd*[7] held that Mackinnon J's decision was wrong. In this case, S sold cars to B and S retained possession under an arrangement whereby S (dealers) displayed them and had a general authority to resell them in their own name subject only to an obligation to account to B. The advantage to B was that many of S's customers agreed to take such cars on hire purchase from B (a finance company). After B withdrew S's authority to handle the cars S sold some to X and the Judicial Committee held that X obtained a good title to them under a statutory provision of New South Wales law which is identical to s 8 of the Factors Act. Assuming the arrangement between S and B

4 [1895] 2 Ch 415, [1895–9] All ER Rep 882.
5 [1934] 2 KB 305, [1934] All ER Rep 322.
6 [1957] 2 QB 600, [1957] 2 All ER 526.
7 [1965] AC 867, [1965] 2 All ER 105.

involved a separate bailment from B to S following the sale by S to B, the words 'continues in possession' in the sub-section, thought the Judicial Committee, 'were intended to refer to the continuity of physical possession regardless of any private transaction between the seller and purchaser which might alter the legal title under which the possession was held'. On this view of the law, if S sells a caravan to a finance company in order to take it back on hire-purchase the finance company must take physical delivery, and thereby break S's continuity of physical possession, if it is to avoid the risk of S being able to pass title to an innocent purchaser under s 8 of the Factors Act.

The view of the Judicial Committee that the phrase 'continues . . . in possession' refers only to the continuity of physical possession has now been followed by the Court of Appeal in *Worcester Works Finance Co Ltd v Cooden Engineering Co Ltd.*[8] It made no difference that the seller remained in possession unlawfully or without the consent of the buyer. In this case, S sold a car to B but S wrongfully retained possession of the car. S had previously bought the car from X and S, having paid X for it with a cheque that was dishonoured, now agreed to let X retake the car. B sued X in conversion but it was held that X had acquired a good title to it under s 8 of the Factors Act. S was someone who had continued in possession of the car, after his sale to B and the delivery of the car to X was a 'disposition' by which X undertook not to sue S on the cheque in return for a retransfer of the property to X.

Section 8 does of course refer to a person, having sold goods who 'continues *or is*' in possession of the goods but if continuity of possession is broken and they merely come back into S's possession, it seems that S may only pass title under s 8 if he is in possession now *as* seller. Where an unpaid seller of goods regains possession after exercising his right of stoppage in transit he would be in possession once more *as* seller and able therefore to pass title under s 8.[9]

5. *Sale by buyer in possession.*—Section 9 of the Factors Act and what is now s 25 (1) of the Sale of Goods Act 1979 (formerly s 25 (2) of the 1893 Act) are identical subject to the omission of a few words in s 25 (1). By s 9 of the Factors Act,

'Where a person having bought or agreed to buy goods obtains, with the consent of the seller, possession of the goods or the documents of title to the goods, the delivery or transfer by that person or by a mercantile agent acting for him, of the goods or the documents of title, under any sale,

8 [1972] 1 QB 82, [1971] 3 All ER 708, CA.
9 See post, p 143.

pledge, or other disposition thereof (or under any agreement for sale, pledge, or other disposition thereof), to any person receiving the same in good faith and without notice of any lien or other right of the original seller in respect of the goods, shall have the same effect as if the person making the delivery or transfer were a mercantile agent in possession of the goods or documents of title with the consent of the owner.'

The bracketed words are omitted in s 25 (1) of the 1979 Act and s 25 (1) has slightly altered the wording of s 25 (2) of the 1893 Act (which it replaced) by substituting 'has' for 'shall have' in the final phrase.

If B has bought goods and the property has passed to him, any sale by B to X will pass a good title so long as B has a good title without any need for X to rely on s 9 of the Factors Act. Suppose, however, B has agreed to buy goods from A and been given possession of the goods, but the contract provides that the property in the goods shall not pass to B till, say B's cheque is cleared, any sale of the goods before then by B to X will only give X a good title if actual delivery is made to X and if X is in good faith and without notice that ownership still rests with A.[10] In other words, X will have to rely on s 9 and the onus of proof will be on X to show his good faith etc.[11] In *Four Point Garage Ltd v Carter*,[12] Simon Brown J held that where possession passed direct from A to X, X still gets a good title under s 9 of the Factors Act if he is in good faith. B is deemed to have taken constructive delivery from A and A is deemed to have acted as B's agent when he made delivery to X.

Section 9 of the Factors Act refers to someone who has bought or 'agreed to buy' goods, so it cannot relate to someone who has a mere option to purchase as in a hire purchase agreement[13] nor to someone who has only taken goods on sale or return or on approval.[14] On the

10 It is difficult to make sense of the words in the section 'without notice of any lien' of the original sellers because a seller has no lien over goods sold once they have left the possession of the seller: see s 43, post, p 143. Perhaps the words cover the case of a seller who retains possession of the goods but gives possession of documents of title relating to them to the buyer and it is these documents of title that are transferred by the buyers.

11 *Heap v Motorists' Advisory Agency Ltd* [1923] 1 KB 577, [1922] All ER Rep 251.

12 [1985] 3 All ER 12.

13 *Helby v Matthews* [1895] AC 471. The popularity of hire purchase among dealers stems from the fact that if a hirer sells the goods they are generally recoverable even from an innocent purchaser. See p 154, post.

14 *Edwards Ltd v Vaughan* (1910) 26 TLR 545. Of course, a sale by B who has taken goods on sale or return or on approval is an 'act adopting the transaction' under s 18, rule 4 (a) which operates to pass the property to B and thence to X, the purchaser from B, but rule 4 (a) can be excluded by contract as in *Weiner v Gill* [1906] 2 KB 574, p 64, ante.

other hand, a person will be treated as having agreed to buy goods although the ownership cannot pass to him until he fulfils a condition.[15] By s 19 (3) of the Sale of Goods Act,

> 'Where the seller of goods draws on the buyer for the price, and transmits the bill of exchange and bill of lading to the buyer together to secure payment of the bill of exchange, the buyer is bound to return the bill of lading if he does not honour the bill of exchange, and if he wrongfully retains the bill of lading the property in the goods does not pass to him.'

In *Cahn v Pockett's Bristol Channel Steam Packet Co Ltd*,[16] a seller of copper transmitted a bill of exchange for the price together with the bill of lading to the buyer B. B did not signify his acceptance of the bill of exchange but indorsed the bill of lading to the plaintiffs in accordance with a contract for resale of the copper already made. By reason of s 19 (3) the property had not passed to B, because he had not satisfied the condition about acceptance, but B was treated as someone who had 'agreed to buy' the goods, and since the plaintiffs had taken the transfer of the bill of lading in good faith and without knowledge of the original seller's rights, they obtained a good title to the copper under s 9 of the Factors Act.[17]

Section 9 of the Factors Act only applies where B who has 'bought or agreed to buy goods' obtains possession of them 'with the consent of the seller'. However, as with the similar phrase in s 2 of the Factors Act, already considered, s 9 operates although consent has been obtained by means of a deception. In *Du Jardin v Beadman*[18] B

---

15 *Marten v Whale* [1917] 2 KB 480. But someone who agrees to buy the goods under a 'conditional sale agreement' which is a consumer credit agreement, is not someone who has 'agreed to buy' them. The Consumer Credit Act 1974, Sch 4, amended the Factors Act 1889 s 9 to this effect and s 25 (2) of the 1979 Act now embodies the same rule. A 'conditional sale agreement' which is a consumer credit agreement means an agreement for the sale of goods within the meaning of the 1974 Act (ie not more than £15,000 is lent otherwise than to a corporate body) under which the purchase price or part of it is payable by instalments and the property in the goods is to remain in the seller (notwithstanding that the buyer is to be in possession of the goods) until such conditions as to the payment of instalments or otherwise as may be specified in the agreement are fulfilled: s 25 (2) (b) of the 1979 Act. A buyer in possession under a conditional sale agreement that is *not* a consumer credit agreement can still pass a good title under s 9 of the Factors Act.

16 [1899] 1 QB 643.

17 Further, by reason of the proviso to s 47 of the Sale of Goods Act, referred to p 145, post, the seller's right of stoppage in transit, which arose because B had become insolvent while the goods were in transit, was defeated.

18 [1952] 2 QB 712, [1952] 2 All ER 160. However, it seems that if possession is obtained by the buyer fraudulently inducing a mistake as to identity he is not in possession with the 'consent' of the owner: *Folkes v King* [1923] 1 KB 282, 305, per Scrutton LJ.

agreed to buy a Standard car from S and gave S a cheque in payment. S, knowing B intended to show the car to a prospective sub-buyer, allowed him to take away the car and handed him the car's registration book and a receipt. B then resold the car to the plaintiff who received it in good faith and with no knowledge of any defect in B's authority to sell the car to him. The cheque given by B to S was worthless. The court held that B was a person who had 'agreed to buy' the car and had possession of it and its registration book 'with the consent of the owner' within the meaning of s 9 of the Factors Act although that consent had been obtained by larceny by a trick (since the Theft Act 1968, obtaining property by deception). In consequence, the plaintiff was held to have obtained a good title to the car.

It will be noted that the final words of s 9 (in contrast to the final words in s 8) refer to the disposition by B as having the same effect 'as if the person making the delivery or transfer were a mercantile agent in possession of the goods or documents of title with the consent of the owner.' This aspect of s 9 was examined by the Court of Appeal in *Newtons of Wembley Ltd v Williams*.[19] The plaintiffs sold a car to B, payment being made by cheque and the property in the car was not to pass until the cheque was met. B took away the car and its registration book. The cheque was dishonoured and the plaintiffs took all reasonable steps to trace B by informing the police and HP Information Ltd, thereby rescinding their contract with B.[20] Later, B sold the car to X in Warren Street, London, a well-known street market in used cars, X being in good faith and without notice of B's lack of title. X sold the car to the defendant. The court held that B had bought the car and was in possession of it with the plaintiff's consent, but his sale to X was only effective if it was a disposition made in the ordinary course of business of a mercantile agent, because the power of a buyer under s 9 of the Factors Act was no greater than that conferred on a mercantile agent by s 2 of that Act. As B was not in fact a mercantile agent, how could he act in the ordinary course of business of a mercantile agent? Pearson LJ said that B's sale could still be deemed to have been made in the ordinary course of business of a mercantile agent if he acted in a way in which a mercantile agent would normally be expected to act. The court accepted that in view of the established street market in Warren Street for cash sales of secondhand cars, the

19 [1965] 1 QB 560, [1964] 3 All ER 532.
20 On this point, the court followed its earlier decision in *Car and Universal Co Ltd v Caldwell* [1965] 1 QB 535, [1964] 1 All ER 290, ante, p 82.

sale by B to X was made in the ordinary course of business of a mercantile agent so X, being in good faith and without notice of B's lack of title and, through X, the defendant, obtained a good title to the car.

Suppose a thief of goods sells them to X who 'with the consent of the seller', ie the thief, obtains possession of them, does a delivery of them by X to Y under a sale in which X acts as if he were a mercantile agent pass a good title to Y provided Y is in good faith etc? Literally, the answer must be yes,[1] because s 9 of the Factors Act states that the effect of such a sale is as if X were a mercantile agent in possession with the consent of *the owner*. This absurd result is, however, avoided if the word 'seller' at the end of s 9 is substituted for the word 'owner'.[2]

6. *Sale after delivery of writ of execution.*—Section 26 of the Sale of Goods Act 1893 which enabled a debtor to pass a good title to goods after a writ of execution had been issued with respect to such goods was not included in the Sale of Goods Act 1979. It has now been repealed and replaced by the Supreme Court Act 1981 s 138.

7. *Protection of Purchasers of Motor Vehicles.*—Part III of the Hire-Purchase Act 1964 (which was reproduced with minor changes in terminology in Sch 4 of the Consumer Credit Act 1974) gives special protection to the 'private purchaser' of a motor vehicle which is the subject of a hire purchase agreement (or conditional sale agreement). A 'private purchaser' means someone who does not carry on a business as a dealer in motor vehicles or of providing finance for hire purchase transactions in motor vehicles. A 'private purchaser' may be a body corporate. A 'motor vehicle' means a mechanically propelled vehicle intended or adapted for use on roads to which the public has access (s 29 (1)). By s 27, where the bailee of a motor vehicle 'disposes' of it to a private purchaser who takes it in good faith and without notice of the hire purchase

1 See Cornish in (1964) 27 MLR 472.
2 See *Atiyah* p 303. By a somewhat different route the Court of Appeal has recently come to the same conclusion that Y cannot obtain a good title: *National Employers Mutual General Insurance Association Ltd v Jones* [1987] 3 All ER 385, 396. May LJ said that if the original transferor was a thief from the true owner then he had never acquired property in the goods and no purported 'sale' from him or anyone to whom he may have purported to sell the goods could attract the consequences of s 9 of the Factors Act. The transactions were not 'sales' within the definitions of the Act because the essence of a sale is the transfer of the ownership in goods from a seller to a buyer.

agreement, such 'disposition' has effect 'as if the creditor's title . . . to the vehicle had been vested in the debtor . . . immediately before that disposition'. 'Disposition' means any contract of sale or hire purchase agreement. It follows, therefore, that if H has, say, a motor cycle on hire purchase from the O Finance Co and, before, he has made all the payments necessary to make him the owner of it, he sells it to X who is not a motor dealer or finance company and who is unaware that the vehicle is the subject of a hire purchase agreement, X will obtain a good title to the motor cycle—assuming that the O Finance Co had had a good title to it. Moreover, X will get a good title if he honestly believed that, although the vehicle was once subject to a hire-purchase agreement, all the instalments have been paid.[3] X will still get a good title even if H is convicted of theft, but H's civil and criminal liability is preserved (s 27 (6)).

Further, if the bailee disposes of the motor vehicle to a 'trade or finance purchaser' and the person who is the 'first private purchaser' of it takes it in good faith and without notice of the hire purchase agreement, the disposition to that private purchaser has effect 'as if the title of the creditor . . . to the vehicle had been vested in the debtor . . . immediately before he disposed of it to the original purchaser'. A 'trade or finance purchaser' means a purchaser who carries on a business.

> 'which consists wholly or partly (a), of purchasing motor vehicles for the purpose of offering or exposing them for sale, or (b) of providing finance by purchasing motor vehicles for the purpose of bailing . . . them under hire purchase agreements . . .' (s 29 (2)).

Suppose H has a lorry on hire purchase from the O Finance Co and, before he has made all the payments necessary to make him the owner of it, he sells it to the P Finance Co which lets out on hire purchase to X who is a 'private purchaser' and takes the lorry in good faith without notice of the earlier hire purchase agreement relating to it. If X pays up all the instalments due under his hire purchase agreement he will obtain a good title to the lorry (assuming the O Finance Co had had a good title to it). It will make no difference that X is aware of the earlier hire purchase agreement by the time he pays up his final instalment (s 27 (4)). If the first 'private purchaser' is not in good faith and without notice of the hire purchase agreement affecting the vehicle, the Act gives no protection to any subsequent purchaser whether in good faith or not. Nothing in the Act exonerates the bailee from his liability (civil

---

3 *Barker v Bell* [1971] 2 All ER 867, [1971] 1 WLR 983, CA. It was stressed that ony 'actual' notice will bar X's protection.

or criminal) in disposing of the motor vehicle, nor any trade or finance purchaser (other than one claiming under the first private purchaser) from his liability (civil or criminal), eg liability in conversion to the old owner (s 27 (6)). Section 28 specifies certain presumptions which are to apply when the effect of these statutory provisions are in issue.

The Court of Appeal in *Stevenson v Beverley Bentinck Ltd*[4] held that s 27 does not protect a person who at the time of the disposition to him is a spare-time dealer in motor vehicles even though he made the particular purchase in his private capacity.

TERMS OF THE CONTRACT

Distinction between representations and terms

When a statement is made by the seller of goods to the buyer, relating to the goods, the statement may be a representation which helps to induce the buyer to enter into the contract, or a term of the contract, ie, a statement which constitutes part of the contract itself. It is not always easy to say whether a statement is a mere representation or is a term of the contract, but if a statement is made at the time of the contract (as distinct from during the negotiations) and the seller has special knowledge, as compared with the buyer, of the truth of the statement, it is more likely to be treated by the court as a term of the contract. Ultimately, it depends on the intention of the parties. If a statement is held to be only a representation, then if the statement is false, no damages were obtainable by the buyer at common law unless he could show the seller was fraudulent, i.e. that the seller knew his statement was false or made it recklessly not caring whether it was false or not.[5] Since the Misrepresentation Act 1967, it has been possible for the buyer to claim damages also if the seller is merely negligent. It has always been notoriously difficult to prove fraud, and until the 1967 Act made it possible to claim damages in respect of a misrepresentation made negligently, the law was in a most unsatisfactory state. It was apparently the law that where there had been a misrepresentation made without fraud—that is, an innocent misrepresentation—the buyer could claim the equitable remedy of rescission but that right was lost if the buyer was held to have affirmed the contract, or delayed unreasonably since he discovered the truth, or if he had 'accepted' the goods, eg by retaining the goods for more than a reasonable time

4 [1976] 2 All ER 606, [1976] 1 WLR 483, CA.
5 *Derry v Peek* (1889) 14 App Cas 337, HL.

without giving notice of rejection.[6] Before the 1967 Act, it made all the difference between a buyer having a remedy and having no remedy at all if a statement made by the seller about the goods was held to be a term of the contract rather than a mere innocent misrepresentation, because if the buyer had 'accepted' the goods he could claim damages for breach of a term, but had no remedy then for innocent misrepresentation.

The Misrepresentation Act 1967 s 2 (1) enables a buyer to claim damages for innocent misrepresentation unless the seller proves he had reasonable cause to believe and did believe that the facts represented were true. With regard to the equitable remedy of rescission, the buyer still has the right to seek it if he acts reasonably promptly, ie before he is considered to have affirmed the contract or 'accepted' the goods, but now by s 2 (2) of the 1967 Act the court has a discretion to award damages instead of rescission even where an innocent misrepresentation is made without negligence. The point is that rescission would be an unduly drastic remedy for a minor misrepresentation, for example, as to the mileage done by a car since its engine was last overhauled.[7]

Even since the 1967 Act, it may still be necessary to determine whether a statement of fact made by the seller about goods sold is a term of the contract or a mere representation; only if it is a term of the contract can the buyer obtain damages as of right should the statement turn out to be untrue even though neither fraud nor negligence can be shown. Consider a case decided before the 1967 Act. In *Oscar Chess Ltd v Williams*,[8] the defendant, wanting to take a Hillman Minx car on hire purchase, offered a second-hand Morris in part exchange. The registration book of the Morris indicated that it was a 1948 model and the defendant in good faith confirmed this. The plaintiffs, assuming it was a 1948 model, allowed £290 for it. It was agreed, therefore, that the defendant take the Hillman Minx on

6 Examples familiar from general contract law are *Leaf v International Galleries* [1950] 2 KB 86, [1950] 1 All ER 693, *Routledge v McKay* [1954] 1 All ER 855, [1954] 1 WLR 615 and *Long v Lloyd* [1958] 2 All ER 402, [1958] 1 WLR 753.

7 By s 3 of the Misrepresentation Act 1967 (as amended by s 8 of the Unfair Contract Terms Act 1977), any contractual term which would exclude or restrict any liability for misrepresentation or any remedy available in respect of such misrepresentation is of no effect except in so far as it satisfies the requirement of reasonableness as stated in s 11 of the Unfair Contract Terms Act 1977 and it is for those claiming that the term satisfies that requirement to show that it does. The principal change made in the 1977 Act is that 'reasonableness' is now to be judged according to the circumstances which the parties had, or ought to have had, in contemplation when the contract was made.

8 [1957] 1 All ER 325, [1957] 1 WLR 370.

hire purchase and the plaintiffs bought the Morris from him in part exchange, allowing £290 for it. Eight months later the plaintiffs discovered the Morris was a 1939 model and that its registration book must have been altered by some previous owner. Had the plaintiffs known it was a 1939 model they would have allowed only £175 for it. Mainly because the defendant had no special knowledge as to the car's age when he confirmed the statement in the registration book that it was a 1948 model, the Court of Appeal held that the defendant's assertion was a mere innocent misrepresentation and not a term of the contract. Since eight months had elapsed from the date of the sale, it was too late for the plaintiffs to seek rescission for misrepresentation—they had 'accepted' the goods, and damages were not available for innocent misrepresentation. As a result the plaintiffs had no remedy.

The Misrepresentation Act 1967 which gives a remedy in damages where the misrepresentation is negligent would probably make no difference in a case like *Oscar Chess Ltd v Williams* because the defendant had reasonable grounds for believing the car was a 1948 Morris. This reasoning would not necessarily apply to the sale of a car *by* a dealer.[9]

Emphasis has been placed on misrepresentations made by the seller of goods. It is possible for a seller to be induced to enter into a contract by the misrepresentation of the buyer, as in *Goldsmith v Rodgers*[10] where the potential buyer of a fishing vessel falsely stated he had found defects in it and thereby induced the owner to sell it to him at a reduced price. The Court of Appeal held the seller was entitled to rescind the contract.

Express terms

If a statement made by the seller about the goods is a term of the contract, it may be a condition or a warranty but there is recent authority[11] to the effect that this dichotomy is not exhaustive. The Sale of Goods Act distinguishes these two categories of terms by saying that breach of a condition gives the buyer a right to treat the contract as repudiated, whereas a breach of warranty gives rise to a claim for damages but not to a right to reject the goods and treat the contract as repudiated (s 11 (3)). That does not, however, provide

9 See *Dick Bentley Productions Ltd v Harold Smith (Motors) Ltd* [1965] 2 All ER 65, [1965] 1 WLR 623, CA.

10 [1962] 2 Lloyd's Rep 249.

11 *Cehave NV v Bremer Handelsgesellschaft mbH* [1976] QB 44, [1975] 3 All ER 739, CA.

a test for saying whether any particular term in a contract for sale of goods is a condition or is a warranty. By s 11 (3), whether a term is a condition or a warranty depends on the construction of the contract. Section 61 defines a 'warranty' as collateral to the main purpose of the contract. Certainly a term may be a condition, though called a warranty in the contract. In *Cehave NV v Bremer*[12] the Court of Appeal said that s 11 did not require a rigid division of the terms of a sale contract into 'conditions' and 'warranties'. A term that goods be 'shipped in good condition' was held not to be a condition or a warranty. It was an intermediate stipulation and in those circumstances the court was required by common law principles (expressly preserved by s 62 (2) of the Act) to consider the extent of the actual breach—if it went to the root of the contract the other party was entitled to treat himself as discharged but otherwise(as here) he was not.[13] However, the pull of tradition in sale of goods contracts is strong and it seems that terms as to the time of shipment, delivery, etc are likely to continue to be treated as conditions. In *Bunge Corp v Tradax*,[14] a term agreed by a buyer to name the vessel to take the goods bought was held to be a condition and the seller therefore entitled on breach to repudiate even though the buyer was only four days late.

A buyer may always elect to treat a breach of condition as a breach of warranty ex post facto by claiming damages instead of repudiating the contract altogether (s 11 (2)). The buyer is bound to do this in the circumstances referred to in s 11 (4) which reads:—

> 'Where a contract of sale is not severable and the buyer has accepted the goods or part of them, the breach of a condition to be fulfilled by the seller can only be treated as a breach of warranty, and not as a ground for rejecting the goods and treating the contract as repudiated, unless there is an express or implied term of the contract to that effect.'

If a contract is severable, then whether a buyer can repudiate the contract after he has accepted part of the goods depends, as we shall see, on the ratio of the breach to the contract as a whole and the probability of repetition of the breach.[15] If it is not severable, then by s 11 (4) the buyer's right to reject for breach of condition is lost as soon as he accepts all or part of the goods.

12 [1976] QB 44, [1975] 3 All ER 739, CA.
13 See also *Hong Kong Fir Shipping Co Ltd v Kawaski Kisen Kaisha Ltd* [1962] 2 QB 26, [1962] 1 All ER 474, CA and *Reardon Smith Line v Hansen-Tangen* [1976] 3 All ER 570, [1976] 1 WLR 989, HL.
14 [1981] 2 All ER 513, [1981] 1 WLR 711, HL.
15 See p 127, post. A contract is not severable merely because the seller has an option to sever it: see *Rosenthal & Sons v Esmail* [1965] 2 All ER 860, 870.

There are certain presumptions with regard to terms as to time. By s 10:

'(1) Unless a different intention appears from the terms of the contract, stipulations as to time of payment are not of the essence of a contract of sale.

(2) Whether any other stipulation as to time is or is not of the essence of the contract depends on the terms of the contract.'

A term as to time of delivery or shipment is prima facie a condition. In *J Aron & Co (Inc) v Comptoir Wegimont*,[16] McCardie J said that an express requirement that goods be shipped at a particular period was a condition precedent to the contract of sale. If the buyer waives a breach of a condition as to the time of delivery, the waiver is binding on the buyer though given without consideration (s 11 (2)). An example of a buyer waiving a breach on the part of the seller of a condition as to delivery date is where, after the breach, the buyer continues to press the seller for delivery. However, if after the buyer has waived such a breach by the seller, the buyer gives reasonable notice that he will not take delivery after a certain date, ie the buyer reimposes the condition as to delivery date, he is entitled to reject the goods if they are not delivered by that date.[17]

Implied terms

Certain terms are implied in contracts of sale of goods. Until the Supply of Goods (Implied Terms) Act 1973 s 55 of the Sale of Goods Act 1893 provided that any such term may be 'negatived or varied by express agreement or by the course of dealing between the parties, or by usage, if the usage be such as to bind both parties to the contract'. The meaning of 'course of dealing' and 'usage' have already been explained.[18] The 1973 Act, following proposals of the English and Scottish Law Commission[19] not only amended the provisions of the 1893 Act relating to implied terms, it also amended s 55 of the 1893 Act so as to restrict contracting out of the obligations of the seller which are implied by those provisions. The Unfair Contract Terms Act 1977 now controls 'contracting out' and the Sale of Goods Act 1979 s 55, provides that any contracting out is subject to the 1977 Act.

The amendments made to ss 12–15 of the 1893 Act by the Supply of Goods (Implied Terms) Act 1973 (and in the case of s 14, by the

16 [1921] 3 KB 435, 440.
17 *Charles Rickards Ltd v Oppenheim* [1950] 1 KB 616, [1950] 1 All ER 420.
18 See p 51, ante.
19 Law Com No 24 (1969).

Consumer Credit Act 1974) are now embodied in ss 12–15 of the Sale of Goods Act 1979. After examining these, the statutory and common law restrictions on contracting out, ie exemption clauses, will be discussed.

1. *Implied undertakings as to title.*—Section 12 of the 1979 Act reads:—

'(1) In a contract of sale, other than one to which sub-section (3) below applies, there is an implied condition on the part of the seller that in the case of a sale he has a right to sell the goods, and in the case of an agreement to sell he will have such a right at the time when the property is to pass.

(2) In a contract of sale, other than one to which subsection (3) below applies, there is an implied warranty that—

(a) the goods are free, and will remain free until the time when the property is to pass, from any charge or encumbrance not disclosed or known to the buyer before the contract is made; and

(b) the buyer will enjoy quiet possession of the goods except so far as it may be disturbed by the owner or other person entitled to the benefit of any charge or encumbrance so disclosed or known.

(3) This subsection applies to a contract of sale in the case of which there appears from the contract or is to be inferred from the circumstances of the contract an intention that the seller should transfer only such title as he or a third person may have.

(4) In a contract to which subsection (3) above applies there is an implied warranty that all charges or encumbrances known to the seller and not known to the buyer have been disclosed to the buyer before the contract is made.

(5) In a contract to which subsection (3) above applies there is also an implied warranty that none of the following will disturb the buyer's quiet possession of the goods, namely—

(a) the seller;

(b) in a case where the parties to the contract intend that the seller should transfer only such title as a third person may have, that person;

(c) anyone claiming through or under the seller or that third person otherwise than under a charge or encumbrance disclosed or known to the buyer before the contract is made.'

In *Rowland v Divall*,[20] the plaintiff bought a car from the

20 [1923] 2 KB 500. It will be noted that the plaintiff was held entitled to recover the full price he had paid and reject the car although he had 'accepted' it. It would seem that, as Atkin LJ said, s 11 (1) (c) of the 1893 Act (now s 11 (4) of the 1979 Act) has no application to a breach of s 12 (1) because there is not really a contract of sale at all if the seller has no right to sell the goods. The decision was followed in a case concerning more complicated facts: *Butterworth v Kingsway Motors Ltd* [1954] 2 All ER 694, [1954] 1 WLR 1286.

defendant and used it for four months before discovering that the car had never belonged to the defendant; the plaintiff then had to hand the car over to the true owner. The Court of Appeal held that the defendant was in breach of the implied condition in s 12 (1) and the plaintiff was entitled to recover the full price he had paid as there had been a total failure of consideration. The reasoning of the court was based on the fact that the plaintiff had paid the price in order to obtain the property in the car, and since he had not received it there was a total failure of consideraion; he had not paid for mere use of the car and therefore no set-off was allowed for the user enjoyed.

It has also been held that where a seller can be stopped by process of law from selling because, for example, the seller has infringed a trade mark of another company, the seller is in breach of s 12.[1]

In *Mason v Burningham*,[2] the plaintiff bought a used typewriter from the defendant for £20 and spent a further £11 10s 0d having it overhauled but then learned that it was stolen property and had to return it to its true owner. In an action for damages for breach of the implied warranty in s 12 as to quiet possession, the plaintiff recovered both the £20 and the amount spent on overhauling the typewriter on the ground that incurring this expense arose 'directly and naturally, in the ordinary course of events, from the breach of warranty' and such loss is, by s 53 (2), the measure of damages for breach of warranty. The implied condition as to title was not relied on in this case but it seems clear that the defendant was in breach of both the implied condition and the implied warranty, and a claim for general damages can be made under either head. However, the implied warranty should not be thought entirely otiose. It seems, for example, that it allows the buyer a longer period of limitation because time would not begin to run until the disturbance of possession has actually taken place.[3] Then again, where an execution debtor sells goods which have been seized by the sheriff in pursuance of a writ of fieri facias the execution debtor (and any purchaser from him) is able to pass the general property and title in the goods, but the execution debtor is in breach of the implied warranty because the title passed is not free from the sheriff's rights. Moreover, the goods are, at the time of the sale subject to an 'encumbrance', assuming that the

1 *Niblett v Confectioners' Materials Co Ltd* [1921] 3 KB 387.
2 [1949] 2 KB 545, [1949] 2 All ER 134.
3 Chitty on *Contracts* (25th edn, 1983) para 4145.

encumbrance was not disclosed or known to the buyer before the sale.[4]

What is now s 12 (3) is a new provision stemming from the 1973 Act. A seller who is doubtful about his title to the goods may expressly sell them on the basis that he is transferring 'only such title as he . . . may have.' There is then no implied condition that he has a right to sell the goods and the implied warranties are modified. Probably, if goods are sold by a sheriff under an execution or by an auctioneer under a distress warrant or if an unredeemed pledge is sold by a pawnbroker, the circumstances are such that the seller will be taken to intend to transfer only such title as he has under s 12 (3).[5] But an outright exemption clause is clearly void because by s 6 (1) of the Unfair Contract Terms Act 1977 liability for breach of the obligations arising from s 12 of the Sale of Goods Act cannot be excluded or restricted by any contract term and that provision applies to all sales whether 'consumer' sales or not (and therefore even to sales by a private individual not selling in the course of a business). The provision does not apply to 'international sales'.[6]

2. *Condition as to description.*—Section 13 reads:—

'(1) Where there is a contract for the sale of goods by description, there is an implied condition that the goods will correspond with the description.

(2) If the sale is by sample as well as by description it is not sufficient that the bulk of the goods corresponds with the sample if the goods do not also correspond with the description.

(3) A sale of goods is not prevented from being a sale by description by reason only that, being exposed for sale or hire, they are selected by the buyer.'

Subsection (3) was introduced by the 1973 Act to clarify the position where, for example, goods are selected by the buyer at a self-service store, without anything being said. In these circumstances, the goods may be regarded as describing themselves either by the words on their packaging or labelling or, perhaps, even by their appearance.

4 *Lloyds and Scottish Finance Ltd v Modern Cars and Caravans (Kingston) Ltd* [1966] 1 QB 764, [1964] 2 All ER 732. See also *Microbeads AC v Vinhurst Road Markings Ltd* [1975] 1 All ER 529, [1975] 1 WLR 218, CA.

5 Section 12, as it originally stood, stated that the terms implied by the section were implied 'unless the circumstances of the contract are such as to show a different intention' and, in the type of case exemplified in the text, the courts held that no condition as to title was implied. See eg, *Payne v Elsden* (1900) 17 TLR 161.

6 See pp 110–118, post.

Unlike s 14, to be considered shortly, this implied condition applies whether or not the seller sells goods in the course of a business. In *Varley v Whipp*,[7] a private person selling a second-hand reaping machine described it as new in the previous year and used to cut only 50 or 60 acres and he was held to be in breach of s 13 when the description given was found to be very far from the truth.

All sales of unascertained goods will be sales by description. So too will many sales of specific goods, particularly where, as in *Varley v Whipp* the buyer has not seen the goods sold, but there can also be a sale by description even though the buyer is buying something displayed before him on a shop counter.[8]

In *Beale v Taylor*,[9] the sellers of a car advertised it as a 'Herald convertible, white, 1961 . . .'. The buyer saw the car before agreeing to buy it and later discovered that while the rear half of the car was part of a 1961 Herald convertible, the front half was part of an earlier model. The Court of Appeal held that the buyer was entitled to damages for breach of the condition implied by s 13. A sale by sample alone would not be a sale by description. The 'description' means any words used in relation to the goods which identifies them. Even a slight divergence from the quantity or size of goods ordered, or the way in which they are to be packed, or their thickness, is prima facie a breach of this condition.[10] In *Re Moore & Co and Landauer & Co*,[11] for example, a buyer agreed to purchase 3,000 tins of Australian canned fruit, packed in cases of 30 tins. When the goods were delivered, it was found that about half the cases contained only 24 tins. The total quantity of tins ordered had been delivered but, nevertheless, there was held to be a breach of s 13 and the buyer was entitled to reject the whole consignment. It will be apparent from this case that a buyer is entitled to reject goods for a breach of s 13 although he has suffered no damage from the breach. The seller may of course protect himself, for example, as to the quantity, by using such phrases as 'more or less' or 'thereabouts' and no doubt the de minimis principle will avail him in some cases.

The House of Lords in *Ashington Piggeries Ltd v Christopher Hill*

7 [1900] 1 QB 513.
8 *Grant v Australian Knitting Mills Ltd* [1936] AC 85, [1935] All ER Rep 209.
9 [1967] 3 All ER 253, [1967] 1 WLR 1193, CA.
10 *Arcos Ltd v E A Ronaasen & Son* [1933] AC 470, [1933] All ER Rep 646.
11 [1921] 2 KB 519; Lord Wilberforce in *Reardon Smith Line v Hansen-Tangen* [1976] 3 All ER 570, 576, [1976] 1 WLR 989, HL, referred to this case as 'excessively technical' and due for fresh examination in the House of Lords. See further, p 125, post.

Ltd[12] stressed that 'description' is different from 'quality'. There, herring meal sold to buyers for use as mink food was contaminated with a substance that made it unsuitable for that purpose. By a four to one majority, however, their Lordships held that there was no breach of s 13—the goods were still properly described as 'herring meal' because they were still *identifiable* as such. Of course, words relating to quality may be necessary to identify the goods—'prime Scotch beef'—and they are then part of the description.

Lord Wilberforce in *Reardon Smith Line v Hansen-Tangen*[13] endorsed remarks by Roskill LJ in *Cehave NV v Bremer Handelsgesellschaft mbH*[14] to the effect that it is not easy to see why the law relating to contracts for the sale of goods should be different from the law relating to the performance of other contractual obligations, ie attending to the nature and gravity of a breach rather than accepting rigid categories of term which do or do not automatically give a right to rescind. Specifically in relation to s 13, Lord Wilberforce said, obiter:—

'Even if a strict and technical view must be taken as regards the description of unascertained future goods (eg commodities) as to which each detail of the description must be assumed to be vital, it may be, and in my opinion is, right to treat other contracts of sale of goods in a similar manner to other contracts generally, so as to ask whether a particular item in a description constitutes a substantial ingredient of the "identity" of the thing sold, and only if it does to treat it as a condition.'

3. *Condition that goods are of merchantable quality.*—Section 14 of the 1893 Act was reworded and rearranged by the 1973 Act and these changes are now embodied in s 14 of the 1979 Act. As before 1973, it begins with a statement of the general principle of caveat emptor—this is now s 14 (1); then follows a reworded implied condition that goods are of merchantable quality—s 14 (2); and a reworded implied condition that goods are fit for their purpose—now s 14 (3).

The present s 14 (1) reads:—

'Except as provided by this section and section 15 below and subject to any other enactment, there is no implied condition or warranty as to the quality or fitness for any particular purpose of goods supplied under a contract of sale.'

The present s 14 (2) reads:—

12 [1972] AC 441, [1971] 1 All ER 847. The sellers were, however, held to be in breach of s 14.
13 [1976] 3 All ER 570, 576–577, [1976] 1 WLR 989, HL.
14 [1976] QB 44, 71, [1975] 3 All ER 739, 756.

'Where the seller sells goods in the course of a business, there is an implied condition that the goods supplied under the contract are of merchantable quality, except that there is no such condition—
   (a) as regards defects specifically drawn to the buyer's attention before the contract is made; or
   (b) if the buyer examines the goods before the contract is made, as regards defects which that examination ought to reveal.'

This is an improved and simplified provision as compared with the old s 14 (2) because it is no longer limited to sales 'by description' and it applies even though the seller has not previously dealt in goods of a similar kind or does not regularly sell such goods. All sales 'in the course of a business' are covered and 'business' is defined to include 'a profession and the activities of any government department, . . . or local or public authority.' It follows that if a wine merchant sells off the van he has been using in his business, or a solicitor sells furniture from his offices, the implied condition applies. On the other hand a private individual selling his lawnmower to a neighbour is not subject to s 14 (2). However, if a private individual sells goods through the agency of a person who disposes of them in the course of a business (eg, an auctioneer) the private seller is subject to s 14 (2) unless the buyer knows he is a private seller or reasonable steps are taken to bring this fact to the notice of the buyer before the contract is made (s 14 (5)).

For the first time, the 1973 Act introduced a statutory definition of 'merchantable quality'. The definition is now contained in s 14 (6) of the 1979 Act:—

'Goods of any kind are of merchantable quality within the meaning of subsection (2) if they are as fit for the purpose or purposes for which goods of that kind are commonly bought as it is reasonable to expect having regard to any description applied to them, the price (if relevant) and all the other relevant circumstances.'

Academic writers have differed as to whether the advent of the statutory definition replaces the old law or is declaratory of it.[15] The Court of Appeal in *Aswan Engineering Establishment Co v Lupdine Ltd*[16] preferred the latter view. It followed that they examined the old case law and, on the basis of the House of Lords decision in *Henry Kendall & Sons v William Lillico & Sons Ltd*,[17] ruled that goods are of merchantable quality if they are suitable for one or more purposes for which they might, without abatement of the price, reasonably

15 Eg, Goode *Commercial Law* (revised edn, 1985) p 261 against *Atiyah*, p 133.
16 [1987] 1 All ER 135, [1987] 1 WLR 1.
17 [1969] 2 AC 31, [1968] 2 All ER 444.

be expected to be used, but they were not required to be suitable for every purpose within such a range of purposes for which such goods are normally bought. However, a differently constituted Court of Appeal shortly afterwards took the view that s 14 (6) was clear and free from technicality and 'it should be sufficient in the great majority of cases to enable the fact-finding judge to arrive at a decision without exploring the intricacies of the prior law'.[18]

The description and price are the key criteria. In *Cehave NV v Bremer Handelgesellschaft mbH*[19] Lord Denning MR said this statutory definition was the best yet devised and thought it appropriate to a contract made before the 1973 Act. In that case the Court of Appeal held that the fact that the goods could only be sold at a reduced price was not conclusive evidence that they were not of merchantable quality. Citrus pulp pellets sold had been used for the purpose for which they were commonly sold, ie for cattle food, and it followed that they must have been of merchantable quality. Clearly, goods sold in the course of business second-hand or at a reduced price are required to be of merchantable quality but the standard of quality properly to be expected will depend very much on the price paid.

In a decision before the 1973 Act, Lord Denning MR said that in the case of second-hand goods, they are merchantable if in usable condition even though not perfect.[20] Goods may be considered to be of 'merchantable quality' though they happen not to be saleable in the place where the seller knows the buyer intends to resell them.[1] When goods are sold under a contract which involves transit of the goods before use, as in a cif or fob contract it may be implied (if the goods are perishable) that they are merchantable not only at the beginning of the journey but will withstand the normal incidents of transit so as to be merchantable on arrival and for a reasonable time thereafter. In *Mash and Murrell Ltd v Joseph I Emmanuel Ltd*[2] the

18 Per Mustill LJ in *Rogers v Parish (Scarborough) Ltd* [1987] 2 All ER 232, 235. The Law Commission, on whose report the statutory definition was based, envisaged that it would replace the common law: Law Com no 24 para 42. The Law Commission's more recent report on *Sale and Supply of Goods* (Law Com no 160, 1987) proposes a new definition, see below, p 110.

19 [1976] QB 44, [1975] 3 All ER 739, 748, CA.

20 *Bartlett v Sidney Marcus Ltd* [1965] 2 All ER 753, 755, [1965] 1 WLR 1013, 1017, CA.

1 *Summer Permain & Co Ltd v Webb & Co Ltd* [1922] 1 KB 55. But on such facts the seller may be in breach of what is now s 14 (3).

2 [1961] 1 All ER 485, [1961] 1 WLR 862. The Court of Appeal reversed Diplock's J's decision on the facts since the potatoes had remained unventilated for five days and nights in hot summer weather so that it was not a normal voyage; [1962] 1 All ER 77n, [1962] 1 WLR 16n.

defendants agreed to sell the plaintiffs a quantity of Cyprus spring-crop potatoes. It was a c & f contract, ie, the price agreed included the cost of the goods and the freight charges. The potatoes were in good condition when they left Cyprus but were found to be affected by soft rot and unfit for human consumption when they arrived in England. Diplock J, assuming as a fact that it was a normal voyage, held that the defendants were in breach of s 14 (2) because, in a contract of this kind involving transit, the condition implied by s 14 (2) required that the goods remain of merchantable quality from the time of shipment through normal transit to the destination, and for a reasonable time thereafter for disposal. Twenty years later, Lord Diplock delivering the opinion of the House of Lords in *Lambert v Lewis*[3] ruled that the implied condition of fitness for purpose under s 14 (3) is a continuing promise that goods will continue to be fit for a reasonable time and it seems likely that this now will be applied to the condition of merchantable quality under s 14 (2).

The condition implied by s 14 (2) (and, indeed the condition implied by s 14 (3) applies not only to the goods actually sold but to any 'goods supplied under the contract'. In *Wilson v Rickett, Cockerell & Co Ltd*,[4] there was a sale by the defendants of Coalite and in the consignment delivered there was an explosive substance that blew up in the plaintiff's fireplace. Despite an argument that the Coalite itself was of merchantable quality, the Court of Appeal held that the 'goods supplied' were not merchantable. 'A sack of coal, which contains hidden in it a detonator, is not fit for burning and no sophistry should lead us to believe that it is fit', said Denning LJ.[5] The Court of Appeal in *Wormell v RHM Agricultural (East) Ltd*[6] held that, although instructions as to the use of goods had to be taken into account in considering whether the goods were fit for the purpose for which they were supplied, if the instructions gave a clear warning that the goods should not be used after a particular time the buyer could not complain that the instructions had rendered the goods unfit merely because he had misunderstood the effect of the warning.

A new limitation introduced by the 1973 Act is that there is no implied condition of merchantable quality as regards defects

3 [1982] AC 225, 276, [1981] 1 All ER 1185, 1191.
4 [1954] 1 QB 598, [1954] 1 All ER 868. In *Geddling v Marsh* [1920] 1 KB 668; [1920] All ER Rep 631, the section was held to apply to a mineral water bottle as well as to the contents although the bottle remained the seller's.
5 [1954] 1 QB 598, 606, [1954] 1 All ER 868.
6 [1987] 3 All ER 75, [1987] 1 WLR 109, CA.

specifically drawn to the buyer's attention before the contract is made. There is no requirement that such defects should be specified in writing though clearly a seller would be well advised to specify them in writing and keep a copy. A limitation or proviso that continues from the pre-1973 law is that if the buyer examines the goods, there is no implied condition of merchantable quality as regards defects which 'that examination' ought to reveal.[7]

4. *Condition of fitness for purpose.*—The present s 14 (3), replacing s 14 (1) of the 1893 Act as it originally stood, reads:—

'Where the seller sells goods in the course of a business and the buyer, expressly or by implication, makes known—
   (a) to the seller, or
   (b) where the purchase price or part of it is payable by instalments and the goods were previously sold by a credit-broker to the seller, to that credit broker,
any particular purpose for which the goods are being bought, there is an implied condition that the goods supplied under the contract are reasonably fit for that purpose, whether or not that is a purpose for which such goods are commonly supplied, except where the circumstances show that the buyer does not rely, or that it is unreasonable for him to rely, on the skill or judgment of the seller or credit-broker.'

By s 61 (1), 'credit broker' means a person acting in the course of a business of credit brokerage carried on by him, that is a business of effecting introductions of individuals desiring to obtain credit—

(a) to persons carrying on any business so far as it relates to the provision of credit, or
(b) to other persons engaged in credit brokerage.

The reference to a credit-broker was introduced by the Consumer Credit Act 1974 and is significant only for a credit sale agreement, i.e., an agreement for the sale of goods under which the purchase price or part of it is payable by instalments but (unlike a conditional sale agreement) the property passes at once.[8]

Suppose a student asks a law bookseller for a book on contract law suitable as a student's textbook. Clearly, there is an implied condition that the book supplied will be fit for the purpose the

7 This is a slight change of wording from the old s 14 (2) which referred to 'such examination' and in *Thornett and Fehr v Beers & Son* [1919] 1 KB 486, it was held that where a buyer of glue examined the barrels from the outside only, although given the opportunity to make a thorough examination, the implied condition was excluded. Perhaps the new wording will prevent a similar decision in future.
8 See post, p 203.

student has expressly specified. There will be a breach of s 14 (3) if the book supplied is a practitioner's book or is an out-of-date edition.

In many instances, the purpose for which goods are required is obvious. If one buys food[9] or underclothing,[10] or a hot water bottle,[11] there is no need to specify in express words the purpose for which the goods are wanted as the purpose is made known 'by implication'. In *Godley v Perry*[12] a six-year-old boy purchased a toy plastic catapult. While he was using it, the catapult broke and the boy lost an eye when part of the catapult entered it. The boy's action against the shopkeeper was successful.[13] However, where goods are required for some special purpose, that purpose must be made known expressly to the seller if the buyer is to be entitled to rely on s 14 (3).[14] Thus, in *Griffiths v Peter Conway, Ltd*,[15] a woman with an abnormally sensitive skin bought a Harris Tweed coat without disclosing this fact to the seller. The Court of Appeal held that when the woman contracted dermatitis from the coat the seller was not liable. There was nothing in the cloth which would have affected the skin of a normal person.

The established interpretation of what is now s 14 (3) was approved by the House of Lords in the case of *Henry Kendall & Sons v William Lillico & Sons Ltd.*[16] Wholesalers K sold a quantity of groundnut extractions to G knowing that G wanted the extractions for the purpose of resale for compounding as food for cattle and poultry. G sold some of the extractions to S knowing S wanted them for compounding for food for pigs and poultry. S did compound the extractions and sold them to H for the purpose of feeding his pheasants. H's pheasants died because of poison in the extractions. H's claim against S was settled out of court. The House of Lords held that S could succeed against G and G could succeed against K. They stressed that where goods are brought for their normal and obvious purpose, then in the absence of anything to the contrary,

9 *Chaproniere v Mason* (1905) 21 TLR 633.

10 *Grant v Australian Knitting Mills Ltd* [1936] AC 85.

11 *Preist v Last* [1903] 2 KB 148.

12 [1960] 1 All ER 36, [1960] 1 WLR 9.

13 The retailer, in his turn, claimed against the wholesaler, and the wholesaler against the importers. These sales were by sample and the claims, brought under s 15 (2), were successful. See p 109, post, for a discussion of s 15 (2).

14 *Manchester Liners Ltd v Rea Ltd* [1922] 2 AC 74, [1922] All ER Rep 605.

15 [1939] 1 All ER 685.

16 [1969] 2 AC 31, [1968] 2 All ER 444. See also *Crowther v Shannon Motor Co* [1975] 1 All ER 139, [1975] 1 WLR 30, CA.

the implied condition applies although the buyer has done nothing specifically to indicate the purpose for which he requires them. In this case, where goods were bought for a special purpose, that purpose must be made known (as it was by G to K and by S to G).

Since the condition implied by s 14 (3) is only that the goods be 'reasonably fit' for their purpose, a seller of pork chops which would have been harmless if properly cooked was held not liable to a buyer who only partly cooked them and became ill.[17] Unlike the pre-1973 implied condition of fitness for purpose, the present condition applies if the seller has not previously dealt in goods of a similar kind. All sales 'in the course of a business' are covered and also covered is a sale by a private person who sells through someone acting in the course of a business, such as an auctioneer, unless the buyer knows the seller is a private individual or reasonable steps are taken to bring that fact to the notice of the buyer (s 14 (5)). Another change in the law is that the provision no longer suggests that, in order to have the benefit of this implied condition, the buyer must positively establish that he relied on the seller's skill or judgment. Instead, there is a proviso that the implied condition does not apply where the circumstances show that the buyer does not rely, or that it is unreasonable for him to rely, on the seller's skill or judgment. This suggests that the onus of disproving reliance is on the seller but the change may not be significant because case law had already indicated that reliance on the seller was readily assumed from the buyer choosing to go to a particular seller unless the seller warned the buyer to rely on his own judgment.

The old proviso that there was no condition of fitness for purpose if goods were sold under a patent or trade name has been deleted. It had already lost most of its meaning.[18]

Section 14 (4), repeating the old s 14 (3), says that an implied condition or warranty as to quality or fitness for a particular purpose may be annexed to a contract of sale by usage.

5. *Conditions applicable in sales by sample.*—Section 15 implies the following condition in contracts of sale by sample:—

'(1) A contract of sale is a contract for sale by sample where there is an express or implied term to that effect in the contract.

(2) In the case of a contract for sale by sample there is an implied condition—

17 *Heil v Hedges* [1951] 1 TLR 512.
18 See eg, *Baldry v Marshall* [1925] 1 KB 260, [1924] All ER Rep 155.

(a) that the bulk will correspond with the sample in quality;[19]
(b) that the buyer will have a reasonable opportunity of comparing the bulk with the sample;
(c) that the goods will be free from any defect, rendering them unmerchantable, which would not be apparent on reasonable examination of the sample.'

The first two limbs of the condition in s 15 (2) explain themselves. The third means that the seller is generally liable if the goods are defective but he escapes liability if the defect in the goods could have been discovered by reasonable examination of the sample, whether in fact the buyer has made any examination or not.

Law Commission proposals

In 1987 the Law Commission published a report[20] on *Sale and Supply of Goods* proposing a replacement of the statutory definition of 'merchantable' quality by one of 'acceptable' quality, consisting of two elements: a basic principle, formulated in language sufficiently general to apply to all kinds of goods and all kinds of transaction; and a list of aspects of quality, any of which could be important in a particular case. The basic principle should be that the quality of goods sold or supplied under a contract should be such as would be 'acceptable' to a reasonable person, bearing in mind the description of the goods, their price (if relevant) and all other circumstances. The following matters should be included in the list of aspects of quality: the fitness of the goods for *all* their common purposes, their appearance and finish, their freedom from minor defects, their safety and their durability. For *non-consumers* only, there should be a restriction on the right to reject goods where the breach is so slight as to make it unreasonable for him to exercise such a remedy.

Contracting out—exemption clauses

Section 55 of the 1893 Act allowed complete freedom to contract out of any of the obligations implied by the Act. As we shall see, the

19 It is no defence that the goods could be made to correspond with the sample by a simple process: *E and S Ruben Ltd v Faire Bros & Co Ltd* [1949] 1 KB 254, [1949] 1 All ER 215 where vulcanised rubber material was sold by sample and the seller was held to be in breach of s 15 although the rubber supplied could have been made to correspond with the sample merely by warming and then pressing out the folds and crinkles.

20 Law Com no 160, Cmnd 137. See also p 132, post.

courts developed various principles by which they sought to limit the effect of exemption clauses, ie, clauses which, typically, sought to exempt the seller from the conditions and warranties implied by ss 12–15 of the Act. The principles are still of importance in non-consumer sales, though less so than before the 1973 Act. It is in relation to consumer sales, however, that the 1973 Act has made the biggest change in the law. The present law is now contained in the Unfair Contract Terms Act 1977. As has already been mentioned, by s 6 (1) of that Act liability for breach of the obligations arising from s 12 of the Sale of Goods Act cannot be excluded or restricted by any contract term. This provision applies to all sales, whether 'consumer sales' or not and applies therefore even to sales by a private individual not selling in the course of a business but it does not apply to 'international sales'.

Consumer sales

Then comes the key distinction between consumer sales and other sales. By s 6 (2) of the Unfair Contract Terms Act 1977 (as amended by the Sale of Goods Act 1979):—

'As against a person dealing as consumer, liability for breach of the obligations arising from—
(a) section 13, 14 or 15 of the 1979 Act . . . cannot be excluded or restricted by any contract term.'

The definition of 'dealing as consumer' is in s 12 of the 1977 Act:—

'(1) A party to a contract "deals as consumer", in relation to another party if—
(a) he neither makes the contract in the course of a business nor holds himself out as doing so; and
(b) the other party does make the contract in the course of a business; and
(c) in the case of a contract governed by the law of sale of goods . . . the goods passing under or in pursuance of the contract are of a type ordinarily supplied for private use or consumption.
(2) But on a sale by auction or competitive tender the buyer is not in any circumstances to be regarded as dealing as consumer.
(3) Subject to this, it is for those claiming that a party does not deal as consumer to show that he does not.'

This definition emphasises (a) the type of goods and (b) the type of buyer. If a private person buys a lorry or elaborate building equipment it would not be a 'consumer sale' but, in these do-ityourself days, it would be a matter of evidence as to whether some kinds of building or decorating materials were of a type 'ordinarily supplied for private use or consumption'. 'Business' includes 'a profession and the activities of any government department or local or public authority' (s 14 of the 1977 Act) so that if a shopkeeper or an accountant buys a fan heater for his office that is surely not a 'consumer sale' though the goods are of a type ordinarily supplied for private use.[1] If a private person purports to be a trade purchaser, perhaps in order to obtain a trade discount, it would not be a 'consumer sale' because he would be holding himself out as buying in the course of a business.

It is clear from the final phrase in s 6 (2) 'any contract term' that exemption clauses in relation to consumer sales are void not only when they are in the contract of sale itself but also when they are in collateral contracts, for example, a contract of 'guarantee' whereby the manufacturer grants the buyer certain rights of repair or replacement. Moreover, by s 13 of the Unfair Contract Terms Act 1977:—

'(1) To the extent that this Part of this Act prevents the exclusion or restriction of any liability it also prevents—
   (a) making the liability or its enforcement subject to restrictive or onerous conditions;
   (b) excluding or restricting any right or remedy in respect of the liability, or subjecting a person to any prejudice in consequence of his pursuing any such right or remedy;
   (c) excluding or restricting rules of evidence or procedure;
and (to that extent) sections 2 and 5 to 7 also prevent excluding or restricting liability by reference to terms and notices which exclude the relevant obligation or duty.
   (2) But an agreement in writing to submit present or future differences to arbitration is not to be treated under this Part of this Act as excluding or restricting any liability.'

It follows, for example, that any term requiring notice of loss to be given within a specified time or any attempt by a seller to avoid liability for consequential loss will, in respect of a consumer sale, be ineffective.

Because exemption clauses in consumer sale contract and notices in shops such as 'no money refunded' continued to be used after these terms became void in 1973, the Director General of Fair Trading using powers under the Fair Trading Act 1973 proposed

1 Contra *Atiyah* p 195.

that their use should constitute a criminal offence. An Order to that effect was made in 1976.[2]

Non-consumer sales

With regard to *non-consumer sales*, a contractual term purporting to exempt the seller from all or any of the provisions in ss 13–15 of the Sale of Goods Act is not automatically void. By s 6 (3) of the Unfair Contract Terms Act 1977, liability under such provision 'can be excluded or restricted by reference to a contract term, but only in so far as the term satisfies the requirement of reasonableness'.

Section 11 (5) provided that it is for those claiming that a contract term or notice satisfies the requirement of reasonableness to show that it does and s 11 (1) specifies that what the requirement amounts to is 'that the term shall have been a fair and reasonable one having regard to the circumstances which were, or ought reasonably to have been, known to or in the contemplation of the parties when the contract was made'. (The 1973 Act allowed matters subsequent to the date of the contract to be considered but put the onus of proof on the buyer to show the term was unreasonable.)

If the seller seeks to restrict liability to a specified sum of money and the question arises whether the sum satisfies the requirement of reasonableness, s 11 (4) says that regard shall be had in particular to (a) the resources which he could expect to be available to him for the purposes of meeting the liability should it arise and (b) how far it is open to him to cover himself by insurance.

Apart from s 11 (4) there is a large element of uncertainty in the application of the 'reasonableness' requirement but Sch 2 of the 1977 Act provides a number of guidelines which were first specified in the 1973 Act. By Sch 2 the matters to which regard is to be had, in particular for the purposes of s 6 (3) are 'any of the following which appear to be relevant':—

'(a) the strength of the bargaining positions of the parties relative to each other, taking into account (among other things) alternative means by which the customer's requirements could have been met;
(b) whether the customer received an inducement to agree to the term or in accepting it had an opportunity of entering into a similar contract with other persons, but without having to accept a similar term;

2 Consumer Transactions (Restrictions on Statements) Order 1976, as amended in 1978. The Order followed a Report of the Consumer Protection Advisory Committee: HC of 1974–75.

114   *Sale of goods*

    (c) whether the customer knew or ought reasonably to have known of the existence and extent of the term (having regard, among other things, to any custom of the trade and any previous course of dealing between the parties);

    (d) where the term excludes or restricts any relevant liability if some condition is not complied with, whether it was reasonable at the time of the contract to expect that compliance with that condition would be practicable;

    (e) whether the goods were manufactured, processed, or adapted to the special order of the customer.'

The House of Lords considered the provisions of Sch 2 in *George Mitchell (Chesterhall) Ltd v Finney Lock Seeds Ltd.*[3] Seed merchants sold some cabbage seed to farmers on terms which purported to limit the liability of the sellers, should the seed prove to be defective, to merely replacing the defective seed or refunding the purchase price—all liability for any loss or damage was excluded. The seed delivered was in fact defective and the crop planted by the buyers was a failure. The House of Lords held that on its true construction the limitation clause was effective to limit the sellers' liability to the replacement of the seed or the refund of the price paid. However, they also held that it would not be fair or reasonable to permit the sellers to rely on the clause because in other cases of seed failure they had negotiated settlement of claims rather than rely on the clause, the cause of the defect was negligence on the part of an associate company of the sellers and the sellers could have readily insured against claims.

The common law

So far as consumer sales are concerned, since the 1973 Act liability for breach of the obligations *implied* by ss 13–15 cannot be excluded or restricted by any contract term, the buyer is less likely to have to rely on the common law. If an exemption clause purports to exclude or restrict liability for breach of an *express* term, the exemption clause may only be relied on by the seller if it satisfies the test of reasonableness (s 3). In a non-consumer sale, if the buyer purchases on the basis of the seller's written terms of business, an exemption clause may only be relied on by the seller if it satisfies the test of reasonableness (s 3). But in both consumer and non-consumer sales, even if the exemption clause satisfies the test of reasonableness, the

3 [1983] 2 AC 803, [1983] 2 All ER 737. The case concerned a contract made between 1973 and 1978, so their Lordships did allow matters subsequent to the date of contract to be considered in determining the reasonableness of the clause.

buyer may be able to rely on principles established by earlier case law.

The courts have long construed strictly any terms which purport to exclude any of the terms implied by the provisions of the Sale of Goods Act. For example, a term excluding 'guarantees' or 'warranties' does not exclude a condition. In *Baldry v Marshall*,[4] there was a clause in the agreement which expressly excluded any 'guarantee or warranty, statutory or otherwise'. The sellers' breach of s 14 was a breach of a condition and the court, therefore, held that their liability was not excluded by that clause. This is the position even though the breach of condition has to be treated as a breach of warranty ex post facto so that only damages can be claimed for breach. In *Wallis, Son and Wells v Pratt and Haynes*,[5] the defendants sold to the plaintiffs seed described as 'common English sainfoin'. After delivery the seed was discovered to be commercially different seed, 'giant sainfoin'. There was a clause in the contract of sale by which 'warranties, express or implied, as to growth or description' were excluded. The House of Lords held that a condition of the contract had been broken so the exemption clause had no application, although the plaintiffs, having 'accepted' the seed by being in possession of it for some time before complaining of breach, had to treat the breach as a breach of warranty ex post facto and could only claim damages.

Further, a clause excluding implied conditions does not exclude any express condition. In *Andrews Bros (Bournemouth) Ltd v Singer & Co Ltd*,[6] buyers ordered a 'new' Singer car from the manufacturers. A clause in the contract of sale excluded all warranties, conditions, and liabilities implied by statute, common law, or otherwise. The car delivered was not 'new' and damages were awarded to the buyer because the exemption clause did not cover breach of an express condition.

It is possible that an express oral term will be held to override a printed or written exemption clause. In *Harling v Eddy*,[7] when the defendant put up a heifer for sale by auction, no bid was made until he said:—'There is nothing wrong with her. I guarantee her.' Bidding did then begin and the heifer was knocked down to the plaintiff. The heifer died of TB four months later. There was a

4 [1925] 1 KB 260, [1924] All ER Rep 155.
5 [1911] AC 394, [1911–13] All ER Rep 989. Approved by the House of Lords in *Henry Kendall & Sons v William Lillico & Sons Ltd* [1969] 2 AC 31, [1968] 2 All ER 444.
6 [1934] 1 KB 17, [1933] All ER Rep 479.
7 [1951] 2 KB 739, [1951] 2 All ER 212.

printed clause in the auctioneer's catalogue excluding liability for any warranty, but the court held that, even assuming the words spoken were a warranty and not a condition, the spoken words prevailed over the printed exemption clause. It was on the basis of those spoken words that the parties contracted and the plaintiff was successful in his claim for damages for breach of the oral warranty.

The common law of fundamental breach and the Unfair Contract Terms Act.—A clause excluding 'any express or implied condition, statement or warranty, statutory or otherwise' will, subject to new statutory rules since the 1973 Act, exclude any condition or warranty.[8] However, it is clear that a failure to carry out the contract at all, for example by delivering entirely different goods from those contracted for, would be a breach of a 'fundamental term', in which case the court will normally construe any exemption clause as not intended by the parties to apply in this situation.[9] For example, in *Pinnock Bros v Lewis and Peat Ltd.*[10] a contract was made for the purchase of 'copra cake'. The court held that the delivery of copra cake adultered with castor oil so as to be poisonous was not a delivery of 'copra cake' at all. As Roche J put it 'a substance quite different from that contracted for has been delivered', and the sellers were not allowed to rely on an exemption clause. On the other hand, the delivery of a consignment of mahogany logs of inferior quality and quantity to those contracted for does not amount to a fundamental breach.[11] It had been asserted by the Court of Appeal in *Karsales (Harrow) Ltd v Wallis*[12] that there was a substantive rule of law to the effect that an exemption clause had no application where there has been a fundamental breach of contract. The House of Lords in the 1966 case of *Suisse Atlantique Société d'Armement Maritime SA v NV Rotterdamsche Kolen Centrale*[13] disapproved of that notion—parties are free to agree that there be no liability even for a fundamental breach of contract but a generally phrased exemption clause will normally be construed as

---

8 *L'Estrange v Graucob* [1934] 2 KB 394, [1934] All ER Rep 16.
9 *Suisse Atlantique Société d' Armement Maritime SA v NV Rotterdamsche Kolen Centrale* [1967] 1 AC 361, [1966] 2 All ER 61.
10 [1923] 1 KB 690.
11 *Smeaton Hanscomb & Co Ltd v Sassoon I Setty Son & Co* [1953] 2 All ER 1471, [1953] 1 WLR 1468. As Devlin J said in the case, it would have been different if pine logs had been delivered.
12 [1956] 2 All ER 866, [1956] 1 WLR 936.
13 [1967] 1 AC 361, [1966] 2 All ER 61.

not applicable to a fundamental breach. The House of Lords approved a dictum of Pearson LJ in an earlier case:

'As to the question of "fundamental breach", I think there is a rule of construction that normally an exception or exclusion clause or similar provision in a contract should be construed as not applying to a situation created by a fundamental breach of contract. This is not an independent rule of law imposed by the courts on parties willy-nilly in disregard of their contractual intention. On the contrary it is a rule of construction based on the presumed intention of the contracting parties'.[14]

In *Photo Productions Ltd v Securicor Transport Ltd*,[15] the House of Lords confirmed that there is no rule of law by which an exemption clause could be eliminated from a consideration of the parties' position when there was a breach of a fundamental term. Whether an exemption clause applied when there was a fundamental breach, breach of a fundamental term or any other breach turned on the construction of the whole contract. Lord Diplock said that in commercial contracts negotiated between businessmen capable of looking after their own interests, 'it is wrong to place a strained interpretation on words in an exclusion clause which are clear and fairly susceptible of one meaning only . . . .' Lord Wilberforce pointed out that any need for this kind of judicial distortion of the English language was banished by making these types of contract subject to the Unfair Contract Terms Act 1977.

By s 3 of the Unfair Contract Terms Act 1977, where the parties have contracted on the seller's written standard terms of business, the seller cannot by reference to any contract term 'claim to be entitled (i) to render a contractual performance substantially different from that which was reasonably expected of him or (ii) in respect of the whole or any part of his contractual obligation, to render no performance at all, except in so far as . . . the contract term satisfies the requirement of reasonableness.' This provision seems to go further than the common law principles of construction but how far it goes is difficult to say. Where s 3 is inapplicable (eg, because standard terms are not used) an exemption clause may be construed as inapplicable because of fundamental breach.[16]

By s 9 (1) of the Unfair Contract Terms Act 1977:—

'Where for reliance upon it a contract term has to satisfy the requirement of reasonableness, it may be found to do so and be given effect

14 *UGS Finance Ltd v Nationale Mortgage Bank of Greece and National Bank of Greece SA* [1964] 1 Lloyd's Rep 446, CA.
15 [1980] AC 827, [1980] 1 All ER 556.
16 Chitty, *op. cit.*, para 890.

accordingly notwithstanding that the contract has been terminated either by breach or by a party electing to treat it as repudiated.'

Section 9 (2) states that where on a breach the contract is nevertheless affirmed by a party entitled to treat it as repudiated, this does not of itself exclude the requirement of reasonableness in relation to any contract term.

Where goods are sold 'with all faults and imperfections', that term saves the seller from liability if the goods delivered are unmerchantable but it would not be construed as saving the seller if the goods delivered are not of the kind and description contracted for at all.[17]

International sales.—The restrictions on contracting out contained in the 1977 Act do not apply to international supply contracts. In these sales, parties are completely free to negative or vary any right, duty or liability which would otherwise arise under ss 12–15 of the 1893 Act.[18] An 'international supply contract' includes a contract of sale of goods made by parties whose places of business are in the territories of different states *and* either (a) the goods are in the course of carriage or will be carried from one State to another; or (b) the offer and the acceptance were effected in different States; or (c) delivery is to be made in a State other than the State where offer and acceptance were effected.

Other contracts for the supply of goods

Apart from contracts for sale of goods and hire purchase (considered in Chapter 3) there are other types of contract for the supply of goods. Sometimes *ownership* passes, as in a contract of barter or exchange and in a contract for 'work and materials', where, for example, in a contract for the repair of a car, the ownership of a new spare part is transferred from the repairer to the owner of the car. In other cases only *possession* passes as where goods are hired to a customer. The Unfair Contract Terms Act 1977, s 7, imposes legislative control over contract terms which exclude or restrict liability for breach of obligation arising by implication of law from the nature of such contracts. Liability in respect of the

17 *Shepherd v Kain* (1821) B & Ald 240. In *Champanhac & Co Ltd v Waller & Co Ltd* [1948] 2 All ER 724, for example, balloons were sold by sample 'with all faults and imperfections' and the fabric of the balloons delivered was perished. It was held that the sellers could not rely on the exemption clause as the bulk did not correspond with the sample. The basic duty for sales by sample, contained in s 15 (2) (a), that the bulk must correspond with the sample, seems to be a fundamental term.

18 Unfair Contract Terms Act 1977 s 26.

right to transfer ownership of the goods, or give possession, or the assurance of quiet possession to the person taking the goods in pursuance of the contract, cannot be excluded or restricted by reference to any such term except in so far as the term satisfies the requirement of reasonableness.

As against a person 'dealing as consumer' liability in respect of the goods' correspondence with description or sample, or their quality or fitness for any particular purpose, cannot be excluded or restricted by reference to any such term. As against a person dealing otherwise than as consumer, such a term is effective only if it satisfies the requirement of reasonableness. The phrases 'dealing as consumer' and 'reasonableness' have already been explained and the same guidelines in Sch 2 of the Act apply to help a court determine whether such a term is reasonable where the customer is not dealing as consumer. It was a curiosity of English law between 1978 and 1982 that, while legislative controls were imposed on contracts that sought to exclude or restrict a supplier's obligations, legislation had not been enacted to clarify what those obligations were. Now, however, by the Supply of Goods and Services Act 1982, in a contract for the transfer of property in goods analogous to a sale of goods contract (such as a contract for work and the supply of materials) and in a contract for the transfer of possession in goods (such as a hire contract), terms are implied as to title, description, fitness for purpose and quality. The detailed provisions of Pt I of the Act which deal with these matters are modelled on ss 12–15 of the Sale of Goods Act.

Fair Trading Act 1973, Part III

The Director General of Fair Trading is empowered to take proceedings in the Restrictive Practices Court or county court for an injunction against a trader who persists in a course of conduct which is detrimental to the interests of consumers by, for example, contravening the duties imposed on him by the Sale of Goods Act. The Director must first use his best endeavours to obtain a satisfactory written assurance but it is not essential that any civil proceedings for breach of contract should have been brought by an individual buyer.

Privity of contract

The implied terms in ss 13–15 only affect the actual parties to the contract, in accordance with the common law doctrine of privity of contract. If a customer buys goods from a retailer, the retailer may be made liable in contract for breach of a term implied by the Sale of Goods Act. The contractual liability is a strict one and it is no defence for the seller to show that the defect is a latent one undiscoverable by the exercise of reasonable care.

In *Frost v Aylesbury Dairy Co Ltd*,[19] the defendants supplied the plaintiff with milk. The milk contained germs of typhoid fever and the plaintiff's wife was infected and later died. The defendants were held liable in damages for breach of s 14 although the existence of the germs could only have been discovered by prolonged investigation. But consider *Preist v Last*,[20] where a man bought a hot-water bottle for use by his wife. After a few days' use by the buyer's wife, the bottle burst and she was scalded. The buyer succeeded in an action against the seller under s 14 to recover the expenses he had incurred in the treatment of his wife's injuries. The wife, however, was not a party to the contract and could not sue the seller under the Sale of Goods Act to recover damages in respect of her injuries.

There will be no privity in the contract of sale as between the customer and the manufacturer unless he is buying direct from the manufacturer. However, the manufacturer may be liable in negligence for personal injuries to the ultimate consumer or for damage to property under the principle of *Donoghue v Stevenson*.[1] Under the Consumer Protection Act 1987, the manufacturer's liability is a strict one subject only to the so-called 'development risks' defence. Further, in the case of many goods such as electrical appliances and motor cars, the buyer is often given a statement of rights by or on behalf of the manufacturer, usually called a 'guarantee' or 'warranty'. This may not create a contract between the manufacturer and the customer in which case the 'rights' are not enforceable. But in certain circumstances a contract is created

19 [1905] 1 KB 608.
20 [1903] 2 KB 148.
1 [1932] AC 562, [1932] All ER Rep 1. Neither at common law nor under the Consumer Protection Act is the manufacturer liable to the ultimate buyer in respect of defective goods that merely cause economic loss. It is true that the House of Lords in *Junior Books Ltd v Veitchi* [1983] AC 520, [1982] 3 All ER 201, took the view that if there is a sufficiently close proximity between the producer of a faulty article and the user, there is a duty to avoid faults being present in the article and liability even if such faults cause only financial loss. Lord Roskill, however, said that as between an ultimate buyer and a manufacturer proximity would not easily be found in everyday transactions because real reliance is placed on the immediate seller, not on the manufacturer. Query, in the light of modern manufacturing advertising and brand advertising. See Borrie *The Development of Consumer Law and Policy* (Hamlyn Lectures, 1984) p 31 and *Atiyah* p 170.

where, for example, a standard manufacturer's guarantee is accepted by the customer, perhaps by signing a card and returning it to the manufacturer, and the guarantee contains a quid pro quo for the manufacturer's undertakings and therefore satisfies the requirement for a valid contract of consideration. The guarantee might give the customer the right to have the free repair of the goods within a specified period of purchase in return for the customer agreeing that 'all common law obligations of the manufacturer to the customer are hereby excluded'. That meant that, if the customer was injured or his property damaged by defects in the goods purchased which were attributable to the fault of the manufacturer, he had given up his right to claim compensation against the manufacturer for the tort of negligence. Now, by s 2 of the Unfair Contract Terms Act 1977, no one may by reference to any contract term or to a notice exclude or restrict his liability for death or personal injury resulting from negligence. In the case of other damage any term or notice is effective only if it satisfies the requirement of reasonableness. Further, by s 5 of the Act, if the goods are 'of a type ordinarily supplied for private use or consumption', the manufacturer's liability for loss or damage cannot be effectively excluded by reference to any contract term or notice contained in or operating by reference to a manufacturer's guarantee. However, the very statutory provision which is aimed at the protection of the consumer throws doubt on the enforceability of the positive undertaking by the manufacturer as to free repair within the guarantee period because there may be no consideration to support such undertaking unless the customer knew of the guarantee before he bought the goods and the purchase from the retailer can be deemed a quid pro quo for the undertaking. It is possible, however, that the return of a guarantee card by the customer to the manufacturer may constitute consideration for the manufacturer's undertaking when the guarantee card contains market research information which is of value to the manufacturer.

Another possibility is that although there be no privity *in the contract of sale* between the customer and the manufacturer, a collateral contract may exist between them. Thus, in *Wells (Merstham) Ltd v Buckland Sand and Silica Co Ltd*,[2] the defendant sand merchants warranted to the plaintiffs who were growers of chrysanthemums that certain sand supplied by them would conform to a certain analysis. Sand conforming to such analysis was suitable for propagating chrysanthemums and three loads were

2 [1965] 2 QB 170, [1964] 1 All ER 41.

ordered by the plaintiffs, one from the defendant direct and two through another company. None of the sand supplied conformed to the analysis and, as a result of using it, the plaintiffs suffered loss. It was held that the plaintiffs were entitled to recover damages for breach of warranty and it was irrelevant that two loads had been purchased indirectly. Edmund Davies J said:

> 'As between A (a potential seller of goods) and B (a potential buyer) two ingredients and two only, are in my judgment required to bring about a collateral contract containing a warranty: (1) a promise or assertion by A as to the nature, quality, or quantity of the goods which B may reasonably regard as having been made *animo contrahendi*, and (2) acquisition by B of the goods in reliance on that promise or assertion.'

Redemption of trading stamps

By the Trading Stamps Act 1964, the holder of 'redeemable trading stamps' which have an aggregate value of not less than 25p is entitled to redeem them for cash. If, however, the holder redeems trading stamps for goods, certain *warranties* are implied by s 4 of the Trading Stamps Act, as amended by the Supply of Goods (Implied Terms) Act 1973:—

> '(1) In every redemption of trading stamps for goods, notwithstanding any terms to the contrary on which the redemption is made, there is—
>
> (a) an implied warranty on the part of the promoter of the trading stamp scheme that he has a right to give the goods in exchange;
>
> (b) an implied warranty that the goods are free from any charge or encumbrance not disclosed or known to the person obtaining the goods before, or at the time of, redemption and that that person will enjoy quiet possession of the goods except so far as it may be disturbed by the owner or other person entitled to the benefit of any charge or encumbrance so disclosed or known;
>
> (c) an implied warranty that the goods are of merchantable quality, except that there is no such warranty—
>
> > (i) as regards defects specifically drawn to the attention of the person obtaining the goods before or at the time of redemption; or
> >
> > (ii) if that person examines the goods before or at the time of redemption, as regards defects which that examination ought to reveal.
>
> (2) Goods of any kind are of merchantable quality within the meaning of this section if they are as fit for the purpose or purposes for which goods of that kind are commonly bought as it is reasonable to expect having regard to any description applied to them and all the other relevant circumstances.'

DELIVERY OF THE GOODS

Meaning of delivery

Section 27 says that it is the duty of the seller to deliver the goods, and of the buyer to accept and pay for them, in accordance with the terms of the contract of sale. The obligations of each party are concurrent, which means that the seller must be ready and willing to give possession of the goods to the buyer in exchange for the price and the buyer must be ready and willing to pay the price in exchange for possession of the goods (s 28). Section 28 is subject to agreement to the contrary, for example, where the seller agrees to give the buyer credit and delivery of the goods is, therefore, made before payment.

'Delivery', according to the definition section (s 61), means 'the voluntary transfer of possession from one person to another'. The most obvious form of delivery is the handing over to the buyer of the actual goods. Delivery of goods stored in a warehouse can be effected by handing over the key to the warehouse and delivery can also be effected by handing over a document of title which represents the goods.

By s 29 (4), if goods are in the hands of a third party, there is no effective delivery until the third person acknowledges (attorns) to the buyer that he holds the goods on his behalf. However, the subsection goes on to state that 'nothing in this section affects the operation of the issue or transfer of any document of title to goods.' This means that where a buyer endorses a bill of lading to a sub-buyer and the goods are in the possession of a third party (eg, a carrier) the transfer of the bill of lading does operate as a delivery of the goods.

Place of delivery

Naturally, the contract itself may specify the place of delivery. By s 29:—

'(1) Whether it is for the buyer to take possession of the goods or for the seller to send them to the buyer is a question depending in each case on the contract, express or implied, between the parties.

(2) Apart from any such contract, express or implied, the place of delivery is the seller's place of business if he have one, and if not, his residence: except that, if the contract is for the sale of specific goods, which to the knowledge of the parties when the contract is made are in some other place, then that place is the place of delivery.'

It follows from s 29 that, subject to anything to the contrary in the contract, the seller's obligation to deliver really amounts simply to being ready and willing that the buyer should take possession of the goods. Section 29 (3) says that where (contrary to the implied rule) the seller is bound to send the goods to the buyer, but no time for sending them is fixed, the seller is bound to send them within a reasonable time. Demand or tender of delivery may be treated as ineffectual unless made at a reasonable hour. What is a reasonable hour is a question of fact (s 29 (5)).

If goods are not in a deliverable state, but need, for example, to be dismantled or assembled, then unless otherwise agreed, the expenses of and incidental to putting the goods into a deliverable state must be borne by the seller (s 29 (6)).

It was held in *Galbraith and Grant Ltd v Block*,[3] that if a seller is bound to send goods to the buyer, he is discharged if he delivers them at the buyer's premises to anyone having apparent authority to receive them, provided the seller has not been negligent. The case concerned the sale of a case of champagne and the sellers agreed to deliver it at the buyer's house. It was sent there and taken in by a respectable looking and apparently authorised person but was not seen again. The court held that sellers were entitled to be paid the price by the buyer unless there had been any negligence on the seller's part.

Delivery of the wrong quantity

Section 30 shows that the seller is under a clear duty, amounting to a condition of the contract, to deliver exactly the correct quantity of goods agreed:—

(1) Where the seller delivers to the buyer a quantity of goods less than he contracted to sell, the buyer may reject them, but if the buyer accepts the goods so delivered he must pay for them at the contract rate.

(2) Where the seller delivers to the buyer a quantity of goods larger than he contracted to sell, the buyer may accept the goods included in the contract and reject the rest, or he may reject the whole.

(3) Where the seller delivers to the buyer a quantity of goods larger than he contracted to sell and the buyer accepts the whole of the goods so delivered he must pay for them at the contract rate.

(4) Where the seller delivers to the buyer the goods he contracted to sell mixed with goods of a different description not included in the contract, the buyer may accept the goods which are in accordance with the contract and reject the rest, or he may reject the whole.

3 [1922] 2 KB 155.

(5) This section is subject to any usage of trade, special agreement, or course of dealing between the parties.

The de minimis rule applies,[4] but otherwise s 30 imposes a strict obligation and is really an exemplification of s 13 which requires goods delivered to correspond with their description. The tender of a smaller or larger quantity of goods than the quantity agreed, or the delivery of the goods contracted for, together with other goods, all constitute a breach of s 30.[5] Thus, if S agrees to sell to B ten tons of coal of a certain description and, on delivery, B finds that only eight tons are of the required description, B is at liberty to accept the eight tons and reject the rest. His acceptance of part of the coal delivered is no bar to his rejection of the rest—s 30 (4) therefore prevails over s 11 (4) in the example. B is also entitled to claim damages. Of course, as was said in relation to s 13, the seller may protect himself by using expressions like 'more or less' or 'about'.

The House of Lords in *Gill & Duffus SA v Berger & Co Inc*,[6] held that where buyers under a cif contract wrongfully refused to pay the sellers on presentation of the correct documents and the sellers properly treated the contract as repudiated by the buyers, subsequent delivery to the buyers of a smaller quantity of goods than contracted for could not give the buyers any rights under s 30 (4) to reject the whole consignment. The sellers were not in the circumstances bound to deliver any goods at all so the possibility of the buyers having any rights under s 30 did not arise and the buyers were liable in damages for breach of contract.

The Law Commission proposed in 1987 that s 30 (4) be replaced by a broader provision allowing for partial rejection by the buyer not only when the unwanted goods are of a different description but also where they are of a different quality, though such right would

---

4 *Shipton, Anderson & Co Ltd v Weil Bros & Co Ltd* [1912] 1 KB 574. Diplock LJ in *Margaronis Navigation Agency Ltd v Henry W Peabody & Co of London Ltd* [1964] 3 All ER 333, 338, said that a contract to deliver a specified quantity of goods was satisfied if that quantity was delivered 'within the margin of error which it is not commercially practicable to avoid'.

5 In *Re Moore & Co and Landauer & Co* [1921] 2 KB 519, a buyer agreed to purchase 3,000 tins of Australian canned fruit, packed in cases of 30 tins. When the goods were delivered, it was found that about half the cases contained only 24 tins. The total quantity ordered was delivered but nevertheless, there was held to be a breach of both s 13 and s 30 and the buyer was entitled to reject the whole consignment. But, as already noted (p 102, ante, Lord Wilberforce in *Reardon Smith Line Ltd v Hansen-Tangen* [1976] 3 All ER 570, 576, referred to this case as 'excessively technical' and due for fresh consideration in the House of Lords.

6 [1984] AC 382, [1984] 1 All ER 438.

not entitle a buyer to reject part only of a 'commercial unit', such as a set of encyclopaedias.[7]

Delivery by instalments

No buyer is bound, unless he agrees, to accept delivery of goods by instalments (s 31 (1)).

Where, however, it is agreed that the goods be delivered by instalments, it is of some importance to know whether it is an indivisible or a severable contract. It will only be a severable contract if it is agreed that each delivery is to be treated as a separate contract and each instalment is to be separately paid for.

First, where it is an indivisible contract, then if the seller is in breach of a condition of the contract in his delivery of the *first* instalment (eg, by late delivery) the buyer is entitled to reject not only that instalment but all subsequent instalments. On the other hand, if the seller is in breach of a condition in his delivery of an instalment subsequent to the first one, the buyer is entitled to damages only and cannot reject either that instalment or subsequent instalments because, some of the goods having already been accepted, he is bound to treat the breach as a breach of warranty *ex post facto* by reason of s 11 (4), examined above.[8] If, however, the total quantity of goods is never delivered by the seller (or part of the total quantity delivered consists of goods of a different description) it seems that the buyer's acceptance of those instalments which have been properly delivered will not prevent him from repudiating the contract altogether and rejecting all goods delivered for breach of s 30.[9]

On the other hand, where it is a severable contract (eg, each instalment is to be separately paid for), s 31 (2) applies:—

> 'Where there is a contract for the sale of goods to be delivered by stated instalments, which are to be separately paid for, and the seller makes defective deliveries in respect of one or more instalments, or the buyer neglects or refuses to take delivery of or pay for one or more instalments, it is a question in each case depending on the terms of the contract and the circumstances of the case whether the breach of contract is a repudiation of the whole contract or whether it is a severable breach giving rise to a claim for compensation but not to a right to treat the whole contract as repudiated.'

7 Law Com no 160, Cmnd 137.
8 See p 97, ante.
9 See p 125, ante and *London Plywood and Timber Co Ltd v Nasic Oak Extract Factory and Steam Sawmills Co Ltd* [1939] 2 KB 343. The buyer may instead retain the goods already delivered (or which comply with the contract) and reject only the rest.

Obviously, the contract itself may say whether a breach by one or other party to the contract in relation to one instalment entitles the other to treat himself as entirely discharged. Apart from that case, s 31 (2) is not very helpful—it depends on 'the circumstances of the case'. However, it has been stated judicially that the main tests are the ratio quantitatively which the breach bears to the contract as a whole and the degree of probability of repetition of the breach.[10] For example, if, when a buyer refuses to take delivery of one instalment of a severable contract, he makes it quite clear he will also refuse all subsequent instalments, the probability of repetition by the buyer of his breach will entitle the seller to treat himself as discharged. So also, if more than half the total quantity of goods to be delivered is discovered to be seriously defective, the ratio of the breach to the whole contract is such that the buyer may treat the whole contract as repudiated.[11] This means that he may refuse to take any further deliveries but, in so far as he has 'accepted' earlier defective deliveries he may only obtain damages in respect of the defects.

On the other hand, in *Maple Flock Co Ltd v Universal Furniture Products (Wembley) Ltd*,[12] there was an agreement for the sale of 100 tons of rag flock, delivery to be at the rate of three loads per week, the weekly deliveries to be separately paid for. It was stipulated that all flock supplied must conform to Government standard. The first 15 loads were satisfactory, the 16th not up to Government standard, and the buyers took delivery of 4 further loads, all satisfactory. The buyers then refused to take any more deliveries. It was held that the buyers were not entitled to do this because there was no probability that the breach would be repeated and the breach that had occurred affected only a small proportion of the flock delivered. In another case, buyers refused to pay for one instalment because they were uncertain whom to pay as the seller company was being wound up, and it was held that the buyers' conduct did not amount to a repudiation of the contract.[13]

Where it is not clear whether a contract is an entire contract or a severable contract, the court will consider whether the parties can really have intended that a breach of one consignment will justify rejection of all consignments. In *Regent OHG Aisenstadt und Barig v*

10 Per Lord Hewart CJ in *Maple Flock Co Ltd v Universal Furniture Products (Wembley) Ltd* [1934] 1 KB 148, 157, [1933] All ER Rep 15, 18, 19.
11 See *R A Munro & Co Ltd v Meyer* [1930] 2 KB 312, [1930] All ER Rep 241.
12 [1934] 1 KB 148, [1933] All ER Rep 15.
13 *Mersey Steel and Iron Co Ltd v Naylor* (1884) 9 App Cas 434.

Francesco of Jermyn Street Ltd. [14] Mustill J considered that a contract for the sale of 62 suits to a retail shop, the number and size of each delivery at the sellers' discretion, was a severable contract. The learned judge rejected an argument that s 31 (2) did not apply to short delivery and held the buyers liable in damages for rejecting all consignments on the basis that one consignment was one suit short.

Delivery to a carrier

Where, in accordance with the contract, the seller is authorised or required to send the goods to the buyer, delivery to a carrier for the purpose of transmission to the buyer is prima facie deemed to be a delivery of the goods to the buyer (s 32 (1)). In such a case delivery to a carrier is performance by the seller of his obligation to deliver the goods and, unless otherwise agreed, the buyer's concurrent obligation to pay the price then becomes operative.

Section 32 (1) does not apply to cif contracts (ie, contracts where the price includes cost of the goods, insurance and freight). In a cif contract, the seller not only has to ship the proper goods at the port of shipment but also has to arrange a contract of carriage and insurance and to tender the shipping documents (the bill of lading, the insurance policy and the invoice) to the buyer. It is the delivery of the shipping documents in cif contracts that represents the seller's obligation to deliver the goods; payment by the buyer will then become due. [15]

Section 32 (1) does, however, apply to fob (free on board) contracts, where the seller's obligation is simply to place the goods on board a ship named by the buyer—that will fulfil the seller's obligation to deliver the goods. [16]

Section 32 (2) which also applies to fob contracts states:—

'Unless otherwise authorised by the buyer, the seller must make such contract with the carrier on behalf of the buyer as may be reasonable having regard to the nature of the goods and the other circumstances of

14 [1981] 3 All ER 327.
15 In cif contracts, the risk passes to the buyer as soon as the goods cross the ship's rail, but the property normally passes only when the shipping documents are handed to the buyer. If the documents are in order, the goods must be paid for, although the goods are already lost: *(C) Groom Ltd v Barber* [1915] 1 KB 316. See p 70, ante.
16 In fob contracts the risk will pass and, prima facie, the property in the goods will pass to the buyer when the goods cross the ship's rail. However, if the goods are unascertained and shipped with other consignments, although the risk will pass to the buyer on shipment, the property in the goods cannot pass to the buyer until they are unconditionally appropriated to the particular contract. In other words, the normal rule in s 18, rule 5(1) determines when the property in unascertained goods passes unless there is an express provision in the contract to the contrary.

the case; and if the seller omits so to do, and the goods are lost or damaged in course of transit, the buyer may decline to treat the delivery to the carrier as a delivery to himself, or may hold the seller responsible in damages.'

From the case of *Thomas Young & Sons Ltd v Hobson & Partners*,[17] it would appear that normally the seller should make a contract of carriage on the buyer's behalf on carrier's risk terms. In that case, electric engines were sold, it being agreed that they be sent to the buyers by rail. The sellers despatched them 'at owner's risk'. They were damaged in transit because they were not made secure in the railway wagons and the buyers refused to accept them. The court dismissed a claim by the sellers for the price since, by s 32 (2), the buyers were entitled to decline to treat delivery to the railway company as delivery to themselves.

Section 32 (3), which applies to fob contracts and other export contracts where it is the buyer's obligation to insure the goods, imposes an obligation on the seller, unless otherwise agreed, where goods are sent by a route involving sea transit, to give such notice to the buyer as may enable him to insure them during their sea transit, and if the seller fails to do so, the goods are at the seller's risk in transit. In *Wimble Sons & Co v Rosenberg & Sons*,[18] the defendants bought goods fob Antwerp. They had details of the freight, the port of shipment and the port of discharge but not the name of the ship. Buckley LJ considered that the information was sufficient to enable them to take out insurance on the goods had they wished and that, therefore, the sellers were not in breach of s 32 (3). Hamilton LJ took the view that the sellers were not in breach of s 32 (3) (on the ground that the sub-section had no application to fob contracts) and the buyers were held liable, therefore, to pay for the cargo which had been lost at sea.

In cif contracts, of course, the seller is obliged to insure the goods so s 32 (3) is inapplicable.

ACCEPTANCE OF THE GOODS

The significance of acceptance

We have seen that by s 27 a buyer is bound to accept and pay for goods in accordance with the terms of the contract. It follows that a

17 (1949) 65 TLR 365.
18 [1913] 3 KB 743. Vaughan Williams LJ agreed with Buckley LJ that s 32 (3) applies to fob contracts but, on the facts, felt that the sellers had not given sufficient notice to enable the buyers to insure and, therefore, that the sellers were in breach of s 32 (3).

failure by the buyer to accept the goods renders him liable for breach of contract unless he has a right to reject them for breach of condition. Furthermore, once a buyer has accepted all or part of the goods he is bound to treat any breach of condition as a breach of warranty ex post facto (s 11 (4)).

Methods of acceptance

By s 34 (1), where goods are delivered to the buyer which he has not previously examined, he is not deemed to have accepted them unless and until he has had a reasonable opportunity of examining them for the purpose of ascertaining whether they are in conformity with the contract.[19]

Section 35 of the 1893 Act was amended by the Misrepresentation Act 1967 and s 35 of the Sale of Goods Act 1979 specifies three possible methods of acceptance:—

> 'The buyer is deemed to have accepted the goods when he intimates to the seller that he has accepted them, or (except where s 34 above otherwise provides) when the goods have been delivered to him, and he does any act in relation to them which is inconsistent with the ownership of the seller, or when after the lapse of a reasonable time he retains the goods without intimating to the seller that he has rejected them.'

The first possibility referred to in s 35 requires clear words of unequivocal conduct and it makes no difference that the buyer has not had a reasonable opportunity to examine the goods. If the buyer signs an 'acceptance note' on delivery he will be considered to have accepted them unless the note can be interpreted as a mere receipt.

The second possibility requires further elaboration:—

> '. . . (except where s 34 above otherwise provides) when the goods have been delivered to (the buyer), and he does any act in relation to them which is inconsistent with the ownership of the seller . . .'

As it originally stood, s 35 did not contain the bracketted words: '(except where s 34 above otherwise provides)'—they were added by the Misrepresentation Act 1967. In 1923, the Court of Appeal in *Hardy & Co v Hillerns and Fowler*[20] had held that if goods have been delivered to the buyer and he resells them and actually despatches all or part of them to the sub-buyer, that was an act 'inconsistent

19 By s 34 (2), unless otherwise agreed when the seller tenders delivery of goods to the buyer, he is bound, on request, to afford the buyer a reasonable opportunity of examining the goods for the purpose of ascertaining whether they are in conformity with the contract.

20 [1923] 2 KB 490, [1923] All ER Rep 275.

with the ownership of the seller' and the buyer was deemed to have accepted the goods under s 35 even though he had not had a reasonable opportunity of examining them to see if they were in conformity with the contract. In the result, when later the goods were found not to conform with the contract, it was too late for the buyer to reject them for breach of condition—damages only could be claimed. The Court of Appeal's decision meant that the provisions of s 35 prevailed over the provisions of s 34. This was reversed by s 4 (2) of the Misrepresentation Act which amends s 35 in the way already shown. The effect of the amendment may be summarised as follows:—

1. If the buyer, having had a reasonable opportunity of examining the goods which have been delivered to him (irrespective of whether in fact he has examined them), despatches all or part of them to a sub-buyer, that is an act 'inconsistent with the ownership of the seller' and the buyer is deemed to have accepted the goods.

2. If, however, the buyer has not had a reasonable opportunity of examining the goods, despatch of all or part of them to a sub-buyer is not now deemed to be acceptance of the goods and, if the facts in *Hardy's* case occurred since the 1967 Act, the decision would be different.

3. A buyer may only reject goods for breach of condition if he is able to let the seller have them back. Where, therefore, the buyer is not able to let the seller have the goods back because the sub-buyer will not return them (this was not so in *Hardy's* case), the buyer has lost his right to reject even though he may not have had a reasonable opportunity of examining them.[1]

4. Dealing with documents of title by the buyer (as distinct from dealings with the goods themselves) had already been considered not to amount to acceptance of the goods in *Kwei Tek Chao (trading as Zung Fu Co) v British Traders and Shippers Ltd.*[2] Devlin J pointed out that in cif contracts, when the documents of title are handed over, the property in the goods passes to the buyer subject to the condition that the property revests if upon examination the goods are found not to conform to the contract. If the buyer sells the documents of title, he sells the conditional property in the goods only and that is not an act inconsistent with the 'reversionary' interest of the seller—in consequence, the buyer is not deemed to have accepted them. Devlin J contrasted *Hardy's* case where the

1 See Atiyah and Treitel *The Misrepresentation Act 1967* (1967) 30 MLR 369, 386.
2 [1954] 2 QB 459, [1954] 1 All ER 779.

buyer physically dealt with the goods themselves by despatching them to sub-buyers but the significance of the *Chao* case has been diminished now that even a dealing with the goods by the buyer is not deemed to be acceptance if he has not had a reasonable opportunity of examining them.

The third possibility referred to in s 35 is that a buyer is deemed to have accepted goods when after 'the lapse of a reasonable time' he retains the goods without intimating to the seller that he has rejected them. It seems clear that a buyer may be considered to have accepted goods even though a latent defect has not come to light and the buyer has not had a reasonable opportunity to discover such defect. In *Bernstein v Pamsons Motors (Golders Green) Ltd*,[3] Rougier J said s 35 was directed solely to what was a reasonably practical interval between a buyer receiving the goods and his ability to return them, bearing in mind the desirability of finality in commercial transactions.

In the 1987 report of the Law Commission on *Sale and Supply of Goods*,[4] it is proposed that a buyer should not lose his right to reject the goods because he has intimated acceptance of them (eg by signing an 'acceptance note') unless he has first had a reasonable opportunity to examine them. In the case of a non-consumer, that should be subject to agreement to the contrary provided it satisfied the 'reasonableness' test under the Unfair Contract Terms Act 1977. Further, in a sale contract, a buyer should not be deemed to have accepted goods merely because he asks for, or agrees to, their repair. In a sale contract, a buyer should not be deemed to have accepted goods merely because they have been delivered to a third party under a sub-sale, gift or other disposition.

Rejection of goods

When a buyer has a right to reject goods for breach of condition, then unless otherwise agreed, he is not bound to return them to the seller. It is sufficient if he intimates to the seller that he refuses to accept them (s 36).

PERSONAL REMEDIES FOR BREACH OF CONTRACT

Breach of the buyer

1. *Failure to take delivery.*—By s 37, when the seller is ready and willing to deliver the goods, and requests the buyer to take delivery,

3 [1987] 2 All ER 220.
4 Law Com no 160, Cmnd 137.

and the buyer does not within a reasonable time after such request take delivery of the goods, he is liable to the seller for any loss occasioned by the neglect or refusal to take delivery, and also for a reasonable charge for the care and custody of the goods. An example of damage caused by the buyer's failure to take delivery would be if the goods have gone bad and harmed other goods in the seller's possession. The seller is still bound to deliver the goods if the buyer is willing to take delivery but there is a proviso to the effect that if the buyer's neglect or refusal to take delivery amounts to a repudiation of the contract, the seller can treat himself as discharged from the obligation of the contract.

2. *Failure to accept goods.*—Section 50 (1) provides the seller with a remedy in damages for non-acceptance where the buyer wrongfully neglects or refuses to accept and pay for the goods. The measure of damages is 'the estimated loss directly and naturally resulting, in the ordinary course of events, from the buyer's breach of contract' (s 50 (2)). That subsection is merely a statutory endorsement of the first rule in *Hadley v Baxendale*[5] but s 50 (3) provides a special rule for the measure of damages where there is 'an available market', ie, the particular goods can be readily sold elsewhere and, if the seller is a dealer, demand for the goods exceeds supply.[6] Section 50 (3) reads:—

> 'Where there is an available market for the goods in question the measure of damages is *prima facie* to be ascertained by the difference between the contract price and the market or current price at the time or times when the goods ought to have been accepted or (if no time was fixed for acceptance) then at the time of the refusal to accept.'

It follows that where there is an available market for the goods, the seller will be entitled to substantial damages only if the market price for the goods is lower than the contract price.[7] If the seller can

5 (1854) 9 Exch 341; approved by the House of Lords in *The Heron II* [1969] 1 AC 350, [1967] 3 All ER 686.
6 See Upjohn J in *W L Thompson Ltd v Robinson (Gunmakers) Ltd* [1955] Ch 177, 187, [1955] 1 All ER 154, 159.
7 If the market price on the day when the goods should have been accepted is lower than the contract price, the seller is entitled to the difference though he retains the goods and later sells them at a price higher than the contract price: *Campbell Mostyn v Barnett* [1954] 1 Lloyd's Rep 65, CA. *Atiyah* p 377, says it is a fair inference from this decision that the position is different where the seller resells immediately on breach at a higher price than the price which rules on the market. The seller should then be entitled only to the difference between the contract and resale prices. *Cf Jamal v Moolla Dawood Sons & Co* [1916] 1 AC 175, PC.

readily dispose of the goods on the market at a price equal to or higher than the contract price he has suffered no loss.

Section 50 (3) will not be applied if the seller is a dealer and although the goods can be readily sold elsewhere, the situation in the trade is such that the supply of such goods outstrips the demand. In *W L Thompson Ltd v Robinson (Gunmakers) Ltd*,[8] the defendants contracted to buy a new Vanguard car from the plaintiff dealers but refused to accept the car when it was ready. The defendants contended that the measure of damages was the difference between the contract price and the market price, and since these prices were the same, the damages were purely nominal. Upjohn J however, felt that as the supply of Vanguard cars at this time exceeded the demand, there was no 'available market' for them, s 50 (3) was inapplicable and the measure of damages was that specified in s 50 (2)—'the loss directly and naturally resulting' from the breach. The seller's direct loss was the loss of profit on the sale—he had sold one less car and was entitled as damages to his loss of profit.[9] Similarly, there may be no 'available market' if goods are specially made to order. If the buyer refuses to accept such goods, the seller is entitled as damages to the cost incurred in making them (if work has already been done) and the loss of profit, though if the goods can perhaps by alteration be made saleable in the general market, the seller is required to do that in accordance with his duty to mitigate damages.[10]

In *Charter v Sullivan*,[11] a buyer refused to accept a new Hillman Minx car when it was ready for delivery and it happened that demand for such cars exceeded supply. Since the contract price and the market price were the same, and the buyer's breach did not affect the number of such cars sold by the seller over any given period, the damages were nominal only whether s 50 (3) or s 50 (2) were applied. The members of the Court of Appeal chose to apply s 50 (2) and agreed that only nominal damages were payable.[12] In *Lazenby Garages Ltd v Wright*,[13] the Court of Appeal held that there was no 'available market' when goods are unique as is the case with

---

8 [1955] Ch 177, [1955] 1 All ER 154.

9 The same principle has been applied in a case of hire of goods: *Inter-Office Telephones Ltd v Robert Freeman Co Ltd* [1958] 1 QB 190, [1957] 3 All ER 479.

10 *Re Vic Mill Ltd* [1913] 1 Ch 465.

11 [1957] 2 QB 117, [1957] 1 All ER 809.

12 Jenkins LJ, obiter, felt that s 50 (3) was never applicable if the sale price was fixed in advance by the manufacturers on the ground that 'available market' meant a place where the price was determined by the law of supply and demand.

13 [1976] 2 All ER 770, [1976] 1 WLR 459, CA.

a second-hand car and since S resold to X at a price higher than he had agreed with B, S suffered no loss from B's breach of contract and so was entitled to no damages. B could not reasonably have contemplated that, in consequence of the breach, S would sell one less car out of the total of his used car sales. Bridge LJ said:

'there was no basis for any proper inference as to what effect on the plaintiffs' (S's) trade would have been felt if the car in question had been sold and delivered to the defendant (B), instead of to the buyer (X) who in fact eventually bought it.'

If a buyer announces in advance of the delivery date agreed that he will not take delivery, that is an anticipatory breach of contract. As with any anticipatory breach of contract, the other party (in this case, the seller) normally has the option of accepting the repudiation and treating the contract as discharged or of continuing to treat the contract as open. In the latter case, the buyer may with impunity change his mind, and in fact take delivery as originally agreed—he would then be under no liability to pay damages to the seller. Apart from that possibility, the seller can claim damages from the buyer and if there is an available market the measure of damages is prima facie the difference between the contract price and the market prevailing at the date the goods ought to have been accepted, irrespective of whether the seller accepted the buyer's earlier repudiation of the contract of not.[14] However, if the seller accepts repudiation of the contract by the buyer and the market price is falling, the seller owes a duty to mitigate the damages by selling the goods on the market at once. On the other hand, if the seller does not accept the buyer's repudiation there is no such duty on the part of the seller to mitigate damages. In *Tredegar Iron and Steel Co Ltd v Hawthorn Bros & Co*,[15] B agreed to buy coal from S at 16s a ton to be delivered during February. On 16 February, B repudiated the contract but informed S of an offer from X to buy the coal at 16s 3d a ton. S declined this offer and insisted on B performing the contract. B continued to decline to take delivery and S early in March sold the coal at 15s a ton. The Court of Appeal allowed S's claim for damages against B at 1s a ton. If the market price rises after the buyer's anticipatory breach the seller

14 Clearly, where the seller does accept the buyer's repudiation and immediately brings an action for damages, the court may have to make an estimate of the probable market price at the date the goods ought to have been accepted if that date has not yet arrived.
15 (1902) 18 TLR 716.

would only be entitled to the difference between the contract price and the market price at the time the goods ought to have been accepted even though he had accepted the buyer's repudiation.

It may be added that though the second rule in *Hadley v Baxendale* is not enacted in the Sale of Goods Act s 54 says that nothing in the Act affects the right of the buyer or the seller to recover interest or special damages in any case where, by law, interest or special damages may be recoverable. Consequently, if a seller can show he has suffered damage which, although it does not arise naturally from the buyer's breach, is 'such as may reasonably be supposed to have been in the contemplation of both parties, at the time they made the contract, as the probable result of the breach' the damage can be claimed for in accordance with the second rule in *Hadley v Baxendale*.

3. *Failure to pay for goods.*—Sections 39 to 48 considered below give to the unpaid seller certain real rights against the goods themselves, but s 49 provides the seller with a personal remedy to sue for the price in two instances. Firstly, where the property in the goods has passed to the buyer, and the buyer wrongfully neglects or refuses to pay for the goods according to the terms of the contract, the seller may maintain an action against him for the price of the goods. Since an action for the price lies only if the buyer's neglect or refusal to pay is 'wrongful', it is not available if the buyer has been given credit and the credit period has not expired and normally it is not available until the seller is willing to deliver the goods, delivery and payment being generally concurrent conditions under s 28. Secondly, where the price is payable on a fixed date and the buyer wrongfully neglects or refuses to pay such price, the seller may maintain an action for the price, although the property in the goods has not passed, and the goods have not been appropriated to the contract. In *Colley v Overseas Exporters*[16] goods were sold fob Liverpool and there was no provision in the agreement making the price payable on a date certain. The seller sent the goods to Liverpool but, owing to the failure of the buyers to name an effective ship he was unable to put them on board. Being an fob contract, the property in the goods would not pass until the goods were put on board so the seller could not sue for the price but only for damages.

16 [1922] 3 KB 302, [1921] All ER Rep 596.

Sections 49 and 50 overlap in that, if the property has passed to the buyer and the buyer wrongfully neglects or refuses to accept the goods, the seller can sue under either section. Of course, a seller has no right to sue for the price if he is no longer in a position to effect delivery which would be the case, for example, if he resold the goods when he learned of the buyer's refusal to take delivery.

Breach by the seller

1. *Failure to deliver the goods.*—Section 51 provides the buyer with a remedy in damages for non-delivery where the seller wrongfully neglects or refuses to deliver the goods to the buyer. It is the counterpart to the seller's remedy, given in s 50, for damages for non-acceptance, already considered. The general measure of damages is similar: 'the estimated loss directly and naturally resulting, in the ordinary course of events, from the seller's breach of contract' (s 51 (2)). Section 51 (3) says that where there is an available market for the goods in question (ie, they are readily obtainable) the measure of damages is prima facie to be ascertained by the difference between the contract price and the (higher) market or current price of the goods at the time or times when they ought to have been delivered or, if no time was fixed, then at the time of the refusal to deliver. Any sub-contracts made by the buyer are generally ignored. In *Williams Bros v Agius*,[17] the seller failed to deliver coal, the contract price of which was 16s 3d a ton. The buyer had made a contract to resell the coal at 19s a ton. At the date of the seller's to deliver, the market price for such coal was 23s 6d a ton. The buyer was awarded as damages 7s 3d a ton, the sum necessary to enable him to buy similar goods on the market; the price at which he had agreed to resell (19s a ton) was irrelevant because the buyer was still able to comply with his obligations under the contract of resale by obtaining coal on the market.

If the seller announces his refusal to deliver before the time for delivery arrives, the buyer may claim as damages the difference between the contract price and the (higher) market price at the time when the goods ought to have been delivered, but if the buyer accepted the seller's repudiation and the market price is rising, he owes a duty to mitigate the damages by buying similar goods on the market at once assuming there is a reasonable opportunity for doing

17 [1914] AC 510, [1914–15] All ER Rep 97.

so.[18] The duty to mitigate does not arise if the buyer does not accept the seller's repudiation but simply waits for the time of delivery as he is entitled to do. In *Tai Hing Cotton Mill Ltd v Kamsing Knitting Factory*,[19] the Judicial Committee ruled that the second limb of s 51 (3) did not apply to anticipatory breach of a contract which did not fix a time for delivery. By virtue of s 51 (2) damages must be assessed by the market price at the time when the goods ought to have been delivered. On the facts there was no clear demand by the buyers for delivery so damages were assessed by reference to the market price one month after the buyers issued their writ, thereby accepting the repudiation of the contract by the sellers. (One month was the period of reasonable notice for delivery that could be required by the buyers.)

Where there is no available market for the goods, then the buyer's damages will depend on the loss directly and naturally resulting from the breach and, under the second rule in *Hadley v Baxendale*, any other damage which ought to have been in the contemplation of the parties as a result of breach.[20] In *Patrick v Russo-British Grain Export Co*,[1] merchants bought some Russian wheat from S at 56s 9d per 480 lb. It was a strain of wheat not generally available on the market. The merchants contracted to resell it at 60s 6d. S failed to deliver the wheat and the court held the merchants entitled to damages to their loss of profit on the resale. It was known to S that the merchants were going to resell the wheat so that loss of profit was clearly within the contemplation of the parties as a probable result of non-delivery.

Again, where there is no available market for the goods, if a seller fails to deliver goods, the buyer may suffer not only loss of profit on

18 *Garmac Grain Co Inc v H M Fauere and Fairclough Ltd* [1968] AC 1130n, [1967] 2 All ER 353, HL. If the market price is falling after the seller's anticipatory breach, the buyer is normally entitled only to the difference between the contract price (say £200) and the market price as at the date when the goods ought to have been delivered (say £230) and not to the difference between the contractual price (£200) and the market price at the date of S's anticipatory breach, (say £250). 'If the action comes to trial before the contractual date for delivery has arrived the court must arrive at that price as best it can' per Bailhache J in *Melachrino v Nickoll and Knight* [1920] 1 KB 693, 699, [1918–19] All ER Rep 857. But if after B accepted S's anticipatory breach he actually bought similar goods at a market price (say £250) which is above the contract price (£200), he can claim the difference even though the market price falls by the date the goods ought to have been delivered.

19 [1979] AC 91, [1978] 1 All ER 515, PC.

20 *Victoria Laundry (Windsor) Ltd v Newman Industries Ltd* [1949] 2 KB 528, [1949] 1 All ER 997, CA; *The Heron II* [1969] 1 AC 350, [1967] 3 All ER 686, HL.

1 [1927] 2 KB 535, [1927] All ER Rep 692.

resale but also loss by reason of having to compensate sub-buyers. If such loss is a direct and natural result of the breach or the buyer can bring himself within the second rule in *Hadley v Baxendale* by showing that a resale was within the contemplation of the parties, he can claim any damages he may have to pay to a sub-buyer for failing to meet his obligations to the sub-buyer as well as his loss of profit on resale, and also any costs incurred in defending an action brought by the sub-buyer if it was reasonable for him to defend such action.[2] This is also the situation where S agrees to sell certain goods to B and S knows that B is going to resell those *same* goods to X so that B can honour his contract with X only by delivering to X those *same* goods, and S then fails to deliver. Even if *similar* goods could be obtained on the market, the market price is not relevant to the measure of damages in such a case. Thus, in *R and H Hall Ltd v W H Pim & Co*,[3] a cargo of wheat of a certain quality and description was sold at 51s 9d a quarter and resold at 56s 9d a quarter. When the seller failed to deliver, the market price of similar wheat was 53s 9d. The House of Lords held that this market price should be disregarded because the buyers could not obtain on the market the particular cargo which they had agreed to resell. As the contract expressly provided for the possibility of resale, the buyer obtained as damages the difference between 51s 9d and 56s 9d a quarter. It might have been otherwise had the resale price been out of the ordinary.

While an action for damages is the buyer's principal remedy should the seller refuse to deliver the goods, the court has a discretion to award a decree of specific performance to the buyer, provided the goods are specific or ascertained. By s 52:

'(1) In any action for breach of contract to deliver specific or ascertained goods the court may, if it thinks fit, on the plaintiff's application, by its judgment or decree direct that the contract shall be performed specifically, without giving the defendant the option of retaining the goods on payment of damages.

(2) The plaintiff's application may be made at any time before judgment or decree.

(3) The judgment or decree may be unconditional, or on such terms and conditions as to damages, payment of the price, and otherwise as seem just to the court.'

If the goods are of a unique or special value to the buyer, an application for specific performance may be successful. Thus,

2 *Hammond & Co Ltd v Bussey* (1887) 20 QBD 79.
3 (1928) 139 LT 50, [1928] All ER Rep 763.

specific performance was granted of a contract for the sale of a ship—damages would have been an inadequate remedy.[4]

In *Sky Petroleum Ltd v VIP Petroleum Ltd*[5] Goulding J held that a court may even grant specific performance of a contract for the sale of unascertained goods where damages would not provide a sufficient remedy, such as where there was no alternative source of supply available to the buyer.

If the property has passed to the buyer a claim may be made for the goods themselves or for damages in conversion. This does not mean that the buyer could thereby obtain higher damages:[6]

Finally, if the buyer has paid the price for goods and the seller fails to deliver, or is in breach of the implied condition as to title under s 12, the buyer may recover the price in an action for money had and received on a consideration that has wholly failed (s 54).

2. *Breach of a condition or warranty.*—Section 53 (1) reads:—

'Where there is a breach of warranty by the seller, or where the buyer elects (or is compelled) to treat any breach of a condition on the part of the seller as a breach of warranty, the buyer is not by reason only of such breach of warranty entitled to reject the goods; but he may—

    (a) set up against the seller the breach of warranty in diminution or extinction of the price; or

    (b) maintain an action against the seller for damages for the breach of warranty.'

The measure of damages is the estimated loss directly and naturally resulting in the ordinary course of events from the breach of warranty (s 53 (2)).[7]

If the seller commits a breach by late delivery then prima facie the buyer is entitled to the difference between the market price at the time when the goods ought to have been delivered and the (lower) market price of the goods when they are actually delivered, plus any damage, for example for loss of use, resulting directly and

---

4 *Behnke v Bede Shipping Co Ltd* [1927] 1 KB 649, [1927] All ER Rep 689. Contrast a case concerning an antique chair: *Cohen v Roche* [1927] 1 KB 169.

5 [1974] 1 All ER 954, [1974] 1 WLR 576.

6 *The Arpad* [1934] P 189, [1934] All ER Rep 326.

7 In *Lloyds and Scottish Finance Ltd v Modern Cars and Caravans (Kingdom) Ltd*, [1966] 1 QB 764, [1964] 2 All ER 732, where the defendants broke an express warranty that the caravan being sold to the plaintiffs was their sole unencumbered property, it was held that the plaintiffs were entitled as damages to compensation for loss arising under a hire purchase agreement relating to the caravan which the plaintiffs had made with a third party, and to expenses incurred by the plaintiffs, in order to mitigate the damage, arising from the defendants' breach, namely, the costs of interpleader proceedings paid by them.

naturally or reasonably contemplated by the parties. If, however, the buyer has made a contract of resale at a price higher than the market price at the time of actual delivery, the damages may be reduced to the difference between the market price at the time when the goods ought to have been delivered and the resale price. In *Wertheim v Chicoutimi Pulp Co Ltd*,[8] S contracted to sell wood pulp to B. S was late in delivering the goods. The market price when the goods ought to have been delivered was 70s a ton, and when the goods were in fact delivered the market price had fallen to 42s 6d a ton. Later B resold the goods at 65s a ton. The Privy Council allowed the buyer only 5s a ton as damages.

In the case of a breach of warranty of quality, the loss claimable is prima facie the difference between the value of the goods at the time of delivery to the buyer and the value they would have had if they had fulfilled the warranty (s 53 (3)). Larger damages, however, will be claimable if, for example, the defects cause consequential loss such as personal injury or damage to other property.

In *H Parsons (Livestock) Ltd v Uttley Ingham & Co Ltd*[9] the plaintiffs, pig farmers, bought from the defendants a hopper for the storage of pig nuts. The hopper supplied was not properly ventilated, nuts stored there became mouldy and pigs fed with them became so ill with a rare type of intestinal infection (which could not have been foreseen) that 254 of them died. The defendants were held to be in breach of s 14 of the Sale of Goods Act as the hopper was not reasonably fit for its known purpose. In interpreting s 53 (2) the majority of the Court of Appeal ruled that for the plaintiffs to recover their loss it was sufficient if loss of the type which in fact occurred could reasonably be supposed to have been in the parties' contemplation as a serious possibility in the event of the breach which in fact occurred. If the loss which could be contemplated was of the type which had in fact occurred, the defendants were liable for the whole of the loss although the quantum was greater than the parties might have contemplated.

THE UNPAID SELLER'S REMEDIES IN REM

'Unpaid seller'

In addition to his personal rights of action against the buyer, already examined, an 'unpaid seller' has certain real rights against

8 [1911] AC 301, [1908–10] All ER Rep 707. The case was approved by the House of Lords in *Williams Bros v Agius* [1914] AC 510; see, p 137 ante, but criticised by Scrutton LJ in *Slater v Hoyle and Smith Ltd* [1920] 2 KB 11, 23–24, [1918–19] All ER Rep 654.

9 [1978] QB 791, [1978] 1 All ER 525, CA.

the goods themselves which are particularly valuable where the buyer is insolvent.

By s 38 a seller is deemed to be an 'unpaid seller' if any portion of the price is unpaid, or if a bill of exchange or other negotiable instrument has been received as conditional payment and has been dishonoured. Furthermore, if a seller sells through an agent and the agent is responsible for paying the seller the price, the agent also has the rights of 'an unpaid seller'.[10]

The unpaid seller has three rights against the goods themselves and they are set out in s 39:—

'(1) Subject to this and any other Act, notwithstanding that the property in the goods may have passed to the buyer, the unpaid seller of goods, as such, has by implication of law—
  (a) a lien on the goods or right to retain them for the price while he is in possession of them;
  (b) in case of the insolvency of the buyer, a right of stopping the goods in transit after he has parted with possession of them;
  (c) a right of resale as limited by this Act.
(2) Where the property in goods has not passed to the buyer, the unpaid seller has (in addition to his other remedies) a right of witholding delivery similar to and co-extensive with his rights of lien and stoppage in transit where the property has passed to the buyer.'

Right of lien

So long as the unpaid seller is in possession of the goods, then though the property in the goods may have passed to the buyer he has a lien over the goods—a right to retain possession of them until payment or tender of the whole of the price. If the property has not passed to the buyer, the unpaid seller has a right of withholding delivery from the buyer. These rights, however, only exist in the following cases:—

(a) where the goods have been sold without any stipulation as to credit; or
(b) where the goods have been sold on credit, but the term of credit has expired; or
(c) where the buyer becomes insolvent (s 41 (1)).

10 If a buyer properly rejects goods for breach of condition, after he has paid the price to the seller, the buyer cannot claim a lien on the goods. Rejection entitles the seller to retake possession, so a buyer should only reject goods when he is certain the seller is solvent and able to repay the price: *J L Lyons & Co v May and Baker Ltd* [1923] 1 KB 685.

It makes no difference that the seller is in possession as agent or bailee for the buyer—he still may have this right of lien (s 41 (2)). When the price *is* paid or tendered, the seller does not have any right to retain the goods, for example, in order to recover the cost of storing the goods during his exercise of the lien.[11]

If *part* of the goods sold have been delivered under an indivisible contract, the unpaid seller can exercise his right of lien or retention on the remainder, unless the part delivery has been made under such circumstances as to show an agreement to waive the lien or right of retention. However, if in a severable contract, one instalment is delivered and not paid for, the seller has no right to refuse delivery of any instalment which *is* paid for.

An unpaid seller loses his right of lien when the goods are delivered to a carrier for transmission to the buyer without the seller reserving the right of disposal, such as by taking a bill of lading in his own name. An unpaid seller also loses his right of lien when the buyer or his agent lawfully obtains possession of the goods or by waiver, as when the seller assents to a sub-sale (s 43). Clearly, the right of lien does not include a right in the unpaid seller to recover back possession once he has given up possession to the buyer, and as soon as the buyer pays or tenders the price the seller's right of lien terminates because he is no longer 'unpaid'. The right of lien may also be defeated or otherwise affected under s 47, considered shortly. The exercise by an unpaid seller of his right of lien or retention or stoppage in transit does not rescind the contract of sale—there is still an obligation on the seller to deliver the goods on payment of the price by the buyer or, for example, by his trustee in bankruptcy.

Right of stoppage in transit

Insolvency of the buyer.—In one circumstance only, the insolvency of the buyer, the unpaid seller has a right to recover goods that have left his possession but are still in the course of transit. This is called a right of stoppage in transit which means that the unpaid seller can resume possession and retain the goods until payment or tender of the price (s 44). A person is deemed to be insolvent, according to s 61 (4) (as amended by the Insolvency Act 1985 Sch 10), if he has ceased to pay his debts in the ordinary course of business, or cannot pay his debts as they become due. The right of stoppage in transit is not properly exercised if the buyer is only thought to be insolvent.

11 *Somes v British Empire Shipping Co* (1860) 8 HL Cas 338.

But it suffices if the buyer is insolvent when the goods would otherwise have arrived although he was not insolvent when the goods were shipped or when notice of stoppage was given. Sir William Scott in *The Constantia*[12] said:

> 'if the insolvency happens before the arrival it would be sufficient I conceive, to justify what has been done and to entitle the shipper to the benefit of his own provisional caution.'

Duration of transit.—Section 45 considers a number of different questions on the duration of transit. Transit ends when the buyer or his agent takes delivery of the goods from the carrier, even if that is done before their arrival at the appointed destination. So too, transit is at an end if, after the arrival of the goods at their appointed destination, the carrier or other bailee (such as a warehouseman) acknowledges to the buyer or his agent that he continues in possession as agent for the buyer or his agent, and it is immaterial that a further destination for the goods may have been indicated by the buyer (s 45 (3)). However, if the goods are rejected by the buyer and the carrier or other bailee continues in possession of them, the transit is not deemed to be at an end, even if the seller has refused to receive them back (s 45 (4)). If the carrier or other bailee wrongfully refuses to deliver, the transit is deemed to be at an end (s 45 (6)).

In the case of part delivery of the goods to the buyer or his agent, the remainder of the goods may be stopped in transit unless the part delivery has been made under such circumstances as to show an agreement to give up possession of the whole of the goods (s 45 (7)).

Since the unpaid seller has no right of stoppage in transit once the buyer or his agent takes delivery of the goods, it follows that if the ship on which the goods are carried is owned by the buyer, the seller's right of stoppage is lost as soon as the goods are handed over to the master of the ship because the master is the buyer's agent. What if the ship is not owned but chartered by the buyer? By s 45 (5):—

> 'When goods are delivered to a ship chartered by the buyer it is a question depending on the circumstances of the particular case, whether they are in the possession of the master as a carrier or as agent to the buyer.'

Ordinarily, it would seem that where the ship has been chartered by the buyer, the goods are during transit in possession of the master as

---

12 (1807) 6 Ch Rob 321, 326.

agent for the shipowner and, therefore, liable to stoppage by an unpaid seller, but the possession of the master will be as agent for the buyer if it is a demise or time charter for a certain period.

How effected.—By s 46, the unpaid seller may exercise his right of stoppage in transit either by taking actual possession of the goods or by giving notice of his claim to the carrier. When such notice is given to the carrier, he is bound to redeliver the goods to, or according to the directions of the seller, at the seller's expense, and a refusal to redeliver would amount to conversion subject to the rule that the carrier has a lien on the goods for the freight due and the expenses of redelivery. Section 46 makes the point that the unpaid seller wishing to exercise his right of stoppage may give notice either to the carrier, 'the person in actual possession', or his principal. In the latter case the notice is only effectual if it is given at such time and under such circumstances that the principal, by the exercise of reasonable diligence, may communicate it to his agent in time to prevent delivery to the buyer.[13]

Defeat of right of lien or stoppage in transit

As a general rule, the unpaid seller's right of lien or retention or stoppage in transit is not affected by any sale, or other disposition of the goods (such as a pledge) which the buyer may have made (s 47). However, if the seller has 'assented' to such a resale, the unpaid seller's rights will be lost. In *D F Mount Ltd v Jay and Jay (Provisions) Ltd*,[14] there was a sale of 250 cartons of tinned peaches, deposited at a wharf, and the buyers explained to the sellers that the price would be paid out of moneys received from a sub-buyer. The sellers made out delivery orders in favour of the buyer. The buyer did sell the peaches to X (and made out a fresh delivery order in X's favour) but never paid the original sellers. The original sellers' claim to exercise a lien on the 225 cartons still remaining at the wharf was not upheld by the court as they were regarded as having 'assented' to the sub-sale to X. The court pointed out that the original sellers knew that the buyers could only pay for the peaches out of money obtained from sub-buyers. The true inference was that the original sellers assented to the resale, in the sense that they intended to

13 If the seller fails to give proper instructions for the redelivery of the goods he is liable in damages to the carrier for the carrier's consequent expenses; *Booth SS Co Ltd v Cargo Fleet Iron Co Ltd* [1916] 2 KB 570, [1916–17] All ER Rep 938.
14 [1960] 1 QB 159, [1959] 3 All ER 307.

146   *Sale of goods*

renounce their rights against the goods and to take the risk of the buyer's dishonesty.

However, a seller cannot be said to have 'assented' to a resale merely because the buyer has informed him of the resale after it has been effected. In *Mordaunt Bros v British Oil and Cake Mills Ltd*,[15] the defendants sold oil to certain merchants and the merchants resold some of this oil to the plaintiffs, giving them delivery orders addressed to the defendants which directed the latter to deliver to the plaintiffs. So long as the merchants were punctual in their payments to the defendants, the latter regularly delivered oil to the plaintiffs. When, however, the merchants fell into arrears with their payments, the defendants claimed to exercise their right of lien as unpaid sellers and refused to make any further deliveries. The court upheld the defendants' claim since, on the facts they had not 'assented' to the resale by the merchants. Pickford J said[16]:—

'In my opinion the assent which affects the unpaid seller's right of lien must be such an assent as in the circumstances shews that the seller intends to renounce his rights against the goods. It is not enough to shew that the fact of a sub-contract has been brought to his notice and that he has assented to it merely in the sense of acknowledging the receipt of the information. His assent to the sub-contract in that sense would simply mean that he acknowledged the right of the purchaser under the sub-contract to have the goods subject to his own paramount right under the contract with his original purchaser to hold the goods until he is paid the purchase-money.'

By s 47 (2), where a document of title to goods has been lawfully transferred to any person as buyer or owner of the goods, and that person transfers the document to a person who takes the document in good faith and for valuable consideration, then, if such last-mentioned transfer was by way of sale the unpaid seller's right of lien or retention or stoppage in transit is defeated, and if such last-mentioned transfer was by way of pledge or other disposition for value, the unpaid seller's right of lien or retention or stoppage in transit can only be exercised subject to the rights of the transferee.

The case of *Cahn v Pockett's Bristol Channel Steam Packet Co Ltd*,[17] has already been mentioned. When the seller of copper transmitted a bill of exchange for the price together with the bill of lading to the buyer, the buyer did not signify his acceptance of the bill of exchange but indorsed the bill of lading to the plaintiffs in

15 [1910] 2 KB 502.
16 [1910] 2 KB 502, 507.
17 [1899] 1 QB 643. See p 90, ante.

accordance with a contract of resale of the copper already made. By reason of s 19 (3) the property had not passed to the buyer, but as we have seen, the plaintiffs obtained a good title under s 9 of the Factors Act (and s 25 (1) of the Sale of Goods Act) because they had bought in good faith from someone who had 'agreed to buy' the goods. The court also held that, by virtue of the proviso to s 47 (now s 47 (2) of the Sale of Goods Act 1979), the original seller's right of stoppage in transit, which arose because the buyer was insolvent and the goods were still in the course of transit, was defeated.

Salmon J in *Mount Ltd v Jay and Jay (Provisions) Co Ltd* said obiter that the proviso to s 47 (now s 47 (2) of the 1979 Act) could apply only if the *same* document which is handed to the buyer is transferred by him to the sub-buyer and therefore the proviso to s 47 did not apply to the facts in *Mount's* case.[18]

Right of resale

Where a seller of goods is left in possession of them, then by s 8 of the Factors Act, if he resells and delivers them to X who takes them in good faith and without notice of the previous sale, X will obtain a good title. The seller will, however, clearly be in breach of contract to the original buyer because, although s 8 gave him power to confer a good title on X, he was under a duty to the original buyer not to exercise that power. Similarly, by s 48 (2), where an unpaid seller who has exercised his right of lien or retention or stoppage in transit resells the goods, the buyer acquires a good title thereto as against the original buyer, but unless the seller has expressly reserved a right of resale in the contract or the special conditions in s 48 (3) are satisfied, resale will render the seller liable in breach of contract to the original buyer.

There are certain instances where a seller not only has a power of resale but is under no duty to anyone to refrain from exercising it. Section 48 (3), which only applies if an unpaid seller has exercised his right of lien or stoppage in transit, provides that where goods are of a perishable nature, or where the unpaid seller gives notice to the buyer of his intention to resell and the buyer does not within a reasonable time pay or tender the price, the unpaid seller may resell

18 However, Salmon J did think that on the facts in *Mount's* case, X could rely on s 25 (2) of the Sale of Goods Act 1893 (now s 25 (1) of the 1979 Act) on the ground that that provision was not confined to cases where the buyer transfers to the sub-buyer the *same* document that he has been given by the sellers—sed quaere, see Borrie (1960) 23 MLR 100.

the goods and recover from the original buyer damages for any loss occasioned by the latter's breach of contract. A resale by an unpaid seller under s 48 (3) will not be a breach by him of the original contract of sale. Similarly, by s 48 (4), where the seller expressly reserves a right of resale in case the buyer should default in payment, and on the buyer making default resells the goods, the original contract of sale is thereby rescinded but without prejudice to any claim the seller may have for damages. Obviously, a resale by an unpaid seller under s 48 (4) will not be a breach by him of the original contract of sale.[19]

It will be noted that s 48 (4) expressly provides that a resale in the exercise of a contractual right rescinds the original contract of sale. It follows that if the seller obtains a better price on the resale he may keep the profit. Finnemore J in *Gallagher v Shilcock*[20] held that a resale in the exercise of the unpaid seller's statutory right under s 48 (3) does not rescind the original contract with the result that, if on the facts the property has passed to the original buyer, any profit made on a resale belongs to the original buyer. That decision was overruled by the Court of Appeal in *R V Ward Ltd v Bignall*.[1] The Court of Appeal held that any re-sale by an unpaid seller under s 48 (3) of all or part of the goods has the effect of rescinding the original contract because such resale is inconsistent with the original contract, and if the property in the goods had passed to the original buyer, the resale divests the original buyer of that property. It follows that:—

1. Any profit made on the resale belongs to the seller; *and,*
2. Any right the seller may have had to sue the buyer for the price on the basis that the property had passed to the buyer (s 49) ceases. The seller may still, however, claim damages from the buyer for non-acceptance under s 50.

AUCTION SALES

Offer and acceptance

Where goods are put up for sale by auction in lots, each lot is prima facie deemed to be the subject of a separate contract of sale

19 It may be added that where a buyer repudiates a contract of sale, the seller may resell the goods and, of course, is not liable in breach of contract to the original buyer for doing so. He may retain any profit made on the resale.
20 [1949] 2 KB 765, [1949] 1 All ER 921.
1 [1967] 1 QB 534, [1967] 2 All ER 449, CA.

(s 57 (1)). Each bid is an offer and the sale is complete 'when the auctioneer announces its completion by the fall of the hammer, or in other customary manner' (s 57 (2)).

A seller has no right to bid himself or through an agent unless the sale is notified to be subject to a right to bid. Any sale that contravenes this rule may be set aside by the buyer as fraudulent. It is also unlawful for an auctioneer knowingly to take a bid from a seller or his agent where the sale is not notified to be subject to a right to bid (s 57 (4)). The auctioneer could be sued for damages if guilty of such unlawful act (s 60).

Section 57 (3) says that a sale by auction may be notified to be subject to a reserve or upset price, and a right to bid may also be expressly reserved by or on behalf of the seller. Where a right to bid is expressly reserved, but not otherwise, the seller, or any one person on his behalf, may bid at the auction.

It was held in *McManus v Fortescue*[2] that where a sale was notified as being 'subject to reserve' and an auctioneer knocked the goods down to the plaintiff for less than the reserve price by mistake, the plaintiff had no right to the goods and the auctioneer was not liable for breach of warranty of authority. The contrasting situation is where an auction is advertised as being held 'without reserve'. There are obiter dicta in *Warlow v Harrison*[3] to the effect that such an advertisement is an offer which is accepted on the highest bidder making his bid. If the auctioneer refused to take such bid, he may be liable in damages for breach of a contract to sell to the highest bidder.

An auctioneer does incur certain obligations when he sells goods. They were listed by Salter J in *Benton v Campbell, Parker and Co.*[4] as follows:—

(1) He warrants his authority to sell.
(2) He warrants that he knows of no defect in his principal's title.
(3) He undertakes to give possession against the price paid into his hands.[5]
(4) He undertakes that such possession will not be disturbed by his principal or himself.

2 [1907] 2 KB 1.
3 (1859) 1 E & E 309.
4 [1925] 2 KB 410, 415–416.
5 If the auctioneer allows the buyer to take delivery without paying the price he can sue in his own name for the full price: *Williams v Millington* (1788) 1 Hy Bl 81, [1755–1802] All ER Rep 124. The auctioneer can also sue in his own name for the full price if the buyer refuses to take delivery: *Chelmsford Auctions Ltd v Poole* [1973] 1 QB 542, [1973] 1 All ER 810, CA.

However, an auctioneer does not warrant his principal's title to sell *specific goods* if he discloses that he is acting for a principal even though he does not name his principal. The facts of the *Benton* case were that an auctioneer had arranged to sell a car on behalf of X who had no title to it and knocked it down at an auction sale to B. B knew that the auctioneer was acting as an agent but not the name of the auctioneer's principal. The true owner later recovered the car from B and the court held B had no claim against the auctioneer. It would have been different if the auctioneer had not disclosed that he was acting as an agent. In the case of unascertained goods, an auctioneer is personally liable where his principal's title is defective not only if he does not disclose he is acting for a principal but also if he merely fails to indicate the identity of his principal.

By the Auctions (Bidding Agreements) Acts 1927 and 1969, it is a criminal offence for a dealer, ie, someone who in the normal course of business attends auction sales to purchase goods with a view to reselling them, to give or receive consideration or reward for abstaining or having abstained from bidding. Moreover, such 'knock-out' agreements entered into by dealers are illegal and upon conviction of an offender, the seller may, as against a purchaser who has been a party to such agreement, treat it as a sale induced by fraud.

Chapter 3

Hire purchase and consumer credit

Obtaining the benefit of the possession and use of goods before one has paid fully for them may take many legal forms. One of the commonest and most popular forms for many years has been hire purchase. To prevent various abuses by traders and the unfairness of one-sided contracts, Parliament intervened in 1938 with the first Hire Purchase Act and there were later statutes regulating the agreements in 1954 and 1964, followed by a consolidating Hire-Purchase Act 1965. Meanwhile, many other forms of credit developed in significance and strong criticism of the anomalies in the varying kinds of legal restriction imposed on different types of lenders and traders was made by the Committee on Consumer Credit, chaired by Lord Crowther, which reported in 1971.[1] As a result, a substantial consumer protection measure, the Consumer Credit Act 1974, was passed by Parliament but implementation of the Act was slow. Following the Act, various Regulations were made to amplify and implement the Act and parts of the Act were brought into effect on different dates; but the Act was only fully brought into effect in May 1985. Much of the protection already accorded to those individuals who took goods on hire purchase is given by the Act to individuals who obtain goods (or services) through other types of credit transaction. Those taking on hire purchase receive additional protection. This chapter first examines fully the law relating to hire purchase, then considers various other forms of consumer credit.

1 Cmnd 4596.

MEANING OF HIRE PURCHASE

Definition

A hire purchase agreement is an agreement by an owner of goods (the creditor) to hire them out to a bailee and to give the bailee an option to purchase conditional on his completing the necessary payments for the goods and complying with the terms of the agreement. In the ordinary form of hire purchase contract, the bailee obtains immediate possession of the goods when the contract is made and the bailee pays a deposit or initial payment, which is usually a certain percentage of the cash price for the goods.[2] The bailee agrees to pay the balance of the cash price together with the hire purchase charges by stated instalments. Only when all such payments have been made does the ownership in the goods pass.[3]

For the purposes of the Consumer Credit Act 1974, a hire purchase agreement is defined in s 189 as

'an agreement, other than a conditional sale agreement,[4] under which—
  (a) goods are bailed or (in Scotland) hired in return for periodical payments by the person to whom they are bailed or hired, and
  (b) the property in the goods will pass to that person if the terms of the agreement are complied with and one or more of the following occurs—
      (i) the exercise of an option to purchase by that person,
     (ii) the doing of any other specified act by any party to the agreement,
    (iii) the happening of any other specified event.'

It is important to note at the outset that the Act regulates every hire purchase agreement which is a regulated 'consumer credit agreement'. This means a personal credit agreement between an

2 In the past, Government orders have often specified a minimum deposit for certain types of goods when a policy of credit restriction prevails. Such orders may also specify a maximum period over which instalment payments may be made. Where an agreement contravenes such an order, it is an illegal contract and neither party may enforce it. Even though neither party has pleaded the illegality, the court of its own motion must apply the overriding principle of public policy that the courts will not assist a plaintiff by enforcing an illegal contract: *Snell v Unity Finance Co Ltd* [1964] 2 QB 203, [1963] 3 All ER 50, CA. Counsel owes a duty to the court to disclose the illegality of any contract being litigated, if he realises this during the course of the proceedings although the point was not pleaded: *Mercantile Credit Co Ltd v Hamblin* [1964] 1 All ER 680, n, [1964] 1 WLR 423.

3 It was held by the Court of Appeal in *Tucker v Farm and General Investment Trust Ltd* [1966] 2 QB 421, [1966] 2 All ER 508, that where there is a hire or hire purchase of livestock, the progeny and produce of the livestock belong to the bailee subject to any express contrary provision in the agreement.

4 See p 154, post.

'individual' (the debtor) and any other person (the creditor) by which the creditor provides the debtor with credit not exceeding £15,000, otherwise than an 'exempt' agreement (s 8 as amended by Order in 1983). An 'individual' includes a partnership or other unincorporated body of persons not consisting entirely of bodies corporate. The creditor is taken to provide the bailee under a hire purchase agreement with fixed-sum credit of an amount equal to the total price of the goods less the aggregate of the deposit (if any) and the total charge for credit. An item entering into the total charge for credit is not treated as credit even if time is allowed for its payment (s 9). By virtue of an Order made under s 16, a hire purchase agreement under which the number of payments to be made by the debtor does not exceed four is an 'exempt' agreement.[5] Regulations have been made under s 20 whereby the total charge for credit includes not only interest charges but also such other payments as insurance premiums and maintenance charges required under contracts which the creditor requires to be made as a condition of making the credit agreement.[6] The Act uses the term 'debtor' as synonymous with the bailee in relation to a hire purchase agreement.

In simple legal terms, a hire purchase agreement is normally a bailment of goods (ie, a delivery of possession of goods) plus the grant of an option to purchase the goods. As with any other agreement, there must be certainty as to the terms if it is to constitute a binding contract. In *Scammell v Ouston*[7] where after considerable correspondence an order was given for a van 'on the understanding that the balance of purchase price can be had on hire purchase terms over a period of two years' and this order was accepted in general terms, the House of Lords held that there was no contract. The language used was so obscure, said Lord Wright, that the court was unable to attribute to the parties any particular intention.

If anyone signs a hire purchase agreement under a mistaken belief that it is a document that is radically different in effect, and this mistake has been induced by misrepresentation, he may plead non est factum (it is not my deed) and he is not bound by it.[8] This defence is not available if the signer was negligent.[9]

---

5 Consumer Credit (Exempt Agreements) (No 2) Order 1985 (SI 1985 No 757).
6 Consumer Credit (Total Charge for Credit) Regulations 1980 (SI 1980 No 51).
7 [1941] AC 251, [1941] 1 All ER 14.
8 *Mercantile Credit Co Ltd v Hamblin* [1965] 2 QB 242, [1964] 3 All ER 592, CA.
9 *Saunders v Anglia Building Society* [1971] AC 1004, [1970] 3 All ER 961, HL.

In *United Dominions Trust Ltd v Western*,[10] the defendant arranged with X, a dealer, to obtain a car on hire purchase. The defendant signed in blank one of the plaintiffs' standard forms and, without the defendant's consent, X completed the form with higher amounts for the price and deposit than were in fact agreed. When the plaintiffs sued on the agreement for amounts due, the defendant argued that the document as completed by X did not represent the defendant's true intentions and was void. The Court of Appeal, however, ruled that the defendant failed to show that, in allowing X to complete the form, he had acted carefully and it was not open to him to assert the agreement was invalid.

Distinction from credit sale and conditional sale

The essence of a hire purchase agreement is that the customer is hiring the goods and is given an option to purchase them—he does not at the time of the contract 'agree to buy' them. It follows also that if, before the customer has exercised his option to purchase, he sells the goods, he cannot confer a good title to them under s 9 of the Factors Act or s 25 (1) of the Sale of Goods Act.[11] This rule was established by the House of Lords in 1895 in the leading case of *Helby v Matthews*.[12]

The facts of *Helby v Matthews* were that the owner of a piano agreed to let it on hire, the bailee agreeing to pay monthly instalments. The terms of the agreement provided that the bailee might terminate the hiring by delivering up the piano to the owner, the bailee remaining liable for all arrears of hire charges. It was also agreed that if the bailee should punctually pay all the monthly instalments, the piano should become his sole property and that until such full payment the piano should continue to be the sole property of the owner. The bailee was given possession of the piano, he paid a few of the instalments, and then pledged it with a pawnbroker as security for an advance. The House of Lords held that on the true construction of the agreement the bailee was under no legal obligation to buy, but merely had an option either to return the piano or to become its owner by payment of all the instalments. In consequence, the bailee was not someone who had 'agreed to buy' the goods within the meaning of s 9 of the Factors Act. He

10 [1976] QB 513, [1975] 3 All ER 1017, CA. But see now Consumer Credit Act 1974 s 61, post, p 188.
11 Ante, p 88. Exceptions to the general rule are considered at pp 163–166, post.
12 [1895] AC 471.

could not, therefore, pass any rights in the piano to a pledgee and the owner was entitled to recover the piano from the pawnbroker without having to tender to him the loan he had given the bailee.

This case ensured the popularity of hire purchase with traders. It was a method of disposing of goods on credit terms which preserved the trader's security in the goods—they could be recovered from anyone to whom the bailee purported to sell or pledge them. It seemed that the trader could not obtain the same security if the customer agreed at the time of the contract to *buy* the goods. This was because the Court of Appeal had held in *Lee v Butler*,[13] just two years before *Helby v Matthews*, that where A 'agreed to sell' furniture to B, B to pay for it by two instalments, the property to pass to B only on payment of the second instalment, a sale by B (who had possession with A's consent) to C before such second instalment was paid would pass a good title to C under s 9 of the Factors Act if C was in good faith. However, according to the much more recent Court of Appeal decision in *Newtons of Wembley, Ltd v Williams*,[14] C would only seem to obtain a good title under s 9 of the Factors Act if B acted in the way in which he would have been expected to act if he had been a mercantile agent. If such point had been taken in *Lee v Butler*, the case might well have been decided differently and, indeed, there might have been no need for the system of hire purchase to have been developed had it been realised that for an innocent purchaser to acquire a good title under s 9, the seller must have acted as if he were a mercantile agent.[15]

Until the Hire Purchase Act 1964, *all* agreements to *buy* goods where the buyer paid for them by instalments were known as *credit sales*. Now, if the property in the goods is to remain in the seller until such conditions as to the payment of instalments or otherwise as may be specified in the agreement are fufilled (as in *Lee v Butler*) these agreements are known as *conditional* sales provided they are 'consumer-credit agreements'.[16] Where the buyer is an 'individual' and the credit does not exceed £15,000 (ie, it is a 'consumer-credit agreement') the 'buyer . . . is to be taken not to be a person who has bought or agreed to buy the goods'.[17] In other words, the buyer is

13 [1893] 2 QB 318, [1891–94] All ER Rep 1200.

14 [1965] 1 QB 560, [1964] 3 All ER 532. See ante, p 91.

15 See paras 21–25 of the 12th Report of the Law Reform Committee: Transfer of Title to Chattels (Cmnd 2958).

16 Hire Purchase Act 1964 s 21 (5) and Hire Purchase Act 1965 s 1 (1). The definition is now embodied in Consumer Credit Act 1974 s 189 and the Sale of Goods Act 1979 s 25 (2).

17 See now Sale of Goods Act 1979 s 25 (2).

treated in the same way as a debtor under a hire purchase agreement and has no power to pass a good title under s 9 of the Factors Act.

Since *credit sale* now means only those agreements to buy goods, the price being paid by instalments, where the property passes at once to the buyer, clearly the buyer as owner may always pass a good title to the goods, on general principles.

Finance companies

Very often, when a customer wishes to take goods from a dealer on hire purchase, the dealer himself is not in a position to provide credit, and the common form of hire purchase transaction is that the dealer sells the goods to a finance company and the finance company, now the owner of the goods, makes the hire purchase agreement with the customer. The dealer will retain the deposit paid by the bailee and receive the balance of the purchase price from the finance company. Under this method, the rights and obligations under the hire purchase agreement exist between the customer and the finance company, and the dealer will not be a party to that agreement. The sale by the dealer to the finance company will, of course, be subject to the Sale of Goods Act except in so far as the obligations implied by that Act have been excluded or varied. In addition the dealer often enters into some sort of 'recourse' agreement, eg, an agreement whereby the dealer guarantees whatever is owing by the bailee to the finance company, or an agreement to indemnify the company against any loss that the company might incur as a result of the termination of the hire purchase agreement. It is a matter of interpretation whether any particular recourse agreement is an agreement of guarantee or indemnity. There is no doubt, however, that a guarantee agreement is of less value from the finance company's point of view than an indemnity agreement because:

(i) if the hire purchase agreement is for any reason void, as is the case of one made with a minor for non-necessary goods,[18] or the debtor is released from liability for any reason,[19] the finance company has a claim against the dealer only if the recourse agreement is one of indemnity; and;

(ii) in certain circumstances the measure of damages payable to

18 *Coutts & Co v Browne-Lecky* [1947] KB 104, [1946] 2 All ER 207, cf *Yeoman Credit Ltd v Latter* [1961] 2 All ER 294, [1961] 1 WLR 828, CA. But see now Minors' Contracts Act 1987.
19 *Unity Finance Co Ltd v Woodcock* [1963] 2 All ER 270, [1963] 1 WLR 455, CA.

the finance company by the bailee for breach of the hire purchase agreement may amount merely to arrears of instalments due which are less than the company's actual loss[20]—only if the recourse agreement is one of indemnity is the dealer liable to the company for the company's actual loss.[1]

Another possibility is that the dealer agrees to re-purchase the goods from the finance company if the hire purchase is terminated for any reason. This may not be so advantageous to the finance company as an indemnity agreement. Subject to contrary agreement, the dealer's obligation will be conditional on the finance company being in a position to deliver the goods to the dealer.[2] Moreover, in *United Dominions Trust (Commercial) Ltd v Eagle Aircraft Services Ltd*[3] the Court of Appeal held that where the dealer agreed to re-purchase an aircraft which had been let out on hire purchase, 'when called on to do so', and the hire purchase agreement was terminated before payment of the full hire purchase price, the finance company were not entitled to enforce the re-purchase agreement because it had not called upon the dealer to re-purchase 'within a reasonable time' of the termination of the hire purchase agreement. The obligations to re-purchase never came into being because the condition precedent *implied* by the Court of Appeal had not been fulfilled.

An alternative method for the finance company to assist in hire purchase transactions is known as block discounting. The dealer enters into hire purchase agreements directly with customers and then assigns his rights under them, together usually with the ownership in the goods, to a finance company. The dealer normally continues to collect instalments as they become due from the bailee but does so now as agent for the finance company.

The licensing system

The Consumer Credit Act 1974 introduced a licensing system administered by the Director General of Fair Trading.[4] Generally, a licence is required to carry on a consumer credit business. A finance company engaging in hire purchase transactions with individuals must have a licence and by s 40, if a regulated hire

20 *Financings Ltd v Baldock* [1963] 2 QB 104, [1963] 1 All ER 443, CA, post, p 181.
1 *Goulston Discount Co Ltd v Clark* [1967] 2 QB 493, [1967] 1 All ER 61, CA.
2 *Watling Trust v Briffault Range Co Ltd* [1938] 1 All ER 525, CA.
3 [1968) 1 All ER 104, [1968] 1 WLR 74, CA.
4 See Borrie *Licensing Practice under the Consumer Credit Act* [1982] Journal of Business Law 91.

purchase agreement is made when the creditor is unlicensed, it is enforceable against the debtor only where the Director has made an order under s 40 that regulated agreements made by the creditor during a certain period are to be treated as if he was licensed. Relevant factors the Director must take into account are how far, if at all, debtors were prejudiced by the creditor's conduct, whether the Director would have been likely to grant a licence had one been applied for and the degree of culpability for failure to obtain a licence. Dealers (credit-brokers by virtue of s 145 of the Act) also have to obtain a licence from the Director (s 147) and by s 149, if a regulated agreement results from an introduction effected by an unlicensed dealer, the agreement is enforceable against the debtor only if the Director makes an order that the agreement be treated as if the dealer was licensed. The same factors as referred to in s 40 are relevant to the Director's determination.

Other types of business requiring a licence from the Director are debt-adjusting, debt-counselling, debt-collecting, and the operation of a credit reference agency, all known as 'ancillary' credit businesses (s 145). A licence is normally a 'standard' one made to the particular applicant for a prescribed period (originally three years but extended in 1979 to 10 years and in 1986 to 15 years) but 'group' licences are obtainable in certain circumstances and such bodies as the Law Society and the various accountancy bodies have obtained such on behalf of their members. A licence is granted only if the applicant satisfied the Director that he is 'a fit person' (s 25) and the Act provides for representations by the applicant against a 'minded to refuse' notice (ss 27 and 34) and an appeal procedure (ss 41 and 42). A licence once granted may at any time be suspended or revoked (s 32). It is an offence to engage in unlicensed trading (s 39).

Bills of Sale Acts 1878 and 1882

Where a mortgage of goods is effected by a document and the goods remain in the mortgagor's possession, the document must be registered under the Bills of Sale Act (1878) Amendment Act 1882 and other provisions of the Act complied with. Otherwise the mortage is void, and the lender will have no rights against the goods though he may recover the loan with reasonable interest, as money had and received.[5]

5 *Davies v Rees* (1886) 17 QBD 408, CA.

The formalities of the Bills of Sale Acts have inhibited the growth in this country of any form of chattel mortgage. A hire purchase agreement is not normally a bill of sale given as security for money lent, but a transaction purporting to be one of hire purchase may, in reality, be a mortgage of goods as security for a loan. A court is not bound by the form used by the parties but can enquire into the real nature of the transaction. If the hire purchase agreement is held to be a sham, covering what is really a mortgage of goods, it will be void unless registered. This can arise where B purports to sell goods to A and then takes them back from A on hire purchase. The facts may show that the real transaction is a loan from A to B on the security of goods—a mortgage transaction dressed up to look like a sale of goods followed by hire purchase to the original owner. A will then have no rights against the goods if the agreement has not been registered as a bill of sale.

The most recent cases on the subject suggest that the transaction will be upheld as a genuine sale from B to A followed by a genuine hire-purchase from A to B even though the *motive* is B's desire to obtain money on the security of the goods, unless it can be shown that both A and B intended that the transaction be of loan and mortgage and did not intend that full ownership should pass to A. Thus, in *Snook v London and West Riding Investment Co*[6] B, who wanted to raise £300 on the security of his car, arranged to sell it to A for £800 and take it back on hire-purchase. The Court of Appeal held that the transactions of sale and hire-purchase were genuine and that, therefore, A could exercise rights of re-possession given to him by the hire purchase agreement. Diplock LJ said that 'for acts or transactions to be a "sham" . . . all the parties must have a common intention that the acts or documents are not to create rights and obligations which they have the appearance of creating'. The majority of the court were not disposed to label the hire purchase agreement a sham merely because it recorded that a deposit of £500 had been paid when the *only* money that had passed was £300 from A to B. Russell LJ explained that if B wanted to raise £300 on a car worth £800, he could agree to sell it for £800 on terms that it be hired back for a deposit of £500 and instalments of, say, £350. The finance company could draw a cheque for £800 in favour of B and B could draw a cheque for the finance company for £500. Instead, as

6 [1967] 2 QB 786, [1967] 1 All ER 518, CA. See also *Stoneleigh Finance Ltd v Phillips* [1965] 2 QB 537, [1965] 1 All ER 513, CA and *Kingsley v Sterling Industrial Securities Ltd* [1966] 1 All ER 37, CA. Cf the earlier case of *Polsky v S & A Services Ltd* [1951] 1 All ER 1062n, CA.

here, one cheque was drawn by the finance company in favour of B for £300.

Block discounting does not seem to be affected by the Bills of Sales Acts. The assignment by the dealer of not merely his contractual rights under hire purchase agreements but also of his interest in the goods is a bill of sale but as block discounting normally consists of absolute assignments and the dealer retains neither possession nor the right to possession, the 1878 Act will not apply.[7]

RIGHTS OF THE OWNER AND BAILEE AGAINST THIRD PARTIES

Rights of the bailee against third parties

The bailee having possession of the goods can bring proceedings in trespass or conversion, as appropriate, against any third party who interferes with his right to possession. Whether or not the bailee is liable to the owner for damage, according to the agreement, makes no difference to the third party's liability to the bailee.[8] Of course, any damages obtained by the bailee must, if the bailee opts to return the goods or if the owner properly retakes possession, be handed to the owner. The bailee's duty to account to his bailor is well established in the cases. The third party, having once paid full damages to the bailee, has an answer to any action brought against him by the bailor.

Rights of the owner against third parties

Normally, the owner cannot sue a third party for any tortious interference with the goods, because during the currency of the hire purchase agreement, the owner does not have an immediate right to possession. However, the owner will have an immediate right to possession and, therefore, be able to sue a third party if the bailment has been determined or if the bailment has become a bailment at will.

In *North Central Wagon and Finance Co Ltd v Graham*,[9] in a hire purchase agreement for a car, the bailee agreed not to sell or attempt to sell it, and it was provided that if the bailee broke any

---

7 Guest *The Law of Hire Purchase* (1966) para 683.
8 *The Winkfield* [1902] P 42.
9 [1950] 2 KB 7, [1950] 1 All ER 780.

stipulation in the agreement 'the owners may terminate the hiring'. The bailee handed the car to an auctioneer to sell and the car was sold. The Court of Appeal held the auctioneer liable in conversion to the owner, because at the time of the sale by the auctioneer the owner had an immediate right to possession of the car. The agreement had become, by its own terms, a hiring at will.[10]

It seems that even if the agreement provides for notice to be given to the bailee in order to terminate the agreement, the auctioneer will still be liable even though no notice was given before the auctioneer sold the car. In *Union Transport Finance Ltd v British Car Auctions Ltd*,[11] the hire purchase agreement for a car provided that if the bailee made any default in his monthly instalments or committed any other breach of the agreement, such as selling the car or offering it for sale, the plaintiffs had the right to declare the agreement terminated by forwarding a notice of default to the bailee's last known address. During the currency of the agreement the bailee instructed the defendant auctioneers to sell the car and the defendants did so. The Court of Appeal held that the contractual right to terminate the agreement on breach, which had not been exercised at the time the bailee instructed the auctioneers to sell the car, did not restrict the plaintiffs' common law right to terminate without notice when the bailee acted in a way which was repugnant to the terms of the agreement. On the evidence, the agreement had been terminated and the plaintiffs had acquired the right to immediate possession as soon as the bailee instructed the auctioneers to sell and the auctioneers were therefore liable in conversion.

The owner may also be able to sue a third party for damages if the goods are destroyed or permanently damaged by the third party—it is an injury to the reversion.[12] Presumably, if the bailee exercises his option to purchase after the owner has recovered such damages

---

10 This is the explanation of the case given by Denning and Hodson LJJ in the later case of *Reliance Car Facilities Ltd v Roding Motors* [1952] 2 QB 844, [1952] 1 All ER 1355.

11 [1978] 2 All ER 385, CA. No reference seems to have been made to the case of *Reliance Car Facilities Ltd v Roding Motors* [1952] 2 QB 844, [1952] 1 All ER 1355. It is not clear whether the Hire-Purchase Act 1965 applied to the agreement because the case report does not specify the hire-purchase price but query whether the decision is correct if the default provisions of the Hire-Purchase Act (or Consumer Credit Act) were applicable. See p 182, post. See also *R H Willis & Son (a firm) v British Car Auctions Ltd* [1978] 2 All ER 392, [1978] 1 WLR 438, CA.

12 *Mears v London and South Western Rly Co* (1862) 11 CB NS 850.

against a third party, the owner would have to account to the bailee.

Lien of third parties

During the currency of a hire purchase agreement the bailee has implied authority to deliver the goods to a third party for repairs provided that is an act which is reasonably incidental to his use on the goods. It follows that a repairer's normal right of lien over goods delivered to him for repair (to secure his repairing charges) is effective against the owner. In *Green v All Motors Ltd*,[13] the bailee of a car agreed to keep it 'in good repair and working condition'. The car met with an accident and the bailee handed it to the defendants for repair, the defendants being aware it was held on hire purchase. The bailee defaulted in his instalments and the owner, having properly terminated the agreement, sued the repairers for possession of the car without tendering the amount due for the cost of repairs. The court held that the bailee had implied authority under the hire purchase agreement to deliver the car to the defendants for repair so that the defendant's lien for the cost of repairs prevailed against the owner.[14] If, however, the agreement has already been properly determined before the goods are handed to the repairer, no lien can be claimed against the owner, irrespective of whether the repairer knew the agreement had been brought to an end.[15] It would seem that a provision in a hire purchase agreement for automatic termination of the agreement *before* goods are handed to a repairer will prevent any lien in favour of the repairer arising.

13 [1917] 1 KB 625.

14 In *Albemarle Supply Co v Hind* [1928] 1 KB 307, [1927] All ER Rep 401, it was held that where a bailee agreed to keep the goods in repair but agreed not to create a lien on them in favour of any third party, a third party who repaired the goods knowing of the existence of the agreement but without knowledge of that contractual limitation was still able to claim a lien on them against the owner on the basis that the bailee had implied authority to create a lien. In *Tappenden v Artus* [1964] 2 QB 185, [1963] 3 All ER 213, the Court of Appeal said that the *Hind* case was based on estoppel. If that were so, the repairer could not claim a lien if he believed the bailee to be the owner because the repairer could not be said to rely on the bailee being held out as having authority to create a lien against the owner. However, it is thought that while a repairer's lien may arise by virtue of the doctrine of estoppel, on the authority of the *Green* and *Hind* cases, the lien normally arises from the notion of the bailee having implied authority to have goods repaired and such implied authority is not affected by a secret limitation of the bailee's authority which is not known to the repairers or by the repairers believing the bailee to be the owner. Cf *Watteau v Fenwick* [1893] 1 QB 346, [1891–94] All ER Rep 897; ante, p 30.

15 *Bowmaker Ltd v Wycombe Motors ltd* [1946] KB 505, [1946] 2 All ER 113.

EFFECT OF SALE OR PLEDGE BY THE BAILEE

General rule

We have seen, when considering the Sale of Goods Act, that as a general rule no one can obtain a good title to goods unless he purchases from someone who has himself a good title: *Nemo dat quod non habet*. Generally, therefore, since a bailee has not the property in the goods himself, a sale by him cannot confer a good title on the purchaser. Both the bailee and any subsequent purchaser are liable in conversion to the original owner though a purchaser may be able to claim the benefit of the bailee's option to purchase under the principle of *Whiteley v Hilt*[16] explained below.

It has already been noted that, since a bailee is not in the position of someone who has 'agreed to buy' the goods, a purchaser from him cannot claim a good title under s 9 of the Factors Act. Further, it has been held that merely handing over the goods to a bailee does not estop the owner from denying his authority to sell.[17] Were the rule otherwise, the owner would always run the risk of losing the ownership of the goods if they came into the hands of a bona fide purchaser from the bailee unless they were indelibly marked as being held on hire purchase. If an owner of goods A sells them and simultaneously takes them back on hire purchase, remaining in possession all the while, and then resells and delivers them to X, we have seen that X may be able to claim a good title under s 8 of the Factors Act.[18]

Exceptional cases

1. *Market overt.*—One risk the owner does run is that if the bailee sells the goods in market overt, then the purchaser, if he is in good faith, will obtain a good title to the goods.[19]

2. *Assignment of option to purchase.*—A bailee normally has the ordinary right of a party to any contract to assign the benefit of the contract to a third party. It follows, therefore, that a bailee who purports to sell will give the purchaser the right to the property in

---

16 [1918] 2 KB 808.
17 *Central Newbury Car Auctions Ltd v Unity Finance Ltd* [1957] 1 QB 371, [1956] 3 All ER 905. See p 77, ante.
18 *Pacific Motor Auctions Property Ltd v Motor Credits (Hire Finance) Ltd* [1965] AC 867, [1965] 2 All ER 105. See p 87, ante.
19 See *Bishopsgate Motor Finance Corpn Ltd v Transport Brakes Ltd* [1949] 1 KB 322, [1949] 1 All ER 37 and p 81, ante.

the goods on paying up the balance of hire purchase instalments and thereby exercising the option to purchase. The bailee's purported sale will have operated, in effect, as an assignment of the benefit of the contract, namely the option to purchase. It is true that both the bailee and the purchaser from the bailee are liable in conversion, but if the purchaser is sued he can claim an interest in the goods, as, in effect, assignee of the option to purchase, and will be liable in damages not for the full value of the goods but only for the balance of the price.[20]

However, if the hire purchase agreement has, under its terms, already come to an end when the bailee sells the goods, the purchaser could not claim to be the assignee of the option to purchase since, at the time of sale, the bailee would no longer have an option to purchase which he could assign. Further, the agreement may specify that assignment of the option is a breach of contract and that exercise of the option is conditional on there having been no breach—here again it would seem that a purchaser from the bailee could not claim to be assignee of the option to purchase. And the agreement may expressly provide that the bailee has no right to assign 'the benefit of the agreement'. In *United Dominions Trust (Commercial) Ltd v Parkway Motors Ltd*,[1] a case concerning the hire purchase of a van, the bailee agreed with the plaintiffs that he would not 'sell, offer for sale, assign or charge the goods or the benefit of this agreement', and his option to purchase was dependent on him not having committed any breach of the agreement. On breach, the owner had the right to end the agreement and retake the goods. After the bailee had defaulted in one payment, he sold the van to X who resold it to the defendants, X agreeing to be responsible for seeing that the balance due under the hire purchase agreement was paid. When the plaintiffs claimed possession, the defendants tendered the balance due under the agreement but the plaintiffs refused to accept it. McNair J held that, on the terms of the agreement itself, by which the benefit of the agreement was not assignable, the defendants could not claim to be assignees of the bailee's option to purchase and the defendants were liable for the full value of the goods.

---

20 In a simple bailment, the bailment is determined at once by any act of the bailee which is entirely inconsistent with the bailment, but hire purchase is a 'complex contract' and because the contract of bailment as such is brought to an end by the bailee's disposition of the goods, it does not follow that the option to purchase is also brought to an end—per Warrington LJ in *Whiteley v Hilt* [1918] 2 KB 808, 822. See also *Belsize Motor Supply Co v Cox* [1914] 1 KB 244.

1 [1955] 2 All ER 557, [1955] 1 WLR 719.

This case has, however, now been disapproved. In *Spellman v Spellman*,[2] Danckwerts LJ doubted whether a contractual prohibition against the assignment of an unconditional option to purchase was effective, and in *Wickham Holdings Ltd v Brooke House Motors Ltd*[3] Lord Denning MR and Danckwerts LJ held that *United Dominions Trust (Commercial) Ltd v Parkway Motors Ltd* was wrongly decided. In the *Wickham Holdings* case, the bailee of a car had paid about three-quarters of the hire purchase price and then wanted to sell it to the defendant dealers. The plaintiff owner gave the dealers a 'settlement' figure of £274 representing the unpaid balance of the hire purchase price but when they bought the car from the bailee they forgot to send a cheque for the agreed 'settlement' figure to the plaintiffs. The plaintiffs sued the dealers in conversion for damages amounting to the full value of the car, ie, £365. A clause in the hire purchase agreement specified that the bailee had no right to assign his rights under the agreement. The Court of Appeal avoided the question of whether the dealers could claim to be assignees of the bailee's rights and concentrated on the question of the measure of damages in conversion. They held the plaintiffs were only entitled to their real loss, ie £274, the amount of the unpaid balance of the total price.

3. *Feeding the title.*—If the general rule applies, and the purchaser from a bailee obtains no title to the goods, the owner may voluntarily relinquish his rights to the goods in return, perhaps, for the payment to him by the bailee of the balance of the total price. Should that be done, the good title obtained by the bailee will go to 'feed the title' of any purchaser from him and any subsequent purchaser of the goods.

However, it was held in *Butterworth v Kingsway Motors Ltd*[4] that if, before the bailee does complete such payments, a purchaser claims a return of his purchase money for breach of s 12 of the Sale of Goods Act, he is entitled to it.

4. *Protection of Purchasers of Motor Vehicles.*—Part III of the Hire Purchase Act 1964 gives special protection to the 'private

2 [1961] 2 All ER 498, [1961] 1 WLR 921.
3 [1967] 1 All ER 117, [1967] 1 WLR 295, CA, followed in *Belvoir Finance Co Ltd v Stapleton* [1971] 1 QB 210, [1970] 3 All ER 664. If the value of the goods is less than the amount of the unpaid balance of the total price, the value of the goods will be the measure of damages. *Chubb Cash Ltd v John Crilley & Son* [1983] 2 All ER 294, [1983] 1 WLR 599, CA.
4 [1954] 2 All ER 694, [1954] 1 WLR 1286. See ante, p 99.

purchaser' of a motor vehicle which is the subject of a hire purchase agreement. These provisions are dealt with in Chapter 2 at pp 92–94.

OBLIGATIONS IN RELATION TO A HIRE PURCHASE AGREEMENT

Obligations of the creditor

Until the Supply of Goods (Implied Terms) Act 1973, the principal obligations of the owner (creditor)—as to title, quality, etc.— depended on the rather uncertain common law unless the agreement came within the current Hire Purchase Act, in which case certain statutory obligations applied. The Hire Purchase Act 1965, for example, applied only if the hire purchase price was not more than £2,000 and the bailee was not a body corporate.

The law has now been simplified in that the obligations implied by the 1973 Act apply to *all* hire purchase agreements. Moreover, these obligations are closely similar to those in sale of goods transactions[5] and the rules as to whether they can be excluded are the same as the act specified for sale of goods contracts.

Because the creditor's statutory obligations are set out in the 1973 Act in wording similar to the seller's obligations in a sale of goods contract and these have been fully discussed in Chapter 2, it is not necessary here to do more than set out the statutory provisions relating to the creditor's obligations in hire purchase. Minor alterations in terminology were made by the Consumer Credit Act 1974 and a small amendment to s 10 (2) of the 1973 Act was made by s 17 (1) of the Supply of Goods and Services Act 1982. However, the obligations set out in ss 8–12 of the 1973 Act are not completely comprehensive and some common law rules, referred to below, continue to apply.

1. *Implied terms as to title.*—By s 8 of the Supply of Goods (Implied Terms) Act 1973 (as amended by the Consumer Credit Act 1974):—

'(1) In every hire-purchase agreement, other than one to which subsection (2) below applies, there is—
   (a) an implied condition on the part of the creditor that he will have a right to sell the goods at the time when the property is to pass; and
   (b) an implied warranty that—

5 See p 98, ante.

(i) the goods are free, and will remain free until the time when the property is to pass, from any charge or encumbrance not disclosed or known to the person to whom the goods are bailed or (in Scotland) hired before the agreement is made, and

(ii) that person will enjoy quiet possession of the goods except so far as it may be disturbed by any person entitled to the benefit of any charge or encumbrance so disclosed or known.

(2) In a hire-purchase agreement, in the case of which there appears from the agreement or is to be inferred from the circumstances of the agreement an intention that the creditor should transfer only such title as he or a third person may have, there is—

(a) an implied warranty that all charges or encumbrances known to the creditor and not known to the person to whom the goods are bailed or hired have been disclosed to that person before the agreement is made; and

(b) an implied warranty that neither—

(i) the creditor; nor

(ii) in a case where the parties to the agreement intend that any title which may be transferred shall be only such title as a third person may have, that person; nor

(iii) anyone claiming through or under the creditor or that third person otherwise than under a charge or encumbrance disclosed or known to the person to whom the goods are bailed or hired before the agreement is made;

will disturb the quiet possession of the person to whom the goods are bailed or hired.'

At common law an implied condition was established that the creditor must be the owner of the goods at the time of delivery to the bailee.[6] This rule seems to be preserved by s 15 (4) of the 1973 Act (as amended) whereby nothing in the earlier statutory provisions 'shall prejudice the operation of . . . any rule of law whereby any condition or warranty, other than one relating to quality or fitness, is to be implied in any hire-purchase agreement.' The common law implied condition is, however, subject to a contractual exemption clause whereas, as we shall see, any clause seeking to contract out of the statutory implied terms is void.

It is necessary also to refer to common law for the remedy available to the bailee if the creditor is in breach of a statutory or common law term as to title. If the bailee has paid any money by way of deposit and/or instalments to the creditor such sums can be recovered as damages or as money had and received for a

6 *Mercantile Union Guarantee Corpn Ltd v Wheatley* [1938] 1 KB 490, [1937] 4 All ER 713.

consideration that has wholly failed, since the basis of a hire purchase agreement, the option to purchase, has gone. This was held to be the law in *Warman v Southern Counties Car Finance Corpn Ltd.*[7] The plaintiff had made a contract with the defendants to take a car on hire purchase and in the contract the defendants were described as owners. The plaintiff paid four out of twelve monthly instalments and then learned that someone else was the true owner of the car. He did, however, pay the balance of the instalments and purported to exercise his option to purchase. After the true owner demanded the return of the car, the plaintiff surrendered it to him and, in this action, claimed against the defendants for damages, namely, all the payments he had made to them in respect of the car. Finnemore J upheld the claim and disallowed the defendants' counterclaim for hire rent during the time that the plaintiff had the use of the car. The plaintiff had not paid instalments merely to have the use of the car but in order eventually to become the owner of the car, and since the defendants could not pass ownership to him there was a total failure of consideration for the instalments paid.

2. *Implied condition as to description.*—By s 9 of the 1973 Act (as amended)—

'(1) Where under a hire purchase agreement goods are bailed or (in Scotland) hired by description, there is an implied condition that the goods will correspond with the description, and if under the agreement the goods are bailed or hired by reference to a sample as well as a description, it is not sufficient that the bulk of the goods corresponds with the sample if the goods do not also correspond with the description.

(2) Goods shall not be prevented from being bailed or hired by description by reason only that, being exposed for sale, bailment or hire, they are selected by the person to whom they are bailed or hired.'

3. *Implied terms as to quality and fitness for purpose.*—Section 10 of the 1973 Act (as amended) reads as follows:—

'(1) Except as provided by this section and section 11 below and subject to the provisions of any other enactment, including any enactment of the Parliament of Northern Ireland, or the Northern Ireland Assembly, there is no implied condition or warranty as to the quality or fitness for any particular purpose of goods bailed or (in Scotland) hired under a hire-purchase agreement.

(2) Where the creditor bails or hires goods under a hire purchase

7 [1949] 2 KB 576, [1949] 1 All ER 711.

agreement in the course of a business, there is an implied condition that the goods supplied under the agreement are of merchantable quality, except that there is no such condition—

(a) as regards defects specifically drawn to the attention of the person to whom the goods are bailed or hired before the agreement is made; or

(b) if that person examines the goods before the agreement is made, as regards defects which that examination ought to reveal.

(3) Where the creditor bails or hires goods under a hire purchase agreement in the course of a business and the person to whom the goods are bailed or hired, expressly or by implication, makes known—

(a) to the creditor in the course of negotiations conducted by the creditor in relation to the making of the hire-purchase agreement, or

(b) to a credit-broker in the course of negotiations conducted by that broker in relation to goods sold by him to the creditor before forming the subject matter of the hire-purchase agreement,

any particular purpose for which the goods are being bailed or hired, there is an implied condition that the goods supplied under agreement are reasonably fit for that purpose, whether or not that is a purpose for which such goods are commonly supplied, except where the circumstances show that the person to whom the goods are bailed or hired does not rely, or that it is unreasonable for him to rely, on the skill or judgment of the creditor or credit-broker.

(4) An implied condition or warranty as to quality or fitness for a particular purpose may be annexed to a hire-purchase agreement by usage.

(5) The preceding provisions of this section apply to a hire-purchase agreement made by a person who in the course of a business is acting as agent for the creditor as they apply to an agreement made by the creditor in the course of a business, except where the creditor is not bailing or hiring in the course of a business and either the person to whom the goods are bailed or hired knows that fact or reasonable steps are taken to bring it to the notice of that person before the agreement is made.

(6) In subsection (3) above and this subsection—

(a) "credit-broker" means a person acting in the course of a business of credit brokerage.

(b) "credit brokerage" means the effecting of introductions of individuals desiring to obtain credit—

(i) to persons carrying on any business so far as it relates to the provision of credit, or

(ii) to other persons engaged in credit brokerage.'

4. *Implied term as to sample.*—By s 11 of the 1973 (as amended):—

'Where under a hire-purchase agreement goods are bailed or (in Scotland) hired by reference to a sample, there is an implied condition—

(a) that the bulk will correspond with the sample in quality; and
(b) that the person to whom the goods are bailed or hired will have a reasonable opportunity of comparing the bulk with the sample; and
(c) that the goods will be free from any defect, rendering them unmerchantable, which would not be apparent on reasonable examination of the sample.'

5. *Implied term as to delivery.*—Nothing is said in the 1973 Act on the point but it seems to be a common law term of every hire purchase agreement that the creditor must deliver the goods to the bailee. Presumably the obligation is to deliver the goods within a reasonable time of the contract if no specific date is fixed by the contract. The duty is a fundamental one so that breach entitles the bailee to repudiate the contract.[8] Unless the goods are of a special or unique kind, the bailee's only other remedy will normally be in damages, not specific performance. In *Bentworth Finance Ltd v Lubert*[9] the Court of Appeal held that in the case of an agreement relating to a motor vehicle, failure to supply the bailee with the car's log book meant that the agreement and its obligations never came into operation.

Exemption clauses

At common law the implied obligations of the creditor could be excluded or modified by the express terms of a hire purchase agreement. The courts, however, did develop various principles by which they sought to limit the effect of exemption clauses. The Supply of Goods (Implied Terms) Act 1973 restricted the contracting out of the obligations implied by statute and the present law is contained in the Unfair Contract Terms Act 1977. By s 6 (1) (b) of the 1977 Act, the implied terms as to title in s 8 of the 1973 Act cannot be excluded or restricted by any contract term. With regard to the terms implied by ss 9–11 of the 1973 Act, the same distinction between consumer agreements and non-consumer agreements is made in s 6 (2) and (3) of the 1977 Act as the 1977 Act provides for in relation to sale of goods contracts.

Reference should be made to the discussion of this distinction in

8 Per Upjohn LJ in *Charterhouse Credit Co Ltd v Tolly* [1963] 2 QB 683, 708, [1963] 2 All ER 432, 440, CA.
9 [1968] 1 QB 680, [1967] 2 All ER 810.

Chapter 2.[10] Suffice here simply to remind the reader that in relation to consumer agreements liability in respect of the obligations as to description, merchantability, fitness for purpose and samples cannot be excluded or restricted by reference to any contract term. So far as non-consumer agreements are concerned, such liability can be excluded or restricted by reference to a contract term but only in so far as the term satisfies the requirement of reasonableness.

In consumer agreements, as any clause exempting the creditor from his statutory obligations is void, the bailee is not likely to have to rely on the common law though the common law is still relevant where an exemption clause purports to exempt a creditor from an express obligation or from an obligation implied by common law. In a non-consumer agreement, the statutory protection of the bailee is more limited but, even if the term satisfies the requirement of reasonableness, he may be able to rely on principles established by the courts. These principles have been examined in Chapter 2 and it is not necessary to spell them out again here.

Remedies of the bailee

If the creditor is in breach of an express or implied *condition* of the contract then the bailee may treat the contract as repudiated and claim damages. By treating the contract as repudiated, the bailee must allow the creditor to retake possession of the goods but the bailee is entitled to recover all moneys paid. There is no equivalent, in relation to hire purchase, of s 11 (4) of the Sale of Goods Act so that acceptance of the goods by the bailee, eg, keeping them for more than a reasonable time without giving notice of rejection, does not bar his right to treat the contract as repudiated. However, if the bailee evinces an intention to go on with the agreement, after he is aware of a breach of condition on the part of the creditor, for example, continuing to pay instalments, this amounts to affirmation of the contract and does bar the bailee's right to treat the contract as repudiated.[11] But in *Farnworth Finance Facilities Ltd v Attryde*,[12] where a bailee repeatedly returned the motor cycle he held on hire purchase and after four months it was still defective, the

---

10 See p 111, ante.
11 It was suggested by the Court of Appeal in *Yeoman Credit Ltd v Apps* [1962] 2 QB 508, [1961] 2 All ER 281, that a bailee could still treat a contract as repudiated after affirmation because the creditor's obligations are continuous. This view was rejected by Lloyd LJ in *UCB Leasing Ltd v Holtom* [1987] NLJ Rep 614, CA.
12 [1970] 2 All ER 774, [1970] 1 WLR 1053, CA.

bailee was held not to have affirmed the contract although he had been paying instalments and had driven 4,000 miles. The Court of Appeal held the bailee was entitled to repudiate the contract.

For breach of either a condition or warranty, express or implied, the bailee may claim damages. The basic contractual principles embodied in *Hadley v Baxendale*[13] and *The Heron II*[14] apply. In *Charterhouse Credit Co Ltd v Tolly*[15] the Court of Appeal held that the measure of damages was the cost of hiring similar goods on similar terms less the value of the use obtained from the goods. Donovan LJ said:—'There is no reason why one should not adopt as the figure of that cost what the hirer had actually had to pay to the company for the like hiring in the present case . . .'[16]

Obligations of the dealer (credit-broker)

If the customer takes goods on hire purchase direct from the dealer, then of course the obligations of the dealer will be those of the creditor, as already described. If, however, the dealer sells the goods to the finance company and the finance company lets them on hire purchase to the customer, the obligations of the owner rest on the finance company and the dealer, not being privy to the hire purchase agreement, cannot be liable in any way to the customer on the hire purchase agreement.[17]

There is authority, however, for the proposition that a collateral contract may be implied at common law between the dealer and the customer. The implied contract rests on the dealer undertaking to cause the finance company to enter into a hire purchase contract with the customer in return for the customer promising to enter into a hire purchase agreement with the finance company. If the dealer made any express warranties about the goods, these may be treated as terms of the collateral contract and the dealer is then liable in damages if such a warranty is broken. Further, the dealer may be liable in damages for negligence, whether he has made any express warranties or not.

The existence of such remedies is particularly useful where the

---

13 (1854) 9 Exch 341.

14 [1969] 1 AC 350, [1967] 3 All ER 686, HL.

15 [1963] 2 QB 683, [1963] 2 All ER 432 followed in *UCB Leasing Ltd v Holtom* [1987] NLJ Rep 614, CA.

16 [1963] 2 QB 683, 706, [1963] 2 All ER 432, 439.

17 Nor can the customer sue the dealer for breach of the implied conditions contained in s 14 of the Sale of Goods Act, since there is no contract of sale between the dealer and the customer: *Drury v Victor Buckland Ltd* [1941] 1 All ER 269.

goods are defective and any remedy against the finance company is blocked by an effective exemption clause. In *Andrews v Hopkinson*,[18] the plaintiff was considering the possibility of taking a certain second-hand car on hire purchase. The dealer told the plaintiff: 'It's a good little bus; I would stake my life on it; you will have no trouble with it.' The car was sold to a finance company which let it out to the plaintiff on hire purchase. A week after delivery of the car to the plaintiff, he was injured in a collision while driving the car owing to a failure of the drag-link joint of the steering which was not safe or fit for use on the highway. The terms of the hire purchase agreement deprived the plaintiff of any remedy against the finance company, but McNair J held that there was an implied contract between the dealer and the plaintiff and the plaintiff was entitled to damages against the dealer for breach of the express warranty, embodied in the words quoted, the warranty forming part of the implied contract.[19] McNair J also considered the dealer liable in negligence on the basis that a dealer in second-hand goods owes a duty to see that goods are not in a condition whereby personal injuries or damage to property might be caused. Since the House of Lords decision in *Hedley Byrne & Co Ltd v Heller & Partners Ltd*,[20] it may be considered that there is a special relationship between the dealer and the customer whereby the dealer owes the customer a duty of care with regard to any statements he makes about the goods and that, therefore, the dealer is liable for any financial loss resulting from careless misstatement made by the dealer. There has, however, been no case establishing that a dealer owes such a duty.

The Unfair Contract Terms Act 1977 makes the dealer's obligations less important because the finance company is less able than in the past to exempt itself from liability by way of exemption clauses. However, the dealer's obligations may be significant

(i) in relation to non-consumer agreements,

18 [1957] 1 QB 229, [1956] 3 All ER 422. The decision followed two earlier cases: *Brown v Sheen and Richmond Car Sales Ltd* [1950] 1 All ER 1102, and *Herschtal v Stewart and Arderny Ltd* [1940] 1 KB 155, [1939] 4 All ER 123. In *Yeoman Credit Ltd v Odgers* [1962] 1 All ER 789, [1962] 1 WLR 215 the Court of Appeal held a dealer liable to pay, as damages to the bailee for breach of warranty, the whole sum which the bailee was liable to pay to the finance company under the hire purchase agreement by way of instalments together with the costs incurred by the bailee in reasonably defending the action brought against him by the finance company for falling into arrears.

19 Obiter, the judge thought that as the transaction between the dealer and the customer was so closely akin to sale, the court could *imply* a term as to fitness for purpose.

20 [1964] AC 465, [1963] 2 All ER 575. See also *Mutual Life and Citizens' Assurance Co Ltd v Evatt* [1971] AC 793, [1971] 1 All ER 150, PC.

(ii) where the finance company is for any reason not worth suing, and
(iii) if the dealer has given express undertakings going beyond the obligations of the creditor which are implied by the 1973 Act, such as an express promise to effect repairs free of charge in certain eventualities.

The Consumer Credit Act 1974 s 145, employs the term 'credit-broker' to include what has previously been called a dealer, ie someone who negotiates a hire purchase agreement. It will have been noticed that by s 10 (3) of the Supply of Goods (Implied Terms) Act 1973, as amended by the 1974 Act, the customer may obtain the benefit of the implied condition of fitness for purpose if he makes known the purpose for which he wants the goods to 'a credit-broker in the course of negotiations conducted by that broker . . .'.

Is the dealer an agent?

Pearson LJ in *Mercantile Credit Co Ltd v Hamblin*[1] said:

'There is no rule of law that in a hire purchase transaction the dealer never is, or always is, acting as agent for the finance company or as agent for the customer. In the typical hire purchase transaction the dealer is a party in his own right, selling his car to the finance company, and he is acting primarily for his own behalf and not as a general agent for either of the other two parties.'

Firstly, then, may the dealer ever be the customer's agent? Pearson LJ thought that a customer *may* authorise the dealer to complete the hire purchase forms by filling in the particulars, but in *Campbell Discount Co Ltd v Gall*,[2] the Court of Appeal held that a customer did not simply by signing such forms confer authority of any kind on the dealer.

Secondly, may the dealer be the finance company's agent? It seems clear that at common law, the dealer has no implied authority to accept on the finance company's behalf an offer to take goods on hire purchase or to make representations about the goods on the company's behalf or to receive a deposit as agent for the company.[3] However, in *Financings Ltd v Stimson*,[4] Lord Denning MR and Donovan LJ took the view that the dealer was agent of the

1 [1965] 2 QB 242, 269, [1964] 3 All ER 592, 600–601.
2 [1961] 1 QB 431, [1961] 2 All ER 104.
3 *Campbell Discount Co Ltd v Gall* [1961] 1 QB 431, [1961] 2 All ER 104, CA and *Branwhite v Worcester Works Finance Ltd* [1969] 1 AC 552, [1968] 3 All ER 104, HL.
4 [1962] 3 All ER 386, [1962] 1 WLR 1184.

finance company for the purpose of receiving notice of the customer's revocation of his offer so that communication by the customer to the dealer of his desire to withdraw his offer was equivalent to communication to the finance company and effective if made before the company had accepted the offer.[5]

In general it is clear from the majority decision of the House of Lords in *Branwhite v Worcester Works Finance Ltd*[6] that at common law the finance company is not responsible for the dealer's acts, receipts or omissions—the dealer is not in law the finance company's agent. In that case the bailee paid £130 as a deposit on a car to the dealer and, when the car was sold to the finance company, the company was credited with the £130 since the company paid the dealer the agreed sale price *less* £130. The dealer fraudulently inserted figures in the proposal form contrary to those agreed by the bailee. The House of Lords *held* unanimously that as the parties to the hire-purchase agreement were not ad idem, the agreement was void and since the finance company could be treated as having received the £130 paid by the bailee this sum was recoverable by the bailee from the finance comany as money had and received on a consideration that had wholly failed. Two of their Lordships, Lords Reid and Wilberforce, found in the alternative in favour of the bailee on the ground that the dealer had received the deposit as agent for the finance company and laid stress on 'the established mercantile background of hire-purchase' whereby a dealer has a standing relationship with the finance company and should be treated realistically as acting on the finance company's behalf. The majority, however, held that the facts did not warrant any conclusion that the dealer received the deposit as an agent for the finance company. On the majority view, the bailee would not have succeeded in recovering the deposit from the finance company if the dealer had absconded with the money before the sale from the dealer to the finance company had been arranged—the finance company could not then have been treated as having received the deposit.

By the Consumer Credit Act 1974, in relation to any hire purchase agreement regulated by this Act,[7] the dealer or credit-

---

5 Pearson LJ disagreed. See also *Northgran Finance Ltd v Ashley* [1963] 1 QB 476, [1962] 3 All ER 973, where the Court of Appeal held that a dealer was not authorised by the finance company to receive offers subject to a condition precedent and, therefore, the company could not be deemed to know of any oral condition attached to the offer.
6 [1969] 1 AC 552, [1968] 3 All ER 104, HL.
7 See p 152, ante.

broker is deemed to be the agent of the creditor for the purposes of receiving a notice of revocation, cancellation or rescission (ss 57, 69 and 102). Moreover, by s 56, if the dealer arranges with a customer for goods selected by the customer to be sold to a finance company introduced by the dealer and the finance company makes a hire purchase agreement with the customer, the dealer is considered to have conducted the 'antecedent negotiations' which are 'deemed to be conducted by the negotiator in the capacity of agent of the creditor as well as in his actual capacity.' 'Antecedent negotiations' are taken to include 'any representations made by the negotiator to the debtor . . . and any other dealings between them' (s 56 (4)). It follows that although the personal liability of the dealer at common law under the authority of *Andrews v Hopkinson*[8] is preserved, the finance company is also liable for any representations or contractual promises made by the dealer. It also seems that where the Act applies, the majority view of the House of Lords in *Branwhite v Worcester Works Finance Ltd*[9] that a dealer is not the finance company's agent for receiving a deposit from the bailee is no longer law. Such deposit paid to the dealer may now be recoverable even if the dealer absconds before the goods are sold to the finance company. Any contractual clause purporting to provide that the dealer is to be treated as the debtor's agent or to relieve the finance company from liability for the dealer's acts or omissions is void (s 56 (3)). (Section 75, important with regard to a debtor-creditor-supplier agreement where the creditor and the supplier *are* not the same person, has no application to a hire-purchase agreement where the creditor (usually a finance company) is also the supplier. But s 56 is sufficient to make the creditor liable for acts or omissions of the dealer.)

By s 175 where the dealer or credit-broker is deemed to receive a notice (or payment) as agent of the creditor, he is deemed to be under a contractual duty to the creditor to transmit the notice (or remit the payment) to him forthwith.

Obligations of the debtor

The common law has become increasingly of less significance because in respect of the principal obligation of the debtor, ie, to pay the instalment charges, typical contractual provisions entitling the owner to repossess, recover compensation, etc., have for some

8 [1957] 1 QB 229, [1956] 3 All ER 422.
9 [1969] 1 AC 552, [1968] 3 All ER 104, HL.

time been subject to statutory restriction. By the Consumer Credit Act 1974, the restrictions exist whenever credit is given to an 'individual' not exceeding £15,000, otherwise than in an 'exempt' agreement.[10] The 1974 Act will clearly apply to most hire purchase agreements that are made but reference will also be made to the common law because this is relevant (i) where no obligation is imposed by the Act; (ii) where the Act does not comprehensively provide the remedies for breach of a statutory obligation, and (iii) where the agreement is outside the Act, eg, where goods are bailed to a limited company rather than to an individual.

1. *To take delivery of the goods.*—If a debtor refuses to take the goods he is liable in damages, but the creditor has no right to wait and sue for the monthly or weekly instalments as they would have become due had the debtor taken delivery.[11] The measure of damages, based on the principle of *Hadley v Baxendale*,[12] ie, the estimated loss directly and naturally resulting from the breach, would seem to be the creditor's loss of profits. In other words, all amounts due that are unpaid less the value of the goods and a discount for earlier return on the capital outlay.

2. *To take care of the goods.*—A bailee is impliedly bound to use reasonable care in looking after the goods. If, therefore, he chooses not to exercise his option to purchase the goods, or if the agreement is determined by reason, for example, of the debtor's failure to keep up his instalments, the debtor will be liable in damages if he or his servants acting in the course of their employment have failed to exercise reasonable care. If the goods are damaged during the currency of the agreement the onus is on the debtor to show that he has taken reasonable care of them.[13] He is not liable for fair wear and tear.

In *Brady v St Margaret's Trust, Ltd*[14] the debtor had broken an express term by which he had agreed to keep a car 'in good order, repair and condition'. The Court of Appeal held that, in assessing the damages, neither the total price nor the price obtained for the car after it had been retaken by the creditors for non-payment of instalments was a guide. As Davies LJ put it:

10 See p 153, ante.

11 *National Cash Register Co Ltd v Stanley* [1921] 3 KB 292.

12 (1854) 9 Exch 341, affirmed by the House of Lords in *The Heron II* [1969] 1 AC 350, [1967] 3 All ER 686.

13 Per Buckley LJ in *Joseph Travers & Sons v Cooper* [1915] 1 KB 73, 88, [1914–15] All ER Rep 104.

14 [1963] 2 QB 494, [1963] 2 All ER 275.

'There ought to be evidence as to what its general condition and value were at the inception of the contract and similarly evidence as to what its general condition and value were at the termination of the contract'.[15]

Should goods let out on hire purchase be lost by theft or Act of God, the agreement will be discharged by frustration and both parties, therefore, free from further liability unless the agreement places a strict liability on the debtor for all loss or damage 'however occasioned'. Presumably, the Law Reform (Frustrated Contracts) Act 1943 will apply.

3. *Liability for loss or damage irrespective of negligence.*—An action for conversion lies against a debtor if he wilfully deals with the goods in a manner inconsistent with the creditor's title, such as selling them coupled with delivery or merely selling them (if that passes title) or wrongfully withholding possession from the creditor after the debtor has opted to return the goods or after the creditor has properly terminated the agreement. An action also lies if the debtor wrongfully detains goods after proper demand by the creditor has been made for them, or if he cannot return them on demand because he has negligently lost them or has voluntarily parted with them.[16]

If the debtor elects to deal with the goods bailed in a way clearly unauthorised by the creditor, by wrongful user or otherwise, he takes upon himself the risk of so doing, and is strictly liable for any damage to the goods occurring thereafter. This is a general principle of bailment.[17]

4. *To pay instalment charges: liability if the debtor opts to terminate.*— At common law the debtor must pay the instalments agreed on to the creditor or his authorised agent subject to whatever option to terminate the agreement and return the goods is given to him by the agreement. If he exercises such option, then according to the Court of Appeal decision in *Associated Distributors Ltd v Hall*[18] he must pay all instalments due at the time, together with any further sum which, according to the agreement, is payable in such circumstances. No question could arise as to whether such sum was a

15 Ibid, at pp 278, 501.
16 *Ballett v Mingay* [1943] KB 281, [1943] 1 All ER 143. (This was an action in detinue. Such actions were abolished by the Torts (Interference with Goods) Act 1977 and an action in conversion would now be brought on similar facts.)
17 See, for example, *Lilley v Doubleday* (1881) 7 QBD 510.
18 [1938] 2 KB 83, [1938] 1 All ER 511.

penalty as that question is only relevant in the event of a debtor's breach of contract. Doubt, however, was thrown on this view by two of the judgments delivered in the House of Lords in *Bridge v Campbell Discount Co Ltd*,[19] and in the later case of *United Dominions Trust (Commercial) Ltd v Ennis*,[20] Lord Denning MR said that a debtor is not to be taken to exercise the option to terminate unless he does so consciously, knowing of the consequences, and avowedly in exercise of the option.

If the agreement is covered by the Act, then by s 99 the debtor may at any time before the final payment under the agreement falls due, determine the agreement by giving notice of termination in writing to any person entitled or authorised to receive the sums payable under the agreement (frequently the dealer). The debtor's liability if he gives such notice, without prejudice to any liability already accrued, is to pay the amount, if any, by which one-half of the total price exceeds the total of the sums paid and the sums due in respect of the total price immediately before the termination, or such less amount as may be specified in the agreement (s 100). There is no such liability if the agreement does not provide for any payment.

By s 100 (3), if the court is satisfied that a sum less than the amount by which one-half of the total price exceeds the total of the sums paid and the sums due in respect of the total price immediately before the termination would be equal to the loss sustained by the owner in consequence of the termination, the court may make an order for the payment of that sum.[1]

If the debtor has contravened an obligation to take reasonable care of the goods the amount the debtor must pay is increased by the sum required to recompense the creditor for that contravention (s 100 (4)) and having determined the agreement, the debtor must allow the owner to retake the goods. In any action brought by the

19 [1962] AC 600, [1962] 1 All ER 385.
20 [1968] 1 QB 54, [1967] 2 All ER 345, 348.
1 In determining the loss sustained by the creditor, the court will presumably be guided by the principles established in *Yeoman Credit Ltd v Waragowski* [1961] 3 All ER 145, [1961] 1 WLR 1124, post, p 180. Thus, suppose the total price for a car is £1,000, the debtor has paid £260 by way of a deposit and instalments and one instalment of £40 is due. The debtor then determines the agreement and returns the car which has been properly taken care of. The creditor sells it for £600. *Prima facie*, the creditor is entitled to claim the £40 due plus the difference between £500 and £300, ie, £200. But the court may on these facts, allow only the £40 due plus £100, ie, the difference between the total price of £1,000 and the total of the sums received from or owed by the debtor and the sale price obtained for the car, this being the loss sustained by the creditor.

creditor to recover possession the court, unless it is satisfied that having regard to the circumstances it would not be just to do so, must order the goods to be delivered to the creditor without giving the debtor an option to pay the value of the goods (s 100 (5)).

By virtue of s 173, any contractual term inconsistent with these statutory provisions, such as a term imposing an additional duty or liability on the debtor is void. It is, however, permissible for the agreement to provide the debtor with more favourable terms on which he may terminate than the Act provides.

By s 103, if an individual serves a written notice on a trader stating that the individual had been a debtor under a specified hire purchase agreement and that the trader had been the creditor, that the individual had made all the necessary payments, and that the agreement has ceased to have any operation, and requiring the trader to give him a notice confirming these statements, the trader must comply with this notice or serve a counter notice to dispute it. In the latter case the trader must given particulars of the way in which he alleges the notice is wrong.

5. *To pay instalment charges: liability if the debtor defaults.*—Should the debtor default in making his payments as required by the agreement, he is liable at common law for all arrears and invariably, the creditor reserves a right in the agreement to terminate the agreement and to resume possession of the goods in such circumstances. The debtor will also be liable in damages for any loss consequent on his breach. The measure of damages depends on whether, by words or conduct, the debtor has repudiated the agreement or not. If he has repudiated the agreement, eg, by writing a letter to the effect that he cannot go on with the agreement, or by failing to pay several instalments, and the company appears to have accepted that repudiation, the measure of damages is in accordance with the principle established in *Yeoman Credit Ltd v Waragowski*.[2] In this case, the plaintiffs let out a van to

2 [1961] 3 All ER 145, [1961] 1 WLR 1124. A criticism of the *Waragowski* measure of damages is that it pays no regard to the fact that the debtor may have an option to terminate the agreement, eg, by making payments up to one-half the price as in *Waragowski* itself. Suppose the price is £3,000 and the debtor pays £750 before defaulting. He is in arrears for a further £750 and then the goods are repossessed and sold for, say, £750. The court will award the £750 in arrears so that the creditor will now have received in all £2,250. As the debtor could lawfully have terminated the agreement by paying £1,500, it is strange that on breach he should be required by the *Waragowski* decision to pay, on these facts, a further £750. See Lord Denning's comments in *Financings Ltd v Baldock* [1963] 2 QB 104, 113–4, and a note by Professor J S Ziegel in (1961) 24 MLR 792.

the defendant on hire purchase, the terms being an initial payment of £72 and 36 monthly instalments of £10 0s 9d with a further £1 to be paid on exercising the option to purchase. The total hire purchase price was £434 7s 0d. The debtor paid the deposit and took delivery but paid none of the instalments and six months later, in accordance with the provisions of the agreement, the plaintiffs retook possession. They sold the van for £205. In an action against the debtor, the Court of Appeal held that the plaintiffs were entitled to arrears of instalments amounting to £60 4s 6d and, as damages for breach of contract, the difference between the total price less the £1 'option money' and the sum of the sale price obtained and the deposit and instalment arrears. The damages allowed, therefore, were £434 7s 0d (less £1) less (£205 plus £72 plus £60 4s 6d), ie, £96 2s 6d.

In *Overstone Ltd v Shipway*,[3] after failing to pay four instalments the debtor wrote a letter saying 'I cannot afford to carry on paying for this car'. The Court of Appeal adopted the measure of damages established in the *Waragowski* case but held that since, in an action of this kind the finance company obtained accelerated receipt of its capital outlay, a discount should be allowed. In *United Dominions Trust (Commercial) Ltd v Ennis*,[4] two members of the Court of Appeal thought that on the facts the debtor had repudiated the agreement but as the repudiation was not accepted by the company (since the company by claiming under a minimum payment clause were treating the contract as continuing) the *Waragowski* measure of damages was not applicable.

If the debtor has not repudiated the agreement but is merely in arrears with, say, two or three instalments, and the creditor exercises a contractual right to terminate the agreement, the creditor may only claim against the debtor the amount of instalments in arrears, damages for any failure on the part of the debtor to take reasonable care of the goods, and the cost of repossessing them. In *Financing Ltd v Baldock*,[5] the plaintiffs let out a truck on hire purchase the terms being an initial payment of £100 and 24 monthly instalments of £28 10s 3d. The total price was £772 16s 0d. The debtor paid the deposit and took delivery but failed to pay the first two instalments and the creditors thereupon exercised their contractual right to end the agreement and repossess the truck. The Court of Appeal held that mere failure to pay two

3 [1962] 1 All ER 52, [1962] 1 WLR 117.
4 [1968] 1 QB 54, [1967] 2 All ER 345.
5 [1963] 2 QB 104, [1963] 1 All ER 443.

instalments did not amount to a repudiation of the agreement and that the plaintiffs were only entitled as damages to the amount of the two instalments in arrears.

However, at common law, creditors can readily avoid that decision by skilled drafting of their contracts. According to the Court of Appeal in *Lombard North Central plc v Butterworth*,[6] if the contract states that prompt payment is a condition of the contract so that failure to pay promptly amounts to a repudiation of the contract, the creditor can accept that repudiation, terminate the contract and claim as damages the loss of the whole of the transaction. Nicholls LJ said he viewed the impact of this with 'considerable dissatisfaction' since it 'emasculates' the decision in *Financings Ltd v Baldock*.

It is possible that the debtor has paid 80 or 90 per cent of the total price before he defaults. Nevertheless, if the agreement entitles the creditor to retake possession on default, the creditor is entitled at common law to do so as well as to retain all instalments paid and claim any arrears due at the time of resuming possession. There seems to be no power in the court to grant any kind of equitable relief.

The common law rules just referred to as to the bailee's liability if he defaults and the measure of damages applicable are of course still directly applicable today in the case of a hire purchase agreement not regulated by the Consumer Credit Act 1974. Even where such an agreement is regulated by the Act, the rules as to measure of damages are generally applicable but the Act imposes restrictions on any contractual right to repossess goods when the bailee defaults and requires the service of a notice of default before any contractual rights consequent on default are effective.

By s 87 (1) of the Act, the creditor must serve a 'default notice' on the debtor before he is entitled by reason of any breach by the debtor of a regulated hire purchase agreement, (a) to terminate the agreement or (b) to demand earlier payment of any sum or (c) to recover possession of goods or (d) to treat any right of the debtor as terminated, restricted or deferred or (e) to enforce any security.

Although this provision refers to 'any breach' it is most important in respect of a breach of the debtor's obligation to pay instalments

6 [1987] QB 527, [1987] 1 All ER 267. Where the Consumer Credit Act applies, s 173 provides that any contractual term is void to the extent that it is inconsistent with a provision in the Act for the protection of the debtor and therefore, a 'time of the essence' clause cannot prevent the operation of ss 87–89 of the Act enabling the debtor to put things right (see post, pp 182–184) or ss 129–136 in relation to time orders (post, pp 185–187).

because it is in respect of breach of this obligation that the agreement usually reserves a right to the creditor to terminate the agreement and repossess the goods. For breach of the debtor's express or implied obligation to take reasonable care of the goods the creditor is generally entitled only to claim damages and the Act does not require the service of a 'default notice' before the creditor is entitled to claim damages or arrears as distinct from the other remedies specified in s 87.

The earlier statutory provision requiring service of a default notice (s 25 of the Hire-Purchase Act 1965) omitted to specify any details that the notice ought to contain though the Court of Appeal in 1971 endeavoured to remedy the omission of the legislature.[7] Now, s 88 (1) of the Consumer Credit Act provides that the notice must be in the prescribed form and specify,

'(a) the nature of the alleged breach;
(b) if the breach is capable of remedy, what action is required to remedy it and the date before which that action is to be taken;
(c) if the breach is not capable of remedy, the sum (if any) required to be paid as compensation for the breach, and the date before which it is to be paid.'

A date specified under s 88 (1) must not be less than 7 days after the date of service of the default notice and the creditor may not pursue any of the remedies mentioned in s 87 before the specified date. The default notice must contain information in the prescribed terms about the consequences of failure to comply with it. It may include a provision terminating the agreement, or for the taking of other action as specified in s 87 (1) at any time after the 7 days or more specified in the notice has elapsed, together with a statement that the provision will be ineffective if the breach is duly remedied or the compensation duly paid. By s 89, if before the 7 days or more specified in the default notice the debtor takes the action required in the notice the breach must be treated as not having occurred. In order to prevent evasion of the default notice procedure by a contractual clause entitling a creditor to repossess, etc, in his absolute discretion, irrespective of any breach by the debtor, s 76 provides that 7 days' notice must be given of the creditor's intention to enforce the agreement by demanding earlier payment of any sum, or by recovering possession of goods, or by treating any right of the debtor as terminated, restricted or deferred. Section 98 allows a creditor to terminate an agreement otherwise than on breach only after giving 7 days' notice of termination.

7 *Eshun v Moorgate Mercantile Co Ltd* [1971] 2 All ER 402, [1971] 1 WLR 722, CA.

The creditor is not entitled to enter any premises to take possession of goods subject to a regulated hire purchase agreement, except under an order of the court and any such entry is actionable as a breach of statutory duty (s 92). Contravention means that the agreement is enforceable against the debtor on a court order only. The creditor is not entitled to take a promissory note or a bill of exchange (other than a cheque) in discharge of any sum payable by the debtor or the surety or to take such a bill as security for the discharge of such sum. Nor is he entitled to negotiate such a cheque except to a banker (s 123). If he does so, this constitutes a defect in his title within the meaning of Bills of Exchange Act.[8]

'*Protected goods.*'—Sections 90 and 91 of the Consumer Credit Act contain provisions restricting the creditor's rights to recover possession of goods when one-third of the total price has been paid. By s 90 (1), at any time when the debtor is in breach of a regulated hire purchase agreement and has paid to the creditor one-third or more of the total price, 'the creditor is not entitled to recover possession of the goods from the debtor except on an order of the court'. This indicates that once one-third of the price has been paid the creditor is not entitled to resume possession by physically retaking them from the debtor. However, there does not seem to be any restriction where the bailee is persuaded voluntarily to surrender possession. This was the decision of the Court of Appeal in *Mercantile Credit Co v Cross*[9] when the statutory restriction embodied in the Hire Purchase Acts 1938–1965 forbad the creditor to *enforce* any right to recover possession from the debtor. The same ruling would presumably be made under the Consumer Credit Act 1974 because by s 173 (3) the debtor's 'consent' given at the time when possession is recovered is equivalent to a court order for possession. In *Bentinck v Cromwell Engineering Co*[10] the Court of Appeal held that the defendants had not contravened the law when they retook possession of goods after the bailee had abandoned them. Again, the decision would be expected to be the same under the Consumer Credit Act because, in such circumstances, the creditor is not recovering possession 'from the debtor'.

It is clear that s 90 (1) does not apply if the debtor exercises his

8 See p 246, post.
9 [1965] 2 QB 205, [1965] 1 All ER 577, CA.
10 [1971] 1 QB 324, [1971] 1 All ER 33, CA. But in this case Lord Denning MR, stressed that the restriction against recovery of possession from the debtor applies also to recovery from a bailee from the debtor: [1971] 1 All ER 33, 34.

option to terminate the agreement—then, the creditor *is* entitled to recover possession without taking the debtor to court.

Goods falling within s 90 are referred to in the Act as 'protected goods' and, if goods are recovered by the creditor in contravention of s 90, then by s 91 the agreement if not previously terminated, will terminate. Moreover, the debtor is released from all liability under the agreement and is entitled to recover from the creditor all sums paid under the agreement. It would seem that these are the only rights of the bailee—he does not have an alternative claim for damages in conversion because the agreement is terminated by wrongful repossession and the bailee has no right to possession.[11]

Special powers of the court.—Whether one-third of the price has been paid or not, any action by the creditor to enforce a regulated agreement or to recover possession will be in the county court. All parties to the agreement and any surety must normally be made parties to the proceedings (s 141). One power the court has is to make a 'time order' (s 129), ie an order for payment by the debtor of any sum owed by such instalments as is thought reasonable.[12] The county court may make a time order whenever it appears to the court just to do so either on an application by the debtor after a default notice or a s 76 or s 98 notice has been served on him or in an action by the creditor to enforce the agreement, eg, in an action for repossession. The order will require the debtor to pay by such instalments, payable at such times, as the court, having regard to the means of the debtor, considers reasonable. Where an offer to pay any sums by instalments is made by the debtor and accepted by the creditor, the court may make a time order giving effect to the offer without hearing evidence of means (s 130). Where the debtor remains in possession of goods after the making of a time order, he is treated as a bailee under the terms of the agreement, notwithstanding that the agreement has been terminated.

On an application by any person affected by a time order, the court may vary or revoke the order (s 130 (6)). For the protection of goods pending proceedings, the creditor may apply to the court for

---

11 *Carr v James Broderick & Co* [1942] KB 275, [1942] 2 All ER 441. There might of course be a claim for damages in trespass if, for example, the creditor's seizure of the goods involved breaking into the bailee's house.

12 Section 129 also provides for another type of 'time order', where the debtor is given time to remedy a breach, other than the non-payment of money, within a specified period. If such order is made by the court, the creditor is not permitted to terminate the agreement or recover possession of goods during the specified period.

an order to protect property from damage or depreciation, and such order may restrict or prohibit the use of property (s 131).

By s 133, in relation to any regulated hire purchase agreement, if it appears just to the court to do so, on an application for an enforcement order or time order, or in an action by the creditor to recover possession of goods, it may:

   (i) make a 'return order' for the return of the goods to the creditor; or

  (ii) make a 'transfer order' for the transfer to the debtor of the creditor's title to certain goods to which the agreement relates and the return to the creditor of the remainder of the goods,

Where a *transfer order* is made, the transferred goods are such of the goods to which the agreement relates as the court thinks just but such an order may be made only where the paid-up sum exceeds the part of the total price referable to the transferred goods by an amount equal to at least one-third of the unpaid balance of the total price (s 133 (3)). Thus, suppose the total price to be £3,000, then, assuming the goods to which the agreement relates can physically be separated, a transfer order may be made in respect of goods to which £1,000 of the total price is referable provided the debtor has paid up at least £1,500. £500 is one-third of unpaid balance of the total price and the paid-up sum (£1,500) does exceed the part of the total price referable to the transferred goods (£1,000) by £500. The part of the total price referable to the transferred goods is the part assigned to those goods by the agreement or (if no such assignment is made) the part determined by the court to be reasonable (s 133 (7)).

Notwithstanding the making of a *return order* or *transfer order*, the debtor may at any time before the goods enter the creditor's possession, claim the goods ordered to be returned to the creditor on payment of the balance of the total price and the fulfilment of any other necessary conditions (s 133 (4)).

The creditor's title to the goods will vest in the debtor when the total price is paid and any other necessary conditions are fulfilled, either in pursuance of a time order or under s 133 (s 133 (5)). If, in contravention of a return order or a transfer order, any goods to which the order relates are not returned to the creditor, the court may (on the creditor's application) revoke the order so far as it relates to those goods and order the debtor to pay the unpaid portion of so much of the total price as is referable to those goods (s 133 (6)).

Where the creditor brings an action or makes an application to enforce a right to recover possession of the goods and proves that a demand for delivery of the goods was made in the default notice or, after the right to recover the goods had accrued but before the action was begun or the application made, he made a request in writing to surrender the goods, then for the purposes of the claim of the creditor to recover possession, the possession of the goods by the debtor is deemed to be adverse to the creditor (s 134). This section assists the proof necessary for a claim for conversion.[13]

Whenever the court makes an order in relation to a regulated hire purchase agreement, it may make the operation of any term of the order conditional on the doing of specified acts by any party to the proceedings or suspend the operation of any term (s 135). The court may also by order amend any agreement or security (s 136).

6. *To give information.*—Section 80 of the Act provides that where a regulated agreement requires the debtor to keep goods to which the agreement relates in his possession or control, he shall, within 7 working days after he has received a request in writing to that effect from the creditor, tell the creditor where the goods are. Failure to comply, if the default continues for 14 days, is an offence.

ENTRY INTO A HIRE PURCHASE AGREEMENT

The whole of this section is based on the Consumer Credit Act 1974. At common law (still relevant for agreements not regulated by the Act) the law relating to the making of the agreement comprises simply the rules about offer and acceptance and revocation of offer in the general law of contract. At common law a hire purchase agreement does not have to be in writing (though it invariably is in practice), there are no special rules about the form of contents of the agreement and, once made, there is no right in either party to cancel it.

Preliminary matters

Disclosure.—Regulations may be made under the Act requiring specified information to be disclosed to the debtor before an agreement is made (s 55). Failure to comply with such regulations

---

13 The measure of damages for conversion was considered by the Court of Appeal in *Wickham Holdings Ltd v Brooke House Motors Ltd* [1967] 1 All ER 117, [1967] 1 WLR 295 to be the unpaid balance of the total price.

before the making of an agreement means that the agreement is not properly executed and, as shown more fully below, this means that it is enforceable only on an order of the court.

Withdrawal.—By s 57, the withdrawal of a party from a prospective agreement has the same results as if the agreement were made and then cancelled under s 69. As we shall see, whether there is a statutory right to cancel depends on where the agreement was signed and is given to one party only, the debtor, whereas of course either party can withdraw from a prospective agreement. Section 57 (2) provides that the giving to a party of a written or oral notice, however expressed, which indicates an intention to withdraw from the prospective agreement operates as a withdrawal from it. Where the post is used, service is deemed to be effected by properly addressing, prepaying and posting a letter and, unless the contrary is proved, to be effected at the time when the letter is delivered in the ordinary course of post.[14] For the purpose of receiving a notice of withdrawal from the debtor, a credit-broker who is the negotiator in 'antecedent negotiations'[15] and any person who, in the course of business, acts on behalf of the debtor in negotiations for the agreement, is deemed to be the agent of the creditor.

An agreement is void if it purports to bind a person to enter as a debtor into a prospective regulated agreement (s 59).

Making the agreement

Form and content.—Regulations as to the form and content of regulated agreements must be complied with. They are intended to ensure that the debtor is made aware of his rights and duties, the amount and rate of the total charge for credit, the protection and remedies available to him under the Act, and other matters it is considered by the Secretary of State desirable for him to know in connection with the agreement (s 60). The Director General of Fair Trading has certain powers to waive or vary any requirement of such regulations.

Signatures.—By s 61 (1) a regulated agreement is not properly executed and, therefore, not enforceable against the debtor except on an order of the court[16] unless,

14 Section 176, bringing into operation s 26 of the Interpretation Act 1889.
15 'Antecedent negotiations' are defined in s 56 and generally mean negotiations conducted by the dealer (credit-broker) in relation to goods to be sold by the dealer to the creditor and then to form the subject-matter of the hire purchase agreement.
16 Retaking of goods is an 'enforcement' of the agreement (s 65 (2)).

(a) a document (in the prescribed form) itself containing all the prescribed terms (and conforming to regulations) is signed (in the prescribed manner) both *by* the debtor (and *by or on behalf of* the creditor), and

(b) the document embodies all the terms of the agreement, other than implied terms, and

(c) the document is, when presented or sent to the debtor, in such a state that all its terms are readily legible.

The court will *not* make an enforcement order if the parts of s 61 (1) (a) unbracketed above are complied with but the remainder of s 61 may be condoned by the court (s 127 (3)). Certainly, the court will not make an enforcement order if the debtor signed blank forms which were to be filled in subsequently by the creditor or dealer.[17] If the debtor is a partnership or an unincorporated body of persons the requirement as to the signatures is that the agreement be signed *by or on behalf of* the debtor and *by or on behalf of* the creditor (s 61 (4)).

Copies.—Where an unexecuted agreement is presented personally to the debtor for his signature, but when he signs it the document does not become an executed agreement (because it has not yet been signed by or on behalf of the creditor), a copy of the unexecuted agreement and of any other document referred to in it must there and then be delivered to him. Similarly if an unexecuted agreement is sent to the debtor for his signature, a copy of it and of any other document referred to in it must be sent to him at the same time (ss 62).

If an unexecuted agreement is presented personally to the debtor for his signature and the document does become an executed agreement when he signs it (because it has already been signed by or on behalf of the creditor) a copy of the executed agreement, and of any other document referred to in it, must be there and then delivered to him (s 63 (1)). Unless s 63 (1) applies or the unexecuted agreement was sent to the debtor for his signature and, on his signing it, it became an executed agreement, then by s 63 (2) a copy of the executed agreement, and of any other document referred to in it, must be given to the debtor within the 7 days following the making of the agreement (typically, the posting of the signed

17 Contrast the common law as exemplified by the Court of Appeal's decision in *United Dominions Trust Ltd v Western* [1976] QB 513, [1975] 3 All ER 1017, p 154, ante.

acceptance of the debtor's offer). In the case of a cancellable agreement, a copy under s 63 (2) must be sent by post.

A regulated agreement is not properly executed and, therefore, not enforceable except on a court order, if the requirements of ss 62 and 63 are not observed (s 65). The court will not make an enforcement order *in the case of a cancellable agreement* if s 62 or s 63 are contravened unless a copy of the agreement and other documents were given to the debtor before proceedings commenced (s 127 (4)).

Notice of cancellation rights.—In the case of a cancellable agreement a notice in the prescribed form indicating the right of the debtor to cancel the agreement, how and when that right is exercisable and the name and address of a person to whom notice of cancellation may be given, must be included in every copy given to the debtor under ss 62 and 63 and if the agreement is complete on the debtor's signature, must *also* be sent by post to the debtor within 7 days following the making of the agreement (s 64). A cancellable agreement is not properly executed if the requirements of this section are not observed, and the court will not enforce it.

The debtor's right of cancellation

If the antecedent negotiations included oral representations made by the dealer or on his behalf when in the presence of the debtor (as distinct, for example from representations made over the telephone), the debtor enjoys a 'cooling-off' period ie, a statutory right to cancel a regulated hire purchase agreement (s 67). There is no such right, however, if the unexecuted agreement was signed by the debtor at premises at which the creditor or the dealer was carrying on business (whether on a permanent or temporary basis). Typically, the right to cancel will arise out of a doorstep transaction where the debtor signs at home but not where he signs at the dealer's shop. By s 68, where the right to cancel does arise, the debtor may serve notice of cancellation at any time between his signing the unexecuted agreement and the end of the fifth day following the day on which he received a copy of the executed agreement required by s 63 (2) or the notice of cancellation rights sent by post as required by s 64 (1) (b) (where the unexecuted agreement is presented personally or sent to the debtor and on his signature becomes an executed agreement). Alternatively, where s 64 (1) (b) does not apply, because regulations dispense with notice of rights, the debtor may serve notice of cancellation at any time between his signing the unexecuted agreement and the end of the fourteenth day following that signature.

A notice of cancellation does not have to be in any particular form and so long as it indicates the debtor's intention to withdraw from the agreement it operates to cancel the agreement (s 69). The notice must be served on the creditor, or on the person specified in the notice required to be given to the debtor under s 64 (1) or on a person such as the dealer (credit-broker) who conducted the antecedent negotiations or on any person who, in the course of business, acted on behalf of the debtor in any negotiations for the agreement or on any person who otherwise is the creditor's agent. A notice of cancellation sent by post is deemed to be served at the time of posting, irrespective of whether or not it is actually received (s 69 (7)).

Consequences of cancellation.—By s 69 (4) a cancelled agreement is generally treated as if it had never been entered into. Section 70 (1) provides that on cancellation any sum paid by the debtor under or in contemplation of the agreement (including any item in the total charge for credit) is repayable and any sum (including any item in the total charge for credit) which but for the cancellation is, or would or might become, payable by the debtor ceases to be so payable. If under the terms of the cancelled agreement the debtor is in possession of any goods, he has a lien on them for any sum payable to him under s 70 (1). Any sum repayable is, by virtue of s 70 (3), repayable by the person to whom it was originally paid. A deposit payable under a hire purchase agreement is often paid to a dealer (credit-broker) and on cancellation is, therefore, recoverable from the dealer. In the alternative, however, under the House of Lords decision in *Branwhite v Worcester Works Finance Ltd*[18] the debtor has a right to recover such deposit from the finance company who are deemed to have received it since the company will have paid the dealer the agreed sale price less the amount of the deposit. (The second part of s 70 (3) has no application to hire purchase as the finance company is both creditor and supplier.)

Where the total charge for credit includes an item in respect of a fee or commission charged by the dealer, the amount repayable under s 70 (1) in respect of that item is the excess over £1 of the fee or commission and if the total charge for credit includes any sum payable or paid to the dealer otherwise than in respect of a fee or commission, that sum is to be treated as if it were such.

18 [1969] 1 AC 552, [1968] 3 All ER 104, ante, p 175.

On cancellation the debtor must, subject to his lien for any sum repayable under s 70, restore any goods he has in his possession to the person from whom he acquired possession (s 72 (4)). Until the goods are so restored, the debtor must retain possession and take reasonable care of them. He is not under any duty to deliver the goods except at his own premises and in pursuance of a request in writing served on him either before or at the time when the goods are collected from those premises. Where the debtor receives such a request at any time during the period of 21 days following the cancellation, and unreasonably refuses or fails to comply with it, his duty to take reasonable care of the goods continues until he delivers or sends the goods back but, if within the 21 days, he does not receive such a request his duty to take reasonable care of the goods ceases at the end of that period. By s 72 (6) the debtor is discharged from any duty to retain the goods or deliver them to any person if he,

(a) delivers the goods (whether at his own premises or elsewhere) to any person on whom a notice of cancellation could have been served under s 69 (other than a person who in the course of business acted on behalf of the debtor in negotiations for the agreement), or
(b) sends the goods at his own expense to such a person.

His obligation to take care of the goods ceases if he delivers the goods as mentioned in (a) above and if he sends the goods as mentioned in (b) above he is under a duty to take reasonable care to see that they are received and not damaged in transit but in other respects his duty to take care of the goods ceases.

These provisions in s 72 do not apply to (a) perishable goods, or (b) goods which by their nature are consumed by use and which were so consumed before cancellation or (c) goods supplied to meet an emergency or (d) goods which had become incorporated in any land or thing not comprised in the cancelled agreement. However, in the case of (c) and (d) the effect of serving a notice of cancellation is that the debtor remains liable to pay the full cash price of the goods. This is because in these cases the only contractual obligations that are cancelled by service of the notice are those relating to the provision of credit or require the debtor to pay an item in the total charge for credit or subject the debtor to any obligation other than to pay for the supply of the goods (ss 69 (2) and 70 (8)).

Breach of a duty imposed by s 72 is actionable as a breach of statutory duty (s 72 (11)).

Sometimes when a hire purchase agreement is made the dealer

agrees to take goods in *part-exchange*. The definition of 'deposit' in the Consumer Credit Act s 189, includes a sum payable by the debtor which is to be or has been discharged by a transfer or delivery of goods. If this does happen and the agreement is then cancelled under s 69, unless the part-exchange goods are returned to the debtor before the end of 10 days beginning with the date of cancellation 'in a condition substantially or as good as' when they were delivered to the dealer, the debtor is entitled to recover from the dealer a sum equal to the part-exchange allowance (s 73 (2)). The debtor has a lien on the goods to which the cancelled agreement relates for delivery of the part-exchange goods or for the part-exchange allowance. The 'part-exchange allowance' is defined in s 73 (7) (b) as:—

> 'the sum agreed as such in the antecedent negotiations or, if no such agreement was arrived at, such sum as it would have been reasonable to allow in respect of the part-exchange goods if no notice of cancellation had been served.'

MATTERS ARISING DURING THE CURRENCY OF A HIRE PURCHASE AGREEMENT

We have already examined the principal obligations of the creditor and the debtor under a hire purchase agreement but there are a number of other matters that may arise during the currency of an agreement governed by the Consumer Credit Act 1974—(1) the creditor's duty to give information to the debtor; (2) the appropriation of payments; (3) the variation of agreements; (4) death of the debtor; (5) early payment by the debtor and (6) judicial control over extortionate agreements.

1. Creditor's duty to give information to the debtor

By s 77, if the creditor receives a request in writing from the debtor and payment of a fee of 50p, the creditor must within the prescribed period of 12 working days[19] give the debtor a copy of the executed agreement (if any) and of any other document referred to in it, together with a statement signed by or on behalf of the creditor of

(a) the total sum paid by the debtor;
(b) the total sum which has become payable but remains

19 Consumer Credit (Prescribed Periods for Giving Information) Regulations 1983 (SI 1983 No 1569).

unpaid, the various amounts comprised in that total sum, with the date when each became due; and

(c) the total sum which is to become payable under the agreement by the debtor, and the various amounts comprised in that total sum, with the date, or mode of determining the date, when each became due.

If the creditor fails to comply with this provision, he is not entitled to enforce the agreement while the default continues and, if the default continues for one month, he commits an offence.

2. Appropriation of payments

By s 81, if a debtor is liable to make payments in respect of two or more regulated agreements to the same person, he is entitled, on making any payment in respect of the agreements which is not sufficient to discharge the total amount then due under all the agreements, to appropriate the sum so paid by him to the sums due under any one of the agreements or to the sums due under any two or more of the agreements in such proportion as he thinks fit. If he fails to make such appropriation, the creditor's normal common law right to appropriate is excluded and the payment is automatically appropriated towards the sums due under the respective agreements in the proportions which these sums bear to one another.

Suppose a man has three different agreements with the same finance company in respect of, say, a refrigerator, a cooker, and a tape recorder, and while there is no payment now due on the refrigerator, £50 is due on the cooker and £30 on the tape recorder. If he sends a cheque for £40 to the company, he has a right to specify that it is a payment in respect of, say, the cooker. On the other hand, if he does not so specify, the finance company must appropriate the amount of the cheque thus: £25 to the cooker and £15 to the tape recorder. It may be that it is only by the application of this section that it can be discovered whether one-half or one-third of the hire purchase price has been paid on a particular article for the purposes of s 99 and s 90.

3. Variation of agreements

By s 82 where, under a power contained in a regulated agreement, the creditor varies the agreement (eg, the rate of interest payable), the variation does not take effect before notice of it is given to the debtor in the prescribed manner. If an agreement varies or supplements an earlier agreement the Act applies as if the later agreement revoked the earlier agreement(s) and contained provisions reproducing the combined effect of the later and earlier agreements and outstanding obligations remain outstanding. Even if the modifying agreements results in the credit exceeding £15,000, it is treated as a regulated agreement (s 82 (3)).

4. Death of the debtor

If a regulated agreement is fully secured, eg by a guarantor, the creditor is not entitled, by reason of the debtor's death—

(a) to terminate the agreement, or
(b) to demand earlier payment of any sum, or
(c) to recover possession of any goods, or
(d) to treat any right of the debtor as terminated, restricted or deferred, or
(e) to enforce any security (s 86).

If, however, the agreement is unsecured or only partly secured, the creditor is entitled, by reason of the debtor's death, to do any of these acts provided he obtains a court order to that effect. The court will make such an order only if the creditor proves he has been unable to satisfy himself that the present and future obligations of the debtor are likely to be discharged (s 128).

Section 86 applies in relation to the termination of an agreement only where (a) a period for its duration is specified in the agreement and (b) that period has not ended when the creditor purports to terminate the agreement, but it does apply even though, under the agreement, any party is entitled to terminate it before the end of the period so specified. Section 86 does not affect the operation of any agreement providing for payment of sums due under the agreement, or becoming due on the death of the debtor, out of the proceeds of a policy of life assurance on the debtor's life.

5. Early payment by the debtor

Section 94 of the Act provides that the debtor is entitled, at any time by notice to the creditor and payment to the creditor of all amounts payable under the agreement (less any rebate allowable under s 95), to discharge his indebtedness. The notice may embody the exercise of any option to purchase conferred on him by the agreement and deal with any other matter arising on the termination of the agreement.

Regulations[20] provide for the allowance of a rebate of charges for credit to the debtor where his indebtedness is discharged (s 95). This provision covers not only where the debtor completes payments ahead of time by virtue of s 94 but also where his indebtedness is discharged on refinancing, on breach of the agreement, or for any othe reason.

Section 97 (1) entitles the debtor (by request in writing) to a statement indicating the amount of the payment required to discharge his indebtedness under the agreement. A creditor who fails to comply with s 97 (1) is not entitled while the default continues to enforce the agreement and, if the default continues for one month, he commits an offence.

6. Judicial control over extortionate agreements

The Moneylenders Acts 1900–1927 (repealed by the Consumer Credit Act 1974) empowered the courts to reopen a moneylending transaction where the interest was excessive and the whole transaction 'harsh and unconscionable'. There was a presumption that the interest was excessive and the transaction harsh and unconscionable if the interest charged exceeded 48 per cent per annum. The Moneylenders Acts did not apply to hire purchase agreements.

Now the Consumer Credit Act ss 137–140, provides for judicial control over all credit bargains including all hire purchase agreements made between an individual and the creditor irrespective of the amount of credit provided (ie, even if it is not a regulated agreement) or whether it is an 'exempt agreement' or small agreement. If the court finds a credit bargain 'extortionate' it may reopen the agreement 'so as to do justice between the parties' (s 137 (1)). To see if the agreement is to be reopened the court will look at any ancillary agreement, eg, a maintenance contract, which is to be taken into account in computing the total charge for credit. A 'credit bargain' is defined as comprising the credit agreement *and* any other transactions which are to be taken into account in calculating the total charge for credit. By s 138 a credit bargain is extortionate if it

    (a) requires the debtor to make payments (whether unconditionally or on certain contingencies) which are grossly exorbitant, or

20 Consumer Credit (Rebate on Early Settlement) Regulations 1983 (SI 1983 No 1562).

(b) otherwise grossly contravenes ordinary principles of fair dealing.

Factors for the court to consider are:—

(a) interest rates prevailing at the time the bargain was made;
(b) the age, experience, business capacity and state of health of the debtor and the degree to which, at the time of making the bargain, he was under financial pressure, and the nature of that pressure;
(c) the degree of risk accepted by the creditor (having regard to the value of any security provided), the creditor's relationship to the debtor, and whether or not a colourable (ie inflated) cash price was quoted for any goods included in the bargain;
(d) any other relevant considerations.

A Deputy High Court judge has stated that the word 'extortionate' does not mean the same thing as 'harsh and unconscionable' under the Consumer Credit Act: 'the test is not whether the creditor has acted in a morally reprehensible manner, but whether one or other of the conditions of s 138 (1) is fulfilled'.[1]

The court may reopen an agreement on the ground that the credit bargain is extortionate on an application by the debtor or any surety to the High Court or county court, or at the instance of the debtor or any surety in any county court proceedings to enforce the agreement or security relating to it or at the instance of the debtor or a surety in other proceedings where the amount paid or payable under the credit agreement is relevant (s 139 (1)). In reopening the agreement the court's powers to relieve the debtor or a surety from payment of any sum in excess of that fairly due and reasonable are to make an order

(a) directing accounts to be taken;
(b) setting aside the whole or part of any obligation imposed on the debtor or a surety by the credit bargain or any related agreement;
(c) requiring the creditor to repay the whole or part of any sum paid by the debtor or a surety under the credit bargain or any related agreement whether paid to the creditor or any other person;
(d) directing the return to the surety of any property provided for the purpose of the security; or

---

1 Per Edward Nugee QC in *Davies v Direct Loans Ltd* [1986] 2 All ER 783, 789. See also *Coldunell Ltd v Gallan* [1986] QB 1184, [1986] 1 All ER 429, CA.

(e) alter the terms of the agreement or any security instrument
     (s 139 (2)).

If the debtor alleges a credit bargain is extortionate, the creditor
has the onus of proving the contrary (s 171 (7)).

SECURITY

Frequently a contract of indemnity or guarantee is entered into to
provide the creditor with some security for the carrying out of the
debtor's obligations. If an indemnity or guarantee is provided by
the debtor or at the debtor's request (express or implied) in relation
to an actual or prospective regulated hire purchase agreement it
comes within the definition of 'security' in s 189 of the Consumer
Credit Act 1974 and the provisions of Part VIII of the Act headed
'Security' apply. By s 105 such an agreement must be expressed in
writing and comply as to form and contents with Regulations made
under the Act. A security instrument is not properly executed unless
the Regulations are complied with, it is signed by or on behalf of the
surety, the document contains all the terms of the security (other
than implied terms) and a copy of the instrument is given to the
surety. If a security is not expressed in writing or is improperly
executed, it is enforceable on an order of the court only.

By s 111 (1), when a default notice (or a s 76 or s 98 notice) is
served on the debtor, a copy of the notice must be served by the
creditor on any surety and if the creditor fails to comply with
s 111 (1) the security is enforceable on an order of the court only.

By s 107, the creditor, within the period prescribed by Regulations, after receiving a request in writing from the surety and
payment of a fee of 50p, must give to the surety a copy of the
executed agreement (if any) and of any other document referred to
in it, a copy of the security instrument (if any) and a statement
signed by or on behalf of the creditor of:

   (i) the total sum paid under the agreement by the debtor;
  (ii) the total sum which has become payable under the
        agreement by the debtor but remains unpaid, and the
        various amounts comprised in that total sum with the date
        when each became due; and
 (iii) the total sum which is to become payable under the
        agreement by the debtor, and the various amounts
        comprised in that total sum, with the date, or mode of
        determining the date, when each becomes due.

If the creditor fails to comply with s 107, he is not entitled, while the default continues, to enforce the security and, if the default continues for one month, he commits an offence.

Section 110 (1) requires the creditor within the period prescribed by Regulations, after receiving a request in writing from the debtor and payment of a fee of 50p, to give the debtor a copy of any security instrument executed in relation to the agreement after the making of the agreement. If the creditor fails to comply with s 110 (1), he is not entitled, while the default continues, to enforce the security and, if the default continues for one month, he commits an offence.

The Act may not be evaded by use of a security—by s 113 (1), if a security is provided, it may not be enforced so as to benefit the creditor, directly or indirectly, to an extent greater than would be the case if the security were not provided, and any obligations of the debtor were carried out to the extent to which they would be enforced under the Act. Thus, if an agreement is enforceable only on a court order made under s 65 (1) because the agreement is improperly executed, any security provided is only enforceable where such an order has been made. Further, if an agreement is cancelled under s 69 or terminated under s 91, the security shall, so far as it is so provided, be treated as never having effect. However, if an indemnity or a guarantee is given in a case where the debtor is a minor, or is otherwise not of full capacity, the reference in s 113 (1) to the extent to which his obligations would be enforced shall be read as a reference to the extent to which they would be enforced if he were of full age and capacity.[2]

ADVERTISEMENTS

Advertisements defined very broadly in s 189, are regulated by Part IV of the Consumer Credit Act and Regulations made under the Act. By s 43, any advertisement published for the purposes of a business carried on by the advertiser indicating he is willing to enter into a hire purchase agreement is covered, provided the advertiser does carry on a consumer credit business. However, the advertisement is not affected by the Act if it indicates (a) that the credit must exceed £15,000 and that no security is required or the security is to consist of property other than land or (b) that the credit is available only to a body corporate. It was held in *Jenkins v Lombard North Central PLC*[3] that where a price sticker attached to a car on a

2 Section 113 as amended by the Minors' Contracts Act 1987 s 4.
3 [1984] 1 All ER 828, [1984] 1 WLR 307, DC.

dealer's premises gave the name and logo of a finance company, that was not sufficient to 'indicate' that the company was willing to provide credit. It was not, therefore, an 'advertisement' that must comply with the Consumer Credit (Advertisements) Regulations.

Regulations in force from 6 October 1980 provide for the form and content of advertisements and they must ensure that, having regard to its subject-matter and the amount of detail included in it, an advertisement conveys a fair and reasonably comprehensive indication of the nature of the credit facilities offered and their true cost (s 44).

If an advertisement conveys information which in a material respect is false or misleading the advertiser commits an offence and information stating or implying an intention on the advertiser's part which he has not got is false (s 46). Where an advertiser commits an offence against Regulations made under s 44 or against s 46, a like offence is committed by the publisher of the advertisement and any person who, in the course of business, devised the advertisement, and, when the advertiser did not procure publication, the person who did procure it (s 47). However, a publisher has a defence if he can prove he received the advertisement in the course of business and did not know and had no reason to suspect that publication would be an offence. Moreover, the advertiser himself has a defence under s 168 if he can prove that the commission of the offence was due to a mistake, or to reliance on information supplied to him, or to an act or omission of another person, or to an accident or some other cause beyond his control, provided that he took all reasonable precautions and exercised all due diligence to avoid the commission of such an offence by himself or any person under his control. The advertiser may not without leave of the court rely on a defence involving the allegation that the offence was due to an act or omission of another person or to reliance on information supplied by another person unless within seven days before the hearing he has served on the prosecution a notice giving such information identifying or assisting in the identification of that other person as was then in his possession.

CONSUMER CREDIT AGREEMENTS (OTHER THAN HIRE PURCHASE) AND CONSUMER HIRE AGREEMENTS

The Consumer Credit Act 1974 covers a much wider range of credit agreement than did the Hire-Purchase Act 1965, now repealed.

Like the Hire-Purchase Act 1965, it applies to conditional sales and, with some modifications, credit sale agreements. But it also governs moneylending transactions and pledges and the old legislation dealing with these transactions, the Moneylenders Acts 1900–1927 and the Pawnbrokers Acts 1872–1960, are also repealed. Further, the 1974 Act covers a wide range of other credit transactions such as check trading, credit card transactions, bank overdrafts, and other types of running account credits and also hire agreements. An agreement which falls partly within one definition in the Act and partly within another (or under two or more definitions at once) is a 'multiple agreement' (s 18). Parts falling under different definitions are treated as separate agreements. Where an agreement falls under two or more categories of agreement at once, it is treated as an agreement in each of the categories in question.

Many of the provisions of the 1974 Act examined above in relation to hire purchase apply with variations to these other types of credit transactions. Other provisions specially applicable to one or more of these other types of credit transactions have yet to be referred to. It is proposed now to refer to each principal type of consumer credit agreement other than hire purchase, and indicate the extent to which the Act applies to it. It will not be necessary to repeat in full provisions of the Act already examined.

(1) Conditional sale agreements

The Act defines a conditional sale agreement as

> 'an agreement for the sale of goods . . . under which the purchase price or part of it is payable by instalments, and the property in the goods . . . is to remain in the seller (notwithstanding that the buyer is to be in possession of the goods . . .) until such conditions as to the payment of instalments or otherwise as may be specified in the agreement are fulfilled' (s 189).

The licensing provisions set out in Part III of the Act apply to finance companies who make conditional sale agreements as they apply to companies making hire purchase agreements. Similarly, the licensing provisions in s 147 apply to dealers who negotiate conditional sale agreements.

The obligations of the seller (creditor) as to title, description, merchantability and fitness for purpose of the goods, implied in any contract of sale of goods by the Sale of Goods Act 1979, apply to conditional sales, as do the rules in the Unfair Contract Terms Act 1977 relating to exemption clauses. Section 14 of the Supply of Goods (Implied Terms) Act 1973 (as amended by the 1974 Act) specifies that s 11 (4) of the Sale of Goods Act 1979 shall not apply to conditional sale agreements that are consumer sales. It follows that a buyer under a conditional sale agreement which is a consumer sale[4] does not lose his right to reject the goods for breach of a condition (express or implied) of the contract merely because he has 'accepted' them, eg, by keeping them after he has had a reasonable opportunity to examine them without giving notice of rejection. However, by s 14 (2) of the 1973 Act (as amended by the 1974 Act) breach of a condition by the seller under such a conditional sale agreement is to be treated as a breach of warranty and not as grounds for rejecting the goods 'if (but only if) it would have fallen to be so treated had the condition been contained or implied in a corresponding hire purchase agreement . . .' The effect of this is that if the buyer *affirms* the contract, ie, he evinces an intention to go on with the agreement after he has become aware of the seller's breach of condition, such as by continuing to pay instalments, he is then limited to a claim in damages.[5]

A conditional sale agreement between an 'individual' (which term includes a partnership or other unincorporated body of persons not consisting entirely of bodies corporate) and a creditor by which the creditor provides the debtor with credit not exceeding £15,000 is a 'consumer credit agreement' under s 8 and, therefore, regulated by the Consumer Credit Act 1974 unless it is an 'exempt agreement'. By virtue of an Order made under s 16 of the Act, a conditional sale agreement under which the number of payments to be made by the debtor does not exceed four is an 'exempt' agreement.[6]

Regulated conditional sale agreements are treated by the Act in the same way as regulated hire purchase agreements. The debtor under a regulated conditional sale agreement has the same right to terminate the agreement under s 99 before the final payment is due as the debtor under a regulated hire purchase agreement.[7] However, by s 99 (4) although the debtor may terminate even after the property has passed to him, this does not apply if he has already sold the goods to another. Moreover, by s 99 (5), if the debtor does properly terminate after the property has passed to him, the

4   See p 111, ante.
5   See p 172, ante.
6   Consumer Credit (Exempt Agreements) (No 2) Order 1985 (SI 1985 No 757).
7   The related point has already been noted p 154, ante, that the buyer under a regulated conditional sale agreement is to be taken not to be a person who has bought or agreed to buy goods for the purposes of s 9 of the Factors Act 1889 and what is now s 25 (1) of the Sale of Goods Act 1979.

property at once revests in the previous owner. A regulated conditional sale agreement is subject to the same requirements as to default and s 76 and s 98 notices, the same restrictions on repossession once one-third of the total price has been paid and the special powers of the court. Also applicable are the provisions of the Act governing entry into agreements, the position of the dealer (credit-broker), the right of cancellation, the obligations of the creditor and debtor to give information, appropriation of payments, variation of agreements, death of the debtor, early payment by the debtor, extortionate agreements, security, and advertisements. These have all been examined fully above in relation to hire purchase.

(2) Credit sale agreements

A credit sale agreement means 'an agreement for the sale of goods, under which the purchase price or part of it is payable by instalments, but which is not a conditional sale agreement' (s 189). The property in the goods passes to the buyer immediately and clearly the agreement is fully subject to the Sale of Goods Act 1979.

The licensing provisions of the Consumer Credit Act 1974 apply to finance companies and dealers engaged in credit sale transactions. On the other hand clearly the buyer (debtor) has no right to terminate the agreement under s 99 of the Act and the restrictions on repossession under s 90 are inapplicable.

Apart from these matters, a credit sale agreement between an 'individual' and the creditor by which the creditor provides the debtor with credit not exceeding £15,000 is a 'consumer credit agreement' under s 8 and, therefore, regulated by the 1974 Act unless it is an 'exempt agreement',[8] or it is a 'small agreement', ie, an agreement for credit not exceeding £50 being an unsecured agreement or one secured by a guarantee or indemnity only (s 17).

Regulated credit sale agreements are governed by the provisions of the Act concerning default and s 76 and s 98 notices, the special powers of the court, entry into agreements, the position of the dealer (credit-broker), the right of cancellation, the obligations of the creditor and debtor to give information, appropriation of payments, variation of agreements, death of the debtor, early payment by the debtor, and security. Even 'small agreements' are covered by the statutory provisions concerning extortionate agreements and advertisements.

8 See p 153, ante.

(3) Consumer hire agreements

Until the Consumer Credit Act 1974 there was no legislative
protection for an individual who took goods on simple hire as
distinct from hire purchase. Obviously he had no right to become
the owner of the goods and because there were no restrictions on
harsh contractual terms and no right of cancellation, the hire
purchase legislation was sometimes evaded by couching an
agreement in the terms of simple hire. As Sachs J said in *Galbraith v
Mitchenall Estates Ltd*[9]:—

> 'It is becoming increasingly apparent . . . that there is a tendency on the
> part of some finance companies, at any rate, to try to ensure that the hirer
> does not have the protection of the Hire-Purchase Acts . . . The sooner
> the legislature is apprised of this tendency and the sooner it takes in hand
> the problem, the fewer will be the occasions when finance companies are
> able to inflict on an unwary hirer, hardships of the type which have
> become manifest in the present case.'

By the Consumer Credit Act, s 15, a consumer hire agreement is,

> 'an agreement made by a person with an individual (the 'hirer') for the
> bailment . . . of goods to the hirer, being an agreement which—
>   (a) is not a hire purchase agreement, and
>   (b) is capable of subsisting for more than 3 months, and
>   (c) does not require the hirer to make payments exceeding £15,000.'

A 'hirer' includes 'the person' (even a corporate body) 'to whom his
[the individual's] rights and duties . . . have passed by assignment
or operation of law' (s 189). A consumer hire agreement is
regulated by the Act if it is not an 'exempt' agreement under
s 16 (6) or a 'small' agreement under s 17. The Secretary of State
has made an Order[10] under s 16 (6) of the Act providing that the
Act should not regulate consumer hire agreements where,

> '(a) the owner is a body corporate authorised by or under any
>   enactment to supply electricity, gas or water; and the subject of
>   the agreement is a meter or metering equipment used or to be
>   used in connection with the supply of electricity, gas or water . . .'

or where the owner is a public telecommunications operator
specified in the order.

By s 17 a consumer hire agreement is a 'small' agreement where
the total amount to be paid by the hirer is incapable of exceeding
£50, being an agreement which is either unsecured or secured by a
guarantee to indemnity only.

9 [1965] 2 QB 473, [1964] 2 All ER 653.
10 Consumer Credit (Exempt Agreements) (No 2) Order 1985 (SI 1985 No 757)
and Telecommunications Act 1984 s 109.

Obligations of the parties.—The Supply of Goods and Services Act 1982 implies certain obligations in all contracts for the hire of goods (including consumer hire agreements) which parallel the obligations of sellers and creditors under the Sale of Goods Act 1979 and the Supply of Goods (Implied Terms) Act 1973. By s 7, there is an implied condition that the bailor has a right to transfer possession of the goods by way of hire for the period of the hire and an implied warranty of quiet possession. Section 8 implies a condition that the goods will correspond with the description of the goods if the goods are hired by description, whether or not they are hired by reference to a sample. Sections 9 and 10 imply conditions of merchantability and fitness for purpose and an implied term, where goods are hired by reference to sample, that the bulk shall correspond with the sample, similar to the terms implied by the Sale of Goods Act. Liability for breach of s 7 cannot be excluded or restricted nor can liability for breach of ss 8–10 as against a person dealing as a consumer. As against a person dealing other than as a consumer, liability for breach of ss 8–10 can only be limited in so far as the term satisfies the 'reasonableness' test of the Unfair Contract Terms Act 1977. The remedies of the hirer for breach of these obligations are as described above for the bailee under a hire purchase agreement.[11]

The hirer has a common law obligation to take reasonable care of the goods hired to him and, if the goods are damaged, the onus of proof is on the hirer to prove there was no fault on his part.[12] The hirer may also be liable in conversion if he does the same kinds of things as would render a debtor in a hire purchase agreement liable in such actions.[13]

Right to terminate.—The Consumer Credit Act introduces for the first time so far as regulated consumer hire agreements are concerned, a statutory right to terminate the agreement by notice in writing to any person entitled or authorised to receive the sums payable under the agreement (s 101). Termination does not affect any liability under the agreement which has already accrued and a notice to terminate cannot expire earlier than 18 months after the agreement was made. Apart from that provision the minimum period of notice (unless the agreement provides for a shorter period) is as follows:—

11 See ante, p 171.
12 *Joseph Travers Ltd v Cooper* [1915] 1 KB 73.
13 See ante, p 178.

(a) if the agreement provides for the making of payments by the hirer at equal intervals: the length of one interval or 3 months, whichever is less;
(b) if the agreement provides for the making of such payments at differing intervals: the length of the shortest interval or 3 months, whichever is less;
(c) in any other case: 3 months.

This statutory right to terminate does not apply to:—

(a) any agreement which provides for the making by the hirer of payments which in total (and without breach of the agreement) exceed £900 in any year; or
(b) any agreement where
    (i) goods are hired for the purposes of a business carried on by the hirer or the hirer holds himself out as requiring the goods for those purposes, and
    (ii) the goods are selected by the hirer and acquired by the owner for the purposes of the agreement at the request of the hirer from any person other than the owner's associate; or
(c) any agreement where the hirer requires or holds himself out as requiring, the goods for the purpose of hiring them to other persons in the course of a business carried on by him; or
(d) any agreement made by a person carrying on a consumer hire business specially exempted by the Director General of Fair Trading.

By s 103, if an individual serves on a trader a notice stating that he was the hirer under a regulated agreement described in the notice, that the trader was the owner, that he has discharged his indebtedness to the trader under the agreement, and that the agreement has ceased to have any operation and requiring the trader to give him a notice signed by or on behalf of the trader confirming that these statements are correct, the trader must, within the prescribed period, comply with the notice or serve a counter-notice that he disputes the correctness of the notice or has no knowledge of any indebtedness. If the trader disputes the correctness of the notice he must give particulars of the way in which he alleges it to be wrong.

If the owner fails to comply with this provision and the default continues for one month, he commits an offence.

Other statutory provisions.—The provisions of the 1974 Act relating to licensing, entry into agreements, the position of the dealer, the right of cancellation, appropriation of payments, variation of agreements and security all apply to consumer hire agreements. The provisions of s 86 apply to the death of a hirer as they do to the death of a debtor. Section 79 provides specially for the duty of the owner under a regulated consumer hire agreement, within the prescribed period after receiving a request in writing from the hirer and payment of a fee of 50p, to give the hirer a copy of the agreement and any other document referred to in it, together with a statement signed by or on behalf of the owner, of the total sum which has become payable but remains unpaid and the various amounts comprised in that total sum, with the date when each became due.

If the owner fails to comply with s 79 he is not entitled, while the default continues, to enforce the agreement and, if the default continues for one month, he commits an offence. If the agreement requires the hirer to keep goods in his possession or control, he must, within 7 working days of receiving a request in writing from the owner, tell the owner where the goods are. Failure to do this continuing for 14 days is an offence (s 80).

Even 'small' agreements are covered by the statutory provisions as to advertisements but s 43 (4) specifies that the provisions do not apply to an advertisement which indicates that the advertiser is not willing to enter into a *consumer* hire agreement.

Although consumer hire agreements are governed by the provisions of the Act concerning default notices, and s 76 and s 98 notices and the prohibition in s 92 on entering premises to recover possession of goods, the restrictions on repossession in hire purchase and conditional sale agreements when one-third of the total price has been paid are, of course, inapplicable—there is no total price in a hire agreement. The owner may repossess, eg, for failure to pay hire charges under a contractual term, entitling him to do so, at any time provided a default notice of s 76 notice has been served and has expired.

However, where the owner recovers possession of goods otherwise than by action, the hirer may apply to the court for an order that the whole or part of any sum paid by the hirer shall be repaid and the obligation to pay the whole or part of any sum owed by the hirer shall cease, if it appears to the court just to do so, 'having regard to the extent of the enjoyment of the goods by the hirer' (s 132). Similarly, if in proceedings relating to a regulated consumer hire agreement, the court makes an order for delivery to the owner of goods, the court may include in the order a like provision. After a default notice or s 76 or s 98 notice is served on him, the hirer may apply to the court and the court may make a time order (s 129). The court may also make a time order in any action brought by the creditor. Conditional or suspended orders may be made by the court but a suspended order may not extend the period for which the hirer is entitled to possession (s 135 (3)).

The statutory provisions relating to early payment by the debtor in a hire purchase or conditional sale agreement, and those relating to extortionate credit bargains have no application.

(4) Loan agreements for fixed-sum credit, other than hire purchase agreements

The Moneylenders Acts 1900–1927 regulated all loans made by moneylenders—they had to be licensed, restrictions were placed on advertising and circulars, forms of contract and interest charges, and 'harsh and unconscionable' transactions could be reopened by the court. But banks and companies exempted by the Department of Trade were not governed by the Moneylenders Acts.

The Moneylenders Acts were repealed by the Consumer Credit Act 1974. Section 9 (1) makes it clear that 'credit' includes a cash loan ('money in any form') and anyone who carries on a consumer credit business requires a licence. Any agreement by an 'individual' to take a loan not exceeding £15,000 is a regulated agreement under the Act whether he takes the loan from a bank or other lender of money, unless it is an 'exempt' agreement[14] or a 'small agreement', ie, an agreement for credit not exceeding £50 being an agreement which is either unsecured or secured by a guarantee or indemnity only (s 17). It is a *fixed-sum credit* if the loan is for a definite sum (whether taken in one amount or by instalments does not matter), say £2,000—eg, a bank loan for £2,000—as distinct from being allowed to debit an account for such sums as one chooses *up to* £2,000—eg, an overdraft arrangement—which is known as a *running-account credit* (s 10).

Suppose A wants to buy a car from B (supplier) and B introduces A to C (creditor) who then lends the purchase price to A. Provided that B and C had 'pre-existing arrangements' and the loan agreement can be taken to have been entered into 'in accordance with, or in furtherance of' such arrangements as laid down in s 187, the loan agreement is known as a debtor-creditor-supplier agreement under s 12 (c). It would also be known as a debtor-creditor-supplier agreement if the agreement provided for C to pay the loan direct to B (a 'restricted use' credit as defined in s 11 and made

14　See p 210, post.

under pre-existing arrangements or in contemplation of future arrangements between B and C: s 12 (b)). Arrangements are to be disregarded if they are for the electronic transfer of funds from a current account at a bank (Banking Act 1987 s 89).

The significance of an agreement being a debtor-creditor-supplier agreement is that, by s 75, if the debtor has a claim in damages against the supplier for misrepresentation or breach of contract (eg, breach of the obligations implied by the Sale of Goods Act), he 'shall have a like claim against the creditor, who, with the supplier, shall be jointly and severally liable to the debtor' for the damages. Subject to any agreement between them, the creditor is entitled to be indemnified by the supplier for loss suffered by the creditor in satisfying this liability including costs reasonably incurred by him in defending proceedings instituted by the debtor. Section 75 applies notwithstanding the debtor has exceeded the credit limit or has otherwise contravened any term of the agreement but does not apply in respect of any single item with a cash price or value not exceeding £100 or more than £30,000.[15]

In contrast to a debtor-creditor-supplier agreement is a debtor-creditor agreement where there are no arrangements between the creditor and any supplier. Section 75 has no application to a debtor-creditor agreement. Thus if C lends A £500, hands the money over to A and A uses it to buy hi-fi equipment from B, then if there are no arrangements between C and B there is no question of C being liable to A if, for example, the equipment is not of merchantable quality. The agreement between A and C is a debtor-creditor agreement and it would make no difference if C paid the amount of the loan direct to B so long as there were still no pre-existing arrangements between C and B and no contemplation of future arrangements between them.

The statutory provisions for default and s 76 or s 98 notices, entry into agreements, the position of the dealer, right of cancellation,[16]

15 Obviously if goods worth, say, £20,000 were bought with the loan, the debtor must have used some of his own money because the loan agreement is only a regulated consumer credit agreement under the Act if the loan does not exceed £15,000.

16 In the case of a debtor-creditor-supplier agreement, if a deposit has been paid to the supplier, the creditor and supplier are jointly and severally liable for repayment. By s 71, if the loan agreement is not a debtor-creditor-supplier agreement for restricted use credit (as defined in s 11), ie, it is a cash loan, the agreement continues in force after cancellation so far as it relates to repayment of credit and payment of interest. No interest is payable on the amount repaid if the debtor repays the whole or a portion of a credit before the expiry of one month following service of the notice of cancellation or, in the case of a credit repayable by instalments, before the date on which the first instalment is due.

the obligation of the creditor to give information, appropriation of payments, variation of agreements, death of the debtor, early payment by the debtor, and security apply as they do to hire purchase agreements.

Exempt agreements.—Exempt loan agreements for fixed sum credit are (i) debtor-creditor-supplier agreements where the credit is repayable in four instalments or less and (ii) debtor-creditor agreements where the annual percentage rate of charge for credit does not exceed 13 per cent or the London and Scottish Clearing Banks' base rates plus 1 per cent if this is higher.[17]

Even 'small' agreements are covered by the statutory provisions concerning pre-contract disclosure, extortionate agreements and advertisements.

(5) Loan agreements for running-account credit

Section 10 (1) of the Act defines a running-account credit as:—

'a facility under a personal credit agreement whereby the debtor is enabled to receive from time to time (whether in his own person or by another person) from the creditor or a third party cash, goods and services (or any of them) to an amount or value such that, taking into account payments made by or to the credit of the debtor, the credit limit (if any) is not at any time exceeded.'

Where the credit does not exceed £15,000 it is a regulated agreement under the Act unless it is a small agreement, ie, an agreement for credit not exceeding £50 being an agreement which is either unsecured or secured by a guarantee or indemnity only (s 17) or is an 'exempt' agreement under s 16.[18]

The phrase 'credit limit' in s 10 (1) is defined by s 10 (2). It means 'as respects any period, the maximum debit balance which, under the credit agreement, is allowed to stand on the account during that period, disregarding any term of the agreement allowing that maximum to be exceeded merely temporarily.' Running-account credit is taken not to exceed the £15,000 limit if either

(a) the credit limit does not exceed £15,000 or
(b) whether or not there is a credit limit, and if there is, notwithstanding that it exceeds £15,000, the debtor is not

17 Consumer Credit (Exempt Agreements) (No 2) Order 1985 (SI 1985 No 757).
18 See p 212, post.

enabled to draw at any one time an amount which exceeds £15,000 or the agreement provides that if the debit balance rises above a given amount (not exceeding £15,000) the rate of the total charge for credit increases or at the time the agreement is made it is probable, having regard to the terms and any other relevant consideration, that the debit balance will not at any time rise above £15,000 (s 10 (3)).

An example of an *unlimited* overdraft agreement which is nevertheless a regulated consumer credit agreement is given in Sch 2 of the Act (Example 6)—G Bank grants H (an individual) an unlimited overdraft with an increased rate of interest on so much of any debit balance as exceeds £2,000. The stipulation for increased interest above £2,000 brings the agreement within s 10 (3). An overdraft agreement will be implied if, eg, a bank in practice allows a current account to be overdrawn from time to time.

Many people have running-account credits with shops. Suppose retailer L agrees with M (an individual) to open an account in M's name and, in return for M's promise to pay a specified minimum amount each month into the account and to pay a monthly charge for credit, agrees to allow to be debited to the account, in respect of purchases made by M from L, such sums as will not increase the debit balance at any time beyond the credit limit, defined in the agreement as a given multiple of a specified minimum sum. Provided the credit limit is not over £15,000, this is a regulated agreement for running-account credit.

Special statutory provisions governing regulated agreements for running-account credit are ss 78 and 108 on the creditor's duty to give information. By s 78 (1), within the prescribed period of 12 days after receiving a request in writing from the debtor and payment of a fee of 50p, the creditor must give to the debtor a copy of the regulated agreement (if any) and any other document referred to in it, together with a statement signed by or on behalf of the creditor showing the state of the account, the amount (if any) currently payable by the debtor and the amounts and due dates of any payments which, if the debtor does not draw further on the account, will later become payable. Section 78 (4) provides that the creditor must give the debtor statements in prescribed form showing the state of the account at regular intervals of not more than 12 months and, where the agreement provides for the periodic making of payments by the debtor or the periodic charging to him of interest, statements must be given showing the state of the account at the end of any period during which there has been a movement in the account.

Section 108 requires a creditor under a regulated running-account credit in relation to which security is provided, within the prescribed period after receiving a request in writing to that effect from the surety and payment of a fee of 50p, to give to the surety a copy of the executed agreement (if any) and of any other document referred to in it, a copy of the security instrument (if any), and a statement signed by or on behalf of the creditor showing the state of the account, the amount (if any) currently payable under the agreement and the amounts due and due dates of any payments which, if the debtor does not draw further on the account, will later become payable under the agreement.

Section 76 which requires a creditor to serve on a debtor a 7 days' notice in order to enforce a term of a regulated agreement to demand earlier payment of any sum, or to recover possession of goods, or to treat any right conferred on the debtor as terminated, restricted or deferred, does not prevent a creditor 'from treating the right to draw on any credit as restricted or deferred and taking such steps as may be necessary to make the restriction or deferment effective' (s 76 (4)). Thus, a bank may stop honouring cheques on an overdrawn account without having to serve a 7 days' notice. Section 87 (2) contains a similar exception with regard to default notices and s 98 (4) contains a similar exception in respect of termination notices.

The statutory provisions concerning entry into agreements, right of cancellation, appropriation of payments, variation of agreements, death of the debtor, early payment by the debtor and security generally apply to running-account credit agreements. However, by s 74 an agreement enabling the debtor to overdraw on his current account is excluded from the provisions of Part V of the Act, ie, those provisions concerning entry into agreements and the right of cancellation—if the Director General of Fair Trading so determines, as he has done. The Banking Act 1979 s 38, amended s 74 of the Consumer Credit Act to the effect that the Director general of Fair Trading 'shall make a determination' excluding overdrafts from the provisions of Part V of the Consumer Credit Act 'unless he considers it would be against the public interest to do so'. It is, therefore, not normally necessary for an overdraft agreement to be in any particular form.

Exempt agreements.—Exempt agreements for running account credit are:—

(i) Debtor-creditor-supplier agreements where the credit provided in each period is repayable in one instalment. This is often referred to as normal trade credit such as is given when a customer can charge his purchases from a retailer and is given a bill each week, month or other period which the customer is required to settle in one amount. Also, if a charge card company (such as American Express) enables the card to be used in shops, restaurants, etc. and a monthly bill is sent which the customer is required to settle in one amount, the arrangement is exempt.

(ii) Debtor-creditor agreements where the annual percentage rate of charge for credit does not exceed 13 per cent or the London and Scottish Clearing Banks' base rates plus 1 per cent, whichever is the higher.[19]

(6) Credit-token agreements—Check trading and credit cards

Check trading and credit card arrangements are examples of loan agreements for fixed sum credit and running-account credit respectively but are also subject to a number of special provisions applicable to what s 14 (1) refers to as 'credit-token agreements'. A credit-token is,

> 'a card, check, voucher, coupon, stamp, form, booklet or other document or thing given to an individual by a person carrying on a consumer credit business, who undertakes—
> (a) that on production of it (whether or not some other action is required) he will supply cash, goods and services (or any of them) on credit, or
> (b) that where, on the production of it to a third party (whether or not any other action is also required), the third party supplies cash, goods and services (or any of them), he will pay the third party for them (whether or not deducting any discount or commission), in return for payment to him by the individual.'

A credit-token agreement is a regulated agreement for the provision of credit in connection with the use of a credit token (s 14 (2)). 'Use of an object to operate a machine provided by the person giving the object or a third party shall be treated as the production of the object to him (s 14 (4)).' So cards to operate cash dispensing machines are covered unless, say, the customer's account is debited at once and, therefore, no credit given.

19 The Consumer Credit (Exempt Agreements) Order 1980 (SI 1980 No 52).

A typical check trading arrangement is where on payment of, say, £1, S issues T (an individual) with a trading check under which T can spend up to £50 at any shop which has agreed, or in future agrees, to take S's trading checks. The trading check is clearly a credit-token under s 14 (1) (b). Since S and the various shops which will take S's trading checks will have made 'pre-existing arrangements' and S's agreement with T can be taken to have been entered into 'in accordance with, or in furtherance of' such arrangements as laid down in s 187, the agreement between S and T is known as a debtor-creditor-supplier agreement under s 12 (b). It would still be a debtor-creditor-supplier agreement even if further shops are added after the issue of the credit-token to T (s 11 (4)). The significance of an agreement being a debtor-creditor-supplier agreement is that, by s 75, if T has a claim in damages against the shop for misrepresentation or breach of contract, he has a like claim against S who, with the shop, are jointly and severally liable. Subject to any agreement between them, S is entitled to be indemnified by the shop for any loss suffered by S in satisfying this liability including costs incurred by S in defending proceedings instituted by T. Section 75 applies notwithstanding that T has exceeded the credit limit or otherwise contravened any term of the agreement but does not apply in respect of any single item with a cash price not exceeding £100 or more than £30,000.

Exactly the same points can be made about a typical credit card arrangement whereby S Bank issues T (an individual) with a credit card under which T can spend up to, say £500, at any shop or supplier of services which has agreed, or in future agrees, to accept S Bank's credit cards. S Bank pays the shop or supplier of services direct (normally after deducting a discount) and, in due course, T repays S Bank. Section 75 applies so that S Bank can be made liable by T in respect of any misrepresentation or breach of contract on the part of the shop or supplier of services.[20] However, there are differing legal views on whether the full protection of s 75 applies to credit card holders who first took out cards before 1 July 1977, when s 75 came into force. Access and Barclaycard take the view that the protection does not extend to such cardholders but announced in 1978 that they were willing voluntarily to accept liability for defective products and services, the liability being

---

20 A credit card scheme is exempt from the application of the Act if the cardholder is required to settle the bill *in full* at the end of each month (or other accountancy period) as with American Express. The card is then termed a 'charge' card rather than a credit card. See p 213, ante.

limited to the amount of the transaction debited to the cardholder's account.[1]

It has been decided that, where a cardholder uses his card to make payment for goods or services, and the card issuing company becomes insolvent before it has paid the supplier of the goods or services, the supplier has no direct claim against the cardholder.[2]

Section 51 makes it an offence to give anyone a credit-token if he has not asked for it. Unless the credit-token agreement is a small debtor-creditor-supplier agreement (ie, where the credit does not exceed £50), a request must be contained in a document signed by the person making the request.

It has been held that sending out a plastic card expressly providing for credit subject only to conditions printed thereon did constitute an offence under s 51.[3]

The statutory provisions as to entry into agreements and cancellation apply to regulated credit-token agreements but s 70 (5) allows recovery on cancellation of a sum payable for the issue of the credit-token only if the credit-token is returned. Section 66 provides that a debtor is not liable under a credit-token agreement for use made of the credit-token by anyone unless the debtor had previously accepted it or the use constituted an acceptance of it by him. He accepts a credit-token when it is signed, or a receipt for it is signed, or it is first used either by the debtor himself or by a person who, pursuant to the agreement, is authorised by him to use it.

Normally, by s 83, a debtor under a regulated consumer credit agreement is not liable to the creditor for any loss arising from use of the credit facility by another person not acting, or to be treated as acting, as the debtor's agent. But, by s 84, this does not prevent the debtor under a credit-token agreement from being made liable to the extent of £50 (or the credit limit if lower) for loss to the creditor from use of the credit-token by other persons during a period beginning when the credit-token ceases to be in the possession of any authorised person and ending when the credit-token is once more in the possession of an authorised person. Thus, a debtor's risk of loss from misuse, if he loses his credit card, is limited to £50. Moreover, he is not even liable up to £50 unless there are contained in the

---

1 See Annual Report of the Director General of Fair Trading 1978 p 31.
2 *Re Charge Card Services Ltd* [1987] Ch 150, [1986] 3 All ER 289. The card used was a charge card but Millett J indicated that the principle of his judgment applied to both charge cards and credit cards.
3 *Elliott v Director General of Fair Trading* [1980] 1 WLR 977.

credit-token agreement particulars of the name, address and telephone number of a person to whom notice of loss or theft is to be given and there is no liability for any use of the credit-token after the creditor has been given oral or written notice that it is lost or stolen, or is for any other reason liable to misuse.

A debtor may be liable fully for loss to the creditor from use of the credit-token by a person who acquired possession of it with the debtor's consent but, again, not in respect of any use of the credit-token after the creditor has been given written or oral notice that it is lost or stolen, or is for any other reason liable to misuse and not if the requisite particulars of the person to whom such notice should be given were not contained in the credit-token agreement.

Section 85 provides that whenever, in connection with a credit-token agreement, a credit-token (other than the first) is given to the debtor, the creditor must give him a copy of the executed agreement (if any) and of any other document referred to in it.

The statutory provisions for default and s 76 and s 98 notices apply save that the creditor may prohibit further use of a trading check or credit card without having to give 7 days' notice (s 76 (4), s 87 (2) and s 98 (4)).

Cheque cards.—A cheque card is different from a credit card. When a cheque card is given by a bank to a customer, the bank undertakes to honour cheques drawn by the customer up to, say, £50 whenever a payee takes the cheque in reliance on the cheque card, whether the customer has funds in his account or not. Since a customer is entitled to draw a cheque and use his cheque card even if there is no money in his current account, the agreement between the bank and the customer is a consumer credit agreement. The customer may use the cheque card any number of times and the agreement is an agreement for running-account credit under s 10. It seems probable that the debit balance will not at any time rise to £15,000 so it will be a regulated agreement but it is *not* a credit-token agreement under s 14 (1) (b) because payment by the bank to a retailer, who takes the customer's cheque in reliance on the cheque card, is payment of the cheque, not payment for the goods supplied by the retailer. The bank will have no obligations with regard to the quality of goods bought or otherwise in respect of any breaches by the retailer because the consumer credit agreement is not a debtor-creditor-supplier agreement—the bank and retailer are not treated as having made 'pre-existing arrangements' so long as the bank is willing to make payments of cheques 'to suppliers generally' (s 187 (3)).

(7) **Pledges**

Where an 'individual' receives a loan not exceeding £15,000 on the security of goods whose possession he hands over to the creditor, this is a pledge and a regulated consumer credit agreement. Any article which is the subject of a pledge is a 'pawn' by virtue of s 189 of the Act and 'pledge' means the pawnee's rights over the article taken in pawn. The 'pawnee' and 'pawnor' include any *person* (even an incorporated body) to whom the rights and duties of the original pawnee or pawnor, as the case may be, have passed by assignment or operation of law. The Pawnbrokers Acts 1872–1960 are repealed but a number of the provisions in the Consumer Credit Act 1974 ss 114–122, are modelled on the earlier statutory provisions.

When a person takes any article in pawn under a regulated agreement, he must at the time he receives the article give to the person from whom he receives it a 'pawn-receipt' in the prescribed form (s 114 (1)). It is an offence to take an article from an individual who is known to be, or appears to be, a minor. It is also an offence for a creditor to fail to observe the requirements of s 114 (1) or to fail to observe the requirements of ss 62–64 as to supplying copies of unexecuted and executed agreements or to fail to give notice of cancellation rights (s 115).[4]

Redemption.—A pawn is redeemable at any time within 6 months after it is taken and, subject to that, it is redeemable within the period fixed by the parties for the duration of the credit secured by the pledge, or such longer period as they may agree (s 116). If the pawn is not redeemed within the 'redemption period' it is nevertheless still redeemable until realised by the pawnee under s 121 except where the property in it passes to the pawnee under s 120 (1) (a). No special charge may be made for redemption of a pawn after the end of the redemption period, and charges in respect of safe-keeping may not be at a higher rate after the end of the redemption period than before. The pawnee must deliver the pawn to the bearer of the pawn-receipt on surrender of the pawn-receipt and payment of the amount owing, at any time when the pawn is redeemable (s 117 (1)). This provision does not apply if the pawnee knows or has reasonable cause to suspect that the bearer of the pawn-receipt is neither the owner of the pawn nor authorised by the owner to redeem it (s 117 (2)). The pawnee is not liable to anyone in tort for delivering the pawn where s 117 (1) applies, or refusing to

4 See ante, pp 190–191.

deliver it where the person demanding delivery does not comply with s 117 (1), or s 117 (1) does not apply, by reason of s 117 (2).

A person, not in possession of the pawn-receipt, who claims to be the owner of the pawn or to be otherwise entitled or authorised to redeem it, may do so at any time it is redeemable by tendering to the pawnee either (a) a statutory declaration in prescribed form or, (b) where the pawn is security for fixed-sum credit not exceeding £25 (or running-account credit not exceeding £25) and the pawnee agrees, a statement in writing in the prescribed form signed by the claimant (s 118). On compliance with either of these requirements, s 117 applies as if the declaration or statement were the pawn-receipt, and the pawn-receipt becomes inoperative for the purposes of s 117.

If any person who has taken a pawn under a regulated agreement refuses without reasonable cause to allow a pawn to be redeemed, he commits an offence. Failure to deliver may, in any case, amount to theft, but even if it does not, s 28 of the Theft Act 1968 allowing a court to make an order of restitution applies as if the pawnee had been convicted of theft (s 119).

By s 120—

'(1) If at the end of the redemption period the pawn has not been redeemed—
  (a) notwithstanding anything in section 113, the property in the pawn passes to the pawnee where the redemption period is six months and the pawn is security for fixed-sum credit not exceeding £30 or running-account credit on which the credit limit does not exceed £30, or
  (b) in any other case the pawn becomes realisable by the pawnee.
(2) Where the debtor or hirer is entitled to apply to the court for a time order under section 129, sub-section (1) shall apply with the substitution, for "at the end of the redemption period" or "after the expiry of five days following the end of the redemption period".'

Realisation.—Section 121 provides that when a pawn has become realisable the pawnee may sell it, after giving the pawnor (except in prescribed cases) not less than a prescribed period of 14 days notice of intention to sell, indicating in the notice the asking price and other prescribed particulars.[5] Within the prescribed period after the sale of 20 working days, the pawnee must give the pawnor certain information in writing as to the sale, its proceeds and expenses. If the net proceeds (sale price less expenses) are not less than the sum

5 Consumer Credit (Realisation of Pawn) Regulations 1983 (SI 1983 No 1568).

which would have been payable for its redemption, the debt is discharged and any surplus paid to the pawnor. Otherwise, the debt is treated as the amount by which the net proceeds of sale fall short of the sum which would have been payable for redemption.

Should the pawnor allege that the sale price is less than the true market value of the pawn, the pawnee must prove that reasonable care was used to ensure that the true market value was obtained. Similarly if the pawnor alleges the expenses were unreasonably high.

Other statutory provisions.—The loan for which a pawn is given as security may be a fixed-sum credit or a running-account credit. The statutory provisions relating to both these types of credit have been outlined above and apply as appropriate to pledges. No agreement secured by a pledge falls within the definition of a 'small agreement' in s 17.

Chapter 4

Negotiable instruments

MEANING OF NEGOTIABILITY

Choses in action

Common law.—When a person has the possession or actual enjoyment of something, he is said to have a *chose in possession*. If, however, he merely has the right to claim or demand something by action, as, for example, a debt that is owed to him, then he has a *chose in action*. At common law it was not possible for the holder of a chose in action (other than the Crown) to transfer or assign it so that the assignee could sue on it in his own name. The assignor might have granted the assignee a power of attorney permitting the assignee to sue the debtor in the name of the assignor, but the assignee could not compel the assignor to do this. Further, the debtor, the assignor and the assignee could all agree that the assignor's right be transferred to the assignee, and that would be effective by virtue of the doctrine of novation which allows for the substitution of a new agreement for an old one, provided all concerned are parties to the new agreement. Apart from these two possibilities, no effective assignment of a chose in action could be achieved at common law.

Equity.—The Court of Chancery was prepared to enforce an assignment of a chose in action without requiring the assignment to be in any particular form. It was prepared to enforce not only assignments of equitable choses in action, that is, choses in action of its own creation, such as a claim to a share in a trust fund or a legacy, but also assignments of legal choses in action, such as a debt arising from money lent or goods sold and not paid for. If the assignee of a legal chose in action wished to sue the debtor, the assignor had to be joined in the action, but if he refused to be joined as co-plaintiff he could be made co-defendant. However, the assignee only obtained such rights against the debtor as the assignor had, that is to say, he could not claim any greater rights than those enjoyed by the assignor. If, therefore, the debtor could have claimed any set-off or raised any other claim by way of defence against the assignor which had arisen before the debtor received notice of the assignment, the same defences could be raised against the assignee. The assignment, in other words, was *subject to equities*.

Statute.—By s 136 of the Law of Property Act 1925,[1] all debts and other choses in action are assignable in law, provided the assignment is absolute and not merely by way of charge, is in writing, and express notice in writing is given to the debtor. An effective assignment of a chose in action under this section enables the assignee to sue the debtor in his own name. The assignee, however, still cannot obtain a better title or obtain any better rights than the assignor; the assignment is *subject to equities*.

Negotiable instruments

The position today is that the assignment of a chose in action can be a legal assignment if the requirements of s 136 are complied with, or an equitable assignment which requires no formalities and can be effected orally or in writing or by handing over a document indicating the obligation assigned.[2] In either case, the assignee obtains no better rights than the assignor. Certain types of legal choses in action, however, were long regarded by merchants as being in a special category, with particular characteristics recognised by the custom of merchants, which custom was incorporated into the common law by way of the law merchant. These special types of choses in action, which became known as negotiable instruments, were transferable and the transferee able to sue in his own name at common law even before the Judicature Act. Moreover, negotiable instruments could be transferred easily by delivery (or by delivery and indorsement) without notice to the debtor, and, in certain circumstances, it was possible for a transferee to obtain a better title and better rights than the transferor. The latter possibility, the characteristic of 'negotiability', marks out the special distinguishing feature of a negotiable instrument. Those

1 Formerly s 25 (6) of the Judicature Act 1873.
2 An equitable assignment of an equitable chose in action must be in writing and signed by the assignor or his agent; s 53 of the Law of Property Act 1925.

types of choses in action which are treated by the custom of English merchants as having this characteristic may be accepted by the courts as being negotiable instruments.[3] With regard to the most important types of negotiable instruments, statute has recognised them as such, for example bank notes, bills of exchange (including cheques), promissory notes, bankers' drafts and dividend warrants.[4] References in this chapter to sections are, unless otherwise stated, to sections of the Bills of Exchange Act 1882.

A transferee of a negotiable instrument can obtain a good right and title to it even though the transferor had no title or a defective title to it, provided the instrument was in a negotiable state and the transferee took it in good faith, for value, and without any notice of defects of title. A bank note or a bill of exchange which is payable to 'bearer' can be transferred simply by delivery and is, therefore, in a negotiable state without the need for the transferor to indorse his signature. A bill of exchange, however, payable not to 'bearer' but to a specified person, ie, an 'order' bill of exchange, requires the indorsement of that person before it is in a negotiable state. Suppose a £5 note is stolen from C by X and handed to D in payment for goods sold by D to X. Because a bank note is a negotiable instrument, and is in a negotiable state without the need for any indorsement, D has a good right to retain the £5 note if he took it in good faith and without knowledge of the theft even though the transferor was a thief and had no title to the £5 note. If a cheque made payable to C is stolen by X before C has indorsed it, it is not in a negotiable state, because a cheque made payable to a specified person and not to bearer requires indorsement by the payee for it to be transferred, and if X hands it to D, D cannot claim to have a good

---

3 *Goodwin v Robarts* (1876) 1 App Cas 476; *Picker v London and County Banking Co* (1887) 18 QBD 515. Usage over a long period is not necessary, as shown by the use of *Bechuanaland Exploration Co v London Trading Bank* [1898] 2 QB 658, where bearer debentures were held to be negotiable on the basis of recent mercantile usage: see also *Edelstein v Schuler & Co* [1902] 2 KB 144.

4 'The obligation upon a negotiable instrument must be either the payment of money or the delivery of a security for money' (Jacobs *Bills of Exchange, etc* (4th edn, 1943) p 17). Inter alia, a share warrant is a negotiable instrument (*Webb, Hale & Co v Alexandria Water Co* (1905) 93 LT 339) and so is a scrip certificate giving the holder a right after payment of instalments due, either to a share warrant or a share certificate (*Rumball v Metropolitan Bank* (1877) 2 QBD 194). Circular notes and Treasury Bills are also negotiable instruments. Postal orders and money orders are not negotiable instruments and in fact are marked 'not negotiable' on their face. A so-called travellers' 'cheque' is not a bill of exchange because payment is made conditional on a counter-signature and on correspondence between the signature and the counter-signature, but it is probably a negotiable instrument: *Chitty on Contracts* (25th edn, 1983), para 2555.

title to it though he may well have given value and been in good faith and had no knowledge of the theft. It makes no difference whether X has forged C's indorsement or not.

BILLS OF EXCHANGE

Examples of use

(1) Let us assume that a company called A Adams Ltd in London has sold goods to the value of £1,000 to B Berens in Amsterdam, payment to be in sterling, and A Adams Ltd owes a debt of at least a similar amount to C Chinon in Paris. By using a bill of exchange, A Adams Ltd can obtain payment from B Berens and at the same time discharge at any rate £1,000 of its debt to C Chinon.

£1,000   London, 1 July 1988

Three months after date pay to C Chinon or order the sum of One thousand pounds, value received.

To B Berens,
    55 Kapstraat, Amsterdam.   A Adams Ltd

A Adams Ltd, the drawers of this bill of exchange, have directed B Berens (the drawee) to pay a sum of money to C Chinon (the payee) at a definite time in the future, and the bill will be delivered to the payee. Bills of exchange may alternatively be drawn payable to 'bearer' and may be made payable 'on demand' instead of at a fixed or determinable future time. B Berens is not in any way bound by the obligation contained in the bill unless and until he signifies his agreement to comply with it by *acceptance*, ie, by writing on its face 'Accepted' and signing his name, or by merely signing his name.[5] He is thereafter termed the 'acceptor' of the bill, and is primarily liable to pay the bill on the agreed date; A Adams Ltd, as the

5 See post, p 234. Section 53 (1) provides that 'a bill, of itself, does not operate as an assignment of funds in the hands of the drawee available for the payment thereof, and the drawee of a bill who does not accept as required by this Act is not liable on the instrument'. It follows that the holder of an unpaid cheque has no equitable claim on the drawee-banker: *Hopkinson v Forster* (1874) LR 19 Eq 74.

drawers, are sureties. The payee may retain the bill until it matures, ie, becomes due for payment, and then present it to the acceptor for payment. If he wishes, however, the payee may prefer to sell it and transfer his rights under the bill to D, by indorsing his signature on the back. If D does buy the bill, he is said to discount it. D may similarly indorse it to E and the bill can go through several hands before it is due for payment. If, say, F is the holder of the bill when the bill matures, F will then present it to the acceptor for payment. If, for any reason, B refuses to pay, the bill is said to have been dishonoured by non-payment, and B can be sued for the amount of the bill by F; alternatively, F can claim the amount of the bill from A, the drawers, or from any indorser. The drawer and indorsers are jointly and severally liable on it. Any indorser who is thereby required to pay the amount of the bill to the holder, can claim in his turn from the drawer or from a previous indorser. In other words, each person who signs the bill (whether as drawer or indorser) acts as surety for the acceptor as regards any subsequent party to the bill.[6]

(2) A bill of exchange may also be employed where a seller of goods wishes to receive prompt payment and the buyer wants, say, four months' credit; its use will satisfy both parties to the contract of sale. A Adams Ltd has sold goods to B Brown Ltd in the following example. B Brown Ltd, the drawees, will no doubt be willing to accept this bill of exchange because it gives them the four months' credit desired. The drawers have drawn the bill of exchange in favour of themselves as payees. A Adams Ltd will doubtless not wish to retain the bill and postpone obtaining payment for the goods sold for four months, but will instead 'discount' the bill, probably with a Bank, for say £290. The bank will thus have bought the bill and will be able to claim £300 from the acceptors when it falls due; the £10 difference between these two figures gives the bank interest at 10 per cent per annum.

---

6 By s 55 (1) the drawer engages that on due presentment, it shall be accepted and paid according to its tenor, and that if it be dishonoured he will compensate the holder or any indorser who is compelled to pay it, provided the requisite proceedings on dishonour be duly taken. This means that, provided a holder gives notice to the drawer of B's refusal to accept or pay the bill, the holder can make the drawer liable. (The drawer is precluded from denying to a holder in due course the existence of the payee and his then capacity to endorse). Similarly, by s 55 (2) an indorser of a bill engages that on due presentment it shall be accepted and paid according to its tenor, and that if it be dishonoured he will compensate the holder or a subsequent indorser who is compelled to pay it, providing that the requisite proceedings on dishonour (ie, notice) be duly taken.

£300   London, 7 July 1988

  Four months after date pay to our order the
  sum of three hundred pounds, value
  received.

To B Brown Ltd
3 High Street, Onechester.   A Adams Ltd

Bills of exchange are not very frequently used now except in foreign trade, but cheques, which are a form of bill of exchange, are, of course, of great importance as a method of financing both business and consumer transactions. Cheques are bills of exchange, but the drawee of a cheque is always a Bank and a cheque must be payable on demand (s 73).

Let us suppose that one John Dobbs has sold goods to Alan Anderson and sent him an invoice for the price, £200. Alan Anderson, who has an account at the Wessex Bank Ltd may pay this debt by drawing a cheque on his bankers (they are the drawees of the cheque) in favour of his creditor, John Dobbs (the payee). A cheque does not expressly indicate when it is payable but s 10 (1) of the Bills of Exchange Act provides that a bill is payable on demand when no time for payment is expressed. John Dobbs may present the cheque for payment at the Wessex Bank Ltd or have the amount collected for him by his own bank. Alternatively, he may, by indorsing his signature on the back of the cheque, transfer the cheque to another person just as can be done with any other bill.

                  Wessex Bank Ltd
                      5 November 1987

  Pay John Dobbs or order Two Hundred
  Pounds.   £200

                          Alan Anderson

Statutory definition

If the practical operation of a bill of exchange in the above examples has been understood, it will now be easier to understand the definition given in the Bills of Exchange Act 1882 s 3 (1):—

> 'A bill of exchange is an unconditional order in writing, addressed by one person to another, signed by the person giving it, requiring the person to whom it is addressed to pay on demand or at a fixed or determinable future time a sum certain in money to or to the order of a specified person, or to bearer.'

It is necessary to analyse this definition in some detail. Any instrument which does not comply fully with the definition cannot be a bill of exchange, but may operate as an assignment.[7] By s 3 (2),

> 'An instrument which does not comply with these conditions, or which orders any act to be done in addition to the payment of money is not a bill of exchange.'

1. *Unconditional order.*—An order to pay is not a bill of exchange if it is conditional on a certain event happening or a certain thing being done. For example, if the direction of the drawer is that £100 be paid so many days after the arrival of a certain ship at a certain port, that is a conditional instrument because the ship may never arrive. So too, if the direction of the drawer is to pay 'on the attached receipt being signed' the document is conditional and, therefore, not a bill of exchange.[8] On the other hand, where a document contained the words ' the receipt at the back hereof must be signed', it was held that these words were addressed to the payee not to the drawee, the order on the drawee was unconditional, and the document, therefore, a valid bill of exchange.[9]

By s 3 (3) an order to pay out of a particular fund is not unconditional, but an unqualified order to pay coupled with (a) an indication of a particular fund out of which the drawee is to re-imburse himself or a particular account to be debited or (b) a

---

7 A bill of exchange may be drawn in a 'set', ie, in duplicate or triplicate. Foreign bills are often drawn in a set; each part of the set is numbered and contains a reference to the other parts. The liability of the parties to such a bill is governed by s 71 of the Bills of Exchange Act.

8 *Bavins v London and South Western Bank* [1900] 1 QB 270.

9 *Nathan v Ogdens Ltd* (1905) 94 LT 126. Similarly, the words 'to be retained' on an instrument are addressed to the payee and do not make it a conditional instrument: *Roberts & Co v Marsh* [1915] 1 KB 42. The word 'drawee' is printed by mistake for 'payee' in the judgments of Buckley and Phillimore LJJ in this case.

statement of the transaction which gives rise to the bill, is unconditional. Thus, an order to 'pay £500 out of the proceeds of the sale of my house' is not a valid bill of exchange, but an order to 'pay £500', and an indication that having paid this sum the drawee should re-imburse himself from the proceeds of the sale of the house is a valid bill of exchange. The explanation is that in the latter case, the holder of the document is not dependent for payment on the existence of a particular fund or on a particular fund being sufficient to meet the order. A cheque drawn in the ordinary way: 'Pay C or order' £500 is a perfectly good cheque although there is an indication on the cheque that one particular account opened by the drawer rather than another be debited with the amount; it may, for example, be rubber stamped 'client account' or 'No 2 account'.

The direction on a bill of exchange must be imperative not precative. It makes no difference that the order is couched in polite terms but it must be an order. It has been held that a document phrased: 'Mr Nelson will much oblige Mr Webb by paying to J Ruff or order 20 guineas on his account' was a bill of exchange,[10] but a document phrased 'We hereby authorise you to pay on our account to the order of G £6,000' was held not to be a bill of exchange.[11]

A so-called travellers' 'cheque' is not a bill of exchange because payment is made conditional on the customer, who has signed it when it is first issued to him, also countersigning it.

2. *Writing.*—The Act provides that writing includes print (s 2).

3. *One person to another.*—Clearly there must be a drawee,[12] and the section implies that the drawer and drawee are different persons. The Act provides that 'person' includes a body of persons whether incorporated or not, so that a party to a bill of exchange may, for example, be a limited company, a local authority, an unincorporated club, or a partnership. The drawee must 'be named or otherwise indicated in a bill with reasonable certainty'.[13]

If the drawer and drawee are the same person, or if the drawee is

10 *Ruff v Webb* (1794) 1 Esp 130.
11 *Hamilton v Spottiswoode* (1849) 4 Exch 200.
12 If there is no drawee, anyone purporting to accept it is not liable as an acceptor of a bill of exchange, but he can be sued as the maker of a promissory note, p 287, post.
13 Section 6 (1). In *Gray v Milner* (1819) 8 Taunt 739, where no drawee was named but an address was given and the sole resident at that address signed the document as 'acceptor', the document was treated as a valid bill.

228 Negotiable instruments

a fictitious person or a person not having capacity to contract, the holder may, at his option, treat the instrument as a bill or as a promissory note thereby excusing himself from some of the duties of the holder of a bill (s 5 (2)). The commonest example is a banker's draft, where the drawer and the drawee are the same person because it is an order addressed by the bank to itself. A banker's draft is commonly used when a large sum of money has to be paid, for example, £50,000 on the purchase of a house, and the creditor (the vendor in this case) would be unwilling to take a cheque. The procedure is for the purchaser to obtain a draft from his bank for £50,000, the bank debiting its customer's account with the amount. The draft will be an order by the bank on itself in favour of the vendor for £50,000 and the signature written on it on the bank's behalf makes it a safer method of payment from the vendor's point of view than a cheque signed only by the purchaser.

A bill may be addressed to two or more drawees, but an order addressed to two drawees in the alternative, or two or more drawees in succession is not a bill of exchange (s 6 (2)). However, the drawer or any indorser may insert on the bill the name of someone to whom the holder may resort in case of need, ie, a 'referee in case of need'. If, then, the bill is dishonoured by the drawee failing to accept or pay the bill, provided the holder has the bill noted or protested,[14] he *may* present the bill to such referee for payment (s 15).

If the drawee of a bill refuses to 'accept' it, it is said to be dishonoured by non-acceptance, and by giving notice to the drawer and to any indorsers, the holder can claim the amount of the bill from any such prior parties. An unaccepted bill can be negotiated but, in practice, it is improbable that anyone would be willing to discount such a bill.

4. *Signed by the person giving it.*—The bill is of no effect, ie, inchoate, until the drawer signs it. 'Signature' is not defined in the Act. It has been suggested that the Act would seem to permit a mechanically produced signature and certainly a mark may be used if there is evidence that the person signing by mark habitually so signed.[15]

5. *On demand.*—Section 10 (1) provides that,

14 See p 261, post.
15 *Byles on Bills of Exchange* (25th edn by M Megrah and F R Ryder, 1983) pp 12–13.

'a bill is payable on demand—
  (a) which is expressed to be payable on demand, or at sight, or on presentation,[16] or
  (b) in which no time for payment is stated.'

A cheque contains no specific indication that it is payable on demand but is so payable by virtue of this subsection. By s 10 (2),

'Where a bill is accepted or indorsed when it is overdue, it shall, as regards the acceptor who so accepts or any indorser who so indorses it, be deemed a bill payable on demand.'

6. *At a fixed or determinable future time.*—By s 11,

'A bill is payable at a determinable future time within the meaning of this Act which is expressed to be payable—
  (1) at a fixed period after date or sight;[17]
  (2) on or at a fixed period after the occurrence of a specified event which is certain to happen, though the time of happening may be uncertain'.

Bills not payable on demand are often termed time bills.

An instrument expressed to be payable on a 'contingency' is not a bill, and the happening of the event does not cure the defect. Thus a bill payable on X's death is valid but an instrument payable on X's marriage cannot be a valid bill as X may never be married, and even if X does marry the instrument is still not a valid bill. An instrument payable at alternative times, one contingent and one certain, such as '3 months after sight or when X marries', is not a valid bill.[18] Nor is a document providing for payment 'on or before' a certain date or 'by' a certain date since the option to pay at an earlier date than the date specifically referred to creates an uncertainty in the time of payment.[19]

7. *A sum certain in money.*—The Act provides that the sum payable by a bill is a sum certain although it is required to be paid (a) with interest, (b) by stated instalments, (c) by stated instalments with a provision that upon default in payment of any instalment the whole

16 'At sight or on presentation' means when the bill is sighted by the drawee or presented to him for acceptance.
17 'Sight' here means when the drawee signifies his acceptance, or in the case of refusal, when the bill is 'noted' for non-acceptance (if it has to be noted or is in fact noted) or otherwise when the drawee refuses or fails to accept. For the meaning of 'noting', see p 261, post.
18 *Alexander v Thomas* (1851) 16 QB 333.
19 *Williamson v Rider* [1963] 1 QB 89, [1962] 2 All ER 268, followed reluctantly by the Court of Appeal in *Claydon v Bradley* [1987] 1 All ER 522, [1987] 1 WLR 521.

shall become due, or (d) according to an indicated rate of exchange or according to a rate of exchange to be ascertained as directed by the bill (s 9 (1)).

However, a direction to pay '£65 and all other sums which may be due' is uncertain.[20] So too if part of the sum agreed to be paid is not in fact, by the terms of the instrument, to be paid but is to be treated as a set-off.[1] Where the sum payable is expressed in both words and figures, should there be any discrepancy between the two, the sum denoted in words prevails (s 9 (2)). Where a bill is expressed to be payable with interest, unless the instrument provides otherwise, interest runs from the date of the bill and if the bill is undated from its issue (s 9 (3)). There is no prescribed rate of interest; the plaintiff may properly ask for a reasonable rate around or somewhere above bank rate.[2]

The amount of a bill may be expressed in any currency, but an order to pay money and do something else or an order to pay money or do something, is not a valid bill. It should be noted that by the Decimal Currency Act 1969, bills of exchange (or promissory notes) drawn in shillings or pence after 15 February 1971, are invalid, but any reference thereafter to an amount of money in shillings or pence shall be read as referring to the corresponding amount in the new currency.

8. *To or to the order of a specified person.*—The payee of any bill not payable to bearer must be named or otherwise indicated therein with reasonable certainty (s 7 (1)) and evidence is admissible to explain a *latent* ambiguity. If a bill is payable to a specified person and comes into the hands of someone else of the same name, the latter cannot obtain or pass title.[3]

It may be payable to two or more payees jointly, or payable in the alternative to one of two or more payees. A bill may also by payable to the holder of an office for the time being, eg, the Treasurer of the Fairfield Rugby Club. Since the payee of a bill not payable to bearer must be a 'specified person', if there is a direction on a cheque form to pay 'Wages' or pay 'Cash', it is not a valid cheque or bill. In *Cole v Milsome*,[4] H obtained from the defendant a document in the

20 *Smith v Nightingale* (1818) 2 Stark 375.
1 *Davies v Wilkinson* (1839) 10 Ad & El 98.
2 *Byles* p 382.
3 *Mead v Young* (1790) 4 Term Rep 28.
4 [1951] 1 All ER 311. See also *North and South Insurance Corpn v National Provincial Bank* [1936] 1 KB 328, [1935] All ER Rep 640. Both cases were approved by the Court of Appeal in *Orbit Mining and Trading Co Ltd v Westminster Bank Ltd* [1963] 1 QB 794, [1962] 3 All ER 565. See post, p 283.

form of a cheque for £137 10s 0d drawn by the defendant and payable to 'Cash or order'. H handed it to the plaintiff asking her to pay it into her bank account, and out of her bank account to pay various sums of money which he owed. This the plaintiff did but meanwhile the defendant instructed her bank not to pay the sum. It was held that the plaintiff, although a bone fide transferee, could not sue on the document as it was not a valid cheque since it had not been drawn in favour of a 'specified person' or 'to bearer'. The only effect of such a document is to operate as a mandate by the drawer to his bank to pay the sum named. Thus, unless the instrument is countermanded by the drawer, the bank may properly pay out on it and debit the drawer's account, but it is not a negotiable instrument.

A bill may be drawn payable to the drawer, as where someone wishes to take cash out of his bank account and draws a cheque for the amount 'pay self'. A bill may also be payable to the drawee, as where a bank has made a purchase of, say, shares, for its customer, and the customer, in order to repay the bank, draws a chque on his account 'pay yourselves'.

By s 8, such directions on a bill as 'pay C' or 'pay C or order' or 'pay to the order of C' all have the same meaning and amount to a direction to pay C or the person to whom the instrument is subsequently transferred. Therefore, as a cheque form reads 'Pay . . . or order', merely crossing out the words 'or order' does not render the cheque non-transferable. A bill or cheque is, however, not transferable if it is marked 'not transferable' or if it is made payable 'pay C only', since s 8 (1) provides that when a bill contains words prohibiting transfer, or indicating an intention that it should not be transferable, it is valid between the parties to it but is not negotiable. In consequence, if a bill drawn in favour of 'C only' is indorsed by C to D, D could not sue on the bill in his own name. Once a bill is made not transferable, that restriction cannot be altered. Further, a crossing 'not negotiable' 'on a bill other than a cheque has been held by the Court of Appeal to mean that the bill is not transferable at all.[5]

5 *Hibernian Bank Ltd v Gysin and Hanson* [1939] 1 KB 483, [1939] 1 All ER 166. This case is criticised by *Byles* (pp 81–82) because the words 'not negotiable' are employed in the Act for use only in connection with the crossing on a cheque. The bill here was not only crossed 'not negotiable' but was also made payable to the order of a specified person 'only'. The case could have been decided on the basis that the bill was drawn in favour of a payee 'only', without involving the question of the effect of the words 'not negotiable'. We will see that the words 'Not Negotiable' on the crossing of a *cheque* do not prevent the cheque being transferred but merely prevent it being transferred free from equities. See p 275, post.

A bill payable to a specified person needs to be indorsed by that person if he wishes to negotiate it to someone else.

9. *To bearer.*—By s 8 (3), 'a bill is payable to bearer which is expressed to be so payable, or on which the only or last indorsement is an indorsement in blank'. It follows that a bill may be drawn as payable to bearer at the outset but also, a bill originally drawn in favour of a specified person, ie, an order bill, may become payable to bearer by the payee or subsequent indorsee indorsing the bill 'in blank'. Suppose the bill is drawn in favour of C and when C transfers it, he simply puts his signature on the back without any additional words designating the indorsee, C's indorsement is an 'indorsement in blank', and what was originally an order bill has become a bill payable to bearer. Bearer bills do not require indorsement and can be transferred simply by delivery. In contrast to an indorsement in blank, a special indorsement does designate the indorsee, eg, 'pay D', signed 'C'. An order bill which has become a bearer bill by indorsement in blank can be converted back into an order bill by a holder writing above the indorser's signature a direction to pay the bill to or to the order of himself or some other person (s 34 (4)).

By s 7 (3), 'where the payee is a fictitious or non-existing person, the bill may be treated as payable to bearer'. As will be shown more fully later, when a holder of an order bill claims payment on it, his claim will normally fail if one of the indorsements on which his title rests is forged or unauthorised.[6] Any indorsements, however, on a bearer bill are superfluous since a bearer bill is transferable simply by delivery. In *Clutton v Attenborough & Son*[7] a clerk in the employ of the appellants, by fraudulently representing to his employers that work had been done on their account by one George Brett, persuaded them to draw cheques payable to 'George Brett' in payment for the pretended work. No person of that name was known to the appellants and no one of that name had in fact done any work for the appellants. The clerk, having obtained possession of the cheques, indorsed them in the name of 'George Brett' and negotiated them to the respondents who gave value for them in good faith. The cheques were paid to the respondents by the appellants' bankers, and this was an action by the appellants to recover the amount of the cheques as money paid under a mistake of

6 See p 247, post.
7 [1897] AC 90.

fact. The House of Lords held that as the payee was a 'non-existing person', the cheques could be treated as payable to bearer. Since bills payable to bearer do not require an indorsement to be negotiated, the respondents' title as holders of these cheques in no way depended on forged instruments—the indorsements could be ignored as superfluous. The respondents' title prevailed against the appellants, and the appellants' claim failed.

A contrasting case is *Vinden v Hughes*,[8] where a clerk filled up cheques payable to the order of various persons who were customers of the plaintiffs, which cheques the plaintiffs signed as drawers. The clerk then forged the indorsements and negotiated the cheques to the defendant who was in good faith and gave value. The payees of these cheques were actual customers of the plaintiffs so the cheques could hardly be said to be payable to 'non-existing persons'. The court held that s 7 (3) did not apply—these were order cheques and the defendant's title rested on forged indorsements. In consequence, the plaintiffs were entitled to recover the amounts of the cheques which the bankers had paid to the defendant.

In an earlier case, *Bank of England v Vagliano Bros*,[9] the House of Lords held that the payee is 'fictitious' within the meaning of this subsection, although the name is that of an existing person, if the name of the payee has been inserted by whoever has in fact signed the bill as drawer, by way of pretence, without any intention that the person named as payee should ever receive payment. Bills were made out by a clerk of the respondents, forging the signature of certain customers of his employers as drawers, in favour of other customers of his employers as payees. The respondents' signature as acceptors of these bills was obtained by the clerk, and he then, having forged the signatures of the payees, indorsed the bills to the Bank of England, and the Bank gave cash for them in good faith. The House of Lords held the bills could be treated as payable to bearer since the payees' name had been inserted on the bills without any intention on the part of the real drawer of the bills (the respondents' clerk) that they should obtain payment, and the payees' name was that of a 'fictitious' person. The Bank's title as holders of the bills did not, therefore, depend on a forged indorsement since the bills could be treated as bearer bills. Nor could the acceptors plead that the Bank's title depended on a forged drawer's signature because, by s 54, an acceptor is precluded from

8 [1905] 1 KB 795. See also *North and South Wales Bank Ltd v Macbeth* [1908] AC 137.
9 [1891] AC 107.

denying to a holder in due course the genuineness of the drawer's signature.[10] The Bank were therefore held entitled to debit the respondents' account with the amount of the bills.

Dating

A bill is not invalid by reason that it is not dated[11] nor by reason of being post-dated, ante-dated or dated on a Sunday (s 13). However, if a bill (or acceptance or indorsement on a bill) is dated, the date is deemed to be the true date. It may well cause inconvenience if a bill is not dated, eg, a bill expressed to be payable four weeks after date. Probably, it will be considered dated as of the time it was issued. The Act makes provision in such cases for a holder to insert the true date. If, in good faith and by mistake, he inserts the wrong date, and in every case where a wrong date is inserted and the bill comes into the hands of a holder in due course, the bill is payable as if the date inserted had been the true date (s 12).[10]

Acceptance

The drawee of a bill is under no liability unless he 'accepts' the bill, ie, he signifies his assent to the drawer's order, and no one other than the drawee can be liable as the acceptor of a bill. An acceptance must be written on the bill and signed by the drawee (his signature alone is sufficient) and it must not express that the drawee will perform his promise by any other means than the payment of money (s 17). A bill may be accepted before it has been signed by the drawer, or is otherwise incomplete, or when it is overdue and even after the drawee has previously refused to accept or pay it (s 18).[12] Acceptance may be either 'general', ie, where the drawee assents without qualifications to the drawer's order, or 'qualified', where the effect of the bill as drawn is expressly varied (s 19).[13] The

---

10 See p 244, post, for the definition of a 'holder in due course'.

11 Section 3 (4). By the same subsection, a bill is not invalid by reason that it does not specify the value given or that any value has been given or the place where the bill is drawn or payable.

12 'When a bill payable after sight is dishonoured by non-acceptance, and the drawee subsequently accepts it, the holder, in the absence of any different agreement, is entitled to have the bill accepted as of the date of first presentment to the drawee for acceptance' (s 18 (3)).

13 See post, p 255.

liability of an acceptor is to pay the bill according to the tenor of his acceptance (s 54).[14]

Capacity

The general law of contract applies and capacity to incur liability as a party to a bill is co-extensive with capacity to contract (s 22). By a proviso to s 22, a corporation cannot make itself liable as drawer, acceptor, or indorser of a bill unless it is competent to do so. A company incorporated for the purposes of trade does have implied authority to make itself liable as a party to a bill because such a power is clearly incidental to the performance of its objects. Moreover, if the directors of *any* company determine to have a bill signed on its behalf, a third party dealing with the company in good faith (eg, the payee of the bill) is able to make the company liable by virtue of the modification of the ultra vires principle embodied in s 35 of the Companies Act 1985.

A minor will never be liable on a bill even though he might have been liable on the transaction giving rise to it. For example, a minor cannot be made liable on a cheque drawn by him in payment for necessaries.[15] The age of majority was reduced from 21 to 18 by the Family Law Reform Act 1969.

If a bill is drawn or indorsed by a minor, the drawing or the indorsement is effective for all purposes except to make the minor liable. In consequence, the holder can proceed against any other party.[16] Suppose, for example, a cheque is drawn by A on his bank in favour of C who is a minor. C indorses the cheque to D in return for goods sold by D to C. A stops payment of the cheque. D has no right to sue C but C's indorsement was effective to transfer the title in the cheque to D so D has a right of action on the cheque against A. If a minor draws a cheque, his bank has the same right to debit his account on paying the holder as if the drawer were an adult.

14 By s 54 (2), the acceptor of a bill is precluded from denying to a holder in due course: '(a) the existence of the drawer, the genuineness of his signature, and his capacity and authority to draw the bill; (b) in the case of a bill payable to drawer's order, the then capacity of the drawer to indorse, but not the genuineness or validity of his indorsement; (c) in the case of a bill payable to the order of a third person the existence of the payee and his then capacity to indorse but not the genuineness or validity of his indorsement'.

15 *Re Soltykoff, ex p Margrett* [1891] 1 QB 413. It makes no difference that the bill signed by the minor is post-dated to a date after he attains his majority: *Hutley v Peacock* (1913) 30 TLR 42; *Coutts & Co v Browne-Lecky* [1947] KB 104, [1946] 2 All ER 207.

16 *Wauthier v Wilson* (1912) 28 TLR 239.

'Backing' a bill

By s 56 'where a person signs a bill otherwise than as drawer or acceptor, he thereby incurs the liabilities of an indorser to a holder in due course'.

Suppose that A sells goods to B Co Ltd, and it is arranged that A will draw a bill of exchange on B Co Ltd in favour of A, that B Co Ltd will accept it and, because A does not consider that the liability of the company itself is sufficient security, that one of the directors of the company should also sign the bill in his personal capacity. If the bill is drawn and signed by the various parties as arranged, the director's personal indorsement of the bill will render him liable to a holder in due course under s 56. The director is said to be a quasi-indorser of the bill and to have 'backed' it.

Agents and representatives

'No person is liable as drawer, indorser, or acceptor of a bill who has not signed it as such' (s 23). But if a person signs in a trade or assumed name he is liable as if he signed in his own name, and the signature of the name of a firm is equivalent to the signature by the person so signing of the names of all persons liable as partners in that firm. Of course the firm is only bound by such signature if the signer had express or implied authority.

By s 91 a person need not sign a bill by his own hand; it is sufficient if his signature is written on the bill by some other person acting by or under his authority. Thus, A may authorise S to sign a bill as A. In the case of a corporation it is sufficient if the instrument is sealed with the corporate seal instead of signed on the corporation's behalf, but this is not essential.[17]

17 By s 37 of the Companies Act 1985, a bill is deemed to have been made, accepted, or indorsed on behalf of a company if made, accepted, or indorsed in the name of or by and on behalf of or on account of the company by any person acting under its authority. By s 349 of the Companies Act, every company must have its name mentioned in legible characters on all bills purporting to be signed by or on behalf of the company. If this is not done, any officer of the company who signed or authorised the signing of the bill is personally liable to the holder unless the bill is duly paid by the company. However, in *Durham Fancy Goods Ltd v Michael Jackson (Fancy Goods) Ltd* [1968] 2 QB 839, [1968] 2 All ER 987, it was held that where the holders of a bill had prepared it with the name of the company as drawee incorrectly stated, they were estopped from enforcing the personal liability under this section of the director of the company who had signed the bill on behalf of the company without ensuring that the company's name was correctly written out. Abbreviation of a word, if generally acceptable, such as 'Co' for 'Company', is not a breach of this statutory provision: *Banque de l'Indochine et de Suez SA v Euroseas Group Finance Co Ltd* [1981] 3 All ER 198.

Where a person signs a bill but adds words to his signature, indicating that he signs for or on behalf of a principal, or in a representative capacity, he is not personally liable on the bill.[18] Nor is he personally liable if the words adjacent to the signature are printed with the company's name. By that signature, he adopts the printing on the cheque so that the cheque is deemed to be drawn on the company's account and the person signing it is not personally liable.[19] However, merely adding to his signature words which *describe* him as an agent, does not exempt him from personal liability on the bill (s 26 (1)). Thus, a cheque signed 'A V Jones, director' renders A V Jones personally liable; a cheque, however, signed 'A V Jones, director, C A Smith & Sons Ltd', or 'C A Smith & Sons Ltd, per pro A V Jones' would exempt A V Jones from personal liability. In *Rolfe Lubell & Co v Keith*,[20] it was held that where there was an ambiguity as to the capacity in which an indorser had signed, it could be resolved by evidence that the indorser had agreed to sign in his personal capacity.

Section 26 (2) provides that 'in determining whether a signature on a bill is that of the principal or that of the agent by whose hand it is written, the construction most favourable to the validity of the instrument shall be adopted'. In *Elliott v Bax-Ironside*,[1] a bill was addressed to the Fashions Fair Exhibition, Ltd and accepted thus: 'Accepted payable at the Westminister Bank Ltd, Piccadilly Branch, H O Bax-Ironside, Ronald A Mason, directors, Fashions Fair Exhibition Ltd'. The same two directors of the company also signed the bill on the back: 'Fashions Fair Exhibition Ltd, H O Bax-Ironside, Ronald A Mason, directors', the name of the company being inserted, in the case of the indorsement on the back of the bill, by means of a rubber stamp, and in the case of the acceptance, in writing. The payee sued the directors in their personal capacity as indorsers of the bill and the Court of Appeal held that they were personally liable. If the indorsement were treated as that of the company, it gave no greater validity to the bill than was already contained in the acceptance, and under s 26 (2) the construction most favourable to the validity of the instrument meant in this context that the indorsement represented the directors' personal liability.

18 He would be liable to the holder for breach of warranty of authority if he had no authority to sign: *Polhill v Walter* (1832) 3 B & Ad 114.
19 *Bondina Ltd v Rollaway Shower Blinds Ltd* [1986] 1 All ER 564, [1986] 1 WLR 517, CA.
20 [1979] 1 All ER 860.
1 [1925] 2 KB 301, [1925] All ER Rep 209.

The question then arises, if someone does sign a bill in a representative capacity, are the principals, on whose behalf he purports to sign, liable? By s 25:

'A signature by procuration operates as notice that the agent has but a limited authority to sign, and the principal is only bound by such signature if the agent in so signing was acting within the actual limits of his authority.'

In *Morison v Kemp*,[2] a manager was authorised by his employers who were insurance brokers to draw cheques 'per pro' for the purposes of his employers' business. The manager drew cheques 'per pro' his employers in favour of a bookmaker to pay off his private betting losses and the bookmaker cashed the cheques. It was held that the employers were entitled to recover the amount of the cheques from the bookmaker as the bookmaker must be taken to have had notice that the cheques were signed for purposes outside the employers' business. Section 25 gives the principal a defence where his agent has exceeded his authority even against a holder in due course.[3]

In the case of a limited company, assuming it has capacity to bind itself by a bill and may under its Articles authorise its managing director to sign on its behalf, it would seem that if a managing director signs a bill per pro the company, since it is within the usual authority of a managing director, unlike a manager, to sign bills on behalf of the company, the company will be liable to anyone taking the bill unless that person has knowledge of any lack of authority or the circumstances are such as to put him on enquiry.[4]

Mistake

No claim can be made against a party who has signed a bill under a mistake that it is a radically different document in effect from what it really is, if such mistake was induced by a misrepresentation and provided the signer was not negligent. In *Foster v Mackinnon*,[5] the defendant, 'a gentleman advanced in life', signed a bill as an indorser mistakenly believing that he was signing a guarantee, the

2 (1912) 29 TLR 70.

3 See *Morison v London County and Westminster Bank* [1914] 3 KB 356, [1914–15] All ER Rep 853. However, if a bank collects payment of a cheque indorsed by A 'per pro P' without P's authority, it is entitled to protection from an action in conversion by s 4 of the Cheques Act 1957 assuming that the bank has not been negligent.

4 *Dey v Pullinger Engineering Co* [1921] 1 KB 77, [1920] All ER Rep 591.

5 (1869) LR 4 CP 704, affirmed by the House of Lords in *Saunders v Anglia Building Society* [1971] AC 1004, [1970] 3 All ER 961.

mistake arising from a fraudulent representation by the acceptor of the bill as to the nature of the document. It was held that as the defendant had not been guilty of any negligence in signing he was not liable on the instrument; it was not his deed: non est factum. Such signature by way of indorsement is ineffective for all purposes so that no one can claim to be holder through such indorsement. It will be difficult for an adult literate person to succeed in the defence of non est factum.

Stamping

Stamp duty on bills of exchange (and promissory notes) was abolished by the Finance Act 1970 s 32.

NEGOTIATION OF A BILL

How a bill is negotiated

By s 31, a bill is negotiated when it is transferred from one person to another in such a manner as to constitute the transferee the holder. As we have seen, in the case of a bearer bill this is done by simple delivery, and in the case of an order bill it is done by indorsement and delivery. It follows, and s 2 makes it explicit, that the holder of a bearer bill is the person in possession of it, and in the case of an order bill, the holder is the person in possession of it if he is either the payee or an indorsee.

An indorsement, in order to operate as a negotiation of a bill, must be written on the bill itself (normally it is put on the back) and be signed by the indorser, the simple signature of the indorser alone being sufficient,[6] but it must be an indorsement of the entire bill (s 32). A slip of paper may be attached to the bill—an allonge—if there is no further space on the bill itself.[7] As a rule, as has been said,

6 '. . . an indorsement on a bill of exchange may be by writing in pencil' per Abbott CJ in *Geary v Physic* (1826) 5 B & C 234, and a mistake by the indorser in his signature does not prevent the indorsement being effective.

7 Where a bill purports to be indorsed conditionally, eg, 'Pay D on his obtaining his degree', the payer *may* disregard the condition and pay D irrespective of whether the condition has been fulfilled or not (s 33). A 'restrictive indorsement', is one where further negotiation is prohibited, eg, 'Pay D only', in which case further negotiation is indeed prohibited, or one where the negotiation is mere authority to deal with the bill as thereby directed, eg, where C indorses a bill 'Pay D or order for collection' in which case while D or someone to whom it is subsequently indorsed can enforce payment from the acceptor or other persons liable on the bill, such sum is then held on C's behalf (s 35).

the indorser's signature renders him liable as a surety on the bill. However, any indorser (or drawer) may negative or limit this liability, eg, by adding to his signature the words 'sans recours' (s 16). Further, where a person has to indorse a bill in a representative capacity, eg, as a personal representative or trustee in bankruptcy, he may negative personal liability (s 31 (5)) and/or negative liability on the part of the estate (as allowed by s 16).

The holder of a bill

From the preceding paragraph it is clear that the 'holder' of a bill need not necessarily be the person rightfully entitled to it. If a thief steals a bearer bill, being now the person in possession of it, he is undoubtedly the 'holder' of it. Of coure, he has no rightful title to it and cannot sue on it, but by delivering it to D who takes it in good faith and for value, D will obtain a good title to it though the thief did not have a good title (s 38 (3) (a)). If D is not in good faith then like a thief he has no title to the bill; he is a 'holder' and the bill has been 'negotiated' to him but he is not the rightful owner, and cannot sue on it. The reason, as will be developed shortly, is that where there is a 'defect' on the bill (eg, it has been stolen, or taken by fraud or undue influence) no one can sue on it unless he has taken it in good faith and has no knowledge of the 'defect'.

Holder for value: consideration

Where there is no 'defect' on the bill, a holder can always claim on it if he is simply a holder for value and by virtue of s 30 (1), every party whose signature appears on a bill is prima facie deemed to have become a party thereto for value. Section 27 provides:—

(1) Valuable consideration for a bill may be constituted by—
   (a) Any consideration sufficient to support a simple contract;
   (b) An antecedent debt or liability. Such a debt or liability is deemed valuable consideration whether the bill is payable on demand or at a future time.
(2) Where value has at any time been given for a bill the holder is deemed to be a holder for value as regards the acceptor and all parties to the bill who become parties prior to such time.

The recent case of *Polloway Ltd v Abdullah*[8] involved the common

---

8 [1974] 2 All ER 381, [1974] 1 WLR 493, CA. Alternatively, the Court of Appeal thought there was consideration in the auctioneer taking the cheque in place of legal tender.

situation of an auction sale and the purchaser being required as a condition of the sale to pay 10 per cent of the purchase price of the property to the auctioneers as agents for the vendor. The purchaser drew a cheque as such a deposit in favour of the auctioneers as payees and subsequently stopped payment of the cheque. The vendors treated this conduct as a repudiation of the contract of sale and resold the property. The Court of Appeal held the auctioneers entitled to judgment against the drawer of the cheque on the basis that they had provided consideration for it. The consideration was their warranty that they had the vendor's authority to sign a memorandum of the sale on the vendors' behalf and to receive the cheque in diminution of the drawer's obligation to pay the full purchase price for the property.

It will be noted from s 27 (1) that, as regards bills of exchange, 'past' consideration is good consideration. Suppose C sell goods to A for £10 and subsequently A signs a cheque in C's favour for £10 in consideration of the goods he has already acquired, the consideration for the cheque is an 'antecedent debt' and, under s 27 (1), C is a holder for value of the cheque. In that example, C, the payee of the cheque, is A's creditor but consider the case of *Oliver v Davis and Woodcock*. [9] D owed money to O and W then drew a cheque in favour of O in order to pay off D's debt. W later stopped her cheque and it was *held* by the Court of Appeal that O was not a holder for value of W's cheque—O was not W's creditor, ie, there was no 'antecedent debt' owing from W to O, and there was no evidence that in taking the cheque O had given consideration by agreeing with W not to enforce his right against D.

Section 27 (2) is of assistance to the holder *either* (a) where he has not himself given value for a bill to anyone, *or* (b) where he has given value only to someone who is not a party to the bill. Thus,

(a) Suppose the holder of a bill obtained it as a gift but value was given for the bill by the payee or by some other previous holder—the holder may sue the acceptor or anyone who became a party prior to the time when value was last given. Therefore, if P signs a cheque in favour of Q for the price of goods sold by Q to P, and Q indorses the cheque to R as a gift, R may not sue Q on the cheque, but he may sue P—R is a holder for value to that extent under s 27 (2).

(b) The case of *Diamond v Graham* [10] is an example of this point. D

9 [1949] 2 KB 727, [1949] 2 All ER 353, CA.
10 [1968] 2 All ER 909, [1968] 1 WLR 1061, CA.

agreed to draw a cheque in favour of H for £1,650 as a loan provided that G made out a cheque in favour of S for £1,665. Until G's cheque was in D's possession, D did not release the stop he had put on his cheque in favour of H. G's cheque was dishonoured and D sued G upon it. The Court of Appeal *held* that there was nothing in s 27 (2) that required that value should have been given directly by the holder (D in this case) to another party to the bill (in this case, G) as long as value had been given. D had given consideration for G's cheque when he released his own cheque in favour of H and was, therefore, entitled to succeed in his action against G who had become a party to the cheque prior to the time that D gave that consideration for it.[11]

If a person becomes a party to a bill gratuitously in order to lend the value of his name to another, eg, to enable that other to raise money on the bill, he is termed an 'accommodation party' and s 28 provides that he is liable on the bill to a holder for value and it is immaterial whether when such holder took the bill he knew such party to be an accommodation party or not. If the person who becomes a party to a bill gratuitously signs as acceptor, the bill is termed an 'accommodation bill'. Let us take as an example, A wanting to borrow about £970 for six months and unable to do so, at any rate on reasonable terms. B, an eminently creditworthy person, though not prepared himself to lend A the money is willing to lend A the value of his name. A may draw a bill on B for, say, £1,000 in favour of himself and payable six months hence. B is willing to accept the bill and with B's signature as acceptor on it, A is readily able to discount the bill with a bank at a low rate of interest. The bank will give A, say, £970 on the bill. When the bill is due for payment, A will pay the amount of the bill to the bank or put B in funds to enable him to do so. The risk on B of having become an 'accommodation party' is that he is liable to pay the holder for value on maturity of the bill irrespective of whether A puts him in funds.

By s 27 (3), where the holder of a bill has a lien on it, he is deemed to be a holder for value to the extent of the lien. If, therefore, A draws a bill for £100 on B in favour of himself and B accepts gratuitously (ie, B is an accommodation party), should A indorse the bill and hand it to C as a security for a loan of £75, C has a lien on the bill and is deemed to be a holder for value to the extent of

11 By contrast, in *Oliver v Davis and Woodcock*, O gave no consideration to anyone *after* W signed the cheque in O's favour. It would have been different if, after W signed the cheque, O had agreed to forbear from claiming his debt from D.

£75. He can sue A or B on the bill for that amount. So too, if the payee of a cheque for £100 asks his bank to collect payment of the cheque for him and he happens to have an overdraft at the bank standing at £50, the bank is a holder for value of the cheque to the extent of £50.[12] The bank will be a holder for value to the full amount of a cheque it is asked to collect if that amount is less than the payee's overdraft.[13]

Holder in due course

As we have seen, where there is no 'defect' on the bill, the holder can claim on it simply by being a holder for value within s 27. That is not, however, sufficient if there is a 'defect' on the bill. Then, it is necessary for the holder to show he is a 'holder in due course' within s 29 or has taken the bill directly or indirectly through a holder in due course by virtue of s 29 (3). Let us suppose that a bill drawn in favour of C has been negotiated by C to D as a result of fraud or misrepresentation or duress or undue influence on D's part, or for an illegal consideration; there is a 'defect' on the bill. Let us then suppose D negotiated it for value to E. E will undoubtedly be a holder for value but because there is a 'defect' on the bill, E can only take the bill free from the defect in the title of D and successfully sue on the bill if he is a holder in due course, which means, inter alia, taking it without notice of any defect in the title of D. If it is established that E is a holder in due course, then the defect is said to be 'cured'; E can sue the various parties to the bill.[14] Further, if E subsequently negotiated the bill to F (whether for value or not) then even though F himself may not be a holder in due course because, say, he has notice of the defect in the title of D, provided F was not a party to any fraud or illegality effecting the bill, he has all the rights of a holder in due course as regards the acceptor and all parties to the bill prior to the holder in due course (s 29 (3)).

The Court of Appeal held in *Jade International Steel, Stahl and Eisen GmbH & Co KG v Robert Nicholas (Steels) Ltd,*[15] that where the

12 *M'Lean v Clydesdale Banking Co* (1883) 9 App Cas 95. See also *Midland Bank Ltd v R V Harris Ltd* [1963] 2 All ER 685, [1963] 1 WLR 1021 and *Re Keever (a Bankrupt) ex p Trustee of Property of Bankrupt v Midland Bank* [1967] Ch 182, [1966] 3 All ER 631, post, p 285.

13 *Barclays Bank v Astley Industrial Trust Ltd* [1970] 2 QB 527, [1979] 1 All ER 719.

14 Section 38 (2) provides that a holder in due course holds the bill free from any defect of title of prior parties as well as free from mere personal defences available to prior parties among themselves and may enforce payment against all parties liable on the bill.

15 [1978] QB 917, [1978] 3 All ER 104, CA.

drawers of a bill discounted the bill and subsequently, on dishonour, the indorsers (who were holders in due course) had recourse against the drawers and the drawers again held the bill, the drawers' title derived from the holder in due course and they had the rights as such under s 29 (3) to claim against the acceptor. Judgment was given irrespective of the acceptor's counterclaim that the goods (of which they were the buyers from the drawers of the bill) were substandard. There is a discretion in the court not to give judgment on a dishonoured bill only when the action is between immediate parties to the bill—here the drawers ceased to be an immediate party when they discounted the bill.

Section 29 (1) provides:—

'A holder in due course is a holder who has taken a bill, complete and regular on the face of it, under the following conditions; namely,

(a) that he became the holder of it before it was overdue, and without notice that it had been previously dishonoured, if such was the fact;

(b) that he took the bill in good faith and for value, and that at the time the bill was negotiated to him he had no notice of any defect in the title of the person who negotiated it.'

One may analyse this important definition as follows:—

1. *Complete and regular on the face of it.*—If someone takes a bill which is lacking in any material particular (eg, the amount or the payee's name is omitted or appears to have been materially altered), he cannot be a holder in due course. If there is any discrepancy between, say, the payee's name on the front of the bill and his indorsement on the back, a holder cannot claim to be a holder in due course.[16]

2. *Before it was overdue.*—A bill payable on demand is deemed to be overdue when it appears on the face of it to have been in circulation for an unreasonable length of time. What is an unreasonable length of time for this purpose is a question of fact (s 36 (3)).[17]

16 However, if a bill is made payable to 'Major Henry Smith' it is a perfectly good indorsement if the payee signs 'Henry Smith'. Of course, even if there is a real discrepancy between the payee's name on the front of the bill and the indorsement on the back, a holder for value can sue on it if the title of the transferor was good: *Arab Bank Ltd v Ross* [1952] 2 QB 216, [1952] 1 All ER 709.

17 Prima facie, every indorsement is deemed to have been effected before the bill was overdue unless it bears a date after maturity of the bill (s 36 (4)).

In the case of a bill other than a bill payable on demand, it is due and payable on the last day of the time of payment as fixed by the bill, or if that is a non-business day, on the succeeding business day.[18] Non-business days mean a Saturday, a Sunday, Good Friday, Christmas Day, a bank holiday, and a day appointed by Royal proclamation as a public fast or thanksgiving day.[19]

If a bill is overdue, it is still valid and can be transferred but it cannot be transferred so that the transferee obtains a better title than the transferor; thus, no one can be a holder in due course after a bill is overdue.

3. *Without notice that it had been previously dishonoured, if such was the fact.*—A holder of a bill is not generally under any duty to present it for acceptance though it is usually desirable to ascertain whether the drawee is willing to accept, because if he does accept, he becomes liable on the bill and the credit of the bill is strengthened, and if he refuses to accept, ie, dishonours the bill by non-acceptance, the holder can, by giving notice to parties liable on the bill, immediately sue any such party for the amount of the bill.[20] If, however, a bill has been presented to a drawee and he has dishonoured it by non-acceptance or by non-payment, a subsequent holder can be a holder in due course only if he is without notice of such dishonour. If such subsequent holder has notice of the dishonour, he takes the bill subject to any defect of title attaching to it at the time of dishonour (s 36 (5)).

4. *In good faith.*—By s 90, 'a thing is deemed to be done in good faith, within the meaning of the Act, where it is in fact done honestly, whether it is done negligently or not'. Careless failure to read a warning communication or advertisement that a bill is stolen does not amount to mala fides,[1] but purchasing a bill at a considerable undervalue may be evidence of mala fides.[2]

5. *For value*—A holder in due course must himself have given value though past consideration is good enough.

18 Bills of Exchange Act 1882 s 14, as amended by the Banking and Financial Dealings Act 1971 s 3.
19 Bills of Exchange Act 1882 s 92, as amended by the Banking and Financial Dealings Act 1971 s 3.
20 See p 258, post.
1 *Raphael v Bank of England* (1855) 17 CB 161.
2 *Jones v Gordon* (1877) 2 App Cas 616.

6. *No notice of any defect in the title of the person who negotiated it.*— 'Notice' means actual though not formal notice, that is to say, either knowledge of the facts or a suspicion that there is something wrong combined with a wilful disregard of the means of knowledge. In *Earl of Sheffield v London Joint Stock Bank*,[3] a moneylender advanced money to clients on the security of negotiable instruments. The moneylender deposited these instruments with the defendant bank as security for the loan of a larger amount than he himself had advanced to his clients. The bank knew the nature of the moneylender's business and that he was in the habit of lending money on such securities. The moneylender became bankrupt. The House of Lords held that the bank were not holders in due course of the instruments because it had knowledge of facts which were calculated to put it on enquiry as to the moneylender's authority to deal with the instruments. In the result, the bank had no better title to the instruments than the moneylender and that upon payment to the bank by the moneylender's clients of the money he had lent to them, the bank had to give up the instruments.

It was held by the House of Lords in *R E Jones Ltd v Waring and Gillow Ltd*[4] that the original payee of an order bill cannot be a holder in due course of it. If, therefore, as a result of a third party's fraud, A is induced to draw a cheque in favour of C, A will have a good defence to any claim on the cheque by C although C may be completely innocent of the fraud. A would not, however, have a good defence to a claim on the cheque made by any subsequent holder of it who has no knowledge of the fraud and who, in all other respects, is a holder in due course.

By s 123 of the Consumer Credit Act 1974 a creditor may not take a bill of exchange (other than a cheque) in discharge of any sum payable by the debtor under an agreement regulated by that Act or by any surety in relation to the agreement. Similarly, the creditor may not take a bill of exchange (including a cheque) as security for the discharge of such a sum. A cheque may be taken in discharge of a payment due under a regulated agreement but negotiation may only be made to a banker (s 123 (2)). If a creditor does take a bill in contravention of s 123, then by s 125 of the same Act he is not a holder in due course and is not entitled to enforce the instrument.

---

3 (1888) 13 App Cas 333. Cf *London Joint Stock Bank v Simmons* [1892] AC 201, where the house of Lords held that when a broker fraudulently deposited with a bank negotiable instruments belonging to his client, the circumstances did not put the bank on enquiry.
4 [1926] AC 670.

Where the creditor negotiated the bill to someone who is a holder in due course, the debtor or surety referred to will be liable to the holder in due course but is in such case entitled to an indemnity against the creditor.[5]

Section 29 (2) provides that the title of a person who negotiates a bill is defective if he obtained the bill or the acceptance thereof by fraud, duress, or force and fear, or other unlawful means, or for an illegal consideration, or when he negotiates it in breach of faith or under such circumstances as amount to fraud.

Presumption.—Every party whose signature appears on a bill is prima facie deemed to have become a party thereto for value. Further, every holder of a bill is prima facie deemed to be a holder in due course. If, however, in an action on a bill it is shown that the acceptance, issue, or subsquent negotiation of the bill is affected with fraud, duress, or force and fear, or illegality, the burden of proof is shifted, unless and until the holder proves that subsequent to the alleged fraud or illegality value has in good faith been given for the bill (s 30).[6] Once the holder has proved that he gave value in good faith for the bill, the defendant in the action is liable unless he can establish that the holder lacks one of the other qualifications of being a holder in due course, eg, that he took the bill when it was overdue.

As will be seen shortly, where an indorsement is forged or unauthorised, that is something more than a 'defect' on the bill, and a subsequent holder has no title to the bill and no right to sue on the bill even though he does satisfy the definition of a holder in due course in s 29 and, inter alia, has no knowledge of the indorsement being forged or unauthorised.

The effect of a forged or unauthorised indorsement

A forged or unauthorised indorsement is wholly inoperative and anyone taking the bill after such an indorsement has no title to it, or right to sue on it, even though he may have no knowledge that the indorsement is forged or unauthorised. The only proviso to this rule

5 It seems that a person can be a holder in due course of an instrument although he discounts it with knowledge of its having been taken by the transferor in violation of s 123 because neither the taking of the instrument nor its negotiation is deemed to be a defect in title for the purposes of s 29 of the Bills of Exchange Act: *Chitty on Contracts*, para 2493.

6 See *Bank für Gemeinwirtschaft v City of London Garages Ltd* [1971] 1 All ER 541, [1971] 1 WLR 149, CA.

in s 24 is if the party against whom it is sought to retain or enforce the payment of the bill is precluded (ie, estopped) from setting up the forgery or want of authority. An unauthorised signature may be ratified unless it amounts to a forged signature which would be the case if put on the bill for a fraudulent purpose. Thus, if a cheque is made payable to a company, and a minor clerk in the company's employ without authority indorses the cheque on behalf of the company to creditors of the company, prima facie the creditors have no title to the cheque, but the company can ratify the unauthorised indorsement if not put on for a fraudulent purpose, and the creditors (the indorsees) could then sue on the cheque.

As an example of the main rule in s 24, suppose a cheque is drawn in favour of C and indorsed by C to D. It is then stolen from D by a thief who forges D's indorsement and negotiates the cheque to E who indorses it to F who indorses it to G. G has no knowledge of the forgery and in all respects complies with the definition of a holder in due course in s 29—that is, he would be a holder in due course but for the forgery. G has no title to the bill because it rests on a forgery. However, he will have rights against E or F by virtue of s 55 (2). When E indorsed the cheque to F he impliedly guaranteed that it was a valid bill and that the signatures on it of the drawer and the previous indorsers were valid signatures; F made a 'guarantee' to the same effect when he indorsed the cheque to G. In the result, because one of the earlier indorsements (D's) was forged, E is liable for the amount of the cheque to G or if G chooses to claim it from F, E is then liable to indemnify F. Section 55 (2) reads:—

> 'The indorser of a bill by indorsing it—
>
> (a) engages that on due presentment it shall be accepted and paid according to its tenor, and that if it be dishonoured he will compensate the holder or a subsequent indorser who is compelled to pay it, provided that the requisite proceedings on dishonour be duly taken;
>
> (b) is precluded from denying to a holder in due course the genuineness and regularity in all respects of the drawer's signature and all previous indorsements;
>
> (c) is precluded from denying to his immediate or a subsequent indorsee that the bill was at the time of his indorsement a valid and subsisting bill, and that he had then a good title thereto.'

An example of the application of the proviso to s 24 is *Greenwood v Martins Bank Ltd.*[7] A man's wife repeatedly forged her husband's

---

7 [1933] AC 51, [1932] All ER Rep 318; followed in *Brown v Westminster Bank* [1964] 2 Lloyd's Rep 187.

signature on cheques and drew out money from his bank account which she applied to her own purposes. The husband became aware of the forgeries but kept silent for eight months. When he finally determined to disclose the forgeries to his bank his wife committed suicide. The husband sued his bank to recover the sums his bank had paid out of his account on cheques on which his signature had been forged by his wife. The bank had given value to the wife on each of these cheques (the wife's name appeared on them as payee) but, of course, the bank's title to each cheque rested on the forged signature of the drawer. However, the House of Lords held that the plaintiff owed a duty to his bank to disclose the forgeries when he became aware of them and, as a result of failing to fulfil that duty, had deprived the bank of the opportunity of bringing an action in tort against the wife until after her death when, under the then existing law, any such action abated. The House of Lords felt, therefore, that the husband was estopped from saying that the signatures were forgeries and he was not entitled to recover.

Negotiation of a bearer bill

When an order bill is negotiated it is indorsed, and by his signature the indorser makes himself liable to the holder as a surety for the amount of the bill.[8] When the holder of a bill payable to bearer negotiates it by delivery without indorsing it, he is termed a 'transferor by delivery'[9] and is not liable on the instrument. However, by s 58, he warrants to his immediate transferee being a holder for value that the bill is what it purports to be (ie, a valid bill), that he has a right to transfer it, and that at the time of the tranfer he is not aware of any fact which renders it valueless (eg, is not aware that payment has been stopped). If the holder of a bearer cheque transfers it without indorsement in exchange for goods, he is not normally liable on the cheque if it is dishonoured and, further, he is not liable on the consideration for which he transferred the cheque, (ie, for the price of the goods—the transferee will normally be considered to have taken the cheque as payment for the goods and thereby takes the risk of the cheque being dishonoured). However, if the holder of a bearer cheque transfers it without indorsement in respect of an antecedent debt or, for example, the

8 See p 224, ante.

9 A transferor of a bearer bill may indorse it though that is not necessary to transfer it. If he does indorse it, he is liable as an indorser on the instrument to a holder in due course (s 56). See p 236, ante.

transferee cashes it for the holder's convenience, the holder is liable to the transferee.[10]

Section 58 refers to bearer bills, originally drawn as such or bills that originally were order bills, but have been indorsed in blank, and to order bills indorsed 'sans recours'. As has been seen, by s 16, any indorser (or the drawer) can insert a stipulation 'sans recours' or 'without recourse to me' which negatives his liability on the instrument.

An order bill transferred by delivery without indorsement is not governed by s 58. Instead, s 31 (4) applies:—

> 'Where the holder of a bill payable to his order transfers it for value without indorsing it, the transfer gives the transferee such title as the transferor had in the bill, and the transferee in addition acquires the right to have the indorsement of the transferor.'

Thus, if D transfers to E an order bill for value without indorsement, E is merely an equitable assignee of it until it is indorsed—E would have to join D in any action he may wish to take against prior parties and such action would be subject to the same defences that could have been raised in an action brought by D alone. If D refuses to put his endorsement on the bill, E may sue D to compel him to do so and by s 39 of the Supreme Court Act 1981, the court may, if D disobeys a court order to indorse the bill, order the indorsement to be made by someone nominated for that purpose who may or may not be the transferee himself. If the transferee does obtain the transferor's indorsement at some time after he obtained delivery of the bill, the indorsement does not relate back, so that if the transferee receives notice before the indorsement that there is some defect on the bill, for example, that the transferor obtained it by fraud, he will be affected by such notice and cannot claim to be a holder in due course.[11]

Delivery

Section 21 (1) provides that 'every contract on a bill, whether it be the drawer's, acceptor's, or an indorser's, is incomplete and revocable, until delivery of the instrument in order to give effect thereto'. This means, for example, that mere indorsement by the payee of an order bill is not effective to negotiate it—delivery of it by the payee is required as well. So also, the drawer of a bill is only liable on his signature when he has 'issued' the bill by delivering it to

10 *Chalmers on Bills of Exchange* (13th edn, 1964) pp 194–195.
11 *Whistler v Forster* (1863) 32 LJPC 161.

the payee. Section 2 defines delivery as the 'transfer of possession, actual or constructive, from one person to another', and s 21 (2) provides that as between immediate parties (ie, parties in direct relation to one another, like the payee and the next holder), and as regards a remote party other than a holder in due course, the delivery to be effectual must be made by or under the authority of the party drawing, accepting, or indorsing the bill, as the case may be. On the other hand the delivery may be shown to have been conditional or for a special purpose only and not for the purpose of transferring the property in the bill. Section 21 (2) also provides that if the bill is in the hands of a holder in due course, valid delivery of it by all parties prior to him so as to make them liable to him is conclusively presumed. Moreover, by s 21 (3), in any case where a bill is no longer in the possession of a party who has signed it as drawer, acceptor, or indorser, a valid and unconditional delivery by him is presumed until the contrary is proved.

So far as the liability of an acceptor is concerned, by a proviso to s 21 (1), if an acceptance is written on a bill and the drawee gives notice to or according to the directions of the person entitled to the bill that he has accepted it, that is as effective as delivery of the bill by the acceptor and the acceptance becomes complete and irrevocable.

Inchoate bills

Section 20 provides:—

'(1) Where a simple signature on a blank . . . paper is delivered by the signer in order that it may be converted into a bill, it operates as a prima facie authority to fill it up as a complete bill for any amount . . . using the signature for that of the drawer, or the acceptor, or an indorser; and, in like manner, when a bill is wanting in any material particular, the person in possession of it has a prima facie authority to fill up the omission in any way he thinks fit.

(2) In order that any such instrument when completed may be enforceable against any person who became a party thereto prior to its completion, it must be filled up within a reasonable time, and strictly in accordance with the authority given. Reasonable time for this purpose is a question of fact.

Provided that if any such instrument after completion is negotiated to a holder in due course it shall be valid and effectual for all purposes in his hands, and he may enforce it as if it had been filled up within a reasonable time and strictly in accordance with the authority given.'

To take an example, if A takes out his cheque book and signs a cheque form as a drawer but does not complete the cheque and does not deliver it to anyone, should this inchoate instrument be stolen and filled in, A is under no liability to anyone on his signature, not even to a holder in due course.[12] Suppose instead, however, that A signs the 'blank cheque' and delivers it to an agent to fill up the spaces with the amount and the payee's name for the purchase of a television set; in other words, A hands it to an agent 'in order that it may be converted into a bill'. The agent fills up the amount for his own private debts. It has not been completed according to the authority given by A so A is prima facie not liable on his signature. But if, after it has been completed, it comes into the hands of a holder who has no knowledge that it has been filled up contrary to A's instructions and who is in all respects a holder in due course, he can enforce payment against A.[13] In *Griffiths v Dalton*,[14] an undated cheque was regarded as wanting in a *material particular* and, while the payee had prima facie authority to fill in the date under s 20, as 18 months had elapsed since the issue of the cheque which was more than a reasonable time, the payee as held unable to enforce payment against the drawer.

A bill is inchoate if, for example, it is drawn payable to the drawer's order, and has a third party's indorsement on it as a 'backer' but no indorsement of the drawer-payee. Thus, in *McDonald & Co v Nash & Co*,[15] the appellants sold certain goods to A & Co, who, being unable to find the purchase price, sought financial assistance from the respondents. At a meeting between all three parties, the respondents agreed to indorse or 'back' bills of exchange drawn by the appellants on A & Co, to the appellants' order. The bills were so drawn, accepted by A & Co, and indorsed by the respondents. The respondents then handed the bills to the appellants who subsequently indorsed their name as payees above the respondents' signature. The respondents denied liability, but the House of Lords held that, from the agreement entered into, the respondents must be taken to have intended to make themselves

---

12 *Baxendale v Bennett* (1878) 3 QBD 525.

13 Cf *Smith v Prosser* [1907] 2 KB 735, where forms of promissory notes were left by A with an agent who was directed that they were not to be used without instruction from A. The agent filled them up without instructions and they came into the hands of someone who took them in good faith and for value. *Held:* As they had not been delivered by A to the agent 'in order that' they be issued as negotiable instruments, A was not liable on them.

14 [1940] 2 KB 264.

15 [1924] AC 625, [1924] All ER Rep 601, applied in *Yeoman Credit Ltd v Gregory* [1963] 1 All ER 245, [1963] 1 WLR 343.

liable to the appellants on the bills. Although when the bills were handed to the appellants they lacked the appellant's indorsement as payee and the bills were therefore, not complete, the appellants had implied authority under s 20 to complete them by inserting such indorsement. The respondents were in consequence liable on the bills. The effect of completing a bill under s 20 is retrospective— when the appellants did indorse a bill, it operated as an indorsement in blank so that the bill could be treated as having been indorsed to the respondents and then reindorsed for value to the appellants. The further consequence of the appellants' indorsement having retrospective effect was that the bill being treated as complete when it came into their hands, the appellants qualified as holders in due course, assuming that the other requirements of the definition of a holder in due course in s 29 were satisfied. Hence, the respondents' liability to them under s 56:

> 'Where a person signs a bill otherwise than as drawer or acceptor, he thereby incurs the liabilities of an indorser to a holder in due course.'[16]

In *McDonald & Co v Nash & Co*[17] the drawer-payee indorsed the bill *above* the signature of the 'backer', but the result would have been no different if, inadvertently or because space had not been left above the backer's signature, the payee had placed his signature below the backer's. Wright J held in *National Sales Corpn Ltd v Bernardi*[18] that the order of the indorsements on a bill is not conclusive and evidence is admissible to explain the intention of the parties. Nor does it matter that the payee's indorsement is restrictive.[19]

It has been seen that by the proviso to s 20 (2), where an inchoate bill is delivered to someone in order that it may be converted into a bill, even if it is completed contrary to instructions a holder in due course may enforce it as if it had been completed in accordance with instructions. It has already been noted that the original payee of an order bill cannot be a holder in due course.[20]

16 *McDonald & Co v Nash & Co* was decided two years before the House of Lords held in *R E Jones Ltd v Waring and Gillow Ltd*, that the original payee of a bill cannot be a holder in due course. The two cases can only be reconciled on the basis that in the earlier case the payee was also considered to be an indorsee.

17 [1924] AC 625, [1924] All ER Rep 601.

18 [1931] 2 KB 188, [1931] All ER Rep 320, followed by Goddard J in *McCall Bros v Hargreaves* [1932] 2 KB 423, [1932] All ER Rep 854 and by Scarman J in *Lombard Banking Ltd v Central Garage and Engineering Co Ltd* [1953] 1 QB 220, [1962] 2 All ER 949.

19 *Yeoman Credit Ltd v Gregory* [1963] 1 All ER 245, [1963] 1 WLR 343.

20 *R E Jones Ltd v Waring and Gillow Ltd* [1926] AC 670, [1926] All ER Rep 36. See ante, p 246.

254 Negotiable instruments

However, such original payee may be able to rely on the doctrine of estoppel if he has changed his position in reliance on the signature. In *Lloyds Bank Ltd v Cooke*[1] S signed his name on a blank paper and gave it to C with authority to complete it as a promissory note for £250 payable to the plaintiffs and to deliver it to the plaintiffs as security for an advance to be made by them. C fraudulently filled up the paper as a promissory note for £1,000 payable to the plaintiffs and thereby obtained an advance from the plaintiffs for his own purposes. The court held that S was estopped from denying C's authority and was liable for £1,000 to the plaintiffs.[2]

The limitations of the authority of *Lloyds Bank Ltd v Cooke*[1] were explained by Lord Greene MR in *Wilson and Meeson v Pickering*.[3]

'Apart from some specific representation of authority or some holding out, or some special character of the agent from which his authority would naturally be inferred, the rule that a person who signs an instrument in blank cannot be heard, as against a person who has changed his position on the faith of it, to assert that the instrument as filled in is a forgery or that it was filled in in excess of the agent's authority, is confined to the case of negotiable instruments.'

In the *Pickering* case a blank cheque crossed 'not negotiable' was handed to an agent to be completed and the signer was held not liable on it when the agent filled it in for more than the amount specified and in favour of a personal creditor of the agent.[4]

THE DUTIES OF A HOLDER

Presentation for acceptance

A holder of a bill other than a cheque may present it to the drawee to be accepted. It is generally desirable for any holder of a time bill to ascertain whether the drawee is prepared to accept the bill because if the drawee accepts the bill, it is more readily negotiable, and if he refuses or acceptance cannot be obtained (ie, there is a dishonour of the bill by non-acceptance) then the holder has, on giving notice, the right to claim at once the amount of the bill from

---

1 [1907] 1 KB 794.

2 Section 20 could not be relied on by the plaintiffs because the paper had been completed contrary to instructions and, as the original payees, the plaintiffs could not be holders in due course.

3 [1946] KB 422, 427, [1946] 1 All ER 394, 397.

4 Even had the instrument been a negotiable instrument the result would no doubt have been the same because the payee of the cheque never acted on the signature of her prejudice—the debt owed to her was not extinguished.

the drawer or any indorser and presentment for payment to the drawee is unnecessary (s 43). In the case of bills payable on demand a holder can of course present the bill to the drawee at any time for actual payment. Only in the following instances is there a statutory duty on a holder to present a bill to the drawee for acceptance—

(1) where a bill is payable after sight, presentment for acceptance is necessary in order to fix the maturity of the instrument;

(2) where a bill expressly states that it shall be presented for acceptance, or where a bill is drawn payable elsewhere than at the residence or place of business of the drawee, it must be presented for acceptance before it can be presented for payment (s 39).

Section 40 provides that when a bill payable after sight is negotiated, the holder must either present it for acceptance or negotiate it within a reasonable time. If he does neither, then the drawer and endorsers are discharged from liability. Section 40 (3) provides that in determining what is a reasonable time regard is had to the nature of the bill, the usage of the trade with respect to similar bills, and the facts of the particular case.

Section 41 lays down rules as to presentment for acceptance and excuses for non-presentment. Presentment must be by or on behalf of the holder to the drawee or some person authorised to accept or refuse to accept for him, at a reasonable hour on a business day before the bill is overdue. Where authorised by agreement or usage, presentment through the Post Office is sufficient. Even where presentment for acceptance is normally required, presentment is excused and a bill may be treated as dishonoured by non-acceptance where for example, the drawee is dead or after the exercise of reasonable diligence, presentment cannot be effected. When a bill is duly presented for acceptance and is not accepted within the customary time (ie, 24 hours) the person presenting it must treat it as dishonoured by non-acceptance (s 42). If he does not treat it as dishonoured and gives notice to the drawer and indorsers, then the holder loses his right of recourse against any party who has not received notice.

Qualified acceptance.—The holder always has a right to refuse to take a qualified acceptance and if he does not obtain an unqualified acceptance from the drawee he may treat the bill as dishonoured by non-acceptance. Types of qualified acceptances are specified in s 19:—

(a) conditional, where payment by the acceptor is dependent on the fulfilment of some condition, eg, giving up bills of lading;
(b) partial, ie, an acceptance to pay part only of the amount for which the bill is drawn;
(c) local, ie, an acceptance to pay only at a particular specified place and not elsewhere, eg, 'payable at the Midland Bank, Westminster, only';
(d) qualified as to time, as where a bill is drawn payable three months after date and the drawee accepts payable six months after date;
(e) acceptance of some one or more of the drawees, but not of all.

If a holder does take a qualified acceptance and the drawer or an indorser has not authorised the holder to do so, or does not subsequently assent, such drawer or indorser is discharged from his liability on the bill. If a holder gives such parties notice of a qualified acceptance, any party who does not within a reasonable time express his dissent to the holder is deemed to have assented to the holder taking it. In the case of a partial acceptance, however, if the holder takes that, provided notice is given to prior parties, they are liable for the balance, and their assent to the holder taking a partial acceptance is unnecessary (s 44).

Presentment for payment

If a bill is not payable on demand, it must be presented by the holder for payment on the day it falls due, and if it is not so presented, the drawer and indorsers are discharged (s 45 (1)). Thus, in *Yeoman Credit Ltd v Gregory*,[5] a bill had been accepted 'payable at the NP Bank', but because the holder was informed by the acceptor's agent that there were no funds at the NP Bank and that presentment should be made at the M Bank, the bill was presented on the correct day at the M Bank who refused payment. On the following day, presentment was made to the NP Bank who also refused payment. Megaw J held that as the bill has not been presented at the NP Bank on the correct day, the indorser was discharged from liability.

If a bill is payable on demand, it must be presented within a reasonable time of its issue in order to render the drawer liable, and within a reasonable time of its indorsement in order to render the

5 [1963] 1 All ER 245, [1963] 1 WLR 343.

indorser liable (s 45 (2)).[6] If the drawee has given a general acceptance to the bill, *he* remains liable for the limitation period from the date of the maturity of the bill, whether presentment for payment has been made or not (s 52 (1)). The terms of a qualified acceptance, however, may require presentment for payment to render the acceptor liable, but *punctual* presentment is only necessary to make such acceptor liable if the terms of the qualified acceptance so specify expressly (s 52 (2)).

Due presentment.—Due presentment for payment is explained in s 45; generally, it is presentment by the holder or by someone authorised to receive payment on his behalf at the proper place, which means the place specified in the bill, or if none, at the drawee's address as shown in the bill, or if none, at the drawee's place of business if known, or if not, at his ordinary residence, if known. As a last resort, presentment may be made to the drawee wherever he can be found, or at his last known place of business or residence. Presentment must be at a reasonable hour on a business day, and must be to the person designated by the bill as payer, or to some person authorised to pay or refuse payment on his behalf, but if no such person can be found at the proper place for presentment, presentment is deemed to have taken place (s 45 (5)). Presentment through the Post Office is sufficient, if authorised by agreement or usage (s 45 (8)).

Excuses for delay and non-presentment.—Delay in presentment is excused when caused by circumstances beyond the control of the holder, and not imputable to his default, misconduct, or negligence (s 46 (1)). Presentment is entirely excused by waiver, express or implied, or where after the exercise of reasonable diligence, presentment cannot be effected, or where the drawee is a fictitious person. As regards the drawer, presentment is not required if the drawee or acceptor is not bound, as between himself and the drawer to accept or pay the bill (as where the drawee has accepted for the drawer's accommodation) and the *drawer* has no reason to believe that the bill would be paid if presented. Similarly, as regards an indorser, presentment is not required if the bill was accepted or

6 In determining what is a reasonable time, regard is paid to the nature of the bill, the usage of the trade with regard to similar bills, and the facts of the particular case (s 45 (2)).

made for the accommodation of such indorser, and such indorser has no reason to expect that the bill would be paid if presented.

When a bill is paid, the holder must forthwith deliver it up to the party paying it (s 52 (4)).

Notice of dishonour

A bill is dishonoured before it matures if the drawee refuses or fails to accept it. On such dishonour by non-acceptance, the holder must notify the drawer and any indorser of the dishonour in order to preserve his rights against them. Similarly, a bill is dishonoured at maturity by non-payment if the drawee or acceptor refuses or fails to pay the bill. On dishonour by non-payment, the holder must notify the drawer and any indorser in order to preserve his rights against them (s 48).[7] To ensure that each prior party remains liable to the holder, the holder should advise every party of a dishonour by non-acceptance or non-payment, since any drawer or indorser who does not receive notice is discharged.[8] However, if the holder gives notice of a dishonour only to his immediate transferor E it will be in the interests of E to pass on the notice to his transferor D and so on; if E did not pass back such notice then the holder could sue him but he would be unable to claim from D. Notice of dishonour must be given by the holder or someone on his behalf or by an indorser who is liable on the bill or someone on his behalf (s 49 (1)).

Where a bill has been dishonoured by non-acceptance and notice of dishonour is not given, the rights of any holder in due course subsequent to the omission are not to be prejudiced by the omission.[9]

Where a bill is dishonoured by non-acceptance, and due notice of dishonour is given, it is not necessary to give notice of a subsequent dishonour by non-payment unless the bill has in the meantime been accepted.

Suppose a bill is indorsed by the payee C to D and further indorsed in succession to E and F. It is dishonoured by non-payment by B the drawee. F gives notice to E and to C. No other notices are given. Because of the notice received by E, F can claim

7 By s 52 (3), to render the acceptor of a bill liable, it is not necessary to give him notice of dishonour by non-payment.

8 Nor may the holder claim against such person on any contract underlying the bill or the indorsement on the bill: *Peacock v Pursell* [1863] 14 CBNS 728.

9 To be a holder in due course, a holder must, inter alia, be a holder who is without notice of any dishonour by non-acceptance.

from him. Further, because C received notice also, that notice given by the holder 'enures for the benefit of all subsequent holders and all prior indorsers who have a right of recourse against the party to whom it is given' (s 49 (3)). The fact that C received notice enures, therefore, to the benefit of E and E can claim from C. Also the fact that E and C received notice enures to the benefit of any subsequent holder to whom F may negotiate the bill.

Form of notice.—Notice may be given in writing or orally and the return of a dishonoured bill to the drawer or an indorser is deemed a sufficient notice.

Time for giving notice.—Notice of dishonour may be given as soon as the bill is dishonoured and must be given within a reasonable time thereafter. Where a party to a bill receives due notice of dishonour, he has after the receipt of such notice the same period of time for giving notice to antecedent parties as the holder has after the dishonour. Where a notice of dishonour is duly addressed and posted, the sender is deemed to have given due notice of dishonour, notwithstanding any miscarriage by the post. In the absence of special circumstances,[10] notice is not deemed to have been given within a reasonable time by s 49 (12) unless:

(a) where the person giving and the person to receive notice reside in the same place, the notice is given or sent off in time to reach the latter on the day after the dishonour of the bill;

(b) where the person giving and the person to receive notice reside in different places, the notice is sent off on the day after the dishonour of the bill, if there be a post at a convenient hour on that day, and if there be no such post on that day then by the next post thereafter.

In a recent case, Mackenna J considered that the persons concerned resided in the same place if it was reasonable in all the circumstances to send the notice by hand rather than using the post.[11]

---

10 It may be reasonable in 'special circumstances' for a party to wait until a bill is back in his hands before giving notice, eg as where presentment had been made by the holder's bank. *Lombard Banking Ltd v Central Garage and Engineering Co Ltd* [1963] 1 QB 220, [1962] 2 All ER 949.

11 *Hamilton Finance Co Ltd v Coverley Westlay Walbaurn and Tosetti Ltd* [1969] 1 Lloyd's Rep 53.

Notice of dishonour *posted* before the bill is dishonoured is effective unless it is *received* before the bill is dishonoured.[12]

Where a bill when dishonoured is in the hands of an agent, such as the holder's bank, then the bank must either himself give notice to the parties liable on the bill or give notice to his customer. In either case the bank has the same time for giving notice as if he were the holder and if the notice is given to the customer, the customer upon receipt of such notice has himself the same time for giving notice as if the agent had been an independent holder (s 49 (13)).

Excuses for non-notice and delay.—Delay in giving notice is excused where the delay is caused by circumstances beyond the control of the party giving notice, and not imputable to his default, misconduct or negligence. When the cause of delay ceases to operate the notice must be given with reasonable diligence (s 50 (1)). Notice of dishonour is dispensed with altogether when, after the exercise of reasonable diligence, notice as required by the Act cannot be given to or does not reach the drawer or indorser sought to be charged. It is also dispensed with by waiver, express or implied. As regards giving notice of dishonour to the drawer, notice is dispensed with (a) where the drawer and drawee are the same person (eg, as with a banker's draft), (b) where the drawee is a fictitious person or a person not having capacity to contract, (c) where the drawer is the person to whom the bill is presented for payment, (d) where the drawee or acceptor is as between himself and the drawer under no obligation to accept or pay the bill (eg, where a drawer of a cheque has insufficient funds in his bank account to meet the cheque) and (e) where the drawer has countermanded payment. As regards giving notice of dishonour to an indorser, notice is dispensed with (a) where the drawee is a fictitious person or a person not having capacity to contract, and the indorser was aware of the fact when he indorsed the bill, (b) where the indorser is the person to whom the bill is presented for payment, (c) where the bill was accepted or made for his accommodation.

---

12 *Eaglehill v J Needham Builders Ltd* [1973] AC 992, [1972] 3 All ER 895, HL. On the facts of this case there was no evidence as to whether the dishonour of the bill or the receipt of the notice of dishonour came first in point of time—both occurred on the same date. The House of Lords held that in these circumstances the events were presumed to take place in the proper order, ie, first, the dishonour and then receipt of the notice of dishonour.

Noting and protesting

Where a foreign bill has been dishonoured by non-acceptance it must be duly 'noted and protested' for non-acceptance and where such bill, which has not been previously dishonoured by non-acceptance, is dishonoured by non-payment it must be duly 'noted and protested' for non-payment. If it is not so noted and protested, the drawer and indorsers are discharged (s 51). Noting and protesting are not necessary to render the acceptor liable (s 52 (3)).

An inland bill is defined in the Act and any other bill is a foreign bill. By s 4 (1):—

> 'An inland bill is a bill which is or on the face of it purports to be
> (a) both drawn and payable within the British Islands, or
> (b) drawn within the British Islands upon some person resident therein.'[13]

It follows from this definition that if a bill purports to be a foreign bill, a holder may show that it is in fact an inland bill so as to excuse the need for noting and protesting it on dishonour.

The requirement of noting and protesting a foreign bill on dishonour involves handing the bill to a Notary Public who again formally presents the bill for acceptance or payment. Upon redishonour, the notary makes a memorandum on the bill of his initials, his charges, the date, and a reference to his register where the details are entered, and he attaches a slip to the bill giving the 'answer he receives'. This is the *noting* which must be done on the day of dishonour or the next succeeding business day. The *protest* is the formal document recording the fact of the dishonour and containing a copy of the bill. The protest may be drawn up at any time after the noting. Delay in noting or protesting is excused when the delay is caused by circumstances beyond the control of the holder and not imputable to his default, misconduct, or negligence. Protest is entirely dispensed with by any circumstance which would dispense with notice of dishonour (s 51 (9)).

By s 94, where the services of a Notary cannot be obtained at the time and place where the bill is dishonoured, any householder or substantial resident of the place may, in the presence of two witnesses, give a certificate signed by the witnesses attesting the dishonour of the bill, and this certificate will operate in all respects as if it were a notarial protest.

---

13 'British Islands', for the purposes of the Act, means any part of the United Kingdom of Great Britain and Northern Ireland, the islands of Man, Guernsey, Jersey, Alderney, and Sark.

There is no duty on a holder to note and protest an inland bill, nor where a bill does not appear on the face of it to be a foreign bill. However, certain special procedures, not considered further here, can only be resorted to if a bill has been noted and protested— acceptance for honour, protest for better security, and payment for honour.[14]

DAMAGES

Whenever a holder of a bill is entitled to judgment for the amount of a bill from any party liable, or a party who has been compelled to pay the bill is entitled to recover from a party liable to him, the damages recoverable consist of:

(a) the amount of the bill,
(b) interest thereon (generally 5 per cent) from the time of presentment for payment of the bill if the bill is payable on demand, and from the maturity of the bill in any other case, and
(c) the expenses of noting, if any, and, where protest is necessary (as with foreign bills) and protest has in fact been extended, the expenses of protest (s 57).

DISCHARGE OF A BILL OR OF PARTIES

A bill is discharged when all rights of action under it are extinguished. The simplest example is where the holder of a bill presents it to the acceptor at maturity and the acceptor pays it, without knowledge that the holder has a defective title, if that be the case. All rights under the bill are extinguished and the bill discharged.[15] On the other hand if a bill has been indorsed by the payee C to D and then to E and to F, and the bill is dishonoured by non-payment, F the holder, may obtain payment from, say, D. The

14 These procedures are provided for in ss 65–68 and s 51 (5).
15 A bill is not discharged simply because it is lost. If a bill is lost before it is overdue, the holders may apply to the drawer for another bill, giving security to the drawer if required to indemnify him in case the bill alleged to have been lost is found again. If the drawer refuses to give such a duplicate bill, he may be compelled by the court to do so (s 69). It is clear from that provision that, whereas the holder has a right to obtain execution of a duplicate by the drawer, he cannot claim execution of it by the other parties. However, by s 70, in any action on a bill, the court may order that the loss of the instrument shall not be set up provided an indemnity be given against the claims of any other person on the instrument in question.

effect of F being paid by D is not to discharge the bill, because there are still rights subsisting under it, for example the right of D to recover payment from C or from the drawer or from the acceptor. The effect of F being paid by D is not to discharge the bill, but it would discharge one of the parties to the bill, namely the intermediate party, E.

Thus, payment of a bill by the acceptor discharges the bill but payment by an indorser only discharges subsequent indorsers.[16] Let us deal, in turn, with the various ways in which a bill may be discharged.

1. Payment in due course

A bill is discharged by payment in due course by or on behalf of the drawee or acceptor. By s 59 this means payment made at or after the maturity of the bill to the holder thereof in good faith and without the drawee or acceptor having notice that the holder's title is defective. Thus, if a holder has obtained a transfer of the bill by fraud, and the acceptor pays the amount of the bill to him at maturity, without knowledge that his title is defective, the bill is discharged. Again, suppose A draws a cheque for £5 payable to bearer and hands it to C from whom it is stolen. A payment by A's bank to the thief, in good faith and without knowledge that the thief's title to the cheque is defective, is a payment in due course and the bank can debit A's account with the amount. A would be under no further liability to C than he would be if he had paid his debt to C with a £5 banknote and the banknote was stolen after being given to C.

On the other hand, if someone is in possession of an order bill after an essential indorsement has been forged, he cannot be a 'holder' and by s 24 has no right to give a discharge for the bill. If the acceptor pays such a person, he has not paid the bill in due course, the bill is not discharged, and the acceptor is still liable to pay the amount of the bill to the true owner.

Thus, suppose a bill is drawn by A on B in favour of C and indorsed by C to D. It is then stolen from D by a thief who forges D's indorsement and negotiates the bill to E who indorses it to F who indorses it to G. G has no title to the bill because it rests on a forgery,

---

16 Alternatively, when a bill is paid by an indorser, he may strike out his own and subsequent indorsements and again negotiate the bill (s 59 (2)). However, if a bill payable to or to the order of a third party is paid by the drawer, while the drawer may enforce payment against the acceptor he may not reissue the bill.

irrespective of whether G took it in good faith or not, and if B pays G this is not a payment in due course—B is still obliged to pay D. However, B may be able to recover the amount he paid to G as money paid under a mistake of fact, at any rate if the mistake is immediately corrected. The demand must be made within a reasonable time because otherwise, in our example, G may be prejudiced by losing his remedies against E and F through failure to give them notice of dishonour in time or G may have released securities given to him. In *London and River Plate Bank v Bank of Liverpool*[17] the forgery was discovered only after six weeks, and it was held that it was too late for the acceptor to recover the money he had paid out. In *Imperial Bank of Canada v Bank of Hamilton*[18] a cheque for five dollars was certified by the drawer's bank and then fraudulently altered by the drawer to 500 dollars and negotiated to X who was in good faith and obtained the payment of that sum from the drawer's bank. The bank discovered the fraud the following day and gave notice to X. The bank was held entitled to recover 495 dollars from X—X would not be prejudiced by losing any remedy against prior parties because he could still proceed against the fraudulent drawer.[19] Notice of dishonour to the drawer of a cheque is not required where the drawee is under no obligation to the drawer to pay the cheque (s 51 (2) (c)).

In the case of an accommodation bill, where the acceptor gratuitously accepts a bill so as to lend the value of his name, if the bill is paid in due course by the party accommodated, the bill is discharged (s 59 (3)).

2. Acceptor the holder at maturity

When the acceptor of a bill is or becomes the holder of it at or after its maturity in his own right, the bill is discharged (s 61). If a bill is paid by the acceptor before maturity and the acceptor then negotiates it to X who is not aware of the earlier payment, X may recover against all prior parties.[20]

17 [1896] 1 QB 7, [1895–9] All ER Rep 1005.
18 [1903] AC 49, PC. See also *National Westminster Bank Ltd v Barclays Bank International Ltd* [1975] QB 654, [1974] 3 All ER 834.
19 Even the holder in due course of a cheque whose amount has been raised can only enforce it according to its original tenor except against a party who made, authorised or assented to the alteration and subsequent indorsers. See also *Barclays Bank Ltd v W J Simms, Son and Cooke (Southern) Ltd* [1980] QB 677 and [1979] 3 All ER 522. See s 64, post, p 265.
20 *Burbridge v Manners* (1812) 3 Camp 193, 194.

3. Renunciation

When the holder of a bill *at or after* maturity absolutely and unconditionally renounces his rights against the acceptor the bill is discharged. The renunciatioin must be in writing, unless the bill is delivered up to the acceptor (s 62 (1)).

If *in like manner* a holder renounces his rights against a particular indorser of the bill, *before, at or after* maturity, that indorser will be discharged—so will subsequent indorsers. If a holder renounces his rights against a party before maturity and then negotiates the bill to a holder in due course, who is ignorant of the renunciation, the holder in due course is not affected by renunciation (s 62 (2)).

4. Cancellation

Where a bill is intentionally cancelled by the holder, or his agent and the cancellation is apparent on the bill, the bill is discharged (s 63 (1)). For example, if the holder crosses out the acceptor's signature or writes 'cancelled' on the bill or burns the bill, that is a discharge of the bill.

So also, any party liable on a bill may be discharged by the intentional cancellation of his signature by the holder or his agent. In such case, any indorser who would have had a right of recourse against the party whose signature is cancelled is also discharged (s 63 (2)). An unintentional or mistaken cancellation is inoperative but where a bill or any signature on the bill appears to be cancelled, the burden of proof rests on the party who alleges that the cancellation was made unintentionally, or under a mistake, or without authority (s 63 (3)).

5. Alteration of bill

By s 64:—

> 'Where a bill or acceptance is materially altered without the assent of all parties liable on the bill, the bill is avoided except as against a party who has himself made, authorised, or assented to the alteration, and subsequent indorsers.
> Provided that,
> Where a bill has been materially altered, but the alteration is not apparent, and the bill is in the hands of a holder in due course, such holder may avail himself of the bill as if it had not been altered, and may enforce payment of it according to its original tenor.'

Suppose a bill is drawn by A on B for £100 in favour of C who

266 Negotiable instruments

indorses it to D, who alters it to £1,000 before indorsing it to E. E indorses it to F. The effect of this material alteration of the amount of the bill is to avoid the bill except as against D who has made the alteration and E who is a subsequent indorser. F can sue E or D for £1,000, but has no rights against C, B or A unless any one of them authorised or assented to the alteration. However, if the proviso applies, and the alteration was a non-apparent one (i.e., not noticeable on reasonable scrutiny by a holder), provided F is a holder in due course, C, B and or A are liable to the extent of £100 to F or to E, whom F may have made liable for the full £1,000.[1]

Section 64 (2) refers to the following alterations as material: alteration of the date, the sum payable, the time of payment, the place of payment, and where a bill has been accepted generally, the addition of a place of payment without the acceptor's assent. If, after a bill is completed, an alteration is made to the place where the bill was drawn, this alteration is only material if it affects the rights of parties which might be the case if, after the alteration, the bill is a foreign bill.[2]

Alteration by pure accident is not within s 64.[3]

6. Limitation Act 1980

Under the Limitation Act 1980, action upon a bill against a party liable on it is barred after a lapse of six years from the accrual of the cause of action against that party. For example, action against the acceptor of a bill is barred six years after the maturity of the bill, and action against the drawer or indorser of a bill is barred six years after the party it is desired to sue has received notice of dishonour.

CHEQUE

Definition

The Act defines a cheque as a bill of exchange drawn on a banker payable on demand (s 73).

Section 2 of the Act refers to a 'banker' in this way: ' "Banker" includes a body of persons whether incorporated or not who carry on the business of banking.' The Banking Act 1987 provides

---

1 See also *Bank of Montreal v Exhibit and Trading Co* (1906) 22 TLR 722.
2 *Koch v Dicks* [1933] 1 KB 307, [1932] All ER Rep 476.
3 *Hong Kong and Shanghai Banking Corpn v Lo Lee Shi* [1928] AC 181.

minimum criteria to guide the Bank of England in determining whether a body may be an authorised bank.

A post-dated cheque, not being payable on demand, is not strictly a cheque but operates as a bill of exchange. We have already seen that by s 13 (2) of the Act a bill is not invalid by reason only that it is post-dated. If a banker in error pays a post-dated cheque before the date, he has no right to debit the drawer's account until the date arrives, and even then the banker has no right to debit the drawer's account if the drawer has meanwhile countermanded payment.

Differences between cheques and other bills

Except as otherwise provided in Part III of the Act, the provisions of the Act applicable to bills of exchange payable on demand apply to cheques. However, there are certain important differences between cheques and other bills. In the first place, the drawee of a cheque is always a banker and a cheque is never 'accepted' so the rules in the Act relating to presentment for acceptance have no application, and normally a holder of a cheque has no rights against the drawee-banker.[4] Notice of dishonour by non-payment is rarely needed in order to claim against the drawer of a cheque because non-payment is almost always due to lack of funds or countermand by the drawer, both of which, as we have seen, are valid excuses for not giving notice to the drawer (s 50 (2) (c)).[5] However, notice of dishonour for non-payment is normally necessary in order to claim against an indorser of a cheque. The provisions in the Act relating to 'crossings' do not apply to bills other than cheques, and in certain circumstances the banker on whom a cheque is drawn is given statutory protection if he pays out on a forged indorsement, whereas there is no such protection for the drawee of a demand bill who is not a banker. Further, the drawer of a cheque, unlike the drawer of other bills payable on demand, is not discharged from liability by the holder's failure to present the cheque for payment within a

4 In a number of Commonwealth countries, the bank on which a cheque is drawn may 'certify' it by marking it, for example, 'approved'. This is a representation that at the time of certification the drawer has sufficient funds in the bank to meet the cheque but it will not give the holder any right of action against the bank unless the case of *Hedley Byrne & Co v Heller & Partners Ltd* [1964] AC 465, [1963] 2 All ER 575 were considered to impose a duty of care on the bank. A more formal method of certification has been developed, for example, in Canada whereby the bank immediately debits the customer's account when it certifies the cheque.

5 See p 260, ante. See also *Barclays Bank Ltd v W J Simms Son and Cooke (Southern) Ltd* [1980] QB 677, [1979] 3 All ER 522.

reasonable time, unless the banker on whom the cheque is drawn fails. This point requires further treatment.

By virtue of s 123 (2) of the Consumer Credit Act 1974, the creditor shall not negotiate a cheque taken by him in discharge of a sum payable under a regulated agreement except to a banker. Where he does so, in contravention of this provision, this is a defect in title so that a holder will only be a holder in due course able to enforce the cheque if he had no notice it had been negotiated contrary to s 123 (2) (s 125 (2)).

Presentment for payment.—In accordance with s 45 (discussed above[6]) Bingham J in *Barclays Bank plc v Bank of England*[7] ruled that where bank A (the presenting bank) receives from a customer for collection a cheque drawn on bank B (paying bank) and the cheque is dealt with through the inter-bank clearing system, the presenting bank's responsibility to its customer to collect payment is discharged only when the cheque is physically delivered to the branch of the paying bank where the drawer has an account. By s 45 a bill payable on demand must be presented for payment to the drawee within a reasonable time after its issue in order to render the drawer liable and within a reasonable time of its indorsement in order to render the indorsers liable. That rule applies also to the indorsers of cheques but generally, presentment to the drawee (the paying bank) is not necessary to render the drawer of a cheque liable, his liability lasting for the six-year limitation period from the date of the cheque. However, s 74 provides that presentment for payment within a reasonable time is in certain circumstances necessary in order to render the drawer liable.

(1) Where a cheque is not presented for payment within a reasonable time of its issue, and the drawer or the person on whose account it is drawn had the right at the time of such presentment as between him and the banker to have the cheque paid and suffers actual damage through the delay, he is discharged to the extent of such damage, that is to say, to the extent to which such drawer or person is a creditor of such banker to a larger amount than he would have been had such cheque been paid.

(2) In determining what is a reasonable time regard shall be had to the nature of the instrument, the usage of trade and of bankers, and the facts of the particular case.

(3) The holder of such cheque as to which such drawer or person is discharged shall be a creditor, in lieu of such drawer or person, of

6 See p 256, ante.
7 [1985] 1 All ER 385.

such banker to the extent of such discharge, and entitled to recover the amount from him.

To illustrate the operation of s 74, suppose A has £1,000 in his bank account and draws a cheque on that bank in favour of C for £200. C delays more than a reasonable time[8] in presenting the cheque for payment, and A's bank then fails and goes into liquidation. The bank is able to pay only 25p in the pound. A is regarded as creditor of the bank for £800 and will, therefore, receive £200 in the liquidation. A's liability to C will be discharged and C will obtain only £50 in the bank's liquidation.

The provision can only operate where there is delay in presentment for payment, the paying bank (ie, the bank on which the cheque is drawn) fails, and the drawer had funds in his bank account which could have been used to meet the cheque if it had been presented within a reasonable time.

Mutual duties of banker and customer

When a customer has deposited money with a banker on current account, he is a creditor of the banker though since demand for repayment is necessary before there is an enforceable debt, time does not begin to run against the customer until he has made a demand for repayment and it has been rejected.[9] Both the customer and his banker have, however, rights and duties that go beyond the ordinary creditor-debtor relationship.

Among the banker's duties to his customer are—

1. *To obey the mandate.*—A banker may only pay out of a customer's account if that customer or his authorised agent on his behalf has signed the cheque. In *Ligget (Liverpool) Ltd v Barclays Bank*[10] where a bank, which had been mandated by a company to pay cheques when drawn by two directors, paid a cheque drawn by one director only, it was not entitled to debit the company's account. However, in so far as cheques paid contrary to the mandate had gone in payment of the company's creditors, the bank was entitled to be subrogated to the position of those creditors.

8 Reasonable time for presenting a cheque for payment, in this context, seems to be 24 hours of receipt; where the holder uses a bank to collect payment, the question of reasonable time depends on the reasonableness of the banking practice adopted.
9 *Joachimson v Swiss Bank Corpn* [1921] 3 KB 110, [1921] All ER Rep 92. With a deposit account, if the customer must give notice of his intention to withdraw, time does not begin to run against him until the expiration of such notice.
10 [1928] 1 KB 48, [1927] All ER Rep 451. See also *National Westminster Bank Ltd v Barclays Bank International Ltd* [1975] QB 654, [1974] 3 All ER 834.

A bank has no right to debit a customer's account for the amount
of a cheque on which the customer's signature has been forged
because the bank has then no mandate from the customer to pay.[11]
Brewer v Westminster Bank Ltd,[12] is a difficult case on this point. A
joint executors' account was held at the defendant bank by two
executors, one of whom was the beneficiary of the estate. The bank's
mandate was to honour only cheques drawn on the account by both
the executors. The beneficiary's co-executor forged the beneficiary's signature on cheques drawn on the executors' account, adding
his own signature. McNair J refused to grant a declaration asked for
by the beneficiary that the bank had wrongly debited the executors'
account with the amounts of these cheques. The learned judge held
that since the bank's obligation was to the two executors jointly, no
action could be maintained unless each executor was in a position to
sue, which was not the case as the fraudulent executor had no right
to sue. This decision was, however, widely criticised by both
academic writers and judges. Professor Goodhart took the view that
where joint account holders have authorised their bank to honour
cheques only if they are signed by all the account holders, this, as
well as being a joint agreement with the bank, amounts to a
separate agreement between each joint account holder severally
and the bank.[13] Bingham J followed this view in *Catlin v Cyprus
Finance Corpn (London) Ltd*[14] and when the bank honoured a cheque
signed by only one of two joint account holders—the husband in
relation to a joint husband and wife account—the wife was held
entitled to claim from the bank.

A bank must pay only according to its customer's direction and as
a general rule, if it pays anyone whose title rests on a forged
indorsement and is, therefore, not entitled to receive payment, the
bank has no right to debit its customer's account. However, there
are statutory provisions, to be considered shortly, which, for
example, protect a banker who pays the amount of a cheque to
someone whose title rests on a forged indorsement. Further, where
the bank's error is occasioned by the customer's breach of his duty to
draw his cheques properly, the bank is protected. In *London Joint*

11 The customer may be estopped from denying the validity of his signature, as in
Greenwood v Martins Bank Ltd [1933] AC 51, [1932] All ER Rep 318. See p 248, ante.
However, a customer is not estopped simply because he has failed to examine a bank
statement from which he may have discovered that his signature on cheques was
being forged.
12 [1952] 2 All ER 650.
13 (1952) 68 LQR 446.
14 [1983] QB 759, [1983] 1 All ER 809.

Stock Bank Ltd v Macmillan and Arthur,[15] a clerk in the employ of the
respondents used to prepare cheques for signature. He prepared a
cheque payable to bearer for one of the respondents to sign, saying it
was for petty cash, with the amount of £2 written in figures but with
the space for the amount in words left blank. After the partner
signed the cheque, the clerk altered the figure of '£2' to '£120' and
filled in the space for the amount in words: 'One hundred and
twenty pounds'. The clerk cashed the cheque and the respondents
brought an action to recover from their bank £118. The House of
Lords, however, held that the action must fail because a customer
owes a duty to his bank to take reasonable care in drawing his
cheques not to leave spaces on the cheques whereby the amount can
readily be altered. Lord Finlay LC said that if a customer draws a
cheque in a manner which facilitates fraud he is guilty of a breach of
duty to his bank and is responsible to the bank for any loss that is a
natural consequence of the breach of duty.

The duty of a drawer to see that the amounts on a cheque cannot
readily be altered does not extend to see that there is no space
between the payee's name and the printed words 'or order'. In
Slingsby v District Bank Ltd,[16] solicitors, Messrs Cumberbirch and
Potts, prepared a cheque for signature by the plaintiffs, two
executors, the cheque being drawn on the defendant bank in favour
of a stockbroker. There was a space between the name of the payee
and the printed words 'or order' and, after the executors had signed
the cheque, one of the solicitors fraudulently inserted in the space
'per Cumberbirch and Potts', indorsed the cheque 'Cumberbirch
and Potts' and paid it into a bank to the credit of a company in
which he was interested. The defendant bank paid out the amount
of the cheque and debited the plaintiffs' account. The Court of
Appeal held, inter alia, that in leaving a blank space between the
name of the payee and the words 'or order' the executors were not
guilty of any breach of duty towards the defendant bank and the
bank had no right to debit the plaintiffs' account with the amount
of the cheque.

It seems that the customer's obligation to take reasonable care in
drawing cheques to draw them in such a way that fraud is not
facilitated does not go very far. In *Tai Hong Cotton Mill Ltd v Liu
Chong Hing Bank Ltd*,[17] the Privy Council ruled that a customer is

15 [1918] AC 777, [1918–19] All ER Rep 30.
16 [1932] 1 KB 544, [1931] All ER Rep 143. This decision might not be followed
today when drawing a line after the payee's name has become the common practice
of bank customers.
17 [1986] AC 80, [1985] 2 All ER 947.

under no obligation to check his periodic bank statements so as to enable him to inform the bank of any unauthorised debit items. If the customer is actually aware that unauthorised cheques have been drawn on his account, he is under a duty to inform the bank but is under no obligation to take reasonable precautions to prevent or seek out such cheques. The Privy Council expressed the view that forgery of cheques was a risk of the service that banks offered to their customers and the bank must in effect be an insurer against forgery on behalf of its customer. Only the imposition of an express obligation on the customer could alter that position.

It should be mentioned that there is no duty on the acceptor of a bill of exchange to see that the amount cannot readily be altered. In *Scholfield v Earl of Londesborough*,[18] the defendant accepted a bill for £500 and there were spaces that could be used to alter the amount in words and figures. The drawer of the bill did alter the amount of the bill to £3,500 and indorsed it to a holder in due course. The court held there was no duty on an acceptor to ensure that the amount on a bill cannot easily be altered and that the defendant was, therefore, liable only for £500.

2. *To honour cheques.*—A bank is bound to honour its customer's cheque to the extent that he is in credit or to the extent of any agreed overdraft.[19] If the customer is a trader (or, for example, a solicitor) breach of this duty entitles the customer to general damages without proving actual loss, for injury to his commercial or professional credit, and may recover any actual loss if proved as special damage.[20] A non-trader will only receive nominal damages unless the damage he has suffered is alleged and proved as special damage.[1] In any case, the holder has no claim against the bank on

18 [1896] AC 514, [1895–9] All ER Rep 282.

19 If a bank has misled a customer into thinking he has sufficient funds to meet a cheque, by an error in the customer's pass book or statement of account, the bank is bound to honour the cheque: *Holland v Manchester and Liverpool District Banking Co* (1909) 25 TLR 386; *Holt v Markham* [1923] 1 KB 504, [1922] All ER Rep 134.

20 *Fleming v Bank of New Zealand* [1900] AC 577.

1 *Gibbons v Westminster Bank Ltd* [1939] 2 KB 882, [1939] 3 All ER 577. Because of this rule, it is sometimes thought that, for a private customer, bringing an action for libel based on the bank's answer when refusing to pay the cheque may be a more worthwhile course to follow. In a New Zealand case words instructing the payee to 'present again' have been held to be capable of a defamatory meaning (*Baker v Australia and New Zealand Bank* [1958] NZLR 907), but British banks prefer to use the words 'refer to drawer' (or 'R/D') and, although the matter is not beyond doubt, those words were considered by Scrutton LJ in *Flach v London and South Western Bank Ltd* (1915) 31 TLR 334, not to be capable of a defamatory meaning. See also *Jayson v Midland Bank Ltd* [1968] 1 Lloyd's Rep 409.

which the cheque is drawn. A bank may not close a current account which is in credit without giving the customer reasonable notice[2] and even if the account is not in credit, the bank must give reasonable notice before withdrawing agreed overdraft facilities.[3]

The bank's duty to honour cheques ceases on the customer countermanding payment and also on receiving notice of the customer's death (s 75). In *Curtice v London City and Midland Bank Ltd*[4] Curtice drew a cheque on his bank, and the same day he countermanded payment by telegram. The telegram was put into the bank's letter box, and because of want of care on the part of the bank's servants, two days elapsed before the telegram was brought to the notice of the bank manager. The cheque had meanwhile been paid. In an action by the customer for money had and received, the Court of Appeal held that the bank was not liable since the cheque had not been effectively countermanded even though it was due to the carelessness of the bank's servants that notice of the customer's desire to stop the cheque was not received in time.[5] Further, a bank is not bound to rely on an unconfirmed telegram or telephone message and such attempted countermand may only be acted upon by the bank to the extent of postponing payment.

Contrast *Burnett v Westminister Bank Ltd*[6] Burnett had current accounts with the A and B branches of the bank. As the bank had introduced a computer which could read the magnetic characters of a cheque but not ordinary ink, the cheque book issued by the A branch bore on its cover (for the first time) a statement that cheques must not be used to draw on any other account. Burnett did not read this prohibition and on a cheque for £2,300 he altered it in ink so that it was addressed to the B branch. Shortly afterwards he told the B branch, first by telephone and then in writing, not to pay the cheque but as the computer was blind to the alteration the cheque was collected from the A branch and Burnett's account there was debited. Mocatta J held that Burnett was entitled to have his account credited with the £2,300 as he had never instructed the bank to debit his account at the A branch with that sum. The judge did not consider that Burnett had *agreed* to the provision on the cheque book cover.

2 *Prosperity Ltd v Lloyds Bank Ltd* (1923) 39 TLR 372.
3 *Rouse v Bradford Banking Co Ltd* [1894] AC 586.
4 [1908] 1 KB 293.
5 If the bank had been sued in negligence, it may well have been held liable but the measure of damages in negligence may not be the same as in an action for money had and received.
6 [1966] 1 QB 742, [1965] 3 All ER 81.

A bank's duty to honour cheques also ceases on receiving notice of the customer's mental incapacity, and if the customer is a joint-stock company, on notice of the commencement of the winding-up of the company. Commencement of the winding-up of a company means the time of presentation of a petition or the time of passing a resolution for voluntary winding-up if that precedes a petition.[7] Similarly the service on the banker of a garnishee order nisi suspends the banker's duty to honour cheques until the order or summons is discharged and it matters not that the balance to the customer's credit in his current account is in excess of the judgment debt.[8] However, if a named sum is expressed in the garnishee order *nisi* as the limit attachable, being the amount of the judgment debt together with an estimated allowance for costs, this sum will be earmarked by the banker to a suspense account and the balance can continue to be operated by the customer.

3. *To take reasonable care.*—Even where a cheque drawn on behalf of a company contains the authorised signatures, if the bank knows or ought to know that it has been drawn for an unauthorised purpose it is liable to the company should it pay out on the cheque.[9]

4. *To observe secrecy.*—A bank is under a duty of secrecy in relation to the financial affairs of its customer, but there are certain exceptions. In *Tournier v National Provincial and Union Bank of England*,[10] Bankes LJ said that the qualifications to the rule could be classified under four heads: (a) where disclosure is under compulsion of law, eg, an order of the court under the Bankers' Books Evidence Act 1879, (b) where there is a duty to the public to disclose (eg, in wartime where the customer's account indicates he is trading with the enemy), (c) where the interests of the bank require

---

7 Companies Act 1985 s 524.

8 *Rogers v Whiteley* [1892] AC 118. The garnishee procedure is available only to debts 'owing or accruing' from a third party to the judgment debtor and normally no money is 'due' from the bank to the holder of a current account until demand, but the court of Appeal held in *Joachimson v Swiss Bank Corpn* [1921] 3 KB 110, [1921] All ER Rep 92, that the service of a garnishee summons may be taken as a demand. By s 38 of the Administration of Justice Act 1956, a deposit account is now subject to attachment by way of garnishee although, generally, the money is only withdrawable by notice or subject to some other condition being satisfied.

9 *Selangor United Rubber Estates Ltd v Cradock* [1968] 2 All ER 1073, [1968] WLR 1555; *Karak Rubber Co Ltd v Burden (No 2)* [1972] 1 All ER 1210, [1972] 1 WLR 602.

10 [1924] 1 KB 461, 473, [1923] All ER Rep 550.

disclosure (eg, where the bank is suing on an overdraft) and (d) where the disclosure is made by the express or implied consent of the customer (eg, where the customer authorizes a reference to his bank). Where none of these exceptions apply, as in the case of *Tournier* itself—bank informed customer's employers that his account was overdrawn and that he was suspected of gambling, as a result of which his employment was not renewed—the bank is liable in damages to its customer.

5. *To collect cheques paid in.*—A bank is under a duty to collect for its customer's account cheques paid in by the customer. The bank acts then as a collecting bank and may obtain the protection of s 4 of the Cheques Act 1957 if its customer has a defective title to the cheque.[11]

Crossed cheques

Where a cheque bears across its face an addition of the words 'and company' or any abbreviation thereof between two parallel transverse lines, or simply two parallel transverse lines, in either case with or without the words 'not negotiable', the cheque is said to be crossed generally (s 76). Such a cheque will only be paid by the bank on which it is drawn (the paying bank) through another bank and not over the counter. It is therefore a hindrance for someone who obtains the cheque wrongfully, because he could only obtain payment through a bank, the loss may be discovered meanwhile and the cheque stopped. The statutory provisions as to crossed cheques in ss 76–81 apply also to banker's drafts, dividend warrants, 'Pay Cash' documents, conditional orders, and to warrants and similar documents issued by a public officer.[12]

If the cheque bears across its face the addition of the name of a banker, it will only be paid by the paying bank to the bank which is so named; the cheque is then said to be specially crossed whether there are transverse parallel lines on the cheque as well or not.

Neither a general or special crossing prevents the cheque being transferred but if the crossed cheque bears on it the words 'not negotiable' no one can claim to have a better title than the previous holder, ie, no one can claim to be a holder in due course taking the

11 See p 280, post.
12 Cheques Act 1957 s 5.

cheque free from defects (s 81).[13] Thus, where a cheque crossed 'not negotiable' was given in respect of gaming tokens, and therefore for an illegal consideration, the indorsee had no better title than the payee and had no right of action against the drawer.[14]

If a cheque is issued uncrossed, a holder can cross it generally or specially and if it is issued crossed generally, a holder may turn the crossing into a special crossing. A holder may also add the words 'not negotiable' to a crossing and a banker asked to collect an uncrossed or generally crossed cheque may cross it specially to himself.

Where a cheque is crossed specially, the banker to whom it is crossed may again cross it specially to another bank for collection, and where an uncrossed cheque or cheque crossed generally is sent to a banker for collection he may cross it specially to himself (s 77). By s 78, a crossing authorised by the Bills of Exchange Act is a material part of the cheque, and it is not lawful for any person to obliterate it or, except as authorised by the Act, to add to or alter the crossing.

Where a cheque is crossed specially to more than one banker, except when crossed to an agent for collection being a banker, the banker on whom it is drawn must refuse payment. If he does pay such a cheque, or if he pays a cheque crossed generally otherwise than to a banker, or if crossed specially otherwise than to the banker to whom it is crossed, or his agent for collection being a banker, he is liable to the true owner of the cheque for any loss sustained (s 79). Therefore, where a bearer cheque is crossed and handed to C, if a thief of the cheque obtains payment of the cheque across the counter, the paying banker would be liable to C. There is statutory protection for the paying banker, however, if the cheque does not at the time of presentment appear to have been crossed, or to have had a crossing which has been obliterated, and the banker is in good faith and without negligence.

Statutory protection of a paying banker

We have already seen that if a customer draws a cheque on his bank, the bank owes him a duty to obey his directions. If the cheque is

13 If the words 'not negotiable' appear on an open cheque (ie, a cheque which is crossed) they are presumably intended to have the same effect as when they appear on the crossed cheque: Chorley *Law of Banking* (6th edn, 1974) p 57. If the words 'not negotiable' appear on a bill of exchange, other than a cheque, they have been held to mean that the bill may not be transferred at all. See p 231, ante.

14 *Ladup v Shaikh* [1983] QB 225.

payable to bearer, then the bank can properly debit the drawer's account with the amount of the cheque if it pays in good faith any bearer of it whether rightfully entitled or not—it is a payment in due course and a good discharge of the cheque under s 59. However, in the case of an order cheque, the bank on which it is drawn may only debit the drawer's account in favour of the payee or some other person to whom the cheque has been properly negotiated. Otherwise, it is liable in conversion to the true owner of the cheque. That is the general rule for order cheques but the paying bank may be able to claim statutory protection if it does pay someone who has no title at all to the cheque. The relevant statutory provisions are ss 60 and 80 of the Bills of Exchange Act and s 1 of the Cheques Act 1957.

The Cheques Act 1957 resulted from the Report of the Mocatta Committee on Cheque Endorsement published in the previous year. The main purpose of the Act was to make it unnecessary for the payee of a cheque or a subsequent indorsee to indorse the cheque before paying it into his own bank account or for the credit of a joint or partnership account when the payee is one of the holders of the account. Indorsement of a cheque is still necessary to effect the negotiation of an order cheque and it is the practice of banks to require an indorsement when cashing uncrossed cheques across the counter.The Cheques Act merely amended the law in certain limited respects and, in the absence of consolidating legislation, there is at present some overlapping between the statutory provisions that give the paying banker certain protection when paying someone who has no title.

1. *Under s 80 of the Bills of Exchange Act.*—Section 80 reads:—

'Where the banker, on whom a crossed cheque is drawn, in good faith and without negligence pays it, if crossed generally, to a banker, and if crossed specially, to the banker to whom it is crossed, or his agent for collection being a banker, the banker paying the cheque, and, if the cheque has come into the hands of the payee, the drawer, shall respectively be entitled to the same rights and be placed in the same position as if payment of the cheque had been made to the true owner thereof.'

To illustrate the operation of this section, let us suppose A draws a crossed cheque in favour of C from whom it is stolen and the thief forges C's signature in order to negotiate the cheque to D. If A's bank pays the amount of the cheque to D's bank, assuming that it is not crossed specially to some other bank, and A's bank in making this payment is in good faith and not negligent, A's bank has a right under s 80 to debit A's account with the amount of the cheque although D has no title to the cheque. Furthermore, by virtue of the same section, since the cheque came into the hands of the payee C before it was stolen, A is under no further liability to C either on the cheque or on the underlying debt for payment of which the cheque was drawn. C's only remedy is to claim the amount of the cheque from D who has no title to it as it rests on a forged indorsement.

2. *Under s 60 of the Bills of Exchange Act.*—Wider protection for a banker paying the amount of a cheque to someone other than a person rightfully entitled to the cheque is given by s 60. Firstly, s 60 applies to uncrossed cheques as well as to crossed cheques and secondly, it applies even though the paying banker has been negligent provided he has acted 'in the ordinary course of business'.

Section 60 reads:—

> 'When a bill payable to order on demand is drawn on a banker, and the banker on whom it is drawn pays the bill in good faith and in the ordinary course of business, it is not incumbent on the banker to show that the indorsement of the payee or any subsequent indorsement was made by or under the authority of the person whose indorsement it purports to be, and the banker is deemed to have paid the bill in due course, although such indorsement has been forged or made without authority.'

Using a similar illustration to that given for the application of s 80, suppose A draws a cheque (crossed or uncrossed) in favour of C from whom it is stolen and the thief forges C's indorsement in order to negotiate the cheque to D. If A's bank pays the cheque to D's bank or, if uncrossed, cashes it for D over the counter, then provided A's bank has acted in good faith and 'in the ordinary course of business' ie, in accordance with normal banking practice, A's bank is entitled to debit A's account with the amount of the cheque.[15] The drawer of the cheque A is under no further liability to the payee C provided, as in our illustration, the cheque came into his hands before it was stolen.[16]

Neither s 80 nor s 60 gives any protection to a paying banker

---

15 In *Carpenters' Co v British Mutual Banking Co* [1938] 1 KB 511, [1937] 3 All ER 811, Slesser and Mackinnon LJJ (Greer LJ contra) said that negligence did not preclude the protection of s 60, but it has been suggested that for most purposes due care and action in the ordinary course of business are synonymous: *Chorley* p 93.

16 *Charles v Blackwell* (1877) 2 CPD 151.

where its customer's signature as drawer is forged, or where there has been a material alteration of the cheque.[17]

3. *Under s 1 (1) of the Cheques Act 1957.*—Section 1 (1) of the Cheques Act reads:—

'Where a banker in good faith and in the ordinary course of business pays a cheque drawn on him which is not indorsed or is irregularly indorsed, he does not, in doing so, incur any liability by reason only of the absence of, or irregularity in, indorsement, and he is deemed to have paid it in due course.'

Suppose A draws a cheque on the X bank in favour of C from whom it is stolen. The thief, instead of negotiating it, is able to open a bank account in the same of C at the Y bank and the Y bank collect payment of the cheque for their new customer under the erroneous impression that he is C. Since the Cheques Act 1957, the Y bank would not require its customers to indorse the cheque before collecting it for him. If the X bank pay the amount of the cheque to the Y bank in good faith and in the ordinary course of business, the X bank is entitled to debit A's account.

It is s 1 of the Cheques Act that gives the paying banker protection where there is no indorsement on the cheque and the same section is applicable to give protection if there is an irregular indorsement, eg, there is a discrepancy between the name of the payee as it appears on the face of the cheque and an indorsement on the back. Section 60 of the Bills of Exchange Act, on the other hand, gives protection to the paying banker where there is a forged or unauthorised indorsement on the cheque.

If, in our illustration of the application of s 1 of the Cheques Act, the cheque were uncrossed and the thief sought payment of it across the counter from the drawer's bank, the X bank, the bank could not claim the protection of s 1 if it paid the cheque without requiring his indorsement because it is 'in the ordinary course of business' for a paying bank to demand indorsement when cashing a cheque across the counter. If indorsement were demanded by the paying bank, presumably the thief would forge C's indorsement and the paying bank could claim the protection of s 60. It seems clear that a paying bank cannot claim the protection of s 1 where any indorsement, other than that of the person who presents the cheque for payment, is missing or is irregular.

17 *Slingsby v District Bank Ltd* [1932] 1 KB 544, [1931] All ER Rep 143. Section 60 does not apply to a banker's draft but by the Stamp Act 1853 s 19, the paying bank obtains similar protection with regard to such instruments.

Section 1 (2) gives similar protection to a paying bank where the instrument is a banker's draft, or though not a bill of exchange the instrument is 'intended to enable a person to obtain payment' from the bank of the sum mentioned in the document, eg, a 'Pay Cash' document or a conditional order or a dividend warrant.

Statutory protection of the collecting banker

At common law, if a banker collected a cheque for his customer and that customer had no rightful title to it, he would be liable in conversion to the true owner. Statutory protection, however, is given to the collecting banker provided he can establish that he has acted without negligence by s 4 (1) of the Cheques Act.[18]

'Where a banker, in good faith and without negligence—
  (a) receives payment for a customer of an instrument to which this section applies; or
  (b) having credited a customer's account with the amount of such an instrument, receives payment thereof for himself,
and the customer has no title, or a defective title, to the instrument, the banker does not incur any liability to the true owner of the instrument by reason only of having received payment thereof.'

Section 4 (2) expressly refers to cheques as 'instruments' to which the section applies and also covered are dividend warrants and 'Pay Cash' documents which, though not bills of exchange, are both 'intended to enable a person to obtain payment 'from the bank of the sums mentioned in the documents, bankers' drafts, and any warrants or similar documents issued by a public officer. It will be noted that a collecting bank can only claim the protection of s 4 if it is collecting payment of a cheque for 'a customer' or if before collection it has already credited 'a customer's' account with the amount of the cheque. A bank collecting a cheque for someone as a casual service could not claim to be collecting it for a customer, but it is clear from the cases that a person who has handed in a cheque for an account to be opened is immediately 'a customer' within the meaning of s 4. As Atkin LJ put it in *Taxation Comrs v English, Scottish and Australian Bank*[19] 'the contrast is not between a habitué and a newcomer, but between a person for whom the bank performs a casual service, such as, for instance, cashing a cheque for a person

18 Prior to 1957, protection was afforded to a collecting banker in the case of crossed cheques only by s 82 of the Bills of Exchange Act as amended by s 1 of the Bills of Exchange (Crossed Cheques) Act 1906.
19 [1920] AC 683, 687.

introduced by one of their customers, and a person who has an account of his own at the bank'. It would seem that if the bank gave its customer cash across the counter for the cheque and the bank therefore did not credit the customer's account with the amount of the cheque but were, in effect, purchasing or discounting the cheque, the bank would not be entitled to the protection of s 4 and would be liable in conversion to the true owner if an indorsement in the cheque were forged; on the other hand, if there were no such forgery, clearly the bank would be a holder for value of the cheque and may also be a holder in due course.[20]

A more difficult question is whether a bank may claim the protection of s 4 of the Cheques Act if it not only credits its customer's account with the amount of a cheque before collection but also agrees to the customer drawing on the account before the proceeds of the cheque are collected. Section 82 of the Bill of Exchange Act applied only where a bank collected a cheque for a customer and, therefore, did not apply if a bank credited the customer's account before clearance, but by s 1 of the Bills of Exchange (Crossed Cheques) Act 1906, a bank was deemed to collect for a customer notwithstanding that he credited his customer's account before clearance. However, under that provision, if there was a contract whereby a bank agreed to the customer drawing on the amount before the proceeds of the cheque were collected the bank would have been collecting the cheque for itself and therefore not entitled to statutory protection. But s 4 (1) (b) of the Cheques Act does expressly protect a banker who, having credited the customer's account receives payment for himself, and would now seem to give protection in this situation.[1]

We have seen that the main purpose of the Cheques Act 1957 was to make it unnecessary for the payee of a cheque or a subsequent indorsee to indorse the cheque before paying into his own account, and s 4 (3) provides that a banker is not to be treated as negligent by reason only of his failure to concern himself with the absence of, or irregularity in, indorsement.[2]

There are many reported cases where the courts have found a bank negligent in collecting a cheque for a customer.[3] For example,

---

20 See post, p 285.

1 See also *Chitty* para 2642.

2 It seems certain that a bank collecting for someone other than the payee must see that there are indorsements on the back of the cheque linking the payee with the present holder and that they are not irregular.

3 For an examination of the cases, see Borrie 'Problems of the Collecting Bank' (1960) 23 MLR 16.

it has long been held negligent for a bank to collect for a customer who is an employee a cheque drawn by third parties in favour of the customer's employer and apparently indorsed by the employer, or a cheque drawn by the customer's employers in favour of a third party. In *Lloyds Bank Ltd v Savory & Co*,[4] bearer cheques drawn by a firm of stockbrokers in the City of London were paid to the credit of a housewife's private account at Redhill. The bank was held negligent because it had failed to inquire of the housewife when she opened the account the name of her husband's employers. If it had done so, it would have discovered that he was a clerk employed by the stockbrokers. In *Midland Bank Ltd v Reckitt*[5] cheques were signed 'R by T his attorney', and paid by T into his own overdrawn bank account. T's bankers, having noticed from the form of the cheques that the money was not T's money, were held by the House of Lords to be negligent in omitting to ask to see T's power of attorney or to make any other enquiry as to T's authority to pay the moneys into his own account. Another example of a similar sort of case is *Marquess of Bute v Barclays Bank Ltd*.[6] One McGaw, in his capacity as manager of farms belonging to the Marquess of Bute, made applications to the Department of Agriculture for Scotland for hill sheep subsidies. McGaw left the Marquess's employment and subsequently warrants drawn by the Department (similar in effect to cheques) were sent to McGaw in satisfaction of his applications. Each warrant was made payble to 'D McGaw (for the Marquess of Bute)'. McGaw applied to a branch of the defendant bank for permission to open a personal account with the warrants and the bank did so, collecting the amounts of these warrants for McGaw's newly opened personal account. The court held that the defendant bank was liable in conversion to the Marquess and could not claim statutory protection because it had not discharged the onus of proving that it had acted without negligence. McNair J pointed out that the warrants clearly indicated that McGaw was to receive the money as an agent and it is elementary banking practice that such documents should not be credited to a personal account of the named payee without inquiry.

In *A L Underwood Ltd v Bank of Liverpool*,[7] where a cheque was

4 [1933] AC 201, [1932] All ER Rep 106.
5 [1933] AC 1, [1932] All ER Rep 90.
6 [1955] 1 QB 202, [1954] 3 All ER 365.
7 [1924] 1 KB 775, [1924] All ER Rep 230. Exceptionally, a company's agent may have implied authority to indorse a cheque payable to the company and to pay it into his own account; *Australia and New Zealand Bank Ltd v Ateliers De Constructions Electrique de Charleroi* [1967] 1 AC 86, PC.

made payable to a one-man company, it was held negligent for a bank to collect it for the private account of the 'one man' who was also the managing director. Broadly, whenever the terms of a cheque would raise a doubt in the mind of a bank cashier of ordinary intelligence and care as to whether the customer has a good title to it, the bank owes a duty to make inquiries as to the customer's title.

In most of the decided cases, the collecting bank has not been able to establish that it has acted 'without negligence'. However, in *Orbit Mining and Trading Co Ltd v Westminister Bank Ltd*,[8] the bank did succeed in this defence. Two directors of the plaintiff company, W and E, were authorised jointly to sign cheques on the company's behalf. When W went abroad he left some cheque forms signed by him in blank for use by E in the company's business. E completed them 'Pay Cash or order', added his own signature, and the words 'for and on behalf of' the company, and paid them into the defendant bank for collection for his own private account. The Court of Appeal held that the bank had not been negligent and were therefore protected by s 4 of the Cheques Act. The court took the view that 'Pay Cash or order' is not itself a suspicious form of drawing, and that as the bank did not know of E's connection with the plaintiff company and E's own signature on the cheque was illegible, there was nothing to indicate to the bank that their customer E was concerned with the drawing of the cheque.

Another recent decision, showing perhaps a trend in favour of a more lenient attitude towards banks, is *Marfani & Co Ltd v Midland Bank Ltd*.[9] A cheque for £3,000 was signed on behalf of the plaintiff company in favour of E. K (an employee of the plaintiffs) obtained possession of the cheque, and calling himself E, sought to open an account at a branch of the Midland Bank in the name of E. The bank agreed to do this and obtained a reference from A who knew K as E and had been a valued customer of the bank for six years. The bank collected the cheque for K (known as E) and after a few weeks K withdrew all the money from his account and left the country. The Court of Appeal held that the bank had acted according to the current practice of bankers and, relying on A's reference, was not negligent in failing to ask for identification or inquire as to K's employment. However, Diplock LJ in this case did emphasise that the onus of showing that the bank took reasonable care lies on the bank. Generally, where the customer is in possession of the cheque

8 [1963] 1 QB 794, [1962] 3 All ER 565.
9 [1968] 2 All ER 573, [1968] 1 WLR 956, CA.

at the time of delivery for collection, and appears on the face of it to be the holder, the bank may assume that the customer is the owner of the cheque unless there are facts which are known or ought to be known to the bank which should cause it to suspect that the customer is not the true owner. In *Thackwell v Barclays Bank plc*,[10] Hutchison J applied Diplock LJ's dicta and held that, on the facts, the circumstances in which the cheque in issue had been presented for collection were so unusual that the bank ought to have been put on inquiry and its failure to make inquiries amounted to negligence, disentitling it from the protection of s 4 of the Cheques Act.[11]

Even if a collecting bank is held not to be protected by s 4 of the Cheques Act because of negligence, the damages it must pay in conversion to the true owner may be reduced by contributory negligence on the part of the owner. A decision to this effect by Donaldson J in 1971[12] was inadvertently reversed by s 11 (1) of the Torts (Interference with Goods) Act 1977 which reads: 'Contributory negligence is no defence in proceedings founded on conversion . . .' However, the decision was in effect restored by the Banking Act 1979 s 47:—

> 'In any circumstances in which proof of absence of negligence on the part of a banker would be a defence in proceedings by reason of section 4 of the Cheques Act 1957, a defence of contributory negligence shall also be available to the banker notwithstanding the provision of section 11 (1) of the Torts (Interference with Goods) Act 1977.'

Where a cheque is drawn by A in favour of a creditor, and A's employee forges the payee's signature and pays it into his own account at the same bank on which the cheque is drawn, the fact that as paying bank it is protected from liability by paying in good faith and in the ordinary course of business (s 60) does not assist it if, as the collecting bank, it is unable to establish that it has acted without negligence.[13]

Crossing 'account payee'.—This crossing has no legislative sanction but may afford greater protection to the true owner of a cheque. Its effect is to put the collecting bank under a duty to make inquiry to see that it collects for the payee named on the cheque or that its customer has the payee's authority. It does not restrict the

10 [1986] 1 All ER 676.
11 However, the plaintiff payee of the cheque failed in his action for conversion against the collecting bank on the principle of *ex turpi causa non oritur actio*.
12 *Lumsden & Co v London Trustee Savings Bank* [1971] 1 Lloyd's Rep 114.
13 *Carpenter Co v British Mutual Banking Co* [1938] 1 KB 511, [1937] 3 All ER 811.

negotiability of a cheque,[14] but if the bank does not make such inquiry it would be liable if it collected for someone other than the true owner.[15] It is best for a drawer to combine this crossing with a 'not negotiable' crossing because otherwise, should the cheque be indorsed in blank and then stolen, it may come into the hands of a holder in due course who could compel payment by the drawer.

Bank as holder for value or holder in due course.—A bank can only show it is a holder in due course of a cheque if, inter alia, it has given value for the cheque. Value is deemed to have been given by the collecting bank if there is an express or implied agreement with its customer to apply the cheque in the reduction of an overdraft or to allow him to draw against it before the proceeds have been cleared or if, in fact, it has given cash for the cheque across the counter or if it has a lien on the cheque.[16] However, as Atkin LJ said in the *Underwood* case:[17]

'the mere fact that the bank in their books enter the value of the cheques on the credit side of the account on the day on which they receive the cheques for collection does not without more constitute the bank a holder for value.'

By s 2 of the Cheques Act,

'A banker who gives value for, or has a lien on, a cheque payble to order which the holder delivers to him for collection without indorsing it, has such (if any) rights as he would have had if, upon delivery, the holder had indorsed it in blank.'

As was held by Megaw J in *Midland Bank Ltd v R V Harris, Ltd*,[18] where the bank has given value for a cheque, eg, because the customer is by agreement permitted to draw against a cheque

14 *National Bank v Silke* [1891] 1 QB 435.
15 *In Universal Guarantee Property Ltd v National Bank of Australia Ltd* [1965] 2 All ER 98, [1965] 1 WLR 691, PC, the bank was dealing with cheques crossed 'account payee' drawn in favour of X, apparently indorsed by X and paid in by the customer drawing the cheque, leading merely to two contra items in the customer's account. The Judicial Committee thought there was nothing suspicious in this to put the bank on inquiry which might have led to the early discovery of fraud committed by the customer's employee.
16 If a customer is overdrawn when he pays in the cheque, the bank is deemed to be a holder for value to the extent of the overdraft, whether there was any agreed arrangement for paying off the overdraft or not. See p 242, ante, on the application of s 27 (3) and *Barclays Bank Ltd v Astley Industrial Bank* [1970] 2 QB 527, [1970] 1 All ER 719.
17 [1924] 1 KB 775.
18 [1963] 2 All ER 685, [1963] 1 WLR 1021 followed in *Re Keever, a Bankrupt, ex p Trustee of Property of Bankrupt v Midland Bank* [1967] Ch 182, [1966] 3 All ER 631.

before it is cleared, the lack of any indorsement by the customer before paying it into the bank for collection and crediting to his account is immaterial—the bank is still a holder for value. It follows that if the customer was payee of the cheque and yet gave no value for it, nevertheless the bank could enforce payment against the drawer. In *Westminster Bank Ltd v Zang*[19] the House of Lords held that s 2 did not restrict the protection accorded collecting banks to cases where they are to collect for the holder and for no one else because the words 'for collection' appear in the section without any qualification. In consequence, if the holder of a cheque, X, without indorsing it, pays it into a bank to be credited to the account of Y, the bank may enforce it if it has given value for or has a lien on it. Zang drew a cheque for £1,000 in favour of one Tilley who was managing director of Tilley Autos, Ltd. Without indorsing the cheque, Tilley paid it into the Westminster Bank for the account of Tilley Autos Ltd. The cheque was dishonoured and the Westminster Bank claimed to be holders in due course of the cheque and therefore entitled to succeed in an action against Zang. The House of Lords held (i) that s 2 of the Cheques Act applied as the cheque was handed over to the bank 'for collection' although the holder handed it to the bank for the account of someone else's account, and the bank were, therefore, holders of the cheque; but (ii) that the bank failed to establish that it had agreed to allow Tilley Autos Ltd to draw on the amount of the cheque before it was cleared and, therefore, the bank were not holders for value or holders in due course. Moreover, it could not claim to have given value by using the cheque to reduce the company's overdraft as it had continued to charge interest on the amount of the cheque.

If the bank has not only given value but fulfils all the particulars of the definition of a holder in due course, by reason, inter alia, of being in good faith and having no knowledge of any defect in the title of its customer, it has a good defence to any claim in conversion even if it could not, because of negligence, claim the protection of s 4 of the Cheques Act. Of course, the collecting bank cannot claim to be a holder in due course of a cheque if its title rests on a forged indorsement; nor if there is an irregular indorsement on it because the cheque would not then be 'complete and regular on the face of it' as required by the definition of a holder in due course in s 29 of the

19 [1966] AC 182, [1966] 1 All ER 114. The House of Lords did not determine the question whether value may be deemed to be given by a collecting bank which, without prior agreement, does allow the cheque to be drawn against before the proceeds have been cleared.

Bills of Exchange Act, and s 2 of the Cheques Act covers only the absence of indorsement, not an irregular indorsement.

Cheque as a receipt

By s 3 of the Cheques Act, 'an unindorsed cheque which appears to have been paid by the banker on whom it is drawn is evidence of receipt by the payee of the sum payable by the cheque'.[20]

PROMISSORY NOTES

Section 83 (1) of the Bills of Exchange Act defines a promissory note as follows:—

> 'A promissory note is an unconditional promise in writing made by one person to another signed by the maker, engaging to pay, on demand or at a fixed or determinable future time, a sum certain in money, to, or to the order of, a specified person or to bearer.'

The various phrases in the definition that are similar to the phrases in the definition of a bill can be understood by reference to the explanation given earlier of the latter definition. Clearly the note must contain a promise so that an IOU, which is merely an acknowledgement of a debt and no more, cannot be a promissory note. While the promise must be unconditional, s 83 (3) provides that a note is not invalid by reason only that it contains a pledge of collateral security with authority to sell or dispose thereof.

In the following example, Alan Adams is the maker of the promissory note and Charles Smith the payee.

£1,000   London, 1 July 1988

Three months after date I promise to pay
Charles Smith or order the sum of one
thousand pounds for value received.

                          Alan Adams

---

20 Even before the Cheques Act, a paid *indorsed* cheque was prima facie evidence of payment: *Egg v Barnett* (1800) 3 Esp 196.

It is provided by s 85 (1) that a promissory note may be made by two or more makers, and they may be liable thereon jointly, or jointly and severally according to its tenor, and by s 85 (2) that where a note runs 'I promise to pay' and is signed by two or more persons, it is deemed to be a joint and several note. If the note is a joint note, the holder has only one cause of action on it, so that if he sues only one or some of the makers and the judgment is unsatisfied, no action may then be brought against the other makers. On the other hand, if the makers' liability is joint and several, a holder of the note has as many causes of action on the note as there are makers. By s 83 (2) an instrument in the form of a note made payable to its maker's order is inchoate and not a valid note until it is indorsed by the maker and there is a general provision that a promissory note is inchoate until delivery to the payee or bearer (s 84).

A note which is or on the face of it purports to be both made and payable within the British Islands is an inland note—any other note is a foreign note (s 83 (4)), but where a foreign note is dishonoured, it need not be protested for dishonour (s 89 (4)).

Only if a note is made payable at a particular place by a provision in the body of the note must it be presented for payment to the maker (at that place) to render him liable on it, and even then presentment need not be punctual. No presentment to him is necessary to render him liable on the note in any other case (s 87 (1)). However, presentment to the maker for payment is necessary to render an indorser liable and that means punctual or 'due presentment', ie, within a reasonable time of the indorsement in the case of demand notes, and on the last day for payment in the case of time notes (s 87 (2)). Presentment must be at the place specified in the body of the note, if any, to render an indorser liable. If the place at which presentment to the maker should be made is merely specified in a memorandum, added perhaps after the maker's signature, presentment to the maker either at that place or elsewhere is sufficient to render the indorser liable (s 87 (3)).

Generally speaking, the law relating to bills of exchange applies also to promissory notes, and the maker of the note corresponds to the acceptor of a bill, ie, the maker is the person primarily liable on a note and the indorsers are in the position of sureties. The maker engages that he will pay it according to its tenor and is precluded from denying to a holder in due course the existence of the payee and his then capacity to indorse. Further, although where a note payable on demand has been indorsed, it must be presented for payment to the maker within a reasonable time of the indorsement or the indorser is discharged (s 86 (1)), the maker remains liable for the six year limitation period from the date when the note matures.

By s 86 (3), a holder of a demand note is treated as the holder in due course of it although more than a reasonable time has elapsed between its issue and its negotiation to him—it is not deemed to be overdue because a promissory note is treated as a continuing security.[1]

NEGOTIABLE INSTRUMENTS AND CONFLICT OF LAWS

A number of difficult problems arise if a bill of exchange drawn in one country is accepted, negotiated, or payable in another country, and similarly, if a promissory note made in one country is negotiated or payable in another. When the effect of some transaction that has taken place on a bill or note is considered by the English courts, whether English law or some other law is to be applied depends largely on the rules found in s 72 of the Bills of Exchange Act.[2] Whether any document can be treated as a negotiable instrument is a matter for English law to determine if the alleged negotiation took place in England.[3]

Before examining the various rules, it should be realised that a negotiable instrument may embody several distinct contracts. For example, the original contract in a bill of exchange is that between the drawer and the payee and the 'supervening contracts' are those represented by the acceptance of the bill and each indorsement. By and large, the liability of each party is governed by the law of the place where the particular contract to which he is party was made.

1. Form

As a general rule, 'the validity of a bill as regards requisites in form' for example, whether the bill contains an unconditional promise, 'is determined by the law of the place of issue', the 'place of issue' being where the drawer delivers the bill to the payee (s 72 (1)). However, where a bill is issued out of the United Kingdom, it is not invalid by

1 The position is, therefore, different from that of the holder of a bill who cannot be a holder in due course if the bill has been in circulation for more than a reasonable time: s 36 (3). See ante, p 244.

2 The section has been described by the editor of *Cheshire* as verging 'perilously on the unintelligible'. Cheshire *Private International Law* (9th edn, 1974) p 260.

3 *Picker v London and County Banking Co* (1887) 18 QBD 515.

reason only that it is not stamped in accordance with the law of the place of issue. Further, where a bill issued out of the United Kingdom is valid as to form by the law of the United Kingdom, it may, for the purpose of enforcing payment thereof, be treated as valid between all parties who negotiate, hold, or become parties to it in the United Kingdom.

The formal validity of the supervening contracts, such as acceptance or indorsement, is determined by the law of the place where such contract was made. The contract between the payee and his indorsee, for example, is made where the bill is delivered to the indorsee.

2. Interpretation and legal effect

Generally, the interpretation of the drawing, indorsement, or acceptance, of a bill is determined by the law of the place where such contract is made (s 72 (2)). As an example, whether an acceptance of a bill is unconditional or qualified is determined by the law of the place where the drawee accepted the bill. In *Embiricos v Anglo-Austrian Bank*[4] a cheque was drawn in Roumania on an English bank payable to the plaintiffs and stolen. It was clearly a 'foreign bill' because an 'inland bill' is defined in the 1882 Act as one which is both drawn and payable within the British Islands, or which is drawn within the British Islands upon some person resident there, and any other bill is a 'foreign bill'. An indorsement was forged in Austria and the cheque was negotiated to a bank in Vienna. The Vienna bank indorsed the cheque to the defendants who were their London agents and the defendants collected the amount from the bank on which the cheque was drawn. By the law of Austria, a holder could obtain a good title through such a forged indorsement and, since Austrian law governed the interpretation of the indorsement, the defendants were held not liable in conversion. It has been argued that the decision in *Embiricos v Anglo-Austrian Bank* is an application of the general rule governing the transfer of property in tangible movables, namely, that the lex situs applies, and that s 72 of the Bills of Exchange Act has no application to the question of the validity of transfers.[5] However, the Court of Appeal did expressly rely on s 72 of the Act in *Koechlin v Kestenbaum Bros*.[6] Here, a bill was drawn in France on the defendants in favour of one

4 [1904] 2 KB 870.
5 Dicey and Morris *Conflict of Laws* (9th edn 1973) pp 856–858.
6 [1927] 1 KB 889.

M Vidgerhaus, and accepted by the defendants. The bill was indorsed by the payee's son, E Vidgerhaus, who signed in his own name, and transferred the bill in France to the plaintiffs. By French law this was a valid indorsement and the Court of Appeal held that, since by virtue of s 72, French law governed the question of whether the indorsement was valid or not, the plaintiffs obtained a good title to the bill.

By a proviso to s 72 (2), where an inland bill is indorsed in a foreign country the indorsement shall as regards the *payer* be interpreted according to the law of the United Kingdom'. Thus, the acceptor of an inland bill is liable to a holder only if he claims through indorsements that are valid by English law, but the proviso has no application if the dispute is between two claimants to the instrument and is not a claim against the acceptor.[7]

3. Duties of a holder

'The duties of the holder with respect to presentment for acceptance or payment and the necessity for or sufficiency of a protest or notice of dishonour, or otherwise, are determined by the law of the place where the act is done or the bill is dishonoured' (s 72 (3)). The language of this provision, as Cheshire comments, is obscure. It would seem that the duties of a holder as to how he should present a bill for acceptance or payment are determined by the law of the place where such presentation is to be made and the need for and sufficiency of a notice of dishonour or protest is determined by the law of the place where the dishonour takes place.

4. Judgments in foreign currency

The traditional rule that a judgment for a sum of money must be expressed in sterling was embodied in s 72 (4) of the Bills of Exchange Act. The rule was abrogated by the House of Lords in *Miliangos v George Frank (Textiles) Ltd,*[8] and s 72 (4) of the Bills of Exchange Act (together with s 57 (2) which provided for the measure of damages for bills dishonoured abroad) were repealed by the Administration of Justice Act 1977 s 4. Judgment in respect of a bill expressed in a foreign currency may now be entered in the foreign currency concerned.

---

7 *Alcock v Smith* [1892] 1 Ch 238. The distinction is surely an unsatisfactory one.
8 [1976] AC 443, [1975] 3 All ER 801. See also *Barclays Bank International Ltd v Levin Bros (Bradford) Ltd* [1977] 2 QB 270, [1976] 3 All ER 900.

5. Determination of the due date

'Where a bill is drawn in one country and is payable in another, the due date thereof is determined according to the law of the place where it is payable' (s 72 (5)). Therefore, where a bill is payable in another country, it is important to know whether the law of that country provides for days of grace. French law, for example, does not.

Chapter 5

Insurance law

THE CONTRACT OF INSURANCE

Definition

A contract of insurance is a contract whereby, in consideration of
the payment of a premium, the insurer agrees to take upon himself a
risk borne by the insured and to compensate the insured for any loss
if the risk insured against does in fact occur.

The insurers will be either an insurance company[1] or Lloyd's
underwriters.

Types of insurance contracts

A wide variety of happenings which involve a risk to an individual
or to a corporation may be insured against. A man may insure his
house and its contents against the risk of fire or burglary, and he
may insure himself against the risk of personal accident. A business
may wish to insure, inter alia, against the risk of legal liability to
third parties. These are familiar types of insurance, but there is no
limit to the risks which insurers may be prepared to insure against;
the risk of loss of a parliamentary candidate's deposit and the risk of
rain during one's holiday are examples of less well-known risks which
can be the subject of insurance contracts. Insurance by the owner of a
motor vehicle against the risk of legal liability to third parties is in a
special category because this type of insurance has been compulsory

---

1 A company is not able to start an insurance business unless it is authorised by the
Secretary of State for Trade and Industry under the Insurance Companies Act 1982
or exempted by the Act. An insurance company with its head office in the U.K. must
possess the standard solvency margin (s 32). The Policyholders Protection Act 1975
makes provision for indemnifying policyholders when authorised insurance
companies fail to meet their liabilities.

since the Road Traffic Act 1930. One very important branch of insurance law concerns marine insurance, but this is governed largely by special rules contained in the Marine Insurance Act 1906 and it is not proposed to examine it here.

In all the various types of insurance contracts mentioned, if the risk insured against does not occur then of course no payment is made to the insured. However, in life assurance, some payment is bound to be made by the insurance company at some time because death must take place eventually.

Although the types of insurance contracts are many, there is one broad division that can be made. Most insurance contracts are indemnity contracts, that is, they bind the insurer to pay the amount of the insured's actual loss up to the amount covered by the insurance policy. One of the facets of the principle of indemnity, to be examined more fully below, is that if the insurer does pay out on the policy he is subrogated to any right of action which the insured may have against anyone who is legally liable for bringing about the loss. On the other hand, contracts of life assurance and most accident or sickness insurance contracts are not indemnity contracts; the insurer's liability is to pay certain fixed sums as specified in the policy, on the death, accident or sickness of the insured.[2] Because these contracts are not indemnity contracts the insurer cannot, having paid out on such policies, claim any right of subrogation to rights of action which the insured or his personal representatives may have against anyone who is legally liable for causing the death or accident. Such rights of action may be pursued by the insured himself (or his personal representatives) and the insured may retain both the policy moneys paid to him *and* any damages obtained in the action.

Contracts of insurance are not confined to contracts for the payment of a sum of money but include contracts for some benefit corresponding to the payment of a sum of money. This was the ruling given by Templeman J in *Department of Trade and Industry v St Christopher Motorists Association Ltd.*[3] The defendant association, in return for an annual sum paid by a member, agree to provide a chauffeur service, in the event that the member is unable to drive

2 An accident policy *may* be an indemnity policy. For example, in *Theobald v Railway Passengers' Assurance Co* (1854) 10 Exch 45, a policy provided (i) for the payment of £1,000 to the assured's executors if he were killed in an accident, and (ii) for compensation up to an amount not exceeding £1,000 for the expense and pain and loss caused to him by accident. The second part of the policy was held to be an indemnity policy. See also *Blascheck v Bussell* (1916) 33 TLR 74.

3 [1974] 1 All ER 395, [1974] 1 WLR 99.

himself, for example, because of an accident or being disqualified from driving. However, Megarry V-C held in *Medical Defence Union Ltd v Department of Trade*[4] that because a medical or dental practitioner who was a member of the Medical Defence Union merely had the right to have his request for help in relation to legal proceedings and indemnities fairly considered and he had *no right* to require the Union to conduct legal proceedings for him or to indemnify him, the contract between a member and the Union was not a contract of insurance.

If an insurer effects an insurance contract which it is not authorised to make under the Insurance Companies Act 1982 (or that Act's predecessors), the contract is illegal and void and therefore unenforceable not just by the insurer but also by the insured. This 'unfortunate state of affairs', as Kerr LJ recently described it, arises because the prohibition under the Act was not limited to effecting contracts of a class for which the insurer had no authority but extends to carrying out unauthorised insurance business, eg paying out on claims.[5]

Form and renewal

A contract of non-marine insurance does not have to be in writing, but by s 100 of the Stamp Act 1891 (as amended by the Finance Act 1970 s 32), in the case of a *life policy*, an insurer who does not issue a stamped policy within one month of receiving the first premium is liable to be fined. Liability to pay such a penalty would not affect the validity of an oral contract but naturally, in practice, life assurance contracts are invariably in writing. Before the Finance Act 1970, all other kinds of insurance policies also had to be stamped and in practice *all* insurance contracts are still in writing.

The contract may result from the intending insured completing a proposal form, prepared by the insurers and containing questions for answer by the insured, and forwarding it to the insurers. The completed proposal form is the offer and the contract is normally made when the insurer accepts the offer by agreeing to issue a policy. On receiving the proposal form the insurance company may issue an interim certificate, termed a cover note, bringing about a temporary binding contract of insurance, which usually provides either that it is to be in force until the insurers indicate that they

---

4 [1980] Ch 82, [1979] 2 All ER 421.
5 *Phoenix General Insurance Co of Greece SA v Administratia Asigurarilor de Stat* [1987] 2 All ER 152, 178.

accept or reject the proposal, or that it is to be in force for a specified period subject perhaps to a right in the insurers to determine it earlier by indicating rejection of the proposal.[6] Where a policy has been in existence and is subject to renewal, the insurers may send to the insured a temporary cover note for use during a period following expiry of the policy—this is treated merely as an offer to renew by the insurers and there is no binding contract unless there is some conduct on the part of the insured showing he accepts the offer.[7]

Most insurance policies last for a fixed period, usually for a year, and are only renewable on the agreement of both parties to the contract. In the case of life policies, it would clearly be inequitable if, after insurers had been receiving annual premiums for 20 or 30 years, they were entitled to refuse to renew the policy when the assured's expectation of life is diminished. The rule for life policies is that either the assured always has a right to renew provided he keeps up the premiums or that the policy continues subject to forfeiture for non-payment of premiums, depending on the terms of the policy.

It was held in *Stuart v Freeman*,[8] that if a life policy provides for *forfeiture* on non-payment of premium, a claim can be made on the policy even if death occurs after a premium has fallen due and has not been paid, provided it is paid within the days of grace permitted. It is less certain what the position would be if the policy, instead of subsisting till forfeiture by non-payment of premium, is expressed to be *renewable* by payment of premium. Often the policy itself settles any doubt by clearly providing that the policy moneys are payable if death occurs during the period of grace whether payment of the premium is made before or after the death.

Since renewal of policies other than life policies is conditional on mutual agreement between the insurers and the insured, as a general rule no claim can be made for any loss that occurs after the expiry of the period of the policy for which a premium has been paid, even though days of grace are allowed for payment of the next premium, the loss occurs during the days of grace and the premium is then paid before the days of grace expire. Of course, such a claim could be made if the policy expressly provided that loss occurring during the days of grace is covered.

6 The conditions of the policy itself do not apply to the cover note unless, as is usual, these conditions are incorporated expressly or by a reference in the cover note to a signed proposal form which incorporates them: *Re Coleman's Depositories* [1907] 2 KB 798, [1904–7] All ER Rep 383.
7 *Taylor v Allon* [1966] 1 QB 304, [1965] 1 All ER 557.
8 [1903] 1 KB 47. See also *McKenna v City Life Assurance Co* [1919] 2 KB 491.

In the case of a contract effected with Lloyd's Underwriters, in place of the proposal form there is a 'slip', containing brief details of the risk to be insured, prepared by an insurance broker on behalf of his client. When one underwriter initials the slip for a certain percentage of the risk, the initials represent an offer to be bound on behalf of his syndicate of underwriting members, to the extent indicated, and on the terms of the slip at the time when he saw it but he retains the right to modify that offer to accord with different terms inserted by underwriters taking subsequent lines. The broker will then seek the initials of other underwriters until the risk is covered 100 per cent. Once the slip is fully subscribed, it constitutes a binding contract and all the underwriters are deemed to have offered to be bound for their respective proportions on the terms of the slip in the finally amended form whether or not they knew of subsequent amendments.[9] The subsequent signing of a policy is a formality only.

Regulations have been made under the Insurance Companies Act 1982 as to the form and content of insurance advertisements, ie advertisements inviting persons to enter into contracts of insurance (s 72). Anyone who knowingly issues a misleading statement or promise thereby inducing another person to enter into an insurance contract is guilty of an offence (s 73). No insurance company or member of Lloyd's may enter into a long-term insurance contract (eg life assurance) unless a statutory notice is sent to the intended assured containing a form of notice of cancellation. The assured under such a contract has a cooling-off period in which he may withdraw from the transaction—the right may be exercised within 10 days of receipt of the statutory notice or at any time if no notice is sent (ss 75 and 77).

THE PRINCIPLE OF INSURABLE INTEREST

Common law

At common law, it was possible for A to take out an insurance policy for his own benefit on the life of B, a complete stranger.

The contract of insurance was legal and enforceable although the insured had no interest in the subject matter of the insurance apart from the insurance money itself. However, a contract of indemnity insurance could not be enforced unless the insured did have an interst at the time of the loss. It would have been a valid contract for

9 *Jaglom v Excess Insurance Co Ltd* [1972] 2 QB 250, [1972] 1 All ER 267.

A to take out an insurance policy for his own benefit on the goods of
B, in which A had no interest or rights of any kind, but since the
principle of indemnity insurance is compensation for actual loss,
unless A owned the goods at the time of their loss or had then some
other interest in them, he could make no claim on his insurance
contract in respect of loss.

The classic definition of insurable interest was given by
Lawrence J in *Lucena v Crauford*:—[10]

> 'A man is interested in a thing to whom advantage may arise or prejudice
> happen from the circumstances which may attend it. . . . And whom it
> importeth, that its condition as to safety or other quality should continue
> . . . To be interested in the preservation of a thing is to be so
> circumstanced with respect to it as to have benefit from its existence, or
> prejudice from its destruction . . .'

A mere hope or expectation of interest is not enough.

Statute

1. *The Life Assurance Act 1774.*—By the Life Assurance Act 1774,
unless the person for whose benefit or account a life policy is effected
has an interest in the life assured at the time the contract of
assurance is made, the assurance is null and void and, indeed, an
illegal contract.[11] Further, it is not generally lawful to make any
policy of life assurance unless the name of the person for whose
benefit or account the policy is effected, is stated in the policy.
However, by virtue of s 50 of the Insurance Companies Amendment Act 1973, it is lawful to make a policy for the benefit of
unnamed persons within a specified class or description provided
that the class or description is stated with sufficient particularity to
make it possible to establish the identity of all persons who at any
time are entitled to benefit under the policy. As we shall show more
fully when dealing particularly with life assurance, a man has an
insurable interest, inter alia, in his own life, in the life of his wife, and
in the life of anyone who owes him money, though only up to the
amount of the debt. So long as the person for whose benefit the
policy is effected has that insurable interest at the time the policy is
taken out, it is a valid insurance and may properly be kept up by the
payment of periodic premiums although the debt meanwhile is
repaid. Where the person for whose benefit or account the policy is

10 (1806) 2 Bos & PNR 269, 302, 127 ER 630, 643. But see *General Reinsurance
Corpn v Forsakringsaktiebolaget Fennia Patria* [1983] QB 856.
11 *Harse v Pearl Life Assurance* [1904] 1 KB 558, [1904–7] All ER Rep 630.

effected does have an interest in the life assured, 'no greater sum shall be recovered . . . than the amount or value of the interest . . .', but life assurance, not being a contract of indemnity, does not require an insurable interest to exist at the time of death.[12]

Despite its name, the Life Assurance Act 1774 applies to other insurances besides life assurance. Section 2 of the Act provides:—

'. . . it shall not be lawful to make any policy or policies on the life or lives of any person or persons *or other event or events* without inserting in such policy or policies the person or persons name or names interested therein or for whose use, benefit or whose account such policy is to be made or underwrote.'

However, the Act specifically exempts from its scope 'ships, goods or merchandise' and a motor vehicle policy covering third party liability has been held to be an insurance of 'goods'.[13] Furthermore, Kerr LJ in *Mark Rowlands Ltd v Berni Inns Ltd*[14] said that s 2 of the Act 'does not apply to indemnity insurance but only to insurances which provide for the payment of a specified sum on the happening of an insured event.' It follows that, as insurance on a building is an example of indemnity insurance, while the principle of indemnity requires an insurable interest to exist at the time of loss (otherwise no claim could be made) the name of the insured need not be inserted in the policy.

If a contract is illegal under the Life Assurance Act, then in accordance with the ordinary rule relating to money paid under illegal contracts, any premium that may have been paid cannot be recovered.[15] There is an exception, however, if the parties are not in pari delicto. For example, in *Hughes v Liverpool Victoria Legal Friendly Society*[16] the defendants' agent who knew that the plaintiff had no insurable interest in the lives of the various persons on whose lives she was taking out insurance policies, fraudulently represented that the policies would be valid. The Court of Appeal allowed the plaintiff to recover premiums she had paid on the ground that, although the policies were illegal under the Act, the parties were not in pari delicto.

It is possible for a person with no interst or only a limited interest in a building to take out insurance on it for the full value of the building, provided it is clear that he is taking out the policy for the

12 *Dalby v India and London Life* (1854) 15 CB 365, 387. See p 315, post.
13 *Williams v Baltic Insurance Assocation of London Ltd* [1924] 2 KB 282.
14 [1985] 3 All ER 473, 480.
15 *Harse v Pearl Assurance* [1904] 1 KB 558, [1904–7] All ER Rep 630.
16 [1916] 2 KB 482, [1916–17] All ER Rep 918.

benefit of the other persons intersted as well as in respect of his own interest (if any). In *Re King, Robinson v Grey*[17] a lessee of a factory was required by terms of his lease to effect an insurance for the full value of the property in the joint names of the lessor and the lessee, and to apply any insurance moneys obtained in reinstatement. The lessee did effect such insurance and subsequently the factory was damaged by fire. Reinstatement was impossible because the local authority had purchased the property compulsorily. Could the lessor make any claim on the insurance moneys? The Court of Appeal held that the purpose of the insurance covenant referred to was to enable the lessor to make certain that the moneys would only be payable against a joint receipt and the lessor would be in a secured position to see that the lessee performed his obligation of reinstatement. The policy was, therefore, construed as having been taken out solely for the benefit of the lessee (who also had paid the premiums) and, since the covenant of reinstatement gave the lessee an insurable interest in the full value of the premises, he was solely entitled to the policy moneys.

2. *The Gaming Act 1845.*—By this Act all contracts or agreements by way of gaming or wagering are null and void. A contract purporting to be a contract of insurance will be void under this Act unless the insured has an insurable interest in the event upon which the insurance money is payable or a reasonable expectation of acquiring one.[18]

Clearly, all contracts illegal under the Life Assurance Act are void under the Gaming Act. The latter Act also covers insurance on goods, so that a contract for the insurance of goods is void unless at the time of the contract the insured had some interest in the goods or an expectation of acquiring one.

It was held in *Macaura v Northern Assurance Co Ltd*,[19] that since neither a shareholder nor a simple creditor of a company (as distinct from a debenture holder) has an insurable interest in assets belonging to the company, any claim on a policy effected by such a person on goods belonging to the company must fail because, independently of the Gaming Act, a claimant under an indemnity policy must have an interest at the time of loss.

17 [1963] Ch 459, [1963] 1 All ER 781.
18 *Howard v Refuge Friendly Society* (1886) 54 LT 644.
19 [1925] AC 619, [1925] All ER Rep 51. It is possible, however, for a shareholder to insure his shares against a fall in value because of the failure of an undertaking in which the company is engaged: *Wilson v Jones* (1866), LR 2 Exch 193; on appeal (1867) LR 2 Ex 139.

Since a bailee of goods is, subject to the contract of bailment, normally under a legal liability in negligence for loss or damage to the goods, he has an insurable interest in the goods. So does a bankrupt remaining in possession of his estate.[20] In *Macaura's* case, where the shareholder merely allowed the timber belonging to the company to lie on his land but owed no duty in respect of its safe custody, Lord Buckmaster took the view that he had no insurable interest in the timber.[1] A creditor has no insurable interest in his debtor's goods unless he has a lien over them or is mortgagee of them.[2]

A bailee of goods has an insurable interest in the goods bailed to him to the extent of the full value of the goods. It is a matter of construction of the insurance policy taken out by a bailee whether he is insuring only in respect of his own loss or liability to the owner or to the full value of the goods. In the former case, he can recover only to the extent of his loss or liability as where a firm insured goods which were its own or 'in trust or on commission for *which they are responsible*' and they sold certain goods in which the property and risk passed to the buyer but which remained in the firm's possession—the policy was held not to cover the buyer's interest in such goods.[3] But where a wharfinger takes out insurance to cover goods 'in trust or on commission' such insurance covers his own interest, eg, a lien for warehouse rent, *and* the interests of the owners although the owners may not have assented to or ratified the insurance.[4] The wharfinger would of course be trustee of any insurance moneys received in excess of his own interest. Lord Campbell CJ urged that 'goods in trust' meant goods with which the insured was entrusted in the ordinary sense of the word, not just goods held in trust in the strict technical sense.[5]

In *Hepburn v A Tomlinson (Hauliers) Ltd*[6] the respondent hauliers agreed to carry cigarettes for the Imperial Tobacco Company and to keep the goods insured with full comprehensive cover against loss. Without any negligence on the respondents' part, the goods

20 *Marks v Hamilton* (1852) 7 Exch 323.
1 [1925] AC 619, 628, [1925] All ER Rep 51, 55.
2 *Wolff v Horncastle* (1798) 1 Bos & P 316; *Westminster Fire Office v Glasgow Provident Investment Society* (1888) 13 App Cas 699. But the creditor can take out a solvency insurance policy whereby he insures against non-payment of the debt and he may, as has been seen, insure the life of his debtor.
3 *North British and Mercantile Insurance Co v Moffat* (1871) LR 7 CP 25.
4 *Waters v Monarch Fire and Life Assurance Co* (1856) 5 E & B 870.
5 (1856) 5 E & B 870, 880. See also *John Rigby (Haulage) Ltd v Reliance Marine Insurance Co Ltd* [1956] 2 QB 468, [1956] 3 All ER 1.
6 [1966] AC 451, [1966] 1 All ER 418 HL.

were stolen. The respondents had taken out a Lloyd's policy which covered 'all risks' of loss or damage in transit and referred to 'tobacco the property of Imperial Company'. The House of Lords *held* that on the wording of the policy, the respondents had covered the full value of the goods; they were, therefore, entitled to recover although they had themselves suffered no loss—they must of course account to the owner for the policy moneys recovered.[7] By analogy with a bailee's right to insure and recover the full value of bailed goods, the head contractor under a building or engineering contract who took out a contractor's all risks policy was entitled to take out a single policy covering the whole of the risk, including cover for all contractors and sub-contractors in respect of loss or damage to the entire contract works.[8] It was commercially conveneint for one policy to cover the whole risk and it followed that a sub-contractor was entitled under such a policy to recover in respect of the entire contract works as well as his own property. Each insured person was insured in respect of the whole contract works.

Anyone with no insurable interest or only a limited insurable interest in goods may insure them for the benefit of someone who has an insurable interest, provided the intention is clear. Thus, in *Prudential Staff Union v Hall*[9] it was held that a trade union could properly insure the safety of goods belonging to members provided it held itself as trustee for any policy moneys payable.

THE EFFECT OF NON-DISCLOSURE, MISREPRESENTATION OR BREACH OF CONTRACT

The principle of disclosure

A contract of insurance is one requiring utmost good faith—it is a contract uberrimae fidei. This means that the insured person owes a duty to disclose before the contract is made every material fact of

---

7 Lord Reid said that the bailees had an insurable interest in the full value of the goods and it was, therefore, irrelevant whether the bailee *intended* unilaterally to insure for the benefit of the owners: 'If there were any question whether the policy is a wagering policy intentions would be relevant, but no such question arises in this case and it could hardly arise in a case of this character'. Lord Reid thought it could be different if someone without an insurable interest insured on behalf of an undisclosed principal—then, under the ordinary law of agency, the undisclosed principal could only come in to take advantage of the contract if the agent intended to act on his behalf. Lord Pearce, however, thought that if the insurers could affirmatively prove that the bailee had no intention to insure on behalf of the owners, his insurance *quoad* the owner's interest was gaming and he could not recover.

8 *Petrofina (UK) v Magnaload Ltd* [1984] QB 127, [1983] 3 All ER 33.

9 [1947] KB 685.

which he knows or ought to have known, the reason being that the insurer can only evaluate the risk on the basis of what he is told by the proposed insured. If a material fact is not so disclosed, the insurer has a right at any time to avoid the contract.[10]

A fact is material if it would influence the judgment of a prudent insurer in deciding whether to accept the risk and, if so, in fixing the premium.[11] It makes no difference that the insured himself, whether acting reasonably or not, thought the fact to be not material. As the Law Reform Committee commented in 1957: 'it seems that a fact may be material to insurers, in the light of the great volume of experience of claims available to them, which would not necessarily appear to a proposer for insurance, however honest and careful, to be one which he ought to disclose'[12] One fact that is material is the refusal of a previous proposal to take out similar insurance, or possibly even insurance of a different kind.[13]

In *Anglo-African Merchants v Bayley*,[14] the owner of a large quantity of clothing who wanted it insured informed his broker that it was 'government surplus' but Lloyd's underwriters who provided the insurance were informed by the brokers that the goods were 'new clothes'. Megaw J held that the fact that the goods were government surplus was material as such clothing involved an abnormally high risk of theft and that the underwriters were entitled to avoid liability for non-disclosure.

There is no duty on the insured to disclose facts which he does not know[15] (unless his ignorance is due to negligence) or which diminish the risk or which the insurers know or ought to know.[16]

10 The duty of the utmost good faith is reciprocal though it is rare for the insurer to be sued on the basis that he has failed to disclose material circumstances which might affect the insured's decision to enter into the contract of insurance: see *Banque Keyser Ullmann SA v Skandia UK Insurance Co Ltd* [1987] 2 All ER 923, [1987] 2 WLR 1300.

11 *Mutual Life Insurance Co of New York v Ontario Metal Products Co Ltd* [1925] AC 344, 351–352. It follows that evidence is admissible from brokers and underwriters on the question of whether a fact is material.

12 Cmnd 62. All three judges in the Court of Appeal in *Lambert v Co-operative Insurance Society Ltd* [1975] 2 Lloyd's Rep 485, were critical of the existing law. Cairns LJ said he shared the view expressed by the Law Reform Committee Report that the law might well be changed (at p 493).

13 *Locker and Woolf Ltd v Western Australia Insurance Co Ltd* [1936] 1 KB 408.

14 [1970] 1 QB 311, [1969] 2 All ER 421. The insurance broker is agent for the insured only. By the Insurance Brokers (Registration) Act 1977, the description 'insurance broker' may be used only by those qualified and registered under the Act and such brokers are subject to Rules and a code of conduct drawn up and supervised by the Insurance Brokers Registration Council.

15 *Joel v Law and Crown Insurance Co* [1908] 2 KB 863.

16 *Mann, MacNeal and Steeves v Capital and Counties Insurance Co* [1921] 2 KB 300.

The duty on the insured to disclose all material facts of which he knows continues up to the time the contract is made. Thus, in *Looker v Law Union and Rock Insurance Co Ltd*,[17] a proposed assured stated in his proposal form for life assurance that he was free from disease or ailment, whereas at the time of the acceptance of his proposal by the company, the assured was in a critical condition from an attack of pneumonia from which he died soon afterwards. It was held that the insurers were not liable on the insurance policy to the assured's personal representatives, on the ground that it is incumbent on a proposer to inform the insurers of any material change before contract in the nature of the risk undertaken by them. If, as is usual except for life policies, the insurers' consent is required in order to effect a renewal, all material facts which have come to light before such consent is given must be disclosed.[18] As Cresswell J said in *Pim v Reid*,[19]

'it may be very material for the company to know of any change in the extent of the risk to enable them to determine whether or not they will continue the insurance.'

The answering of questions in a proposal form by the insured is not conclusive that he has complied with his duty of disclosure but, as Scrutton LJ said in one case, failure on the part of the insurers to ask a particular question does involve the insurers in risk,[20]

'The insurance companies . . . run the risk of the contention that matters they do not ask questions about are not material for, if they were, they would ask questions about them.'

In *Woolcott v Sun Alliance and London Insurance Ltd*[1] there was no proposal form when the plaintiff applied to a building society for a mortgage on a house he was buying and the application form merely asked that he specify the amount for which he wanted the building society to insure the property. The building society had a block insurance policy with the defendants and the plaintiff's name was added to the policy records when his application for a mortgage was accepted. The plaintiff at no time disclosed that he had several convictions, including one for robbery for which he had been sentenced to twelve years' imprisonment. When the plaintiff made a claim after the house was destroyed by fire the insurance company refused to pay and Caulfield J agreed they were entitled to do so.

17 [1928] 1 KB 554.
18 *Re Wilson and Scottish Insurance Corpn* [1920] 2 Ch 28, [1920] All ER Rep 185.
19 (1843) 6 Man & G 1, 25.
20 *Newsholme Bros v Road Transport and General Insurance Co* [1929] 2 KB 356, 363.
1 [1978] 1 All ER 1253, [1978] 1 WLR 493.

The absence of a proposal form in no way modified the duty of disclosure.

An exception to the duty of disclosure has been created by the Rehabilitation of Offenders Act 1974. Failure to disclose a 'spent' conviction will not amount to a breach of the duty or entitle insurers to disclaim liability. A 'spent' conviction does not include any conviction which has resulted in a sentence of imprisonment for life or for a term of more than $2\frac{1}{2}$ years but for other sentences the Act prescribes a 'rehabilitation period' at the expiry of which the conviction becomes 'spent'. Imprisonment for more than six months (but not more than $2\frac{1}{2}$ years) involves a rehabilitation period of 10 years. Imprisonment for not more than six months involves a rehabilitation period of seven years and other detailed provisions are given.

Return of premium.—Where there has been a non-disclosure of a material fact, since the insurer has a right to avoid the policy, he has never been 'at risk', and therefore any premiums that have been paid are recoverable, there being a total failure of consideration.

Misrepresentations

False statements which the insured may make in the course of negotiations or in his proposal form may be misrepresentations or breaches of terms of the contract, depending on the construction of the contract. In the case of a misrepresentation, whether it is fraudulent or innocent, provided it is as to a material fact (as already defined) the insurer has a right to avoid the contract. Thus, in *London Assurance v Mansel*,[2] in answering questions in the proposal form as to what other proposals on his life the proposer may have made, the proposer answered that he was 'insured now in two offices for £16,000 at ordinary rates. Policies effected last year'. This was a half-truth as proposals on the assured's life had been declined by several offices, and therefore the answer amounted to a misrepresentation. Since this was a material matter the insurers were entitled to have the contract set aside.[3] Damages are also claimable for

2 (1879) 11 Ch D 363. Cf *Mutual Life Assurance Co of New York v Ontario Metal Products Co Ltd* [1925] AC 344 (facts undisclosed held not material).

3 By s 2 (2) of the Misrepresentation Act 1967, where a misrepresentation is not fraudulent, a court may, instead of granting the equitable remedy of rescission, award damages in lieu if of opinion that it would be equitable to do so. But the right of an insurance company to avoid a contract for any breach of the insured's duty of good faith is a *common law* right and s 2 (2) may not apply to this—see *Chitty on Contracts* (25th edn, 1983) para 3690.

fraudulent misrepresentation and, since the Misrepresentation Act 1967, for negligent misrepresentation.

Any premiums paid are recoverable by the insured only if the misrepresentation was innocent, but if, as in *London Assurance v Mansel*, the insurers are seeking rescission of the contract for misrepresentation, on the principle that 'he who comes to equity, must do equity', rescission may be granted by the court only on terms that premiums are repaid irrespective of whether the insured's misrepresentation is innocent or fraudulent.

Of course, there may be misrepresentation by the insurer giving rise to civil remedies for the insured and, by the Insurance Companies Act 1982 s 73 it is a criminal offence to induce any person to enter into a contract of insurance with an insurance company by knowingly or recklessly making any misleading, false or deceptive statement or forecast or by any dishonest concealment of material facts. Provision is made in s 72 of the same Act for Regulations as to the form and content of insurance advertisements.

Warranties

There is usually little doubt whether statements made by the insured are merely representations or contractual warranties, because the proposal form normally contains a declaration in which the proposer agrees that the truth of his answers shall form the basis of the contract. Alternatively the policy itself may contain a provision that these answers shall form the basis of the contract and be deemed to be incorporated in the contract. In either case the answers are terms of the contract and unless they can be treated as a description of the risk (to be examined shortly), these answers are warranties the accuracy of which is a condition precedent to the insurer's liability, whether the answers are material to the risk or not: warranties are thus equivalent in effect to conditions in any other type of contract. *Dawson's Ltd v Bonnin*[4] concerned the insurance of a lorry against fire. The proposal form required the proposer to state the full address at which the lorry would be garaged, and inadvertently the wrong address was inserted. A claim was made under the policy when the lorry was lost by fire. The House of Lords held that as the proposal form was clearly expressed

---

4 [1922] 2 AC 413. See also *Condogianis v Guardian Assurance Co* [1921] 2 AC 125. If a policy contains the provision that 'This policy will be indisputable on any ground other than fraud', liability cannot be avoided for mere non-disclosure, innocent misrepresentation or breach of warranty.

by the terms of the policy to be the 'basis of the contract', the answer in the proposal form involved a contractual promise as to its accuracy. Since the answer was not accurate the insurers had a right to avoid liability for breach of warranty. It made no difference that the answer was not material, ie, the premium would have been no different if the correct address had been shown, nor that the inaccuracy was innocent.

If an answer in a proposal form amounts to a warranty merely as to facts existing at the date the policy is effected, and these facts were correctly stated, there is no breach of warranty merely because of a later change in the facts. In *Woolfall and Rimmer Ltd v Moyle*[5] a proposal form for an employer's liability policy contained the question and answer: 'Are your machinery, plant and ways properly maintained, fenced and guarded and otherwise in good order and condition? Yes.' A claim was made on the policy following an accident caused by a defective board in the scaffolding. There was no evidence that this board was not in good condition when the question was answered. The Court of Appeal held that as the question and answer related only to the existing condition of the machinery, plant and ways, there was no breach of warranty and the insurers were liable to meet the claim. On the other hand, in *Beauchamp v National Mutual Indemnity and Insurance Co Ltd*,[6] the following question and answer in a proposal form relating to an accident liability policy were held to constitute a warranty as to the future, or promissory warranty: 'Are any explosives used in your business? No.' The insured had, apparently, not previously undertaken demolition work and was taking out a policy to cover the demolition of a mill, and the question clearly was intended to relate to that future event. A claim made under the policy after the insured began to use explosives failed on the ground that the use of explosives constituted a breach of the promissory warranty given by the insured. Of course, a claim would have succeeded if it related to an accident occurring before explosives had been used, ie, the insured's claim had vested prior to his breach.

If the insurers successfully avoid liability because there has been a breach of warranty, normally the insurers will never have been at risk and any premiums paid are, therefore, recoverable. However, if the warranty is as to the future, eg, in fire insurance, that a fire will not be lit in a certain room, any premiums paid prior to breach of such warranty are irrecoverable as the insurers will have been at

5 [1942] 1 KB 66, [1941] 3 All ER 304.
6 [1937] 3 All ER 19.

risk prior to such breach. In life assurance, it is common for the policy to provide that in the event of a breach of warranty as to the future, such as a promise by the assured not to go abroad, neither premiums paid before nor those paid after a breach are recoverable. In *Sparenborg v Edinburgh Life Assurance Co.*[7] a life policy effected in 1894 provided that if the assured travelled abroad beyond certain limits 'the assurance shall be void and the premiums paid shall be forfeited'. In 1897 the assured did travel beyond the limit agreed and continued to pay premiums until 1911. He then sought to recover the premiums paid since 1897. The court held on the wording of the clause in the policy quoted above that the premiums paid since 1897 had become forfeited and the assured was not entitled to recover them. Bray J felt he could not limit the meaning of the words 'premiums paid' by holding that they referred only to the premiums paid before 1897.

In *Magee v Pennine Insurance Co Ltd*[8] the insurers agreed to settle a claim made on a motor car policy before learning that, because of misstatements by the insured in the proposal form amounting to breach of warranty, they could have repudiated the policy. The Court of Appeal held by a majority that, as the settlement agreement was made under a fundamental mistake that an enforceable policy existed, the insurers were entitled to avoid liability on it.

Description of the risk

It is possible that a term of the contract may be treated by the courts not as a contractual warranty but merely as a description of the risk being covered. The case of *Farr v Motor Traders Mutual Insurance Society Ltd*[9] is an example of this. In the proposal form for the insurance of a taxi against damage caused by accident, there was a question as to whether the taxi was driven in one or more shifts per 24 hours and the proposer answered 'Just one'. The insurance policy recited that the particulars in the proposal form were the 'basis of the contract'. For a short time the taxi was driven two shifts per day while another taxi was being repaired, but was only being driven one shift per day when the accident occurred on which a claim under the policy was made. The Court of Appeal held that the answer quoted in the proposal form was not a warranty as to the

---

7 [1912] 1 KB 195.
8 [1969] 2 QB 507, [1969] 2 All ER 891, CA.
9 [1920] 3 KB 669.

future, ie, a warranty by the proposer that the taxi would only be driven one shift per day but was merely a description of the risk covered by the policy, ie, the policy only covered the taxi while it was being driven one shift per day. Since the accident happened while the taxi was only being driven one shift per day the insurance company was liable.

Ambiguity

If there is any ambiguity in the policy or in the proposal form, since these documents are devised by the insurers the courts will construe them contra proferentem. In *Provincial Insurance Co v Morgan and Foxon*[10] an insurance was taken out against damage to a lorry and against liability for injury to persons and damage to other vehicles caused by the use of the lorry. In the proposal form appeared the following inquiry: 'State (a) the purposes in full for which the vehicle will be used; and (b) the nature of the goods to be carried.' The answers given were '(a) Delivery of coal; (b) Coal.' The proposers agreed that the answers in the proposal form should be the 'basis of the contract'. One day the lorry was used to deliver both timber and coal, but while the lorry was carrying coal only, a collision occurred between the lorry and a car. The Court of Appeal followed *Farr's* case and determined that the questions and answers were merely a description of the risk covered and, since the lorry was being used only for the delivery of coal when the collision occurred, the insurers were liable. The House of Lords, without differing from the ratio decidendi of the Court of Appeal, took the view that even if the questions and answers did form a contractual warranty, there had been no breach of it since the words 'purposes in full' did not involve the same thing as stating in full the purposes for which the vehicle would be exclusively used, and as a general description of the use of the vehicle the answers were accurate. Thus the House of Lords resolved the ambiguity in the proposal form against the insurers.

Somervell LJ put the point clearly in another case: 'If there is any ambiguity, since it is the defendants' (the insurers') clause, the ambiguity will be resolved in favour of the assured'.[11]

Where the policy provides that certain steps should be taken by the insured after the event insured against occurs, the court is

10 [1933] AC 240, [1932] All ER Rep 899.
11 *Houghton v Trafalgar Insurance Co Ltd* [1954] 1 QB 247, 249, [1953] 2 All ER 1409, 1410.

reluctant to construe such a term as a condition precedent to liability and damages only may be available if there is a breach by the insured.[12] But a clause providing, for example, for notice of claim to be given within a certain period of the accident may be treated as a condition precedent to liability and then the insurers may escape liability if such notice is not given though no damage becomes apparent until after the period of notice has expired. In *Cassel v Lancashire and Yorkshire Accident Insurance Co Ltd*,[13] the plaintiff had an accident policy with the defendant company which provided that in the case of injury from accident the insured should give the company notice in writing of the occurrence of the accident, and also within 14 days of the accident should forward medical certificates of the nature and extent of the injuries received. The plaintiff met with an accident while paddling a canoe in Cornwall. No immediate ill resulted from the accident but eight months later the plaintiff did become ill and he gave notice to the company of the accident and the injuries which he stated were the result. The court held that the plaintiff was not entitled to recover as his notice had not been given within the time limited by the policy.

The Court of Appeal in *Allen v Robles*[14] held that where the insurers have a right to repudiate liability because the insured has failed to comply with a term requiring notification of a claim within a certain period, there is in general no limit on the time within which the insurers may elect whether or not to repudiate liability.

Where notice has to be given 'as soon as possible' after an accident, the court will take all existing circumstances into account. In *Verelst's Administratix v Motor Union Insurance Co Ltd*[15] the insured was killed in a motor accident in India and his personal representative did not know of the existence of an insurance policy until one year later, when notice was given. It was held that the arbitrator was entitled to find that notice had been given, as the policy required, 'as soon as possible'.

In *Lickiss v Milestone Motor Policies at Lloyds*[16] a majority in the

12 *Stoneham v Ocean Railway and Accident Insurance Co* (1887) 19 QBD 237, *Re Bradley and Essex and Suffolk Accident Indemnity Society* [1912] 1 KB 415, [1911–13] All ER Rep 444.

13 (1885) 1 TLR 495. Similarly, it may be a condition precedent to recovery that the insured should provide 'all such proofs and information with respect to the claim as may reasonably be required.' *Welch v Royal Exchange Assurance Co* [1939] 1 KB 294, [1938] 4 All ER 289.

14 [1969] 3 All ER 154, [1969] 1 WLR 1193.

15 [1925] 2 KB 137.

16 [1966] 2 All ER 972, [1966] 1 WLR 1334.

Court of Appeal held that if insurers obtained particulars of the loss from another source so that they are not prejudiced by the insured's failure to tell them, they cannot rely on non-compliance with a condition requiring the insured to give notice to defeat the claim.

Loss of remedy

Waiver.—If the insurers accept payment of a premium after they have knowledge of a material non-disclosure or of a misrepresentation or breach of warranty by the insured, they are treated as having waived the right to repudiate liability.

Thus, in *Ayrey v British Legal and United Provident Assurance Co.*[17] a fisherman, who took out a policy of life assurance, failed to disclose in the proposal form that he was in the Royal Naval Reserve and, therefore, exposed to greater risks. He did, however, disclose this fact verbally to the insurers' district manager. Premiums due under the policy were paid to and accepted by the district manager. The Divisional Court held that the district manager's knowledge of the true facts was the knowledge of the company and that the acceptance of the premiums by the district manager after he had full knowledge of the facts was a waiver by the company of the right to avoid liability for non-disclosure.

However, it is clear that the knowledge of the insurance company's agent is not imputed to the company, if acquired while the agent is filling in the proposal form on the proposer's behalf, because he is then normally considered in law to be acting as agent for the proposer.[18]

---

17 [1918] 1 KB 136.

18 *Newsholme Bros v Road Transport and General Insurance Co* [1929] 2 KB 356, [1929] All ER Rep 442, CA. However, if the proposer is illiterate, the agent will still be acting as the insurers' agent in completing the proposal form and any knowledge he acquires then of a material non-disclosure or misrepresentation will be imputed to the insurers: *Bawden v London, Edinburgh and Glasgow Assurance Co* [1892] 2 QB 534. See also *Stone v Reliance Mutual Insurance Co* [1972] 1 Lloyd's Rep 469, CA. The Law Reform Committee recommended in 1957 that the agent be treated at all times as the insurers' agent, and the knowledge of the agent as being the knowledge of the insurers (Cmnd 62). In January 1977 the Department of Trade published a White Paper on *Insurance Intermediaries* (Cmnd 6715) expressing support for the Bill that has since become the Insurance Brokers (Registration) Act 1977. It said that the right way to improve the standards of insurance *agents* is to make the companies employing them fully responsible for an agent's conduct in carrying out the terms of his agency agreement with the company. It explicitly supported the recommendation of the Law Reform Committee referred to ante that knowledge of the agent should be treated as knowledge of the insurers.

In *O'Connor v B D B Kirby & Co,*[19] a broker (who is, of course, the insured's agent) filled in a proposal form for motor car insurance at the dictation of the intending insured. Owing to mistake, the broker put in the form that the car was garaged although the intended insured had told him it was parked in the street. When a claim was later made on the policy, the insurers repudiated liability and the insured sued the broker for damages. The Court of Appeal held the claim must fail because the duty of a proposer for insurance is to sign a proposal form only after satisfying himself that it is accurate and the sole effective cause of the insured's loss was his failure to do that. However, an insurance broker does owe a duty of care to the intending insured including, for example, a duty to inform him of any exemptions under the policy which may affect the cover given.[20]

Affirmation.—Where insurers affirm a policy as a valid policy after knowledge of any ground there might be for repudiating liability, the right to repudiate liability is lost.[1]

Fraudulent claim

Irrespective of any provision on the point in the policy, if the insured makes a fraudulent claim, for example by dishonestly claiming more than the actual loss in an indemnity policy, the insurer may repudiate liability altogether and avoid the whole policy. However, an excessive or exaggerated claim is not necessarily to be held a fraudulent claim and the policy-holder may still be able to recover his real loss. In *Norton v Royal Fire and Life Assurance Co*[2] the plaintiff grocer insured the contents of his premises against fire. He made a claim on this policy for £274 which the company rejected as excessive and the plaintiff reduced his claim to £187, which the company still resisted. When the plaintiff brought his claim before the court, the defendant pleaded that the claim was a fraudulent one. The trial judge said that what the plaintiff had done was no doubt morally wrong in putting forward a claim he knew to be exaggerated, but he left it to the jury whether it was fraudulent in the sense of showing an intention to deceive and defraud the company by getting out of them money he knew he had

19 [1972] 1 QB 90, [1971] 2 All ER 1415, CA.
20 *McNealy v Pennine Insurance Co* [1978] 2 Lloyd's Rep 18, CA.
1 *West v National Motor and Accident Insurance Union Ltd* [1955] 1 All ER 800, [1955] 1 WLR 343.
2 (1885) 1 TLR 460.

no right to, and that must depend on all the circumstances. The jury found the claim was not fraudulent and the Divisional Court declined to disturb that verdict.

Statements of Practice

Even prior to a critical report of the Law Commission (published in 1980),[3] the representative insurance bodies had publicly recognised that the law's treatment of answers given in proposal forms was capable of working injustice. Statements of Practice (issued in 1977) stated, inter alia, that in non-life policies insurance companies would not unreasonably repudiate liability if an undisclosed fact was not material or if the loss was not connected with the false statement. The Law Commission pointed out, however, that the Statements lacked the force of law and considered that the insured's needs should be provided by legislation. The Government did contemplate legislation but, after consultation with the insurance industry, changes were made to the Statements of Practice and the Government announced in 1986 that it did not propose to proceed with changes in the law.

The current Statement of General Insurance Practice (issued by the Association of British Insurers) applies to policyholders resident in the UK and insured in their private capacity only. The following are among the key provisions relevant to the duty of disclosure and warranties:

'1 (a) The declaration at the foot of the proposal form should be restricted to completion according to the proposer's knowledge and belief.
  (b) Neither the proposal form nor the policy should contain any provision converting the statements as to past or present fact in the proposal form into warranties[4]. . . .
  (d) Those matters which insurers have found generally to be material will be the subject of clear questions in proposal forms.
2 (a) Under the conditions regarding notification of a claim, the policyholder shall not be asked to do more than report a claim and subsequent developments as soon as reasonably possible. . . .
  (b) An insurer will not repudiate liability to indemnify a policyholder . . .
    (iii) on ground of a breach of warranty or condition where the circumstances of the loss are unconnected with the breach unless fraud is involved.'

3 Law Com No 104, Cmnd 8064.
4 This seems to reduce considerably the effect of *Dawsons Ltd v Bonnin* [1922] 2 AC 413, p 306, ante.

INDEMNITY INSURANCE

Principle of indemnity

It has been seen that insurance contracts are broadly divisible into
indemnity contracts on the one hand and contracts of life assurance
and accident or sickness insurance on the other. In the latter case
the insurers' liability is to pay certain sums as specified in the policy
on the death, accident or sickness of the insured. Likewise, a policy
covering the risk of rain on a certain day is not an indemnity policy.

The principle of indemnity insurance which applies to all
insurance contracts other than life and accident insurance is that
the insured cannot recover more than his actual loss. A good
example is *Darrell v Tibbitts*[5] where the landlord of a house obtained
£750 from insurers when the house was damaged by a gas
explosion. The tenant, by the covenants in his lease, was obliged to
reinstate the house and did so with moneys recovered from the local
authority whose negligence had caused the damage. The Court of
Appeal held that the insurers could recover the £750 they had paid
over to the landlord because otherwise, as Brett LJ said, the
landlord would not be indemnified, 'he would be paid twice over'.[6]

Subrogation

For the purpose of furthering the principle of indemnity that the
insured should recover no more than his actual loss, as Brett LJ
asserted in *Castellain v Preston*,[7] the courts have adopted the doctrine

5 (1880) 5 QBD 560.
6 (1880) 5 QBD 560, 562. See also *Castellain v Preston* (1883) 11 QBD 380. If the
insured happens to recover more than his real loss from the third party who has
caused the loss, the insurers have no claim to the excess over the amount they paid
out under the policy: *Yorkshire Insurance Co Ltd v Nisbett Shipping Co Ltd* [1962] 2 QB
330, [1961] 2 All ER 487. However, although that follows from the general
principles of indemnity and subrogation, the correct approach is to construe the
terms of the insurance policy and only if there is ambiguity in the policy, would it be
right to invoke these general principles as a guide. The terms can exclude the
application of the general principles of indemnity: Viscount Dilhorne in *L Lucas Ltd v
Export Credits Guarantee Department* [1974] 2 All ER 889, 897, HL. See also R W
Hodgin 'Subrogation in Insurance Law' (1975) *Journal of Business Law* 114.
7 (1883) 11 QBD 380, 387. Brett LJ's, dicta were quoted with approval by Wynn
Parry J in *Re Miller, Gibb & Co Ltd* [1957] 2 All ER 266, 271, [1957] 1 WLR 703. In
this latter case, the Export Credits Guarantee Department of the Board of Trade had
paid out on a shipments policy of indemnity to a company of exporters, when
payment by importers in Brazil was held up by currency restriction. The export
company was wound up and it was held that when payment was finally made the
Board of Trade was entitled to exercise its rights of subrogation.

of subrogation. When the insurers have paid the insured under an indemnity policy, they are placed in the position of the insured, and, as a general rule, are entitled to sue in the name of the insured. This is how Brett LJ expressed the effect of the doctrine:[8]

'. . . as between the underwriter and the assured the underwriter is entitled to the advantage of every right of the assured, whether such right consists in contract, fulfilled or unfulfilled, or in remedy for tort capable of being insisted on or already insisted on, or in any other right, whether by way of condition or otherwise, legal or equitable, which can be, or has been exercised or has accrued, and whether such right could or could not be enforced by the insurer in the name of the assured by the exercise or acquiring of which right or condition the loss against which the assured is insured, can be, or has been, diminished.'

As a simple example, if goods insured against damage by fire are damaged by fire caused by the negligence of X, when the insurers have paid out under the policy, the insurers, standing in the shoes of the insured, are entitled to sue X but if damages are recovered in excess of the amount paid by the insurers to the insured and the insurers' costs, the balance belongs to the insured. Of course, if X is also insured, the loss would normally fall on X's insurers. But where, for example, two insured cars have a collision, the two insurers may have a knock-for-knock agreement whereby they agree that the damage to each vehicle will be borne by the owner's insurers, irrespective of who is to blame.[9]

In *Mark Rowlands Ltd v Berni Inns Ltd*,[10] landlords leased part of their premises to tenants on terms whereby the tenants covenanted to pay as 'insurance rent' sums equivalent to the premium paid by the landlords to maintain insurance against fire of the leased premises. The lease further provided that, in the event of the premises being destroyed by fire, the tenants were relieved of their repairing obligations and the landlords were required to apply the insurance moneys received on reinstating the premises. The landlords insured the entire building against fire in their sole name. The entire building was destroyed by fire caused by the tenants' negligence. Having paid out the landlords the cost of reinstating the building, the insurers brought an action (in the name of the landlords) claiming damages from the tenants for negligence. The

8 (1883) 11 QBD 380, 387.
9 *Morley v Moore* [1936] 2 KB 359, [1936] 2 All ER 79, *Bourne v Stanbridge* [1965] 1 All ER 241, [1965] 1 WLR 189; *Hobbs v Marlowe* [1978] AC 16, [1977] 2 All ER 41, HL.
10 [1986] QB 211, [1985] 3 All ER 473.

Court of Appeal held that the terms of the lease whereby the tenants were relieved of their repairing obligations in the event of fire did not deprive them of a limited insurable interest in the building and they were entitled to assert that the insurance effected by the landlords was intended to enure for the tenants' benefit to the extent of the tenants' interest. The sensible construction of the parties' intention was that, in the event of damage by fire, the landlords could recover from the insurers and, if they did so, they had no further claim against the tenants for negligence. It follows that, as the insurers' rights depended on those of the landlords, they had no relevant right of subrogation. Certainly there is no right of subrogation against a co-insured—an insurer may not sue one of the co-insured in the name of the other.[11]

Subject to agreement to the contrary, the right of subrogation depends on the insurers having paid the insured before the insured has himself issued a writ against X.[12] Assuming that to be the case, the insurers can compel the insured to let them use his name against an indemnity as to costs.[13] If the insured compromises any right of action he may have against a third party, he is liable to his insurers to the extent that that deprives the insurers of the benefit of subrogation. In *Phoenix Assurance Co v Spooner*,[14] the defendant insured her buildings against fire with the plaintiff company. During the currency of the policy the Plymouth Corporation gave the defendant notice to treat for the buildings under the Lands Clauses Consolidation Act 1845. Before anything had been done under that notice the buildings were destroyed by fire and the plaintiffs paid to the defendant an agreed sum as the amount of her loss. Later, the amount to be paid by the Corporation on taking over the property pursuant to their notice to treat was agreed between the defendant and the Corporation, and the sum was arrived at by taking into account the money paid by the plaintiffs to the defendant under the policy, the Corporation agreeing to indemnify the defendant against any claim which the plaintiffs might make against her. The court held that when the plaintiffs paid the defendant under the fire policy, since a fire policy is a policy of indemnity, the plaintiffs were entitled to all the rights of the defendant in respect of the destroyed property and those rights included a right to be paid by the Corporation the value of the

11 *Petrofina (UK) Ltd v Magnaload Ltd* [1984] QB 127, [1983] 3 All ER 33.
12 *Page v Scottish Insurance Corpn* (1929) 98 LJKB 308.
13 See McCardie J in *John Edwards & Co v Motor Union Insurance Co* [1922] 2 KB 249, 254.
14 [1905] 2 KB 753.

property as it existed at the date of the notice to treat. The defendant could not deprive the plaintiffs of that right by an agreement with the Corporation and, therefore, the plaintiffs were entitled to recover from the amount paid by them to her for the loss insured against.

Insurers who have made payment under a policy will also be able to claim, by way of subrogation, an ex gratia payment given to the insured provided it was given with the intention of diminishing or extinguishing his loss and the insurers have not been excluded by the donor from the benefit of the gift. The only reported cases concern gifts of public money made by governments.[15]

A recent decision of the Court of Appeal, *Morris v Ford Motor Co Ltd*[16] stressed that the right of subrogation is a necessary incident of a contract of indemnity but Lord Denning MR suggested that as the right is an equitable right it is excluded if it would not be just or equitable to compel the person indemnified to lend his name and James LJ said that the right could be excluded by an implied term to that effect. The court was concerned not with a contract of insurance as such but with a contract whereby a firm of cleaners agreed to indemnify factory owners for any liability they might incur arising out of the cleaning services they provided at the factory, including liability arising from the negligence of employees of the factory owners. The factory owners did incur liability in respect of the negligence of one of their employees and the terms of the indemnity contract entitled the factory owners to claim an indemnity from the firm of cleaners. The majority of the Court of Appeal (Lord Denning MR and James LJ) ruled that the firm of cleaners were not entitled to be subrogated to the factory owners' right of action against the employee—although they gave somewhat different reasons, they both thought that to exercise a right of subrogation in these circumstances could lead to industrial dispute and was unrealistic.

Contribution: double insurance

Where two or more indemnity policies have been taken out with different insurers in respect of the same interest in the same subject-matter and the total amount of insurance exceeds the total value of the loss, the insured may recover the total loss from any insurer up to

15 See Ivamy *General Principles of Insurance Law* (5th edn, 1986), pp 485–486.; *Burnand v Rodocanachi* (1882) 7 App Cas 333; *Castellain v Preston* (1883) 11 QBD 380, at 404.
16 [1973] 2 QB 792, [1973] 2 All ER 1084.

the amount of the policy. However, the insurer who pays can claim a contribution from the other insurer in proportion to the amount for which he is liable provided, of course, that the loss arises from a risk that is common to both policies and both are enforceable at the time of the loss.[17]

Thus, suppose a house valued at £5,000, is insured against fire, gas or explosion with A for £3,000 and against fire only with B for £2,000 and loss by fire occurs to the extent of £2,000. The insured can claim the whole of his £2,000 loss from either A or B. If he claims it from A, A can obtain a contribution from B of two-fifths, ie, £800. If, on the other hand, the insured claimed the whole of his loss from B, B could obtain a contribution from A of three-fifths, ie, £1,200. The apportionment in that example is made on a 'maximum liability' basis which seems to be the basis preferred in property cases.

The insured cannot, however, claim the whole of the loss from an insurer if the policy is expressed to be 'subject to average' and the policy does not cover the total value of the property.[18] Nor can the insured recover the whole of the loss from an insurer if the policy contains a clause that the insurer is not liable for more than a rateable proportion of the loss should there be any other insurance covering the same property and there is, in fact, other insurance. In one case,[19] a clause in a fire policy read:

'If, at the time of any loss or damage by fire happening to any property hereby insured, there be any other subsisting insurance or insurances, whether effected by the insured or by any other person, covering the same property, this company shall not be liable to pay or contribute more than its rateable proportion of such loss or damage.'

Baggallay JA explained this clause thus:

'. . . where there are several policies, and where there, in point of fact, is a double insurance, then in order to do away with the old practice of the insured recovering the whole from one of the insurance offices, and then the one from whom it was recovered being put to obtain contribution from the others, this clause was put in to say that the insured should, in the first instance, proceed against the several insurance companies for the aliquot parts for which they are liable in consequence of that condition.'

Where a public liability policy contains a rateable proportion clause, the rateable proportion is assessed on an 'independent

17 *American Surety Co of New York v Wrightson* (1910) 103 LT 663.
18 See p 324, post.
19 *North British and Mercantile Insurance Co v London, Liverpool, and Globe Insurance Co* (1877) 5 Ch D 569, 588.

liability' basis, ie, the liability of each insurer is ascertained as if he were the sole insurer and the total liability to the insured is then divided in proportion to the independent liabilities so ascertained.[20] The total liability of Commercial Union in the case of *Commerical Union Assurance Co Ltd v Hayden* was limited to £100,000 and Lloyd's total liability was restricted to £10,000. Any claim up to £10,000 was held to be one that must be borne equally by the two insurers and a claim for £40,000 must be shared proportionately to their independent liabilities in the ratio of £40,000 : £10,000, ie, £32,000 by Commercial Union and £8,000 by Lloyd's.[1]

For the principle of contribution to operate it is necessary that the same interests are covered by both policies, and this is not so if the landlord and the tenant insure their own interests alone by separate insurances.[2]

In *North British and Mercantile Insurance Co v London, Liverpool, and Globe Insurance Co*,[3] the owners of goods insured his interest and the bailee warehouseman insured his common law liability in respect of the goods. The goods were lost by the negligence of the warehouseman. The warehouseman was paid in full by his insurers and, in an action to determine the liability of the insurance companies inter se, the Court of Appeal held that the owner's insurers were not liable to contribute towards the loss. The policies covered different interests and the principle of contribution, therefore, had no application; the warehouseman was primarily liable for the loss and since he had been indemnified by his insurers, the latter were ultimately liable for the full loss. As Mellish LJ explained, if the owner's insurers had paid out the owner, they would have had not just a right of contribution against the warehouseman's insurers but a right of subrogation against the warehouseman and, in effect, against his insurers.

No indemnity for wilful misconduct

As Lord Atkin said in *Beresford v Royal Insurance Co*[4] 'on ordinary principles of insurance law an assured cannot by his own deliberate

---

20 *Commercial Union Assurance Co Ltd v Hayden* [1977] QB 804, [1977] 1 All ER 441, CA.

1 If the apportionment had been made on a 'maximum liability' basis, Commercial Union would have been liable for $\frac{10}{11}$ of every claim whatever its amount.

2 *Portavon Cinema Co Ltd v Price and Century Insurance Co Ltd* [1939] 4 All ER 601.

3 (1877) 5 Ch D 569.

4 [1938] AC 586, 595, [1938] 2 All ER 602, 604. This principle applies also to non-indemnity insurance, for example, life assurance with which this case was in fact concerned. See p 331, post, for the effect of suicide on a life policy.

act cause the event upon which the insurance money is payable'. If the insured deliberately sets fire to his house he clearly cannot claim on his fire policy. Where a fire policy is taken out in the joint names of the owners and mortgagees and the fire is intentionally caused by the mortgagors, the mortgagees can recover provided that they are quite innocent.[5] The onus of proving that the loss has been caused by the insured's misconduct lies on the insurers.[6] Mere negligence is another matter. As Kerr LJ said in *Mark Rowlands Ltd v Berni Sons Ltd*,[7] an essential feature of insurance against fire is that it covers fires caused by negligence as well as by accident. In *Harris v Poland*[8] the contents of a flat were insured against loss by fire. For purposes of protection against theft, on leaving the flat one day, the insured concealed jewellery in the grate under coal and wood. In the evening she inadvertently lit the fire and the jewellery was damaged. Since the insured had not intentionally caused the damage the insurers were liable on the policy.

It follows from this principle that an indemnity policy taken out by a solicitor could not cover his liability in respect of an intentional criminal act such as entering into a champertous agreement.[9] So too, where the defendants had agreed to indemnify the plaintiffs for any liability in defamation arising from the plaintiffs' paper 'Vanity Fair', the defendants were held not liable to indemnify the plaintiffs for liability in respect of statements in that paper which the plaintiffs knew were libellous.[10] In *Gray v Barr*[11] B shot and killed G in a struggle. B was acquitted of murder and manslaughter but G's personal representatives sued B under the Fatal Accidents Acts and B sought an indemnity, in respect of such damages as he might be required to pay, under his accident

---

5   *P Samuel & Co Ltd v Dumas* [1924] AC 431, [1924] All ER Rep 66.

6   *Slattery v Mance* [1962] 1 QB 676, [1962] 1 All ER 525.

7   [1985] 3 All ER 473, 484.

8   [1941] 1 KB 462, [1941] 1 All ER 204.

9   *Haseldine v Hosken* [1933] 1 KB 822, [1933] All ER Rep 1. Champerty ceased to be a crime by the Criminal Law Act 1967.

10   *W H Smith & Son v Clinton* (1908) 99 LT 840. By s 11 of the Defamation Act 1952, an agreement to indemnify anyone against civil liability for libel in respect of the publication of any matter is not unlawful unless at the time of the publication that person knows that the matter is defamatory and does not reasonably believe that there is a good defence to any action brought upon it.

11   [1971] 2 QB 554, [1971] 2 All ER 949, CA. The case would probably be decided the same way today despite the Forfeiture Act 1982—see note in (1983) 46 MLR 66, 68. The Forfeiture Act modifies the common law rule against a person who has unlawfully killed another benefiting as a result by giving the court a measure of discretion.

liability policy. Members of the Court of Appeal differed as to whether G's death had been caused by an 'accident' within the terms of the policy though even Salmon LJ who thought the death had been caused by an 'accident', said that the policy must be read subject to an implied exception that the policy did not apply to injuries caused by an accident occurring in the course of threatening unlawful violence with a loaded gun. In any event, the Court of Appeal was unanimous in rejecting B's claim on the ground that public policy required that no one who threatened unlawful violence with a loaded gun should be allowed to enforce a claim for indemnity against any liability he might incur as a result of having so acted. On the other hand a liability policy does cover an act of negligence though it may amount to a criminal offence, so that a conviction for 'motor manslaughter' does not prevent the convicted person claiming to recover under a policy of insurance against third party risks if he is held liable in negligence to a third party.[12]

A claim is tainted by illegality and will be disallowed if either the plaintiff needs to plead or prove illegal conduct in order to establish his claim or the claim is so closely connected with the proceeds of crime as to offend the conscience of the court. It follows that a professional handler of stolen goods cannot claim under an indemnity policy for their loss.[13]

No indemnity can be claimed in respect of ordinary wear and tear on property[14] or damage due to the inherent vice or condition of the property.[15]

The extent of the indemnity

General principle.—Obviously the insured cannot recover more than the amount of his policy so that if the contents of a house are

12 *James v British General Insurance Co* [1927] 2 KB 311, [1927] All ER Rep 442. The Court of Appeal in *Haseldine v Hosken* [1933] 1 KB 822, [1933] All ER Rep 1, reserved its opinion on the correctness of the earlier decision, but in *Marles v Philip Trant & Sons Ltd (No 2)* [1954] 1 QB 29, [1953] 1 All ER 651, the Court of Appeal approved the decision in *James*. In *Marcel Beller Ltd v Hayden* [1978] QB 694, [1978] 3 All ER 111, a life policy contained a clause excluding liability where death was due to the insured's own criminal act. The insured was killed whilst driving dangerously and under the influence of drink and the court held the insurers were entitled to repudiate liability. 'Criminal acts' covered all criminal offences which were not offences of inadvertence or negligence.

13 *Euro-Diam Ltd v Bathurst* [1987] 2 All ER 113, 123.

14 *Austin v Drewe* (1816) 6 Taunt 436.

15 *British and Foreign Marine Insurance Co v Gaunt* [1921] 2 AC 41, [1921] All ER Rep 447.

insured to the extent of £500 that is the limit of any claim that may
be made in respect of their loss.

The sum insured is the *maximum* amount that will be paid and, if
the event insured against occurs, the amount to be paid is the actual
loss incurred by the insured up to that maximum. In *Leppard v Excess
Insurance Co Ltd*,[16] the insurance policy on a cottage stated the
amount insured to be £10,000 and this figure was declared by the
insured to be the amount it would cost to replace the property in its
existing form if it was totally destroyed. When the cottage was
totally destroyed by fire the insured claimed that the amount
payable was the cost of replacement. The Court of Appeal,
however, allowed him only the market value of the cottage at the
time of the fire, namely £3,000.

Apart from that point, the extent of the indemnity depends on the
description in the policy of the risks insured against. Every loss that
clearly and proximately results from the event insured against is
covered. 'It is well understood' said Lord Dunedin in a marine
insurance case 'that the question of which (cause) is *proxima* is not
solved by mere point of order in time'.[17] Was the event insured
against the 'dominant' cause of the loss? If so, the policy covers the
loss. Thus, a fire insurance policy will cover not only loss caused
directly by the fire but also loss caused by the efforts of firemen to
put out the fire such as by the use of water hoses. On the other hand,
if the fire merely facilitates loss by leaving property exposed to the
risk of theft, such loss could not be claimed under the fire policy.[18]

If a car is insured against 'loss' and is sold for a worthless cheque,
the seller has voluntarily parted with the property in the car and
therefore there has been no 'loss' of the car, only the proceeds of sale,
and the insurers are not liable.[19]

Exception clauses.—If the proximate cause of loss is something for
which an exception clause in a policy provides that the insurers will
not indemnify the insured, the insured will not be able to claim. In
Wayne Tank and Pump Co Ltd v The Employers' Liability Assurance Corpn

16 [1979] 2 All ER 668, [1979] 1 WLR 512, CA. This was an ordinary indemnity
policy not a 'valued' policy. See p 323, post.

17 *Leyland Shipping Co v Norwich Fire Insurance Society* [1918] AC 350, 363 [1918–19]
All ER Rep 443.

18 *Marsden v City and County Assurance* (1865) LR 1 CP 232. Similarly, under
ordinary fire insurance, consequential loss such as the cost of hiring other premises,
loss of wages and profits, cannot be recovered: *Re Wright and Pole* (1834) 1 Ad & El
621.

19 *Eisinger v General Accident Fire and Life Assurance Corpn Ltd* [1955] 2 All ER 897,
[1955] 1 WLR 869.

Ltd[20] a public liability policy contained an exception clause which provided that the insurers would not indemnify the insured in respect of liability consequent on 'damage caused by the nature and condition of any goods . . . supplied by' the insured. The insured was held liable for breach of contract after equipment installed by the insured in a factory was switched on and caused extensive fire damage. The two causes of fire were the dangerous nature of the equipment and the conduct of the insured's employee in switching it on. In a claim under the policy, the Court of Appeal held the insurers could avoid liability by virtue of the exception clause quoted. The equipment when installed constituted 'goods' and, according to Lord Denning MR and Roskill LJ the dangerous nature of the equipment was the proximate cause of the fire—this was the dominant or effective cause and, therefore, the proximate cause in insurance law, even though more remote in time than the conduct of the insured's employee. Moreover, the whole court held that, in any event, where there were two causes of loss, one within the general words of the policy and the other within an exception clause in the policy, the insurers were entitled to rely on the exception and were not liable for the loss.

Total and partial loss.—Within the amount covered by the policy, the insured can recover the value of his loss. In the case of loss of property, on a total loss the insured can claim the market value of the property at the time of the loss, but if similar property is not available, the cost of restoration may be claimed though some allowance may be made 'new for old'.[1] If partial loss only has occurred, the indemnity claimable is the cost of repairs though sometimes the policy provides that this sum be the difference between the value before fire and the value after fire.

Valued policies.—Though it is rare outside marine insurance, the policy may put a valuation on the property insured in which case the insured is entitled to claim that value on a total loss or a proportion in the case of partial loss. In *Elcock v Thomson,*[2] a mansion was insured against fire, and by a schedule to the policy

20 [1974] QB 57, [1973] 3 All ER 825, CA. The claim against the insurers followed the award of heavy damages against the insured in the well-known case concerning fundamental breach and exemption clauses in contract law: *Harbutt's Plasticine Co Ltd v Wayne Tank and Pump Co Ltd* [1970] 1 QB 447, [1970] 1 All ER 225, CA.

1 *Chapman v Pole* (1870) 22 LT 306, *Westminster Fire Office v Glasgow Provident Investment Society* (1888) 13 App Cas 699.

2 [1949] 2 KB 755, [1949] 2 All ER 381.

its value was agreed at £106,850. The mansion was damaged by fire. Its actual value before fire was £18,000 and its actual value after fire was £12,600. The court held that in order to assess the amount to which the insured was entitled under the policy, the percentage of actual depreciation resulting from the fire should be applied to the agreed value, and that the insured was, therefore, entitled to:—

$$\frac{£5,400}{£18,000} \times £106,850, \text{ ie}, £32,055.$$

However, it should be added that although the mansion was not in fact reinstated, the cost of reinstatement would have been some £40,000 and the court queried whether, if the estimated cost of reinstatement had been less than £32,055, the insurers could have limited their liability to the cost of reinstatement. Insurers may, of course, avoid liability in the case of fraud, misrepresentation or non-disclosure of a material fact and over-valuation may be due to one of those factors.[3] Further, the over-valuation may be so gross as to make the contract a wager and therefore void.[4] When the insurers have paid out under a valued policy, they have the same right of subrogation as with any other indemnity policy, up to the amount paid by them to the insured.

'Subject to average' clause

On general principles, an insured is entitled to claim the full cost of repairs in the case of partial loss provided it comes within the total amount covered by the policy, so that the insured may feel adequately protected although the property is under-insured, since total loss is rare.[5] If, however, the policy contains a 'subject to average' clause, and the property is under-insured, the insurers are liable only for the proportion of the actual loss which the sum insured bears to the value of the property. Thus where property worth £5,000 is insured for only £2,000, if there is a partial loss to the extent of, say, £1,500, without a 'Subject to average' clause in the policy the insurers are liable for £1,500. If the policy does contain a 'subject to average' clause, then the liability of the insurers is only two-fifths of £1,500, ie, £600.

In *Acme Wood Flooring Co v Marten*[6] the plaintiff company was

3   *Thames and Mersey Marine Insurance Co v Gunford* [1911] AC 529.
4   *Lewis v Rucker* (1761) 2 Burr 1167, *Irving v Manning* (1847) 1 HL Cas 287.
5   *Fifth Liverpool Starr Bowkett Building Society v Travellers Accident Insurance Co Ltd* (1893) 9 TLR 221.
6   (1904) 90 LT 313.

insured under a Lloyd's fire policy on timber in the sum of £11,450 and the policy was expressed to be 'subject to average'. The actual value of the timber at risk was £36,500 and the insured suffered a loss by fire of £12,850. The court said that the phrase 'subject to average' in the policy meant that it impliedly included the standard Lloyd's 'average clause' which states:

'Whenever a sum insured is declared to be subject to average, if the property covered thereby shall at the breaking out of any fire be collectively of greater value than such sum insured, then the assured shall be considered as being his own insurer for the difference and shall bear a rateable share of the loss accordingly.'

In the result, the court held the underwriters liable for £4,031 0s 6d representing the proportion of the actual loss (£12,850) which the sum of £11,450 bore to the sum of £36,500.

Reinstatement—fire policies

The ordinary common law rule in insurances on property is that the insured is not bound to use any moneys payable under the policy on reinstating the property. The insured is entitled to be indemnified in cash which he may use as he thinks fit. In two instances, however, the insured is bound to take reinstatement of the property in lieu of money. One is where there is an express term in the policy giving the insurer a right to reinstate the goods or buildings and the insurer chooses to exercise the option. Once the insurer has determined under such a clause to exercise the option and reinstate the property he is bound by that election and cannot limit his expenditure to the sum insured.[7] The other instance is where the insurers are bound to reinstate under s 83 of the Fires Prevention (Metropolis) Act 1774.

Fires Prevention (Metropolis) Act 1774.—Under s 83 of this Act, 'any person or persons interested' in a house or houses or other buildings burnt down, demolished or damaged by fire, which are insured against loss by fire, may request the insurers to lay out the insurance money as far *as it will go* towards the rebuilding, reinstating, or repairing of such buildings, and the insurers are then bound to do so. Similarly, the insurers are also bound to reinstate 'upon any grounds of suspicion' that the assured has been guilty of fraud, or of wilfully setting fire to such buildings. In neither case, however, are the insurers bound to reinstate if, within 60 days of the claim being adjusted, the assured gives a sufficient security that the insurance money will be laid out in reinstating the property, or if the insurance money is in that time settled and disposed of to and

7 *Brown v Royal Insurance Co* (1859) 1 E & E 853, 858.

amongst all the contending parties to the satisfaction and approbation of the governors or directors of the insurance company.

Despite the word in the Act's title, 'Metropolis', s 83 applies throughout the country. The section has no application if the insurers are Lloyd's underwriters.[8] 'Persons interested' include an owner, lessor, lessee, mortgagor and mortgagee, and remainder-man and the statutory right is exercisable by a claim for an injunction to restrain the company from paying the money to the insured unless the latter gives adequate security to apply the money in reinstatement.[9] It may well be that a purchaser is also a 'person interested'. As we shall see, if a fire destroys a building after contract for sale but before completion, the purchaser may, if he is not insured, rely on the provisions of s 47 of the Law of Property Act 1925, by which insurance money payable under the vendor's insurance policy is held by the vendor on behalf of the purchaser. It is not always possible for a purchaser to rely on s 47 and a purchaser may wish, therefore, to demand of the vendor's insurers that they reinstate the property instead of handing over the policy moneys to the vendor.[10]

It is too late for a 'person interested' to demand reinstatement under s 83 if the insurers have already paid the insurance moneys over.[11]

Salvage

Clearly it follows from the general principles of indemnity insurance that if the insured obtains a full indemnity from his insurers under a fire policy, the insurers have a right to any salvage there may be.[12]

LIFE ASSURANCE

Insurable interest

A policy of life assurance is a contract to pay a specified sum on the death of the life assured in consideration of the agreed premium. We have already noted that it is not an indemnity policy so that, for example, if the death of the life assured is caused by the negligence of X, the policy moneys may be retained intact though the assured's

8 *Portavon Cinema Co Ltd v Price and Century Insurance Co Ltd* [1939] 4 All ER 601.

9 *Wimbledon Park Golf Club Ltd v Imperial Co Ltd* (1902) 18 TLR 815. Quaere whether a mandatory injunction can be claimed to compel reinstatement.

10 See M P Picard *Elements of Insurance Law* (2nd edn, 1939) p 111. See also p 344, post.

11 *Simpson v Scottish Union Insurance* (1863) 1 Hem & M 618.

12 *Kaltenbach v Mackenzie* (1878) 3 CPD 467.

personal representatives obtain damages from X. No right of subrogation can arise out of payment by the insurers under a life policy. An endowment policy by which the insurers agree to pay a sum of money on the assured reaching a given age or at death whichever is the sooner is a policy of life insurance.

Although by virtue of the Life Assurance Act 1774, the person for whose benefit a life policy is taken out must have an insurable interest at the time the policy is taken out, since life assurance is not a contract of indemnity, it does not matter that the insurable interest no longer exists at the time of the death of the life assured. In *Dalby v India and London Life Assurance Co*,[13] X insured his life with A Co for £3,000; A Co reinsured X's life with B Co for £1,000. At the time of that reinsurance, A Co had an insurable interest in X's life because it owed a contingent liability to X. X's life assurance with A Co was surrendered so that A Co was no longer under any such contingent liability, but A Co kept up its reinsurance policy. It was held that when X died A Co could claim £1,000 from B Co under the contract of reinsurance.

A man has an unlimited insurable interest in his own life and spouses have unlimited insurable interest in each other's life.[14] Even though when a man takes out a policy on his own life for his own benefit he intends to assign the benefit to another person, it is still a valid policy.[15] Such policy would, however, be void if the assured merely lent his name to another person who paid the premium and was intended all along to have the benefit of the policy, as this is a fraudulent evasion of the Life Assurance Act.[16] An employee has an insurable interest in the life of his employer to the extent of the wages he is entitled to under his contract of service, and a creditor has an insurable interest in his debtor's life up to the amount of the debt even if he has adequate security for the debt.[17]

A partner has an insurable interst in his co-partner's life to the extent of loss he may suffer on the death of the co-partner from the withdrawal of partnership funds, and a surety has an interest in the life of a co-surety to the extent of his proportion of the debt.[18] Since

---

13 (1854) 15 CB 365.

14 *Griffiths v Fleming* [1909] 1 KB 805, [1908–10] All ER Rep 760.

15 *M'Farlane v Royal London Friendly Society* (1886) 2 TLR 755.

16 *Shilling v Accidental Death Insurance Co* (1857) 27 LJ Ex 16.

17 *Law v London Indisputable Life* (1855) 1 K & J 223. Life policies not valid under these general principles may be taken out for limited amounts under the Friendly Societies Acts 1896–1974.

18 A surety also has an interest in the life of the principal debtor because of the surety's quasi-contractual right against the latter if the surety has paid off the creditor: *Lea v Hinton* (1854) 5 De G M & G 823.

the donee of a gift inter-vivos is liable to pay duty on it if the donor dies within seven years of the gift, the donee has an insurable interest in the donor's life and life policies are obtainable with cover reducing in the fifth, sixth and seventh years when under the law reduced duty is payable.[19] Merely being told to expect a benefit under a man's will does not give one an insurable interest in the testator's life.

Married Women's Property Act 1882

By virtue of s 11 of this Act:

'A policy of assurance effected by any man on his own life, and expressed to be for the benefit of his wife, or his children, or of his wife and children, or any of them, or by any woman on her own life, and expressed to be for the benefit of her husband, or of her children, or of her husband and children, or any of them, shall create a trust in favour of the objects therein named, and the moneys payable under any such policy shall not, so long as any object of the trust remains unperformed form part of the estate of the insured, or be subject to his or her debts.'

There is a proviso to the effect that, if it is proved that the policy was effected with intent to defraud creditors of the insured, they are entitled to receive out of the moneys payable on the policy a sum equal to the premiums so paid.

In *Cousins v Sun Life Assurance Society*,[20] a man took out a policy on his life for the benefit of a named wife. The named wife predeceased him and it was held that the policy moneys payable on his death belonged to that wife's estate, though the man had remarried.[1] Had the policy been taken out for the benefit of 'my wife' that would be construed as meaning the man's wife at the date of death[2].

The section applies to endowment policies if one event on which the policy moneys are payable is the death of the assured and, in that circumstance, is expressed to be for the benefit of the assured's wife (or children etc). Thus, in *Re Ioakimidis' Policy Trusts*[3] an endowment policy provided for payment of policy moneys after

19 The seven-year period applies in the case of deaths since 19 March 1968 (Finance Act 1968 s 35); prior to 1968, the period was five years.

20 [1933] Ch 126, [1932] All ER Rep 404.

1 In such a case of the wife predeceasing the husband, the husband has a lien on the policy moneys for premiums paid by him after his wife's death as this is money spent by a trustee to preserve the trust property: *Re Smith's Estate, Bilham v Smith* [1937] Ch 636, [1937] 3 All ER 472. If the named wife is divorced, she does not lose her vested interest under a s 11 policy but by the Matrimonial Proceedings and Property Act 1970, the court may vary the 'settlement'.

2 *Re Browne's Policy* [1903] 1 Ch 188.

3 [1925] Ch 403, [1925] All ER Rep 164.

20 years or on earlier death. It was expressed to be for the benefit of the assured's wife if he died within the 20 years, but otherwise for the benefit of the assured himself. The assured did die within the 20 years and the court held that the wife was entitled to the policy moneys under s 11 of the Married Women's Property Act.

The assured must act like a trustee when he has taken out a policy governed by the provision so that if, for example, he has an option to surrender the policy, he must exercise the option in the best manner for the benefit of those entitled.[4]

Where a policy is effected under this provision and the assured dies, until the Finance Act 1968 the policy moneys were not aggregated with the deceased's general estate for purposes of estate duty, because the deceased had never an interest in the policy moneys. Now, by s 38 of the Finance Act 1968, in the case of deaths after 19 March 1968, all such property is aggregable.[5] Although gifts inter vivos made during the period of seven years before death are subject to estate duty and premiums paid by the assured under a s 11 policy are treated as gifts to the beneficiary of the policy, no duty is payable on that proportion of the policy moneys which correspond to premiums paid in that seven-year period if the premiums were paid as 'part of the normal expenditure' of the assured.[6]

The limits of s 11 of the 1882 Act should be appreciated. If A takes out a policy on his own life and 'nominates' B as a beneficiary that does not itself constitute A a trustee for B and B may have no rights to claim the policy moneys on A's death. Where B is A's wife, husband, or child, a trust may exist under s 11 but otherwise B has no rights unless the nomination can be construed as a declaration of trust or A was B's agent. Similarly, if A takes out a policy on the life of B, B has rights if it can be construed as creating a trust in favour of B as in *Re Webb, Barclays Bank Ltd v Webb*[7] where A (a father) took out a policy 'on behalf of and for the benefit of the life assured' and his child B was named as the life assured—if B died before he became 21, A was entitled to recover part of the interest in the policy. As the policy moneys were payable only if B did reach the age of 21, Farwell J held that a trust for B had been created. One

---

4 *Re Policy of Equitable Life Assurance Society of United States and Mitchell* (1911) 27 TLR 213.

5 This new rule does apply fully where the policy was taken out before 20 March 1968.

6 Finance Act 1968 s 37.

7 [1941] Ch 225, [1941] 1 All ER 321, followed in *Re Foster's Policy, Menneer v Foster* [1956] 1 All ER 432, [1956] 1 WLR 222.

may contrast the case of *Re Engelbach's Estate*[8] where A took out an endowment policy on behalf of B, his one-month-old daughter, the policy moneys being expressed to be payable to B at the end of the endowment period if she survived to that date. She did survive to that date, but Romer J held that the policy moneys should not have been paid to B but to the estate of A who had now died, on the ground that no trust had been created in favour of B. The insurer might have refused to make any payment on the ground that A had no insurable interest in his daughter's life, but as the insurer had made a payment, the court had to consider the difficult issue of who was entitled to the moneys.

Public policy

At common law, neither a person convicted of murder nor his estate may benefit from a policy on the life of the victim. As Hamilton LJ said in *Re Hall's Estate, Hall v Knight and Baxter*,[9] 'a man shall not slay his benefactor and thereby take his bounty'. In *Cleaver v Mutual Reserve Fund Life Association*[10] a husband insured his own life for his wife's benefit. The husband was poisoned by his wife and it was held that neither the wife nor her estate could claim the policy moneys which were recoverable by the husband's executors for the benefit of his estate and in no way recoverable by the wife or any one claiming through her.[11]

8 [1924] 2 Ch 348. The fact that had this policy been one on the father's life it would have created a trust in favour of the daughter under s 11 of the Married Women's Property Act 1882, explains the proposal of the Law Revision Committee that s 11 should be extended to cover endowment and education policies (Sixth Interim Report 32).

9 [1914] P 1, 7.

10 [1892] 1 QB 147.

11 The result would be the same if the wife had killed her husband by manslaughter: *Re Peacock, Midland Bank Executor and Trustee Co Ltd v Peacock* [1957] Ch 310, [1957] 2 All ER 98, and even if the manslaughter were the result of negligence: *Re Hall's Estate, Hall v Knight and Baxter* [1914] P 1, [1911–13] All ER Rep 381 it would still be contrary to public policy for her to benefit from her crime. Under the Forfeiture Act 1982, the court has power to modify what the Act calls the 'forfeiture rule', ie the rule of public policy which in certain circumstances precludes a person who has unlawfully killed another (or been a party to an unlawful killing) from acquiring a benefit in consequence of the killing. However, the court may only make an order modifying the forfeiture rule if 'the justice of the case' requires it, having regard to the conduct of the offender and of the deceased and to such other circumstances as appear to the court to be material. Moreover, the Act only applies to certain types of property interest and an interest in a policy taken out on the life of the deceased is not specified in the Act. The Act would apply if the offender is a beneficiary of a trust of a policy maturing on the deceased's death or where the insurance moneys fall into the deceased's estate (see note in (1983) 46 MLR 66, 69).

For similar reasons of public policy, the assignees in bankruptcy of a forger, who had been executed for his crime, were held not entitled to recover on a life policy taken out by him on his own life.[12] In this case, the policy moneys were not payable at all.

In *Beresford v Royal Insurance Co Ltd*[13] a life policy stated that the policy would be void if the assured should die by his own hand whether sane or insane within one year from the date of the policy. The assured committed suicide while sane after one year from the date of the policy, and, under the existing law, was guilty of a crime. By implication from the policy, since death occurred after one year, the policy money was payable on his death although he had committed suicide while sane. The House of Lords, however, held that it was contrary to public policy to permit the assured's personal representatives to recover the fruits of the assured's crime. It was suggested by Lord Atkin that if, by an express term the policy moneys were payable on a sane suicide, an innocent assignee of the policy before the suicide could have recovered.[14] Since the Suicide Act 1961, sane suicide is no longer a criminal offence but the general principle of insurance law that no claim can be made on a policy if the assured deliberately brings about the event against which he has insured is still applicable. However, if a life policy expressly provides that the policy moneys are payable if the assured dies by his own hand while sane, presumably the general principle gives way to the express terms of the policy.

The Forfeiture Act 1982 does not apply where death is caused by suicide as it refers only to the unlawful killing of 'another'.

MOTOR VEHICLE INSURANCE

Compulsory insurance

Since the Road Traffic Act 1930, it has been compulsory for the user of a motor vehicle to be insured against the risk of liability for death or bodily injury other than the death or bodily injury of certain excepted categories of persons. The Motor Vehicles (Passenger Insurance) Act 1971 extended compulsory cover to passengers and the law is now contained in a consolidating statute, the Road

---

12 *Amicable Society v Bolland* (1830) 4 Bli NS 194.
13 [1938] AC 586, [1938] 2 All ER 602.
14 [1938] AC 586, 600, [1938] 2 All ER 602, 607. Quaere whether the assignee would be protected only if the policy contained a clause protecting the assignee's interest: *Moore v Woolsey* (1854) 4 E & B 243.

Traffic Act 1972. At the time of writing, Regulations are being introduced giving effect to the EC Directive whereby insurance is made compulsory to cover liability for *damage to property* arising out of the use of a vehicle as well as liability in respect of death or bodily injury.

The main provision is s 143 (1) which replaces s 35 of the Road Traffic Act 1930 and s 201 of the Road Traffic Act 1960:

> 'Subject to the provisions of this Part of this Act, it shall not be lawful for a person to use, or to cause or permit any other person to use, a motor vehicle on a road unless there is in force in relation to the user of the vehicle by that person or that other person, as the case may be, such a policy of insurance or such a security in respect of third-party risks as complies with the requirements of this Part of this Act.'

'Road' means any highway and any other road to which the public has access (s 196).[15] By s 158 'policy of insurance' includes a 'covering note' but a valid insurance for the purposes of s 143 (1) must arise from an enforceable contract and if after the expiry of an insurance policy a temporary cover note is sent to the driver, this is no more than an offer to insure and ineffective unless accepted either by communication with the insurers or, for example, by the driver taking his car out in reliance on the cover note.[16]

In parenthesis, one may say that most motorists take out an insurance policy that gives wider cover than the Act requires, for example, covering liability in respect of damage to property as well as covering damage to the vehicle itself and covering the risk of injury to the insured himself. However, the policy often contains an 'excess' clause under which the insured must bear the loss up to a specified figure, the insurer being liable only for the excess over that sum. Certain types of vehicles need not be covered, eg, those owned by local authorities or police authorities or by the Crown or used by Crown servants in the discharge of their duties (ss 144 (2) and 188).

Anyone who is in breach of the compulsory insurance provision contained in s 143 (1) is guilty of a criminal offence. If the user of the motor vehicle is not covered against liability for third party risks, both the owner and the driver can be prosecuted. In

15 It is sufficient if the greater part of the vehicle is on the road and the vehicle is as a whole using the road: *Randall v Motor Insurers' Bureau* [1969] 1 All ER 21, [1968] 1 WLR 1900.

16 *Taylor v Allon* [1966] 1 QB 304, [1965] 1 All ER 557.

Williamson v O'Keeffe,[17] the respondent was driving a friend's car which was only insured while she (the owner) or her brother was driving it. The Divisional Court held that the respondent driver should have been convicted. However, if a driver charged under this section proves that the vehicle did not belong to him and was not in his possession under a contract of hiring or loan, that he was using it in the course of his employment and that he neither knew nor had reason to believe that there was not in force in relation to the vehicle a policy of insurance or security, he will not be convicted (s 143 (2)).

Apart from criminal liability, anyone in breach of s 143 (1) is liable in damages to anyone injured for breach of statutory duty where there is no other effective remedy for the injured party. Thus, in *Monk v Warbey*,[18] the defendant lent his car to X who, owing to the negligence of his driver, injured the plaintiff. X was uninsured and the defendant's motor vehicle insurance was an 'owner only' policy, ie, it only covered user of the car when the owner was driving it. The defendant was clearly in breach of s 35 of the Road Traffic Act 1930 and was liable to the plaintiff for breach of statutory duty. If a motor vehicle is being driven by a servant in the course of his employment, the employer complies with the Act if he has taken out a policy covering the employer's vicarious liability for his servant's torts; the employer is under no obligation under the Act, or by virtue of any implied term in the contract of employment, to cover the servant's personal liability.[19] The owner of a vehicle is under no statutory obligation to take out insurance to cover the risk of a passenger's liability for injury caused to a third party by the passenger's negligence. Permitting someone to 'use' a motor vehicle on the roads (in the words of s 143 (1)) involves enabling someone to control, manage or operate the vehicle.[20]

By s 147, a policy of insurance is of no effect for the purposes of the

---

17 [1947] 1 All ER 307. In *Elliott v Grey* [1960] 1 QB 367, [1959] 3 All ER 733, it was held that even a car that has been jacked up in the road so that the wheels are off the ground and whose battery has been removed so that it cannot be mechanically propelled still has to be covered by insurance. Furthermore, it appears that a car whose engine has been removed still has to be covered by insurance: *Newberry v Simmonds* [1961] 2 QB 345, [1961] 2 All ER 318. However, where a car was purchased for scrap with no gearbox or battery and what was left of its engine rusted, it was held not to have to be insured: *Smart v Allan* [1963] 1 QB 291, [1962] 3 All ER 893.

18 [1935] 1 KB 75, [1934] All ER Rep 373.

19 *John T Ellis Ltd v Hinds* [1947] KB 475, [1947] 1 All ER 337, *Lister v Romford Ice and Cold Storage Co* [1957] AC 555, [1957] 1 All ER 125.

20 *Brown v Roberts* [1965] 1 QB 1, [1963] 2 All ER 263.

Act unless a 'certificate of insurance' is delivered to the insured.[1] Section 145 requires that the policy of insurance must be issued by an 'authorised insurer', ie, one carrying on motor vehicles insurance in Great Britain.

If the insurance policy purports to cover, say, anyone driving the vehicle with the owner's consent, by s 148 (4) the insurers are bound (whether the risk is one against which insurance is compulsory or not)[2] to indemnify the persons or classes of persons coming within that category. Because of the rules of privity of contract, apart from this statutory provision no one other than the insured himself could sue on the contract contained in the policy. In *Kelly v Cornhill Insurance Co Ltd*,[3] a policy purported to cover anyone driving the insured car with the permission of the insured. The insured gave permission to his son to drive without any limitation as to time. After the owner's death but before the policy was due for renewal, the son damaged property through his negligent driving of the car. The House of Lords held that the son was entitled to the benefit of the policy in respect of the claims made against him. He was driving with the permission of his father. The word 'permission' in the policy was not to be construed as a permission which the assured was at all times in a position to cancel.[4] However, where a policy purports to cover anyone driving with the permission of the insured and the vehicle is sold, the buyer cannot claim to be indemnified under the policy because he cannot be considered to be driving with the former owner's permission.[5]

Risks required to be covered.—To comply with the Act, a motor vehicle policy must cover such person, persons or classes of persons as may be specified in the policy in respect of 'any liability' which

1 By s 144 (1) an alternative to an insurance policy covering third-party risks, provided the vehicle is being driven under its owner's control, is the deposit of £15,000 with the Accountant-General of the Supreme Court. Despite inflation this sum has remained the same since 1930! Another alternative is obtaining a 'certificate of security' from an authorised insurer or other person specified in s 146 (2), the security being an undertaking to make good the failure of the owner to discharge his liability to third parties.

2 *Digby v General Accident Fire and Life Association Corpn Ltd* [1943] AC 121, [1942] 2 All ER 319.

3 [1964] 1 All ER 321, [1964] 1 WLR 158, HL.

4 If a policy covers more than the risk of liability to third parties, an insurable interest is required and it may be argued that the policy lapses when the insured dies as he then ceases to have any insurable interest in the vehicle (see post, p 342).

5 *Peters v General Accident and Fire and Life Assurance Corpn Ltd* [1938] 2 All ER 267. A motor vehicle policy is not transferable because it is essentially a personal contract, except with the insurerers' consent. See post, p 344.

may be incurred by him or them for the 'death of or bodily injury to any person caused by, or arising out of, the use of the vehicle on a road' (s 145 (3) (a)). It must also cover the liability provided for by s 155 in respect of emergency treatment of traffic casualties (s 145 (3) (b)). The Court of Appeal held that 'any person' does not include the actual driver of the vehicle.[6] It does, however, include a person deliberately harmed by the motorist and 'any liability' includes liability for deliberately created harm.[7]

It is not compulsory under the Act for the policy to cover:—

(a) liability in respect of the death, arising out of and in the course of his employment, of a person in the employment of a person insured by the policy or of bodily injury sustained by such a person arising out of and in the course of his employment; or

(b) any contractual liability (s 145 (4)).

The former exception of liability for death or injury to passengers (unless carried for hire or reward or under a contract of employment) ended on 1 December 1972. Since that date insurance against the risk of liability to passengers has been compulsory and, by s 148 (3) of the Road Traffic Act 1972, any agreement or understanding whereby the user's liability to passengers is excluded or restricted is void.[8]

By s 154, if an authorised insurer has made a payment in respect of the death of, or bodily injury to, any person arising out of the use of a motor vehicle on a road or in a place to which the public has a right of access, and the person who has died or been badly injured has, to the knowledge of the insurer, received treatment at a hospital in respect of the injury so arising, the insurer must pay the expenses reasonably incurred by the hospital in affording treatment. There is a maximum liability under this provision of £200 for an in-patient and £20 for an out-patient.

Avoidance of certain exceptions to policies.—By s 148 (1), where the insurance policy purports to restrict the insurance of the persons

6 *Cooper v Motor Insurers' Bureau* [1985] QB 575, [1985] 1 All ER 449. The owners of a motorcycle held not to be required by s 145 (3) to insure against the risk of injury to person whom he asked to road test the motorcycle.

7 *Gardner v Moore* [1984] AC 548, [1984] 1 All ER 1100.

8 The Law Commission pointed out in its Second Report on Exemption Clauses (Law Com No 69, 1975, para 77) that s 148 (3) contains serious gaps because it does not cover the use of motor vehicles except on a road, there are many cases where it does not apply at all, it does not cover 'contractual liability' and it does not apply to the Crown.

covered by the policy in certain particulars, these restrictions are of no effect as regards a person killed or injured liability to whom is compulsorily insurable under s 143 (1). Among the particular restrictions referred to in s 148 (1) are restrictions as to the age or physical or mental condition of the driver, the condition of the vehicle and the number of persons the vehicle carried. There is a proviso to the effect that any sum paid towards the discharge of any liability of any person covered by the policy, by virtue only of the subsection, is recoverable by the insurer from that person. Suppose that a motor vehicle policy provides that the policy has no application if the vehicle carried more than four persons and a pedestrian is run over by the negligence of the driver while the vehicle does carry more than four persons. The pedestrian is not prejudiced by the restriction in the policy and any judgment he obtains against the driver can be enforced against the insurers. By virtue, however, of the proviso to s 148 (1), the insurers may then claim the amount from the insured.[9]

Where a policy, covering risks against which it is compulsory to insure, provides that the policy only applied, for example, when the vehicle is being used 'for social, domestic and pleasure purposes', then the insurers are under no liability if the insured incurs liability for the death or injury of a third party while driving the vehicle for business purposes.[10] The third party is prejudiced by that sort of restriction and s 148 (1) has no application. Moreover, even the restrictions particularly referred to in s 148 (1) are fully effective wherever liability is incurred otherwise than in respect of a risk against which it is compulsory to insure. In *Clarke v National Insurance and Guarantee Corpn Ltd*[11] a motor vehicle policy covering inter alia liability to third parties and damage to the car, provided that the insurers were not liable while the four-seater car insured was 'being driven in an unsafe or unroadworthy condition.' There were nine people in the car when an accident occurred and as this meant that the control of the car was seriously impaired the car was held by the Court of Appeal to be in an unroadworthy condition. The insured failed in his claim to be indemnified under the policy in respect of the damage to the car.

By s 148 (2), any condition in the policy relieving the insurer of liability in the event of some specified thing being done or not done after the accident is of no effect as regards a person killed or injured

9 See, eg *Liverpool Corpn v T and H R Roberts* [1965] 1 WLR 938.
10 *Wood v General Accident Fire and Life Assurance Corpn Ltd* (1948) 65 TLR 53.
11 [1964] 1 QB 199, [1963] 3 All ER 375.

liabilty to whom is compulsorily insurable under s 143 (1). A failure by the insured, for example, to notify his insurers of the accident within the time specified by the policy will not prejudice a person injured in an accident who is able to establish that the insured is liable. However, if an insurer has to meet the injured person's claim because of s 148 (2), a proviso permits the insurer to recover the amount paid from the insured if there is a clause in the policy entitling them so to do.

Enforcement of judgment against insurers.—In respect of any liability that is required to be covered under the Act (ie, in respect of compulsory risks), if a judgment is obtained against any person who is insured by the policy and his liability is covered by the terms of the policy, the insurers must pay to the persons entitled to the benefit of the judgment any sum payable under it in respect of the liability together with any costs and interest also payable (s 149 (1)). This provision does not apply unless, before or within seven days after the commencement of proceedings in which the judgment was given, the insurers had notice of the bringing of the proceedings.[12] Nor is there any liability if execution is stayed pending appeal.

The insurers are not liable if, before the accident, the policy was cancelled by mutual consent or by virtue of a provision in the policy, and either:—

(i) before the happening of the accident the certificate was surrendered to the insurer or the person to whom the certificate was delivered made a statutory declaration as to its loss or destruction, or

(ii) after the accident but before the expiration of 14 days from the cancellation, the certificate was surrendered to the insurer or the person to whom the certificate was delivered made a statutory declaration as to its loss or destruction, or

(iii) either before or after the event but within the said period of 14 days, the insurer has commenced proceedings under the Act in respect of failure to surrender the certificate (s 149 (2)).

Again, the insurers are not liable if, in an action commenced before or within three months after the commencement of proceedings by the third party against the insured, they obtain a

---

12 By s 151 a duty is laid upon any person against whom a claim is made in respect of any liability required to be covered by insurance under s 143 (1), to give on demand particulars of his insurance cover as specified in his certificate of insurance.

declaration that apart from any provision contained in the policy, they are entitled to avoid it on the ground that it was obtained by the non-disclosure of a material fact, or by a representation of fact which was false in some material particular or, if they have avoided the policy on that ground, that they were entitled so to do apart from any provision contained in it (s 149 (3)). 'Material' is defined in the Act as 'of such a nature as to influence the judgment of a prudent insurer' (s 149 (5)). Whenever the insurer commences his action for a declaration *after* the commencement of proceedings by the third party, the insurer is only entitled to the benefit of s 149 (3) if before or within seven days after the commencement of the insurer's action for a declaration he has given notice to the third party specifying the non-disclosure or false representation on which the insurer relies. The third party to whom notice of such an action is given is entitled, if he thinks fit, to be made a party to it.[13]

Third Parties (Rights against Insurers) Act 1930

By this Act, which is not confined to motor vehicle insurance but applies to all liability insurance where the insured goes bankrupt or, if a company, goes into liquidation, but before or after that event, has incurred a liability to a third person, the rights of the insured under the policy are transferred to and vest in the injured third party. Suppose, for example, a company has an insurance policy that covers its liability in negligence to members of the public up to £5,000, and someone is injured by the negligence of the company. The injured party obtains judgment against the company for £8,000. If, before or after judgment, the company has gone into liquidation, the injured person can claim directly against the insurers for the amount of the policy, £5,000. Similarly, if the owner of a vehicle has insured himself against the risk of liability for damage to property arising out of the use of the vehicle and such liability is established, the person whose property has been damaged may claim direct from the insurers under the policy provided the insured is bankrupt. The Court of Appeal in *Post Office v Norwich Union*[14] held that no claim could be made against insurers under this Act until the extent of the liability of the insured has been ascertained by judgment or agreement. It is not possible to contract

13 The insurer is not able to rely on any matter of non-disclosure or misrepresentation, as against the third party, which is not specified in the notice: *Zurich General Accident and Liability Insurance Co Ltd v Morrison* [1942] 2 KB 53, [1942] 1 All ER 529.

14 [1967] 2 QB 363, [1967] 1 All ER 577.

out of the Act but an insurer may rely on any defence which he could have raised against the insured, such as relying on an arbitration clause.[15] Before the Act, the injured third party would only have been able to prove as a creditor against the injured's assets. In the case of compulsory motor vehicle insurance the injured person has no need to rely on the Act because s 149 of the Road Traffic Act 1972 gives him a right to enforce the judgment direct against the insurers whether the insured is bankrupt or not.

The Motor Insurers' Bureau

Since 1946, the Motor Insurers' Bureau, by Agreement with the Ministry of Transport (now the Department of Transport), has undertaken to satisfy or cause to be satisfied any judgment, not satisfied within seven days, which has been obtained against a motorist for any liability required by the Road Traffic legislation to be covered by a policy of insurance. The Bureau was incorporated in 1946 by the motor vehicle insurers and they undertake to keep it in funds. Since 1969 the Bureau has also agreed to make payments in respect of personal injury or death caused by the use of a vehicle where the owner or driver cannot be traced. The two Agreements now current were made in 1972.[16]

Agreement relating to uninsured drivers

This Agreement applies only to judgments obtained in respect of compulsory risks. It is not compulsory to insure against the risk of accident to someone asked by the owner to *drive* the vehicle.[17]

Because of the privity of contract rule, the Agreement is strictly speaking enforceable only by the Department of Transport but when sued by an injured third party the Bureau does not in practice take the point and the courts have not raised any such objection

15 *Freshwater v Western Australian Assurance Co* [1933] 1 KB 515, [1932] All ER Rep 791, *Farrell v Federated Employers Insurance Association* [1970] 3 All ER 632, [1970] 1 WLR 1400, CA (insurers entitled to rely on breach of condition by insured in failing to notify them immediately of receipt plaintiff's writ) and *Pioneer Concrete (UK) Ltd v National Employers Mutual General Insurance Association Ltd* [1985] 2 All ER 395 (insurers entitled to rely on breach of condition by insured in failing to notify insurers of proceedings even though not prejudiced thereby). The insurer may not, however, claim a set-off in respect of premiums due under the policy: *Murray v Legal and General Assurance Society Ltd* [1970] 2 QB 495, [1969] 3 All ER 794.
16 The texts of the two Agreements dated 22 November 1972 are published by Her Majesty's Stationery Office.
17 *Cooper v Motor Insurers' Bureau* [1985] QB 575, [1985] 1 All ER 449, CA. See p 335, ante.

independently. In *Lees v Motor Insurance Bureau*[18] a policy taken out
by an employer covered liability for the death or bodily injury of
any person caused by the use of a lorry owned by the employer, but
it excluded 'liability in respect of death arising out of and in the
course of his employment of a person in the employment of the
insured'. An employee in the course of his employment drove the
lorry negligently and killed a fellow employee whose death arose
out of and in the course of his employment. The widow and
administratrix of the deceased employee obtained judgment
against the driver but it remained unsatisfied. The court held that
the Bureau were not liable under their agreement, since liability in
respect of death arising out of and in the course of his employment of
a person in the insured's employment is not a compulsory risk. In
Hardy v Motor Insurers' Bureau[19] the plaintiff was injured by the wilful
and deliberate action of the driver of a van user of which was not
insured against third party risks. The Court of Appeal held that if
the driver had been insured, although he could not have claimed on
the policy himself, having deliberately brought about the risk
insured against, nevertheless the injured party could have recovered from the insurers under s 207 of the Road Traffic Act 1960
(now s 149 of the Road Traffic Act 1972). Hence, the Bureau was
liable to pay under their agreement. The Court of Appeal
recognised the practical reality of the MIB's position in *Gurtner v
Circuit*[20] where a pedestrian injured by a motor cyclist brought an
action against the motor cyclist who had disappeared abroad and
whose insurers were not known. The Court of Appeal allowed the
MIB's application to be added as a co-defendant because it was
vitally concerned with the outcome of the action. Lord Denning MR said 'it would be most unjust if they were bound to stand
idly by watching the plaintiff get judgment against the defendant
without saying a word when they are the people who have got to
foot the bill'.[1]

18　[1952] 2 All ER 511.

19　[1964] 2 QB 745, [1964] 2 All ER 742. Approved by the House of Lords in
Gardner v Moore [1984] AC 548, [1984] 1 All ER 1100.

20　[1968] 2 QB 587, [1968] 1 All ER 328.

1　Lord Denning pointed out that the Minister of Transport could sue for specific
performance of the 1946 agreement with the MIB and compel the MIB to pay the
injured person—this followed from the House of Lords' decision in *Beswick v Beswick*
[1968] AC 58, [1967] 2 All ER 1197. Any such order of specific performance could be
enforced by the injured person for his own benefit. Lord Denning added that if the
Minister hesitated to sue, it may be open to the injured person to make the Minister a
defendant and thus compel performance of the 1946 agreement but this is a more
questionable proposition.

In cases where there is no policy, the Bureau's Agreement only operates if notice of proceedings is given to the Bureau either before or within seven days after the commencement of the proceedings. Moreover, solicitors are advised to give immediate notice to the Bureau of an intention to institute proceedings in a case where there is the least doubt whether the defendant is effectively covered by insurance as required by statute.[2] If proceedings are brought against a person who is covered by a policy of insurance, it will not be necessary for the victim to take any special steps to secure for himself the benefits of the scheme (merely giving notice to the insurers is enough)—even though the insurers may be in a position to repudiate or are insolvent.

Agreement relating to untraced drivers

The 1946 Agreement did not cover anyone injured from the use of a vehicle on the road the owner or driver of which could not be traced. The Bureau did give sympathetic consideration to the making of an ex gratia payment to the victim or his dependants in the case of such 'hit-and-run' drivers but the absolute discretion of the Bureau to make or refuse payment was judicially criticised[3] and a new Agreement was entered into between the Bureau and the Minister of Transport in 1969. The 1969 Agreement on the 'Compensation of Victims of Untraced Drivers' applied to death or injury on or after 1 May 1969 and the current Agreement has applied to death or injury on or after 1 December 1972. Under it the Bureau will accept applications where (a) the applicant cannot trace any person responsible for the death or injury, (b) the death or injury was caused in such circumstances that on the balance of probabilities the untraced person would be liable to pay damages, and (c) the untraced person's liability is one required to be covered by insurance under the Road Traffic Act 1972. The Bureau will not, however, deal with deliberate 'running down' cases. The applicant has a right of appeal against any decision of the Bureau to an arbitrator who will be a Queen's Counsel selected by the Department of Transport from a panel appointed by the Lord Chancellor. It was held by the Court of Appeal in *Perssen v London Country Buses*[4] that no payment could be obtained from the Bureau except by virtue of the terms of the Agreement. The Agreement

2 *Law Society's Gazette* (July 1947) p 134.
3 *Adams v Andrews* [1964] 2 Lloyd's Rep 347, per Sachs J.
4 [1974] 1 All ER 1251, [1974] 1 WLR 569.

made it clear that the obligation to pay only arose if the Bureau itself determined there should be an award *unless* a claimant, being dissatisfied with a decision of the Bureau, appealed to an arbitrator. It followed that if the Bureau determined that no payment should be made and the claimant did not choose to appeal, he had no right to payment and a claim in a court of action for payment should be struck out.

Sale of insured car

If the insurance policy refers to a specified car owned by the insured, it may cease to be operative when that car is sold. In *Tattersall v Drydale*[5] the insured's comprehensive policy which referred to a Standard car belonging to him expressly extended to the policy-holder when driving other cars. At the time of the accident the insured had sold his Standard car and was driving a Riley car. Goddard J held that the interest of the insured ceased when he parted with the specified car and the extending clause fell together with the rest of the policy so that no claim could be made on it. However, in the case of a policy covering third-party risks only, it is a question of construction whether disposal of the specified vehicle results in a lapse of the policy, because no insurable interest is required where the policy covers third-party risks only. In *Boss v Kingston*,[6] B owned a motor-cycle and had an insurance policy covering third-party risks in connection with driving either the motor-cycle he owned, which was described specifically in the policy or other motor-cycles. He was required by the policy to maintain the specified motor-cycle in efficient condition. Later, B sold the specified motor-cycle and was driving another motor-cycle when he was charged and convicted for contravening the Act. The Divisional Court upheld the conviction on the ground that while a person can properly obtain third-party insurance in respect of a motor vehicle in which he has no insurable interest, B's policy lapsed when he sold the named vehicle because it required him to keep the named vehicle in efficient condition and this could not be complied with once he had disposed of it.

EMPLOYERS' COMPULSORY LIABILITY

An employer owes his employee at common law a duty to take reasonable care to provide proper plant and appliances and engage

5 [1935] 2 KB 174, [1935] All ER Rep 112.
6 [1963] 1 All ER 177, [1963] 1 WLR 99.

other employees who are competent. Furthermore, by the Employers' Liability (Defective Equipment) Act 1969, if an employee suffers injury in the course of employment in consequence of equipment provided by his employer and the defect is attributable wholly or partly to the fault of a third party, the injury shall be deemed to be also attributable to negligence on the part of the employer. Statutory duties, in many instances going beyond liability in negligence, are also imposed on employers by the Health and Safety at Work etc Act 1974.

By the Employers' Liability (Compulsory Insurance) Act 1969 an employer must insure against liability for bodily injury or disease sustained by his employees and arising out of the course of their employment. Local authorities, nationalised corporations and certain other employers specified by regulation are exempt.

ASSIGNMENT AND TRANSFERABILITY OF POLICIES

Assignment of rights under policies

Chose in action.—Since the right to receive the proceeds under an insurance policy is a chose in action, it may be assigned like any other chose in action. An equitable assignment is effective without any particular form and a legal assignment may be made if s 136 of the Law of Property Act 1925 is satisfied. A legal assignment under s 136 requires the assignment to be absolute (ie, the assignor's whole interest is transferred), in writing, and written notice to be given to the debtor (or his agent).

Where the insurance is an indemnity policy, since the insured must have an insurable interest at the time of the loss, if he has no such interest at the time of the loss neither he nor any assignee has any claim. Thus, if A has a fire insurance policy on his own house, A can assign the policy to B so that if A's house is burned down B can claim on the policy provided that A still has an insurable interest in the house at the time of the loss. But if, say, A in selling his house to B purports to assign to B the rights under his fire insurance policy, the assignment is a nullity, because A no longer has any insurable interest.[7] Of course if A merely mortgages his house to B and assigns to B his rights under his fire insurance policy, that is a good assignment because A retains an interest in the house.

Life policies.—A legal assignment of a life policy issued by assurance companies or societies was possible before legal assign-

7 *Ecclesiastical Comrs v Royal Exchange* (1895) 11 TLR 476.

ments of choses in action generally were rendered possible by the Judicature Act 1873. Under the Policies of Assurance Act 1867, the assured may assign a life policy in writing either by endorsement on the policy or by a separate instrument (in the words or to the effect set out in the Schedule to the Act), and the endorsement or separate instrument must be properly stamped. The assignee has no right to claim from the insurers unless he gives them written notice of the assignment at their *principal* place of business which they must specify in their policy. The date on which such notice is received governs priorities and any payment made bona fide by an assurance company before the date on which such notice is received is valid against the assignee giving such notice. An assurance company must, on request in writing from the person giving such notice and on payment of not more than 25p, provide a written acknowledgement of its receipt, this being conclusive evidence as to receipt of the notice. Since life policies are not indemnity insurances, there is of course no need for the assured to have an insurable interest at the time of the death. Unlike legal assignment under s 136 of the Law of Property Act, assignment under this provision may be by way of charge.

Transferability of policies

Assignment by A of the fire policy on his house to B is really the assignment of the right to receive the proceeds. The policy still relates to A's house not B's so that the insurers are under no different risk. Clearly it is not possible for A to transfer his fire policy so that it attaches now to B's house unless the insurers agree, and the same point applies if A sells his house to B. On sale, A's policy can only be transferred to B if that is agreed between A and B *and* if the insurers consent. There must, therefore, be a novation.[8]

By s 47 (1) of the Law of Property Act 1925, where insurance money becomes payable to a vendor of property after the contract but before completion, it must be 'held or receivable by the vendor on behalf of the purchaser and paid by the vendor to the purchaser on completion of the sale or exchange, or as soon thereafter as the same shall be received by the vendor . . . '. By s 47 (2) the previous subsection has effect subject to any stipulation to the contrary in the contract of sale, any requisite consents of the insurers, and the

---

8 Similarly if A has a motor vehicle policy on his car and then sells the car to B, the policy can only be transferred to B if the insurers consent: *Peters v General Accident Fire and Life Assurance Corpn Ltd* [1938] 2 All ER 267.

payment by the purchaser of a proportionate part of the premium from the date of the contract. This latter subsection seriously narrows the effect of the provision in s 47 (1). It seems that the insurers' consent must be obtained for the purchaser to claim any right under the provision unless the terms of the policy give the benefit of it to a purchaser.[9] As noted above, possibly a purchaser is a 'person interested' under s 83 of the Fires Prevention (Metropolis) Act 1774 and has the right, before the policy moneys are handed over to the vendor, to demand reinstatement of the property.[10]

9 In the circumstances the purchaser seems well advised to insure the property himself; see Cheshire *Modern Real Property* (11th edn, 1972) p 713 and JGS 'Insurance pending completion' (1963) 107 Sol Jo 128.
10 See p 325, ante.

Index